A Heart in My Head

A Heart in My Head

A Biography of Richard Harries

JOHN S. PEART-BINNS

continuum

Continuum

The Tower Building   80 Maiden Lane
11 York Road   Suite 704
London   New York
SE1 7NX   NY 10038

www.continuumbooks.com

First published 2007

British Library Cataloguing-in-Publication Data
A catalogue record for this book is available from the British Library.

ISBN 0–8264–8154–X

Typeset by Kenneth Burnley, Wirral, Cheshire
Printed and bound by MPG Books Ltd, Bodmin, Cornwall

Contents

Prefatory Notes

Researching this book on Richard Harries has been exhausting; writing it has been exhilarating. No boundary walls were built and there was an absence of 'no trespassing' signs on his life. His cooperation and generosity have been seamless strands. My gratitude is boundless for the way in which my subject has been prepared to respond to all my probing and questions in lengthy correspondence and with specially prepared papers on specific topics. I have had access to private papers to clarify controversial aspects of his episcopate. Above all, it has been wonderful to be the recipient of relaxed, convivial, warm, serious and gastronomic hospitality on the occasions when we met.

I recall Richard Harries asking if I was on email! He has had the unusual experience of encountering someone who is a technological Luddite, neither possessing nor using a computer, who regards the internet and emails as alien; is even reluctant to use the telephone as a form of communication and is propelled on two feet rather than on four wheels.

I have climbed a mountain of published and unpublished material, from which vantage point I have surveyed the surrounding hills and valleys of books, lectures, sermons and speeches. The Bibliography is not exhaustive. It is limited to what I have read and digested. In addition I have studied Richard Harries' contributions to the Oxford diocesan magazine, *The Door*; weekly devotional articles in the *Church Times* over a period of 15 years; speeches and interventions in General Synod; presidential addresses to the Oxford Diocesan Conference; and numerous letters to editors of national newspapers. I have not listed the large number of his reviews which I have read in a wide variety of journals and papers, for example, the *Church Times*, *New Christian*, *New Fire*, *The Tablet*, *Theology* and the *Times Literary Supplement*. Although they reflect his intellectual range of interests they do not, on the whole, materially add to any deeper understanding of his position on subjects and issues which are found more substantially elsewhere.

I have received and read a huge quantity of unpublished material – sermons, addresses, lectures. Of particular interest and importance are his *Ad Clerum* to 'friends and colleagues' of the Oxford diocese; Maundy Thursday Eucharist sermons and those preached on Easter Day and Christmas Day; all the *Prayer* and *Thought for the Day* contributions which have not been collected in books. Great gratitude goes to Richard Harries' personal staff – Christine Lodge (PA) and Michael Brierley (chaplain) – for unearthing and providing me with a wealth of material.

Then there are the detailed and lengthy contributions from a host of people who, asked to write with sensitivity and candour, have done both. Manifest honesty is the dominant mark from admirers and critics alike. Very few people are neutral in their view of Richard Harries, even less in their evaluation of his thought and work. This means that many correspondents have written confidentially or not for direct quotation, but to help me with context and perspective. Some recollections are scattered through the book, others remain, as they were intended, confidential.

Richard Harries has applied rigour in reading and commenting on the manuscript without disturbing my estimation of his life and work to date! There are portions which may or will have caused discomfort. If so, he has winced in private without urging amendments. On the other hand, he has prevented factual errors and unintended faux-pas. Any errors of judgement are mine alone.

There would have been no completed manuscript without the assistance of Annis, my wife, whose encouragement and criticism are constant and intertwined. Overseeing preparation of the manuscript, correcting my errors and wrong emphases, blocking cul-de-sacs which I may have liked to enter, and keeping me, on this occasion, to the tightest of timetables, is all in a day's work for her!

Finally, special thanks to Carolyn Armitage and Andrew Walby of Continuum and to Catherine Butcher, an experienced editor, for their invaluable assistance.

Apologia
Towards a Mosaic

Quarrying and exploring the thought, work and life of Richard Harries has resulted in an endeavour to produce a mosaic. All life is fragmentary. The best mosaics are not perfectly flat and level, since an uneven surface catches the light and reflects in different ways according to the angle of incidence and the materials used. Mosaics carry their own aesthetic integrity and should not degenerate into propaganda or inoffensive decoration. They allow room for the viewer's imagination and interpretation. A mosaic, like an icon, is more than a photograph; an impact rather than a definition.

Richard Harries has a sharp mind, alert, versatile, open to many impressions, influences and ideas, sensitive to beauty, eager for influence. Although he is a liberal thinker, occasionally a radical and his heart beats firmly on the left, it is mainstream, orthodox Christianity that attracts him and to which he wants to be true. Fundamentalism, intolerance and bigotry of any kind are anathema to him as they produce hearts of steel rather than of love. His manners are generous and courteous to those who oppose him. He knows that, contrary to the laws of physics, the greater the friction between people, the colder they become.

What of the fruits of Harries' mind? What of his theology? Does he portray Christianity as primarily a thesis to be argued rather than a religion to be preached; a principle to be enunciated more than a practice to be extended; a tradition to be maintained, not a passion to be communicated? Is his mind receptive rather than constructive? Is he a stimulator or an originator; a conciliator and facilitator with conservative instincts and liberal antennae, or with reforming convictions on a traditional seam? Is his intellect in charge from first to last? May it be that he feels deeply, not sharply; that he loves truly, not passionately? He has rarely flung himself with emotion into any movement of the human mind, not because he lacks resolve or devotion, but because he thinks the victories of emotion are often defeats in disguise. When he fights for a cause he does so with intelligence, determination and restrained fervour without always anticipating the consequences. What of religious 'psychology' whose workings are intricate, intimate and unverifiable? On the one hand I am shadowing and appraising a good, fearless and upright person with an able, sincere and undisguised personality. On the other hand, in slipping beneath the surface, I have encountered an elusive persona, a life filled with paradox: a character that is both open and hidden. Many friends who know him well admit that there are areas into which they cannot delve. Words of Christopher Fry in *Thor, with Angels* are potent ones as I proceed:

1

> To be able to distinguish one thing from another,
> The storm-swollen river from the tear-swollen eyes,
> Or the bare-cracked earth from the burnt-out face,
> Or the forest soughing from the sighing heart.

Through his books, journalism, lectures, radio broadcasts and television appearances, Harries is well known. There is a recognizable glamour about him which can be potentially destructive. As many a contemporary 'celebrity' has found to their cost, the distance between the platform and pillory is slight. Priests and bishops are far from immune. When they forget that the person is the servant of the priesthood, not the priesthood the servant of the person, they enter a personal and spiritual quagmire! Harries admits, 'There must be a strong influence within me to be known. I suppose I need to be known, recognized, respected and appreciated.'

The wider Harries' interests and involvements, the more one would expect to discover a fragmented mind. That is not the case, for there is an essential coherence in his thought and action, an integral unity in diversity. His eyes may seem sometimes to be veiled, but they are used for incisive analysis to bring things into a right perspective before they are evaluated.

These eyes, like his ears, are precision instruments and sometimes are the watchers and sentinels that guard the secrets of deep thought and keep in check unexamined or unanticipated emotions. It is the union of many seeming contradictions in the complex whole of a single personality that attracts and fascinates or parries and perplexes. Harries does not overdose with self-analysis which can lead to introspection and anxiety – snares entangling people in a web of self-regard. Although not self-analytical, he is wholly aware of his capabilities and does not hide his light under a bushel. He may like the limelight but, as anyone who has seen him at after-service parochial bun-fights knows, he lacks the patina of the true extrovert.

One purpose of the book will be to explore his leadership, power and influence. Harries is uncertain of how far he has been a leader in the typical meaning of that word. He champions no party, represents no movement and expresses no tendency. He is independent in his opinions and thinks for himself, although other people's thoughts augment and enhance his own. Apart from their episcopal consecration, it is difficult to discern in many, probably in most, of the bishops any special qualifications for pronouncing judgement on the numerous intricate and profound questions submitted to them. Episcopal consecration conveys no special transformation to compensate for the absence of experience and expertise.

Many people use the term 'C of E' as if it were a self-confessed reproach. Not Richard Harries! He has always valued the *via media* of the Church of England. Not, on the one hand, to hold on with timorous tenacity to theological opinions, moral diktats and ecclesiastical traditions, sacrosanct by time yet disallowed by modern knowledge; nor, on the other, to let go the fundamental verities which are eternally valid, necessary and morally energizing to float on a stream of popular fashion which is equally confident and fleeting. For Harries the *via media* is also a *via dolorosa*, leading him away from comfortable and familiar regions into a country uncharted and unsafe, the 'borderlands' where he is challenged, stimulated and sustained.

In 2006 a book was published, *Public Life and the Place of the Church: Reflections to Honour the Bishop of Oxford*. Within the folds of this richly merited Festschrift, luminaries made their bow and paid tribute to the prodigious and varied thought, interests, activities and achievements of Richard Harries. A Festschrift is celebratory exposure, a thank-offering. My book – part biography, part thought and work – is necessarily different in tone, temper and intention. It has to withstand different rigours and critical assaults. Detachment, accumulated knowledge and just perspective are key ingredients in the portrayal. The biographer's art has been distorted and diminished in recent years. Many biographies have met readers' cravings for intimate details of private lives; of flaws and failings; the seamy, superficial and often irrelevant. Their subjects become their quarries. Sin, not virtue, rings the bookshop tills and publishers reap their rewards. With public figures it can no longer be assumed that the books, articles and letters – and with bishops also sermons, addresses and lectures – are necessarily wholly from their own heads and pens. Richard Harries is an honourable and notable exception to this increasingly pervasive practice.

If principles are to live by, not to stand on, what are those which should guide a biographer? Michael Holroyd, an exemplar of writing biography, claims: 'A biographer's life . . . may have similarities with that of an actor. He must read, learn lines, metaphorically put on the clothes and become his subject – know what it is like to think feel move about the room like him . . .' (*The Times*, 14 September 1974). My approach is to move from stage to canvas, or in this case to mosaic. Biography is an art. But if it is an art, how far are we to define it? Fundamentally a biography must aim at being a truthful record of an individual life. It is more difficult than a work of fiction, for the biographer cannot invent those circumstances which might illustrate best the character to be depicted. Incidents have to be recorded as they are found. They must neither be altered nor ignored, however much that may help bring out an essential truth.

It is my view that a biographer should delight in the chosen subject – otherwise why devote time, labour and mind-extending effort to the task? This does not mean even the slightest hint of hagiography, for the approach must be vigorously objective. My contemplation of 'Who is Richard Harries?' attempts not judgement – it is far too soon for this – but exploration. The life, thought, ministry and episcopate are encapsulated in the title – *A Heart in My Head* (from Samuel Beckett).

In 1973, when there was considerable controversy over the appointment of a new bishop of London, a letter appeared in *The Times* from Harries, then the young vicar of All Saints, Fulham:

> By virtue of their office bishops now have little influence in the church and none at all in the country. The question of who was or was not appointed to the See of London is of little consequence.
>
> Certain bishops, like some priests and many lay people, manage to command respect and a hearing by virtue of their ability, integrity and concern for

the real needs of human beings. Let us hope, and even pray, that the man who has been appointed will prove to be one of these.

Fourteen years later Richard Harries would be appointed Bishop of Oxford. Time to begin gathering fragments for the mosaic.

Chapter One
Waiting in a Transit Lounge

Richard Douglas Harries was born on 2 June 1936 at 98 Bexley Road, Eltham in London SE9. 1936 was not a propitious year. Civil war broke out in Spain; the Rhineland was remilitarized; Italian troops occupied Addis Ababa; and Germany repudiated the Locarno Treaty; in England it was the year of the three kings. And Eltham had not much to sing about even if Bob Hope, who gagged his way along numerous film roads, was born there. Richard's father, a captain in the Royal Signals, was assistant superintendent at the Signals Experimental Establishment at Woolwich. In 1940 he moved to the War Office, working for the next nine months in the Department of Ordnance Services. At this time the Harries family moved to New Quay, a fishing resort in Cardigan Bay, Ceredigion, formerly Cardiganshire, to escape the threat of bombing. Mrs Harries called it her 'skunk hole'. There is still a family holiday home there.

No. 3 Pentregarth, a stone and mud cottage in New Quay, modernized by Great Aunt Jane, was the place where Richard Harries assimilated the joys of childhood. His memories are of 'friendliness to children, in the shops, on the streets and from innumerable relations. The people genuinely liked children'. He did not know that his short time at Pentregarth would be almost the only normal, carefree happiness he would experience until he was an adult. 'There was the Emporium, a rather grand-sounding name for a tiny shop, but it was grand for children because there were large jars full of sweets placed prominently in the window. In childhood there are always a few sheer, unalloyed delights: glass marbles with coloured centres that were certainly more precious than rubies; balsa-wood gliders that flew more beautifully than any bird, and amongst these were piles of new *Beanos* and *Dandys*. Later loyalties widened out to include *Wizard* – I was never a particular fan of the *Rover* but the *Dandy* in particular, of that early period, was magic. The start to the day was the Bakery, a wooden building in which fresh bread was baked daily. The bread was out of this world for smell and taste. Walking back up to Pentregarth with the early morning loaf, it was perhaps only the heat of it that stopped my sister Linda and me from consuming the whole, as opposed to much of it. We scooped it out in hot, delicious handfuls. At the end of August a fair came to New Quay and what a source of pleasure it was, as well as the cause of chagrin and quarrels with mother. We loved the bumper cars at the Dodgems, the bumping rather than the dodging being the object of the exercise as far as we were concerned. The other evening attraction was at the Memorial Hall. Here, once or even twice a week, a film was shown. I was

5

always slightly puzzled why, with all the lonely lanes and lovely spots in the neigh-bourhood, the back rows should have been so popular on these nights for courting teenage couples.'

Dylan Thomas lived and wrote for a time in New Quay and drank hard at the Black Lion. It is now recognized that New Quay was the inspiration for the fictional Llareggub in *Under Milk Wood*.

Richard Harries preferred the Welsh side of his family: 'They seemed more intel-ligent, more interesting and more generous than the English ones. I liked to think of myself as Welsh. Because I was born and brought up in England I have to acknowledge that I am a totally bogus Welshman but I'd rather be a bogus Welsh-man than an authentic Englishman.'

His childhood idyll at New Quay was ruptured when his father's posting was switched from France to America, where he spent three years developing liaison between the Royal Signals and the US Signal Corps, especially in relation to the purchase and use of signals equipment. The family – mother, sister Linda and Richard – followed, sailing from Liverpool on 25 August 1941 on SS Modessa, an orange cargo boat, taken off the India run, part of a huge, very slow convoy going via Iceland and Greenland in order to dodge the U-boats which were then sinking hundreds of Allied shipping every year. They arrived in America on 17 September for what was a relatively short period but not without its influence on young Richard. 'In Washington we lived at 2843 Chesapeake Street, which was an extremely pleasant white shutter-board house on the border between the white and black areas. There seem, in retrospect, to be two factors which have had a lasting influence on my attitudes. First, the warmth and hospitality of the Americans we knew and the good friends that my parents made. We seemed to receive food parcels for a decade afterwards when we had returned to Britain. This has meant that there is a substratum of warmth towards the Americans in my psyche and I don't share the knee-jerk anti-Americanism which is so prevalent in the world today. This is not a consciously constructed attitude, but I suspect that it is there. Second, being on the edge of the black area I could watch, fascinated, a rather dif-ferent way of life to ours. For example, I watched enthralled as a black man managed to gob his tobacco some 20 or 30 yards. More significantly, I made friends with a young black girl who offered me one of her kittens, which I wanted. I sniffed adult disapproval in the air. I expect this distinctive childhood anti-racism has been part of me ever since. I don't think I shared my parents' attitude to the black lady who helped look after us and her fecklessness in their eyes.'

In February 1944 the family returned to England and another experience awaited seven-year-old Richard in Huddersfield where his father was posted. They were billeted on a Yorkshire family, the Broadbents, who offered their house as part of the war effort. Again, Richard's memories are pertinent: 'The two families could not have been more different. My parents, south-east England and my mother somewhat snobbish; the Broadbents, moneyed and totally unpretentious. The Broadbents owned a 'Works', which during the war made small submarines, switch-ing to washing machines after the war. My memory of Molly Broadbent, my

Aunty B, is of a very large lady, arms deep in the washing-up bowl, chain-smoking Craven A cigarettes. My memory of Uncle Brian, her husband, is of a quiet, spectacled man, coming home from work and immediately settling down to his extremely extensive stamp collection. Their only luxuries at that time were Alvis cars, later Rolls-Royces, and Airedale dogs.

Richard had the ability to soak up the atmosphere of a place but was perhaps mistaken that he had breached a divide between north and south. It had been an itinerant life without a focus or stability for a child who needed to be needed. The Broadbent embrace gave him something that was both natural and special, notably the experience of love, acceptance and warmth. Later he thought he knew what it was like to live in an industrial northern town but his slight sojourn was in abnormal times when people of all classes were pulling together and identification was effortless. He had his first sense of freedom doing what he liked, going to the local chippie before watching Huddersfield Town play football, a loyalty which remains. Cinema was alluring too. Above all: 'I developed a taste for voracious reading. The house had an attic full of wonderful pre-war toys, hundreds of beautifully made lead soldiers, for example. It also had shelves of books. I remember reading my way through Percy F. Westerman.'

Huddersfield also meant school. Although Richard had attended school in America, his education had dropped two years behind and he was still doing block capitals when the rest of the class were writing longhand. St David's preparatory school was his one uniformly happy encounter with education.

A complementary view comes from Jennifer Aebischer, née Broadbent, who was five years older than Richard: 'We didn't see a great deal of each other as I was at boarding school at the time, and my parents divided the house in two so the Harries' could have their quarters and we ours. My mother had been anxious before they came in case the two families didn't hit it off, particularly Richard's mother, Greta, and herself. She needn't have worried, as we all got along famously. His father Bill was busy most of the time but Greta was a delightful person. In spite of food shortages Greta concocted amazing "fish" pies, which could include anything – sometimes even fish. On one or two occasions we suspected her and my mother of adding a bit of dog food, but anyway they were delicious and we survived. When the Harries' family left, Greta was expecting Charles and I remember her saying to my mother, "I'm pregnant, Molly, and it's all your fault!" My mother believed in large families.

'I clearly recall seeing Richard in his St David's prep school uniform of royal blue cap and blazer with a thin double-red stripe. He was a nice-looking, amiable boy with particularly large front teeth. We all went swimming, cycling and picnicking on the moors as well as playing games together. Richard and my mother were particular pals. She was a big-hearted, larger-than-life sort of person who one disobeyed at one's peril. She had huge faith in Richard and used to say that whatever profession he took up later she was sure he'd make his mark.'

At this juncture we pause to consider Richard's background and parents. The Welsh Harries' were tenant farmers on the Dynevor Estate near Llandeilo in

Carmarthenshire. Richard's grandfather, Arthur Harries, was brought up on the farm but, like a number of brothers, became an ironmonger in the district. He retired to New Quay, 30 miles away, where all his wife's side, the James', resided. There were generations of established local doctors and, before them, importers and exporters from the quay.

Richard was drawn to 'characters' although he would never be one himself. His grandfather was one: 'Grandpa was a well-built, handsome man, with a strong jaw and nose. "One for the ladies", so it was said, though no doubt his ardent, non-conformist piety kept him in check most of the time. Certainly he was sociable and liked to go down to the village to sit on the Green "clonking" i.e. gossiping with the locals. He also liked to do good and his favourite way was through one of his inventions. He spent much of his time in his little garage opposite No. 2 Pentregarth making things, and he was famous for his "washing machines". These consisted of two baking dishes, one slightly smaller than the other, with holes punched in them, screwed together and fastened on the end of a pole, with a handle on the end. When clothes were put in a tub the handle was pushed up and down, soapy water gushed in and out of the holes and the general agitation of the clothes washed any dirt away. In short, there was a great deal of movement with little expenditure of energy and, above all, the hands were kept dry. These were much in demand. Grandpa never threw anything away. Every piece of string or screw was neatly kept in some container on his workbench.

'His living habits were similarly economical. It is said he refused the State Pension on principle and lived on £1 a week from his savings. His diet was invariable: a rice pudding cooked in the stove by the coal fire in the kitchen, bread, cheese, an occasional boiled egg and some real coffee.

'Talking to Willie Harries once about my grandfather, he said he had been a leader of "the split" – a word which sums up the whole, fissiparous history of Welsh non-conformity. In other words a leading member of the congregation has a row with the minister and ups and offs with half the congregation to build a new chapel nearby. There were many chapels in New Quay and Grandpa settled in the Tabernacle which I attended on one occasion. The minister seemed to take the whole service, including the prayers, with two sermons, one allegedly for children, and the congregation with no vocal part at all except for the reading of the lessons. I can still hear in my mind the reading of the Prologue to St John's Gospel: "In the beginning was the Word . . ." – there was then as long a pause as I have ever heard in church before the reader continued, "And the Word was with God". Similar powerful pauses punctuated the whole reading.

'In Grandpa's bathroom were piles of old copies of the *Readers' Digest* and he himself liked to give guidance to the young in a similar crisp style. Grandpa built a seat for people exhausted on the hill on the way up to Pentregarth and wrote on it "Rest and be thankful". This seat now has a memorial plaque on it to him, a fitting symbol of practical piety.'

Richard's father, William Douglas Jameson Harries, was born on 31 August 1900. He was educated privately and at Sandhurst and, as with many others of the

Harries family, the Welsh language did not follow him to England and beyond. He sat his examination for the Royal Military College on Armistice Day 1918, was commissioned into the Welsh Regiment in 1920 and became signals officer in the lst Battalion, beginning his worldwide service in Waziristan and India. He was a typical military man, straight 'up and down', black was black and white was white. He was technologically trained and gifted. His word was as trusted as his actions were commended; always a gentleman and a person of absolute integrity. In 1925 he was seconded to the Indian Signal Corps. He was moved, as he was promoted, from one country to another. In Washington he was awarded the American Legion of Merit. Usually known as 'Bill', he was deputy director of telecommunications at the War Office and an acknowledged expert in the most sophisticated modern equipment. An obituary notice in *The Daily Telegraph* (October 1991) referring to his responsibilities included, 'matching teleprinters and radar equipment. Not the least of his problems was to ensure that clandestine radios and other "behind-the-lines" devices were available in conditions of tight security, for during the war the Royal Signals were responsible for interpreting innumerable enemy transmissions, both in Europe and the Far East, for the crucial "Ultra" code-breaking operations.' His final position was as commandant of the Signals Training Centre at Catterick. He was a brigadier and awarded a CBE in 1953.

Until after he retired Bill Harries' influence on his son was mostly negative. By temperament he was rather distant. His army career increased and compounded this. He was a highly intelligent man, not fierce, with sporting prowess and a wide circle of friends. He achieved rank by hard work, determination and merit. It was this determination that was a flaw when considering his son's future. In fact, he did not consider what might be best for Richard, of whom he had, through circumstances, insufficient knowledge or understanding. Richard, contrary to surface appearances, had a sensitive, thoughtful interior and later a 'stiff-upper-lip' which was for public consumption only. He would follow his father's well-trodden footsteps into the army where he would be an achiever. When heart and head united in Richard, his sudden move in a completely different direction must have been a painful shock for his father, who had other plans for his son. Of course, Richard had had no early opportunity to explore the father inside the uniform. It was a wonderful delight for him later to enjoy many years of deep friendship with his father. It was greater than mere reconciliation, for there had never been a breach as such: it was love, and both parents were proud of their son's progress and ascent in the Church. Bill Harries was 91 when he died. He had long been a practising Christian and churchwarden at Bosham. On the day of his funeral, 19 October 1991, Richard broadcast this *Thought for the Day*:

Dylan Thomas writing of the death of his father said that old age should always 'Rage, rage against the dying of the light'. This is a view that has often been expressed in the twentieth century, notably by Simone de Beauvoir when her mother died. She held that whenever death comes it is 'an untimely violence'. But not all deaths are like that. My father had lived a full life through momentous years, being loved by family and friends. In his last years he had been well looked after by my sister and her husband. He read much of the mystics, especially Johannes Eckhart. He told me of at least two occasions recently when he had experienced peace and blessedness, when a long passage of time passed without him noticing it. We ought not to over-emphasize the importance of religious experience because they depend on so many factors, but there is no doubt that my father was left with a sense of serenity for days afterwards . . . People used to speak of making a good death, one in which we are at peace with ourselves, with other people and with God. It would be a pity if the idea got altogether lost.

If there is work to be done in our last years, it might involve the laying aside of resentments, the making up of old quarrels, drawing closer to those around us, facing up to that mixture of confused and painful feelings most of us carry around inside; and, through it all, learning to live in the presence of and wait upon God. That is why the old Prayer Book litany prays that we might be delivered from 'Battle, murder and sudden death'. We need time at the end. I will miss the weekly telephone calls to my father; his little list of things he always kept to talk about – for he was a well-organized man to the last; his frank comments about my latest *Thought for the Day*. But I am deeply grateful he went in peace. In a world so full of untimely death, unhappiness and spiritual emptiness, his end time was a blessing I would wish for myself and all of us.

What of Richard's English maternal family? For the most part they made their way in the British Empire. 'I think my mother's side were solicitors in India. Her four brothers all lived and worked in Africa for all, or a significant part of their lives. I disliked their political attitudes as they disliked mine and rare family parties at the time of the Smith regime in Rhodesia, for example, usually erupted into an argument.' When Richard's grandfather, Alan Bathurst Brown, a doctor, returned from the First World War he left his wife and six children, including Richard's mother, and went off with the vicar's daughter to set up a practice in another part of the country. Richard never met him and he was never spoken about. Richard's grandmother refused to give him a divorce and that experience had a lasting effect in various ways on all the children.

Richard's mother was Greta Miriam Harries, née Brown. We need to look at her through his eyes and that of his sister Linda and his brother Charles. In 2003 Richard was asked who had had the most profound effect on his life for publication in a book *Five Gold Rings*. He named his mother: 'I believe that in my early days, months and years I was warmly embraced, affirmed and cherished. Nothing later in life could compare with this influence which has given me a sense of my own identity and worth. My mother said she lost interest in children when they began to develop a mind of their own and certainly she was very different from me! But nothing can be more precious than that early experience of bonding.'

This fulsome tribute has a pinch of hindsight, of descriptive muzziness to it.

More recently he quoted Freud's words: 'He who is the favourite of his mother goes through life with a sense of a conqueror' and confirmation that 'I owe her a sense of emotional rootedness'. If this is all that needs be said then nothing further is required to be written, but the evidence betrays that assumption. In some notes for this author he is perhaps more frank: 'My mother was a very practical, hard-working person but not very bright, and I don't think she ever read more than a page or two of a book in her whole life before falling asleep. But when we expressed our minds there developed a good number of altercations.'

When Richard's sister, Linda (Sims-Williams, born 1938) and his brother Charles (born 1945) describe their mother, a different and significantly more interesting portrait emerges. Richard's sister: 'My mother was very much an independent spirit and, unusually for that time, she took a job as a demonstrator for Brown and Polson, makers of custard powder. My grandmother's circumstances on being left on her own with six children, meant that money was always very tight. This reflected in my mother, who was always very frugal and cost-conscious. She always said, "look after the pennies and the pounds will look after themselves"! She made all her own clothes and recycled anything she could.

'For some reason, my mother was sent to a convent in Belgium some time after the end of the First World War. She clearly showed her independence, even there, and one letter described how she hid in a gym vaulting-horse during assembly for a bet. On being discovered, she was taken to the Mother Superior who, instead of punishing her, gave her a bar of chocolate! She never converted to Roman Catholicism but I suspect her convent education laid the foundation for her Christian faith as, particularly in her later years, she regularly attended the early Holy Communion service.

'In 1930 she went to Africa with Granny to visit her brother Jack and to tour the country. We have many photographs of her big-game hunting. She came back in November 1930 and in 1933 she went out to India on her own where she found a job designing for a group of Indian cloth workers.' It was in India that Greta, aged 28, met 34-year-old 'Bill' Harries, then a captain in the Royal Corps of Signals. They married in June 1934.

After retirement Richard's parents moved in 1969 to Bosham where they were active members of the community and of the parish church. They were drivers for the WRVS Meals on Wheels and Greta was a voluntary driver for Bosham Monday Club. She helped to clean and keep tidy the thirteenth-century church of Holy Trinity, bringing to her work a right intention and a determination to do her best. George Herbert's lines come to mind:

> who sweeps a room, as for thy laws,
> makes that and th' action fine.

In 1983 Greta suffered a stroke. That early indomitable spirit returned. Paralysed on her right side, speechless, unable to read or write, she learned to do her tapestry again using her left hand, friends threading the needles for her. She died four years later in 1987. Richard visited regularly and was much moved when she died peacefully. At the time she was preparing to start on a tapestry kneeler for Christ Church Cathedral, Oxford. Although unable to converse, she could still mouth the words of the Lord's Prayer.

We return to the chronological sequence of Richard's life. It is 1946, his parents are in the Far East, he leaves Huddersfield and is then sent away to boarding school at Haileybury and Imperial Service College Junior School, Clewer Manor, Windsor. This was arranged by his father, setting Richard on a predetermined course towards a future in the army. There were no signs in Richard himself to suggest this was best for him or even remotely of interest to him. His parents would have been surprised at their son's future observations: 'The Masters were made up of those who weren't fit enough to do war service and there were certain resemblances to Evelyn Waugh's *Decline and Fall*. In terms of long-lasting influences, I remember praying desperately that my parents would not have to go abroad, a prayer that was not answered in the way that I wanted, the result being that I have never had any undue expectation that my prayers would get me what I want. You could say that a characteristically British, scarcely Christianized stoicism set in. I was ill for one whole term, with I think measles and chickenpox, the only time I have been ill in bed until a hip operation nearly 60 years later. But being in the sanatorium gave me an opportunity to read the whole series of Biggles books.'

Isolation and loneliness were compounded when Richard went to Wellington College from 1949 to 1954. For most of the time at Wellington Richard was unhappy even when he smiled and said he was 'fine' to any enquirer. The habit of internally withdrawing became a trait embedded in his personality. His parents lived in Singapore so Richard and his sister were shunted between different friends of their parents during the holidays or stayed with their grandmother in Cobham. When they returned to England in June 1948 with three-year-old Charles, his parents took a flat in the Surrey town. 'At Cobham I simply felt myself part of the usual kind of people. That is, people who belonged to the professional classes and sent their children to public schools and lived in the south-east of England and talked in what was called Queen's English.' New Quay remained the *El Dorado*!

Richard did not have the self-confident superiority, swagger or outward ebullience, even brutishness, to be happy in a school he describes as 'rough, tough and arrogant'. Since his time, Wellington's academic standard and cultural life have changed for the better, but during his years there it was not an environment in which he could flourish. He adds, 'In order to be happy at school, in addition to the fundamental need for a stable and loving home background, one needs to do well.'

'Doing well' bore less relation to academic prowess than to sporting achievement. This, at modest least, gave Richard an opportunity to contribute something in this alien environment: 'I did quite well at sport at my prep school and was, I think, a very confident scrum-half. However, I rapidly changed from being small and bouncy to being rather long and brittle. I wasn't really fast enough to be a good centre, and not really heavy enough in the scrum. I was quite good at squash and tennis, but never challenged for the college teams. Then, suddenly, in my last term,

I found I could run and won the major school cross-country race, the Kingsley, by a large margin.'

Academically there were few hints of Richard's future. He admits: 'As far as work was concerned I assume I was of average intelligence, but for nearly all my time there I bumped along near the bottom of the classes I was in with very poor reports, the emphasis in them being on the fact that my lack of ability was only matched by my total lack of application. One interesting reflection in retrospect is as to whether I got pushed into doing the wrong subjects: maths and physics. There are, for example, occasional bright notes in my English reports, despite continuing harping on my punctuation, untidiness on paper etc.'

He continued to read novels with alacrity and understanding. When his tutor went round the dormitory at night he usually found that Richard had gone to bed early to read, and invariably his remark as he knocked on the door and entered was, 'My boy, why aren't you working?'

Richard never felt that Wellington was conducive to making deep and lasting friendships, and he made none! He never felt he belonged. And his results did not bring him close to those who were working hard with the prospect of entry to university. 'I mucked about with those who were either not very bright or did not seem to have very much to them.' However, it was at Wellington that the theatre entered his life. Here was a different world of escape and adventure, which kindled imagination. 'A Canadian high school did a touring production of Thornton Wilder's *Our Town*. This play, with no props except for a few hard-backed chairs, re-created for me, as for so many, a magical world of an ordinary small town . . . In contrast, I never responded to my tutor's enthusiasm for the latest American musicals, films which he delighted to show to other boys. I also played the female lead in the House play. My tutor wrote to my mother on 17 January 1951 referring to my lack of progress in the words "My own guess is that his obvious success in the dormitory play went to his head. I do not mean this at all nastily, but I feel that it upset his sense of values and it disturbed him psychologically, probably more than he realized". It did indeed, not because it went to my head, but because as a result of playing the female lead I was teased in a particularly cruel and unpleasant way.'

At that time Richard's family had no real allegiance to the Church. He had never been sent to Sunday school and his only memory of a clergyman was of a rather unconvincing and ham actor in a single visit to a church once in his holidays. School chapel was 'endlessly boring' but this did not preclude significant pointers to the future. 'A friend of mine – who had ordered two gross of condoms by mail order and was, I suppose, hoping to sell them round the school, though all I think rather more for bravado than for us – suddenly said that there was no God. Without having ever given the subject a moment's thought I replied that there was. This could have just been unthinking conditioning, but it may be that some seed of faith had already, unbeknown to me, got into my psyche. We were all confirmed on a conveyor belt system. I can remember my tutor asking me whether I had thoroughly examined religions other than Christianity, Buddhism for example. Without ever having heard the word Buddhism before I replied that I had and was duly confirmed. But according to my very dim lights I took it as seriously as I could and one sign of this was that there was a voluntary evening Communion service once a week and I occasionally used to go to this, finding in that devotion something that I didn't find in ordinary chapel services. The school chaplain was a jovial fellow who used to enjoy himself drawing beautifully coloured maps of the journeys of St Paul on the blackboard. Not much of this rubbed off on us. I think I got less than 10 per cent in my school certificate Divinity. This wasn't the lowest mark in the school. One boy scored nothing at all and eventually, as a school, we were withdrawn from the exam altogether. Another more positive pointer is that I have the distinct impression of at least two devout masters kneeling in chapel either before or after a service. Perhaps their prayers for us poor boys availed somewhat. Finally, on the religious side, I can remember once in school chapel holding my head up and looking around and thinking to myself "This is not what Jesus meant at all, this is not what he meant at all", though it is possible that the cadences of this sentence have been influenced by my later reading of *The Love Song of J. Alfred Prufrock*.'

Beneath the surface, though never articulated, Richard was beginning to think for himself, distinguishing some moral principles if as yet unformulated and unstructured. He felt 'apart' even if he did not show it publicly. One example concerns the single Jewish boy in his House, perhaps in the whole school, being unmercifully tormented with cries of 'Jew boy', which Richard found appalling: 'But it was just one expression of a boys' environment which was crude, vulgar and distasteful generally. And, looking back after all these years, I think I felt at the time that I didn't really want to be part of it, though to all outward appearances I might have looked as though I was thoroughly enjoying the rough badinage, ragging and mucking about.'

Until his last two terms Richard's tutor was B. 'Bertie' C. L. Kemp who was at Wellington from 1924 to 1953. He was head of the science department, and president of the Masters' Common Room, scoutmaster of the Wellington Troop, in charge of ARP during the war and acting works bursar. He remained unmarried. His parents and sister were all dying of cancer, hence constant trips to visit them in Kent. His successor as tutor writes of Kemp: 'I am not aware that he had any friend or even close associate with whom he could share this inhumanly huge burden, nor his adventitious aids against it. After the last of his family died in 1953 he continued to imbibe the aids, but was overwhelmed by the burdens and therefore resigned.' It is perhaps understandable that with a surfeit of anxieties 'Bertie' Kemp was unable to give boys like Richard the confidence and encouragement they desperately yearned and required. Robert Moss succeeded him and immediately there was a reversal of Richard's fortunes. Here was a tutor who cared and seized on and encouraged the good in a boy's performance. And encouragement begat results! Moss wrote to Richard's father on 30 March 1954 to say: 'Richard has come on phenomenally'. Richard himself is convinced that his tutor clearly saw some spark in him and believed in him.

Richard's father wanted to get Richard into the army young so he left school a term early and took his A levels from home just before doing ten weeks' basic training at Catterick where his father had become commandant. Then, following his father's planned programme, Richard entered Sandhurst in 1954. His late flowering success at Wellington and the accelerating assurance caught from Robert Moss went with him. Sandhurst was accepted on its own terms of working hard and playing likewise. 'I did a lot of sport, representing the academy at athletics in the summer and cross-country running in the winter. I was junior under-officer and eventually passed out tenth, first into my regiment, out of a list of several hundred. I even won the military law prize, even though I hadn't attended a single lecture. Lectures took place on a Saturday when I was away playing sport, so I simply had to get hold of some past papers and that seemed to do the trick! Two factors about Sandhurst were I think significant for my subsequent life. First, there was a glamorous, fast set, which I found fun and amusing and amongst whom I had one or two friends.' His sister, Linda, recalls him 'as very much the dashing, handsome, officer cadet with the usual bevy of glamorous girlfriends. Needless to say, having a sister around at that time in his life was not welcomed. He was a great fan of Elvis and Frankie Laine and was always jiving to music. Years earlier I recollect Richard started to smoke, which placed me in an awful dilemma as to whether or not I ought to write to my parents to tell them!' But Richard resisted the temptation to become properly part of the fast set and go, for example, into a fashionable regiment instead of the unfashionable Royal Corps of Signals. However, he is grateful for Sandhurst: 'Whether one liked it or not, Sandhurst set up standards of discipline which have been part of me ever since – like turning up prepared, in good order, on time, with shoes polished.'

What was Sandhurst thinking of Richard? The reports reveal aspects of his character and progress with cogency. His father's 'pushy' influence for his son may have contributed to a lack rather than a strengthening of self-propelled motivation in science subjects in which Richard had little interest and less motivation. However, there is no evidence that he was drawn to anything in particular! The platoon commander regarded his cadet as 'likeable, cheerful, keen and enthusiastic in all that he does . . . who seems determined to fit in with everyone and everything and to do well.' But initially, in 1955, 'the one thing that may cause trouble is his ability to stay on the A Course and to get a good enough result to get to Cambridge which is his father's desire. This might eventually cramp his style.' On several reports the need 'for more self-confidence and drive' is noted. His early science results, never achieving half the maximum marks, are equally pointed: 'His work has improved but he will have to find more time for consolidation to make up for his rather weak background in physics' and, encouragingly for his future, 'He is learning to make his own decisions and overcoming what I suspect to be strong "parental guidance". Pleasant and forthright, he is more aware of his own limitations than his father is.' Richard continued to mature, to detach himself from the shadow of his father's hopes for him and to begin to exhibit some features which remain recognizable today. Richard was one of the three junior officers in Gaza Company in New College, headed by Jack Crutchley, a very tough Rhodesian, who served in their SAS. The other under-officers were John Magnay who regarded Richard as 'a kind, considerate man but also a very determined athlete on the track who practised and competed with considerable guts and determination. He and I tried to calm fire-eater Crutchley's ambitions from time to time. I was a recruit at the Guards Depot so I marched on my heels in true regimental fashion – Richard always shuffled which amused us both. I lost touch but saw him again when he was at Fulham. He remains the charming and courteous man I knew as a cadet.' Simon Turner has a different memory: 'Richard was rather more studious and less boisterous than some of us. His promotion to under-officer came, I suspect, more as a result of dedication and application than any outward and extravagant show of leadership. He was a very friendly and agreeable colleague.'

Those who knew Richard at Sandhurst were surprised that he did not keep up with them at meetings and reunions. This was not a slight on them or on the Sandhurst years. Like a snake shedding its skin he retains the experience without holding onto the body. He is not 'clubbable'. The nearest acquaintance he has with any 'club' is with the House of Lords!

After Sandhurst, Richard returned to Catterick in 1956 for a young officers' course before going out to Minden in Germany to serve with the 4th Infantry Brigade Signal Squadron. Richard's future was never likely to be in the army although he thought 'it was an easier way of life then than is it now and tended to revolve around sport in the afternoon and social life in the evening'. He returned to Catterick briefly in 1957 to study for and take the mechanical sciences qualifying exam (MSQE), a more advanced one than A level, and required for entry to Cambridge. He then returned to Germany.

Major Ron Fletcher first met Richard in Essen in 1957. 'We were both Royal signals subalterns living in an ex-Wermacht Barracks situated directly opposite a coalmine named Katrina. The pithead wheel operated continuously and gave the whole area a permanent coating of coal dust. We kept fit despite unhealthy surroundings. Each year there was a highly competitive inter-regimental athletics meeting and Richard was appointed officer in charge of athletics. He approached his task with enthusiasm and leadership. He built up the speed and stamina of all participants with alternate sprints and middle distance runs which he led. He had no side and found it easy to mix and converse with all ranks. The regimental padre, a Methodist minister, conducted Matins in a converted barrack room.'

Where were the main pointers to Richard's future? He was easily enticed by national serviceman John Halliburton to go to the Old Catholic Church in Essen, a church in full communion with the Church of England. The liturgy of the Eucharist made an immediate impact and created a 'longing' not experienced in Matins. Major Fletcher noticed Richard was reading with real intent, studying Greek and music in the little spare time available. 'He appeared to do so with foresight and planning. It was evident he had a vocation to the ordained ministry.' Indeed, it was during this time that Richard offered himself for ordination and left the army to go up to Cambridge. This was far removed from what his parents, particularly his father, had planned. But they were not privy to the development and changes within him which were now imperatives. 'The decisive factor during my time in the army was my growth into the Christian faith . . . At Sandhurst, if you thought you would be late for the morning parade at 7.00 or not properly ready, you could always go to Holy Communion. So occasionally I went. By such slender threads are we held. Then as a young officer, I can remember thinking to myself that either Christianity is true, in which case it should be at the centre of my life. Or if it's untrue, I should give it up altogether. So I started to read a little round the subject and, as one does, gravitated to friends for whom it meant something.' One was a young regular officer and former art student, an Anglo-Catholic ordinand who had been rejected or, rather, 'not recommended'. Another friend had read history at university and got within a week of ordination at his theological college before deciding to become a regular soldier instead. He was broad Church of England. Alan Godson was another, a very evangelical national service officer and a brilliant sportsman who also went on to Cambridge to be ordained. Then there was David Watson who had been at Wellington with Richard and who, after ordination, became highly influential in charismatic renewal and a magnet for conversions when he was vicar of St Michael-le-Belfry, York. Sadly, he died young of cancer in 1984, aged 51. Richard met these friends at Catterick when he was studying for the mechanical sciences qualifying examination.

The greatest influence came in the regiment in Germany with Lance-Corporal John Halliburton, a remarkable person, described by Richard as 'the most unsoldierly figure one could imagine'. Halliburton ran everything, including the regimental dance band, the jazz band, the regimental office and the garrison church as well as acting as the regimental interpreter. He sneaked into the back of the officers' mess and in return for some of Richard's sherry discussed theology with him, for which he had a natural aptitude. There was an attractive magnetism about him which influenced Richard. Here was an example of a highly intelligent Anglo-Catholic ordinand who combined deep seriousness with wide sympathies and mischievous merriment. Later Halliburton became vice-principal of St Stephen's House, Oxford; principal of Chichester Theological College; and canon residentiary of St Paul's Cathedral. At some point Richard went into the public library and took out, quite unplanned, a book of essays by Roman Catholic priests explaining why they had been ordained. 'When I had finished reading the book I remember thinking to myself "Wouldn't it be funny if one day I was ordained!". A few months later the thought came back. When I was in Germany, with the prospect of going up to Cambridge to read engineering before me in a few months' time, I remember thinking to myself, "When I retire from the army, after a successful career, wouldn't it be nice to end my life as a country parson". Immediately a following thought came: "If that's what you are meant to be doing, you'd better do it now". That thought took hold of me in a volcanic way and precipitated me out of the army to read theology. It was like falling in love, and I knew I had to act on it.' His experience over that time, and perhaps before as well, is best summed up in the words from *The Cloud of Unknowing*, quoted by T. S. Eliot in *The Four Quartets*: 'The drawing of this love and the voice of this calling'. Love had drawn him and then came the call. It is a phrase which will recur throughout Richard's life.

Chapter Two
Wholly Attending?

1958. Selwyn College, Cambridge and the Theological Tripos. What was in store for Richard, henceforward 'Harries'? The Spirit of God speaks in its own language to each generation. We cannot do without symbols, even in philosophy, as Plato knew; but the symbol must be a real projection of the thing signified, a translation into terms of space and time of some supra-spirit and supra-temporal truth. Faith is a spring of unconscious poetry.

Harries needed heroes who would command his intellectual respect and awaken in him dormant aspirations. A major impact for good and for always was the Norris-Hulse professor of divinity, Donald MacKinnon, a layman, whose idiosyncratic brilliance had been recently transferred from Aberdeen, where he was regius professor of moral philosophy. He had a fourfold influence on Harries: first, through his intellectual seriousness – the pursuit of truth really mattered: second, the fact that a Christian thinker today has to operate on the borderlands, the title of his inaugural lecture, feeling the incursions of those who live on the other side, taking their questions seriously. He also said that, 'Apologetics is the lowest form of Christian life'. Although Harries has tried to be an apologist, he has always been wary of the kind of apologetics offered by G. K. Chesterton and C. S. Lewis, attractive though their writings are in so many ways. Third, facts matter, and Christianity is making assertions which are either true or false. It was at the height of linguistic philosophy when people were concerned about the meaning of Christian propositions. The influence of MacKinnon meant that Harries was sceptical of *Honest to God* (1963) and some of the theologians, such as Tillich, who lay behind it, valuable though he found the book from a pastoral point of view. Fourth, MacKinnon's range of reference was incredibly wide, from Greek tragedy to the Holocaust. Unless theology engaged with the central concerns and features of human existence and illuminated them, then it was trivial.

Imbibing MacKinnon meant that Harries adopted the view that the opposition between theological concern and practical concern is a false antithesis. From this time it was Harries' profound conviction that no theological concern could be genuine that was not a concern for the Church in its relation to the whole range of human life. Too much of what passes today for concern for the nature of the Church is merely a religious concern for the maintenance of a standard of a practice.

MacKinnon's lectures held audiences entranced with a mixture of intellectual passion as he pursued faith and reality in tense equipoise. It needed a nimble intelligence to comprehend his convoluted arguments. No simply sponge-like mind could absorb the twists and turns, so students were in danger of retaining the husk at the expense of the kernel. They had to struggle with the meaning of his lectures. George Steiner captures the aura of MacKinnon, a legend in his own lifetime (1913–1994) in *Theology*, January–February 1995:

> Where to begin? There was the subtly menacing undercurrent in his voice, inimitable, but yet so often imitated; the forward lunge (that's too crude a picture, I know) of his towering, turbulently compact physique; the celebrated mannerisms, the lion's paw drawn across the great head. And there is a whole volume of dicta and anecdotes – many of which have been drawn upon, for example by Tom Stoppard in his play Jumpers – anecdotes which reach back to Donald's Oxford days, when Locke Scholar, in fury at some idiot, announced that he would bite this person, getting under the table and proceeding to do so. Donald going down Trinity Street, seeing a very illustrious colleague and saying 'I am giving a dinner party tonight, why don't you come?' and the colleague saying, 'Donald, it's in my honour.' 'Oh, never mind, come anyway.' The rich family of stories about challenging some student or colleague to reassure him, Donald, about 'am I, I' i.e. Donald's identity. The colleague or interlocutor doing so to the passionate best of his limited ability and Donald morosely remarking, 'It's no good, I don't believe you are.' Story after story a clutch of tales and citations that turn on Donald's fragile, haunted intimations of identity, of the self when it is in the grip of systematic thought or supreme excitement of sensibility.

We will discover that Harries was drawn to people of overtowering intellect yet whose personalities were not ones with which he could identify. It was healthy in preventing the kind of hero-worship which merely adores and mimics. At Cambridge he was developing a distinct identity, but not yet a vivid personality.

Owen Chadwick was master of Selwyn College and Dixie professor of ecclesiastical history. Harries was transfixed by Chadwick's 'magical use of language'. His brilliance as a scholar and devout priest (the two are intertwined) is everywhere known and attested, not least because he has made history live by the use of meticulous scholarship, illuminating hitherto undiscovered byways with unerring perception and judgement, in accessible language. He is a knighted member of the Order of Merit, a former president of the British Academy, Regius professor and vice-chancellor of Cambridge. Is it any wonder that Harries and his fellow theological students held him in highest approbation?

Harries had arrived at Selwyn with a view to reading mechanical sciences, having studied maths and physics before and passed the qualifying exam in the army. According to his application he indicated an interest in literature and music. However, as with most ventures new to him, he now took the Theological Tripos with energy and enthusiasm. At the time the one-year Part I included both Hebrew and Greek, three biblical papers and an introduction to the study of theology.

19

Canon John Sweet, with his deep care for his students and his exact scholarship, was Harries' supervisor and another recognized influence: 'Richard was a delight to teach, especially in Greek, though he had no linguistic capital to draw on except O level Latin, achieved in the army just before he came up. In Part II he continued with Hebrew and added philosophical theology, two of the toughest options. He had a robust and penetrating intelligence which goes in a direct and disciplined way for what the situation requires – as an illustration; after completing elementary Hebrew in the first year, Richard's group, of which he was a leading member, asked me to lay on a course in Aramaic; they were doing the Gospels, so wanted the language of the Jews. The university lecturer in Aramaic, who had few official pupils, was delighted, and I joined in. He, and we, were disappointed when Richard missed a II:i in Part II, because he was academically ambitious, even if not an academic.'

This is an important observation and is linked with other attributes. Harries was a leading figure at Selwyn, athletically and socially. He always had time for unglamorous acquaintances, and he befriended misfits. His appetite for what was practically important in religion was already embedded. Critical comments from his supervisors included his tendency to range more widely than the question set, and 'possibly a little inclined to cling too tenaciously to theories that appeal to him to the exclusion of all else'. Is this why he did not secure the result he anticipated and had been led to expect by his teachers?

Were there other reasons? Was one the person to whom Richard became engaged, a very attractive, sparkling, high-flying medic at Girton College? Canon Sweet remembers Harries saying slightly ruefully that he was going out with a Cambridge Inter-Collegiate Christian Union (CICCU) girl whose desire at the time was to work in a mission hospital. Her name – Josephine 'Jo' Bottomley. Jo was born on 15 April 1940 and her family, on her father's side, included some distinguished nineteenth-century scientists. Her father was an industrial chemist and her mother had been training to be a doctor when she married. Jo was head girl at Benenden before reading medicine and psychology at Cambridge and going on to do her clinical training at University College Hospital. She specialized in paediatrics.

Other interests emerged at Cambridge which later evolved, deepened and had a life of their own. The first was a liking and appreciation of poetry. The second was a love for the visual arts. During vacations a group of friends used an old A40 to tour the Continent. (It belonged to Derek Watson's mother; Derek was Harries' best man and later Dean of Salisbury.) Four of them used to go, as often as not without even a tent, camping outdoors, and devouring picture galleries and churches – culture vultures – for a month in France, Spain or Italy. Harries developed a knowledgeable interest in all aspects of art but it was Christian and, later on, Byzantine art which was his particular passion and for which he would become something of an authority.

In his final year at Selwyn, Harries was awarded a scholarship to do a BD at McGill University in Canada on an exchange programme, but after much thought he changed his mind. With a degree of self-candour he felt he needed time for prayer and reflection before he was spiritually fit for his life's work as a priest. He felt that the BD at McGill would not have taken him much further than his Cambridge degree – and in any case he had fallen in love and did not fancy conducting his engagement from the other side of the Atlantic. Instead, he went to Cuddesdon Theological College, Oxford in 1961. Whether all his needs and aspirations, and those of the Church, would be met there is not without question! Robert Runcie, then principal of Cuddesdon, received a letter from Canon Sweet about the new student: 'His personal faith I would think to be simple – in the best sense of the word – straightforward and simple-hearted; capable of learning a great deal on the devotional side . . . He is refreshingly unecclesiastical, without being in the least bit bolshy; a pleasant, friendly person with a good sense of humour but capable of being fierce . . . He plays all games well and modestly.'

Cuddesdon was a seminary, not a university college, and the disciplined routine of prayer and worship in a sober Tractarian way was fundamental to the students' lives. There was a lot of fasting and parsnips in Lent. On one Easter Day the students heard a sermon on the sin of fornication. Robert Runcie, principal for only a year, was more cautious than he might have been, and perhaps circumstances demanded, after the strict and stern regime of his predecessor, bachelor Edward Knapp-Fisher. Some students had been scared and apprehensive about approaching Knapp-Fisher with their problems, although he exercised real pastoral care to those who could penetrate the rather cold barrier.

Since his death Robert Runcie has not been well-served by several of his too many biographers. Access to the authentic and complex person is found in the pre-Canterbury years when it was possible to know that his views were untarnished, free of a tranche of advisers and speech-writers. His use of memorable words and oft-repeated phrases was more contrived than natural but his marvellous gift of mimicry was all his own. Of the principal, who was also vicar of Cuddesdon, Harries says: 'If you went to the loo a few minutes before an evening lecture you would find him pacing up and down the corridor finely honing in his mind the few brilliant words which he would use to introduce the visiting speaker.' Then, as later, he was capable of stripping an argument to its bare essentials.

Harries owed much to Runcie. There was a touching sight and poignant moment when Harries, after the installation of Jeffrey John as Dean of St Albans in 2005, in the aftermath of the forced retreat from the Reading appointment, stood alone – in his rochet and chimere – on the grass outside the abbey contemplating Robert Runcie's gravestone. What drew Harries to Runcie? 'He was a great human being, very *simpatico*, with an extraordinary ability to relate intuitively to a wide range of people and make them feel better for being alive. With a self-deprecating sense of humour, rooted in a genuine humility, together with a sense of the absurd, he rarely began a talk without some story against himself.' Runcie's own lectures were appreciated as a balance between questioning and tradition. Difficulties were acknowledged and 'were to be lived with on the basis of a Gospel faith'. He was never a man for simple solutions and his panache covered a quivering self-confidence. In his later life this proved a defensive mechanism, a shield against the poison-tipped arrows which were shot from tightly drawn bows. Harries did not acquire this skill, so when the barbed arrows flew over a few very serious controversies at Oxford he could do little but retreat into himself as even many erstwhile friends distanced themselves from him.

We know what Runcie looked for in those seeking ordination, revealed in a July 1964 article published in the *Church Observer*:

(A priest) will not depend on status, nor upon his own abilities, nor upon a system, but upon God. (The primary quality) required is a man's sincerity in prayer and faith and compassion. These may yet be hardly developed, but the relevant signs will consist in obstacles overcome, work voluntarily undertaken and thoroughly performed, and a general attitude of responsibility as a Christian man rather than an interest in the social and ornamental aspects of the priesthood. Then they (the selectors) will look for something which can only be described as a love of God's world and his people. Affectation and pretence are danger signs, and the sociability required of a priest consists in a spontaneity of interest in a world and a society of which he feels himself instinctively and naturally a part.

Runcie's challenge to bring fresh air and insights into Cuddesdon was not fully accepted. Peter Cornwell was a student under the old regime and tutor in the new:

By the time I returned to Cuddesdon to be on the staff, having done a curacy in a bleak housing estate in Hull, things were changing and, of course, Richard came as a student at this moment of change. Robert Runcie sensed that the waters were to become turbulent. Indeed the C of E was to live through the *Soundings* and *Honest to God* era while the Roman Catholic Church was to plunge into the Second Vatican Council. Runcie realized that the questions could no longer be evaded and so worked to fashion a more sinewy, virile intellectual life. The college was opened up theologically – the resources of Oxford were drawn upon – high-flyers like Richard were farmed out to Oxford tutors. David Jenkins, then at Queen's, came out to do seminars. He was then a sure guide through the *Honest to God* business and spotted a lot of Robinson's cruder notions. But throughout, Runcie believed in free debate while providing stability through maintaining a pretty conservative devotional and liturgical regime. We remained at this level very solidly Prayer Book Catholics.

Harries had arrived at Cuddesdon with a reputation for being a theologically bright young thing, although another tutor, Lionel R. Wickham, makes the point that Harries was not the most intellectually gifted or best educated of the students at the time. 'But there was no doubting his gifts. I was always conscious that here was someone whose judgement was to be trusted. He had obvious personal skills: people would take note of what he said and thought; he had an easy manner.'

There were students who were in awe of Harries whose mind was already showing signs of versatility. They were even more in awe of Jo, his fiancée, who became the first fruits of a harvest of fiancées and wives, breaking the Knapp-Fisher mould. But in opening up the college, Runcie, the first married principal in the history of the college founded in 1854, was ever mindful of the Cuddesdon tradition. Women were allowed into the college for half an hour after the Sunday Eucharist, when it was assumed that the grace of the sacrament would keep the lusts of the young men down. The lusts of the young women were not considered. But all the men, married or engaged, were treated as if they were single. It made one wonder a little about what this taught concerning Christian marriage! For the most part colleges of that time made no room either physically or spiritually for those with whom the students intended spending the rest of their lives.

All the changes in the pattern of life and worship had small impact on Harries. Was time well spent on cultivating the spirit of personal devotion and prayer amongst the students? How were they helped in the central task of becoming men of God? Without that, all their accumulating gifts would be as naught. The difficulty was not restricted to Cuddesdon. Although they did learn how to say their prayers, it was in a pseudo-academic community, in time with the ringing of a bell. One priest, an Oxford graduate, went to work in a notorious slum area. He returned to his theological college saying: 'My ministry is concerned almost exclusively with housing – how to get good housing, cheap housing, public housing. I learned almost exclusively nothing in theological college about that which is now nearly all of my ministry. The bell-ringing is not regular. It comes any time of the day and night. So I find it just about impossible to have any prayer life at all.'

There were two significant developments for Harries, one for the present, the other for the future. He spent a great deal of time at Littlemore Psychiatric Hospital visiting patients, taking down case histories and being taught by the chaplain, who was also a medically qualified doctor. This experience did far more for his appreciation of interpersonal relationships than any number of academic courses in pastoral theology and was an essential foundation when later, as a curate in Hampstead, he founded a befriending group of the Samaritans.

The other development, whose significance only emerged much later, was a talk by James Parkes who strove for a new relationship between Church and synagogue. He revealed the extent of anti-Semitism in Christian history. At the time it was no more than a scattered seed but found life in Harries and would eventually lead to his prominence in Christian–Jewish relations. He was also able to spend one term in East Jerusalem, at a time when it was governed by Jordan.

How much time did Harries spend in college? Sufficient for two bouts of inspiration making Cuddesdon worthwhile and vital for his future development. They came from visiting lecturers whose thought entered his life and soul. He introduces the first, Austin Farrer (1904–1968): philosopher, theologian and biblical scholar, then warden of Keble College after 25 years as fellow and chaplain of Trinity College. He gave a series of Holy Week lectures on the Atonement. The impression of the man and the message on Harries was immediate:

He came quietly and quickly up the aisle at Cuddesdon Parish Church, mounted the pulpit and without any ado talked of God for an hour before descending the pulpit and walking quickly out again with as little fuss as he had come in. It was a privilege to hear him talking about God. I also came out of the church with a sense that as he had spoken my mind had gone click, click, click as question after scarcely formulated question seemed to receive an answer and a fresh insight. I would have been hard put to decide whether it was a spiritual experience or an intellectual treat. It was of course both. And this highlights the nature of Farrer's genius.

Farrer was a theologian of unquestioned brilliance, a priest and pastor of undisputed power and a great preacher whose sermons in pulpit and in print invited reading as seed-beds for other people's ministry of the Word. In Harries' published essay 'We know on our knees' in *Divine Action* he acknowledges the electrifying stimulation of Farrer for the sheer splendour of his intellect, 'the imagination of a poet; and the depth of his spirituality, his transparency to God'. For Harries he was *The One Genius*, the title of a book of readings through the year with Austin Farrer which he selected and to which Archbishop Michael Ramsey contributed a foreword. Farrer's writings shaped Harries in decisive ways which are prominently evident in, for example, *Being a Christian* (1981) and *The Real God* (1994) and, above all, in what he has tried to write on the problem of evil and suffering.

Part of Farrer's 'genius' was his vocation to write not only on paper but on human souls. He was someone who, to use a neglected word, edified. Once again we find Harries absorbing thought and spirituality like blotting-paper without having known what it was like to be Farrer who for years wrestled with the academic problem of the historical Jesus. No one could accuse Farrer of ignorance or inexperience in that field of learning. This only serves to make all the more impressive his categorical statement, near the end of his life, referring to the New Testament record, 'I want to say simply that the facts of Christ's earthly life are as solid as rock.'

The other Cuddesdon inspirer was W. (Bill) Vanstone (1923–1999) who gave lectures at Cuddesdon. These were published many years later as *Love's Endeavour, Love's Expense* (1977). He developed the idea of the kenosis of God, not simply in relation to the Incarnation but in creation itself. For Harries the importance is the moral and spiritual appeal of this understanding of God. Some ideas of God are morally and spiritually unacceptable. But today, when Christianity cannot be imposed and is unfashionable, the only way it will make headway is by its intrinsic spiritual attraction.

Love's Endeavour, Love's Expense is one of two classics from Vanstone. This academically brilliant man rejected all overtures to spend his life in quad or court. Instead, for 21 years he initiated work and prayer as a parish priest on a new housing estate at Kirkholt on the outskirts of Rochdale. What jolted Vanstone into writing this book came six months after his arrival in Kirkholt, when he recognized the complete apathy of the people who had no interest whatsoever in whether or not a church should be built. In a flash he knew 'that the importance of the Church lies in something other than its service to, or satisfaction of, the needs of man'. Vanstone's other classic, *The Stature of Waiting* (1982), was the fruit of 12 years as a canon residentiary of Chester Cathedral where he had gone following a severe heart attack. Never a team player, Vanstone wrote, preached and was at the disposal of individuals who sought him out. He never entertained offers of preferment, so-called, and once likened the Church of England to 'a swimming pool in which all the noise comes from the shallow end'.

Andrew Henderson – priest, psychotherapist and former director of social services for Kensington and Chelsea – was a contemporary of Harries at Cuddesdon and found him:

> Socially confident and relaxed, very personable with his fair hair and cavalry twills, he could be relied on to impress visitors with intelligent comment and an unusual fluency in expressing his ideas: and he also laughed a lot and clearly enjoyed the company of those who sparkled in conversation, perhaps finding his own lighter side kindled. That could explain why some now find him short of small talk or sometimes unexciting in the pulpit; the stimulation he needs to take off isn't always there! It was easy to see him then as someone who would be likely to do very well in the Church, but the particular qualities that have made him a national figure as Bishop of Oxford were not especially evident or developed at that early stage. I supposed I detected in him a kindred spirit in that his commitment to the Christian faith and the Church was more about engagement with wider society than immersion in ecclesiastical affairs and paraphernalia. He was not a churchy ordinand. From our time at Cuddesdon, I'd have expected Richard to become ultra-conventional over the years. But he hasn't has he? Like all of us he's far too many-layered to be satisfactorily labelled, and fortunately for the embattled liberal wing of the C of E, his unusual combination of qualities has been a source of great encouragement to us foot-soldiers.

Cuddesdon considered itself a little elitist and there were many admirable features to the training. But did it depend more on the inclinations, efforts and dispositions of individual students than on the principal and staff who, admittedly, were wary of destroying sound traditions in their endeavours for reform? Staff were faced with sorting out problems which could have been foreseen with psychological testing of students at the time of selection. The time was not yet ripe for such tests whose purpose would give a bishop some indication of whether a candidate's personality could withstand the stresses of ordained ministry, or if he had some aberration of personality that was hidden from the eye of the bishop and bishops' selectors. Were future priests and bishops helped to recognize the warning signs of emotional stress, personal muddle and conflict, wavering faith and spiritual anxiety in others as well as in themselves? Was a sharper cutting edge needed?

Harries' formal education at Selwyn College, Cambridge and training at Cuddesdon College, Oxford were over. Often the placing of a newly ordained curate is random, haphazard, incomprehensible, a mismatch, which affects his future priestly ministry in an unfortunate way.

But the opportunities in London, the diocese in which Harries would serve, were wide, with some exceptionally able 'training vicars'. Harries would benefit from being on a staff with several curates, where there was a healthy combination of discipline, continuing training and opportunity for imaginative initiatives. By now his personality was fully formed and has not substantially changed. The friendly demeanour is on the surface. He ploughs his own furrow. His Cambridge and Oxford contemporaries unite in saying he was not an easy person to get to know. There was something rather lofty and, apparently, aloof about him. But they soon realized he was a shy and very private kind of person. Where he would serve his curacy would be paramount in determining his future.

Chapter Three
'A Meteor Streaming to the Wind'

If Harries had been placed in a parish with a large staff he would have benefited from the discipline and 'rough and tumble' of collegial curatical life – and encountered stretching regimes with demonstrative competitiveness among the curates. There were many such parishes in the London area which would have provided an exacting and exciting environment in which to minister.

Instead, Harries was placed at St John's, Hampstead, a parish of 8,787 souls. Only hindsight confirms that this was an excellent choice where his debut as a priest would reveal and test his latent gifts, develop in him new skills and where he would grow without swelling, and provide pointers for his future life and ministry.

St John's, on the corner of Frognal Way and at the end of an attractive, unspoilt row of eighteenth-century houses, has a distinctive spire; the decorative gates came from the canons of Stanmore. The church, begun in 1744, has a barrel vault. There is a bust of Keats by Anne Whitney (a replica of the one in Keats House); and monuments to Norman Shaw, George du Maurier and John Constable. The churchyard is the site of Constable's tomb. The parish included a high proportion of men and women who were at or near the pinnacle of their professions: the business world, universities, with a sprinkling of independently-minded political figures. Hampstead was also the haunt of interesting, wide-awake and intellectually aware writers, artists and actors. Perhaps most important of all was the heady atmosphere in Hampstead in the 1960s. 'It was this in which I was caught up rather than any reforms in Church structures and organizations. It was the time of the Beatles, Carnaby Street, sexual liberation and student riots. A Labour government was elected in 1964 and Harold Wilson instituted his white heat revolution. In Hampstead, the Conservative Home Secretary, Henry Brooke, a member of our congregation, lost his seat and Ben Whittaker, a left-wing member of the Labour Party, was elected.'

In 1959 the Vicar of St John's, Alan Rogers, was invited by the Archbishop of Canterbury, Geoffrey Fisher, to be Bishop of Mauritius. He was succeeded by Francis James Thomas Hall, vicar of St Philip's, Earls Court. He was very large and known as Ele (short for elephant) to his wife, children and intimates. He was a friendly, generous-hearted and contented person with no obvious qualities for training and directing curates. When in 1963 he was seeking a new curate, someone suggested that he should see Richard Harries and his fiancée Jo. They were invited to Sunday lunch and found a welcoming family including 19- and 16-year-old vicarage 'children'. The position was very soon offered and accepted.

Surnames were used throughout the congregation so Richard was Mr Harries or Reverend Harries – except to many young people who referred to him as 'Vic'. Jo was still Miss Josephine Bottomley, then a medical student at University College Hospital, taking her final examinations in June 1964, soon to be a doctor practising for a time in Highgate.

Richard and Jo were married on 29 June 1963 and moved into the attractive sounding curate's house at 1 Holly Bush Vale which Ele's widow, Patricia Hall, describes as 'small and humble and situated in the church-school playground'. One youth says it was 'very primitive where Richard instructed us to eat up the excess of cakes so thoughtfully provided by doting ladies who thought Richard needed fattening up'. But for Richard and Jo it was special, their first home together.

Harries was made deacon in 1963 and ordained priest at Michaelmas 1964 in St Paul's Cathedral. He opened a sermon celebrating 150 years of theological education at Cuddesdon in 2004 with these words:

Gerard Manley Hopkins once wrote to his friend Robert Bridges to say that 'a kind of touchstone of the highest or most living art is seriousness; not gravity, but the being in earnest with your subject – reality'. What Hopkins writes about art, is no less applicable to the priestly life. And as he reminds us, there is a world of difference between genuine seriousness, which can often hide beneath a certain lightness of touch, even levity, and being ponderous or portentous, let alone pretentious, which is merely a façade, a disguise for an absence of true seriousness.

'True seriousness' would become one of Harries' good and gracious qualities. There was also already a predisposition in his thought that may be permanently captured and expressed in the word 'liberal', though numerous exceptions will emerge. That does not mean that he fell prey to those who wanted organized agitations and ginger groups to rock the foundations of the Church. When he became a bishop there were those who expressed disappointment that he could not be recruited as a paid up member of various campaigning ecclesiastical organizations. His published books reflect this. He was asked to write *The Authority of Divine Love* (1983) as part of a series celebrating the Oxford Movement. It is about the nature of authority, and deals with some of the disputed issues over the authority of the Scriptures, tradition and the Church. He says: 'I usually try to steer clear of these themes.'

This was the 1960s. Harries' reforming liberalism does not generally lead him to be an ardent radical, neither is he a natural rebel or revolutionary, but when his conscience is stirred to reach boiling point he acts with decisiveness just short of a pressure cooker exploding. Was there ever a more tumultuous and inebriating time to be ordained in Christ's vineyard! Tumbling from the presses came: *Soundings: Essays Concerning Christian Understanding* in 1962, whose essayists included Geoffrey Lampe, Hugh Montefiore, Harry Williams, George Woods and John Habgood. A year later *Honest to God* by John Robinson and *Objections to Christian Belief* with contributions by Donald MacKinnon, Harry Williams, J. S. Bezzant and

A. R.Vidler (also editor) and many others. These books changed the climate, even the direction, of theological insight. *Soundings* set out to 'establish or re-establish some kind of vital contact with that enormous majority for whom Christian faith is not so much unlikely as irrelevant and uninteresting'. How far the books were successful in appealing to the unthinking masses is doubtful. But within the Church and on its perimeter they were seminal works, particularly *Honest to God*.

Harries' theological beliefs are confidently held. They enter into the inner shrine of the conscience and unite themselves with the intimate loyalties of the heart. He read everything that was new with an enquiring, though not wholly open, mind. He accepted traditional theology as the necessary basis of teaching whilst acknowledging that this traditional theology had in many respects fallen out of accord with modern knowledge and needed to be cautiously but frankly revised. The history of Jesus is a vital part of faith in the Christ. The two may not be severed without cutting the roots of spiritual vitality. We cannot now divide them making Jesus a myth and retaining Christ as a living power. That is at one with the fatuity which would maintain that a foundation is only necessary while the house is being built, but ceases to be important when it has been finished. Rather is it the case that the size and splendour of the building tests and reveals the strength of the foundation. Faith throws back upon the history which created it a glory which illumines as well as transfigures.

St John's, Hampstead was not a church untouched by intellectual difficulties. But an intelligent congregation required more from their clergy and the pulpit than perplexity and an 'uncertain sound'. They were aware that the Church was required to undertake again the difficult, invidious, but in the end salutary, task of setting forth the Gospel in right relation to the sum of knowledge, and thus commending it to the acceptance of an informed and considering people. It is at Hampstead that Harries would learn of the power and the potential of the preacher as well as the pitfalls. From some Church of England pulpits congregations began to hear only the disconcerting exposition of the preacher's doubts. Instead of parading before the people the doubts that shadowed their own minds, and the perplexities which they felt, young preachers like Harries learned how to preach the truths by which they lived, and placed their emphasis on the certitudes of the Church's faith. This is what would make him in, 92-year-old Bishop David Say's words, 'one of the best Church of England broadcasters of the day'.

Theological squalls were not all that faced Christians in the 1960s. As if from nowhere there was an eruption of what was called the 'new morality'. If Christian radicalism had been shooting at a too literal interpretation of the Scriptures, it lengthened its sights and changed its targets, taking aim at creeds and traditional morals. It was a tendency, not a body of tenets. The importance of this fact cannot be overestimated; all the more because the type of behaviour inculcated, or at least allowed, by the new morality seemed often strangely akin to that championed by the old immorality. But whereas hitherto it was often practised in defiance of Christianity and the moral law, and defended on the sole ground that it was pleasant even though wrong, its clamouring adherents claimed that it was truer to the highest principles of morality than the more conventional practice and teaching of the Church.

On questions of morality the Church was in the forefront in publishing the findings of working parties peopled by experts in their fields assisted by rich theological and ethical insights on a range of moral issues. The majority came from the Board for Social Responsibility which, three decades later, Harries came to chair. Many reports not merely contributed to the national debate but led it, including *Ought Suicide to be a Crime?* (1950); *Sterilization* ((1962); *Decisions about Life and Death* (1965); *Putting Asunder (A Divorce Law for Contemporary Society)* (1966); *Abortion* (1966); *Fatherless by Law (The Law and Welfare of Children designated illegitimate)* (1966).

The third seismic shift was labelled 'The New Reformation' and concerned the interior reorganization of the Church. During Harries' curacy from 1962 to 1969 the Church of England was awash with reports which would affect its future bearings. Prominent were *Conversations between the Church of England and the Methodist Church* (1963); *The Deployment and Payment of the Clergy* by Leslie Paul ('The Paul Report') (1964); *Crown Appointments and the Church* (The Howick Commission) (1964); *Alternative Services – First Series* (1965); *Government by Synod* (The Hodson Commission) (1966); *Women and Holy Orders* (1966); *Partners in Ministry* (The Morley Commission) (1967); *Towards Reconciliation* (Anglican-Methodist Unity Commission) (1967); *Intercommunion Today* (1968).

The effect of this deluge of words was intoxicating for those with the appetite for root and branch reforms. They were like the drivers of primitive steam engines who, in order to get a greater degree of pressure, tampered with the safety valves – so that occasionally the engine blew up altogether, with painful results to everybody in range. That would not happen, it was thought, if the Church invited such radicals and rebels to join commissions where their ardour could be softened and their balloons pricked. But they were not sweetened and subdued and, on the whole, were successful in pushing reforms forward. The results would become evident when legislation appeared in the following decades.

Harries was not swept up and away by these windy gusts of reform. He was dubious and apprehensive about the clamour created. Ecclesiastical reorganization never captured his imagination or struck him as of primary importance. Moreover, as a curate he did not have ready access to the surprisingly inferior parish magazine of St John's to state and propagate his views. His energies were concentrated on his ministry in the parish, even if his mind was conceivably elsewhere. Two people were important: one an inspirational preacher, the other a fellow curate.

Joseph McCulloch was already famous as rector of St Mary-le-Bow, with its famous twin pulpits, in the City of London. He was endlessly stimulating, a pioneer and a divine disturber, not an easy person to live with. As St Mary-le-Bow was only open for worship on weekdays, McCulloch was attached to St John's Hampstead for weekend duty. Harries sat at his feet for six years, a huge figure in his life, whom he 'caught' in an obituary notice in *The Independent*, 10 March 1990:

Although I have been fortunate to hear many good preachers, Joseph McCulloch is consistently the best preacher I have listened to. His sermons were almost invariably both highly interesting and profound, the best of them a work of art. During the 1960s at the height of the satire boom, *That Was The Week That Was*, *Private Eye* and all that, he preached a brilliant sermon showing the intimate relationship between satire and Christianity, exploring the nature of satire and Christianity down the ages and its spiritual basis, to end with a devastating line to the effect that it was such a pity that we hadn't got any satirists today.

The three-hour meditation on Good Friday was the place where he really came into his own. The spiritual wrestlings and reflections on the previous year were drawn to a focus and the three-hour period, which went in a flash for the hundreds who came and stayed, gave him the length he needed. In this mature period of his ministry, he was passionately concerned, in an age of apparently dying faith, to communicate religious conviction in a way that people could understand and respond to . . . Always enormously good company, holding forth with a string of anecdotes and witticisms, he could give the impression of being self-centred and difficult. In later years, no doubt partly derived from Jung whom he had read thoroughly, his theology and preaching focused on a contrast between the ego and the true self. He was himself a living example of this theology. The 'clamant ego', to use his phrase, was certainly there. But more significantly, so was the true self, Christ within him. With Joseph you had a sense of the greatness of spirit, that God within him, that led those many who loved him to sit so lightly to his ego and respond with such gratitude to his profound centre.

Michael Langford, five years older than Harries, was an honorary curate from 1963–1967, being also a full-time research student, later professor of philosophy and subsequently of medical ethics at Newfoundland University:

Richard's pastoral gifts were evident, and I recall even now a couple of very tricky family situations which he handled with tact and charity. Even then he had a style that tended to put people at ease. He could be very humorous, but one always felt that there was a real concern for all the people he met . . . We shared a common concern to present a version of Christianity that combined some real sense of personal commitment with an intellectual integrity of some doctrines – such as original sin (e.g. to distance it from 'original guilt').

There were the usual parochial organizations. Harries was dissatisfied with those catering for the under-thirties with their limited programmes and insular activities. He had plenty of idealism to impart and matched innovation with determination. He changed the ethos and direction of some existing organizations and started new ones with help from other people. Peter Lund, chairman of the 18–30 Club:

This was a small group of people who met for coffee after Evensong in the church hall. There were walks, musical evenings etc. but numbers were small. Richard saw the potential of the club but felt that the venue was off-putting to a lot of people. He persuaded some of the church members, with room to host up to 50 young people in more pleasant surroundings, to take turns in hosting them, resulting in well-attended gatherings. The name was changed to 'The Sunday Club' and very well-known speakers were attracted, despite offering no fee, for example Peter Cook came to address a capacity audience. The vicar and older members of the congregation were supportive. One result was the large number of young people at Evensong.

The Friday Club started as a club for choristers and their friends, meeting in the Moreland Hall, a building shared by the church and the parochial school. This was too exclusive for Harries and when he was asked to help with the club he immediately and actively encouraged children from less privileged and difficult backgrounds to attend. The club became an 'open' one and its success was phenomenal. Numbers had to be limited to 200 with a long waiting list. Harries and Michael Langford were in charge, helped by two non-churchgoers – a social worker and a medical researcher – plus less regular adult helpers. The curate's house was next to the hall so Harries was always there when the club opened. Peter Lund is of the opinion that Harries' most important role 'was to convince the trustees responsible for the building that the club was serving a great social need in an area lacking in facilities for young people'. On several occasions 20 or so members were taken on camps including a sort of youth hostel in Yorkshire, and a collection of farm buildings in the Quantock Hills, where they had to do their own catering. These occasions were full of fun and adventure (including, in Yorkshire, getting chased by a bull). The two curates hoped a small degree of Christian influence would rub off. However, the Friday Club was not primarily a source of evangelism, but a kind of social outreach to the community.

Harries chaired a volatile, independent gathering of young people called Arrowline which combined social service with coffee parties in different homes around Hampstead village. Charlotte and Susannah Ellie were members:

Arrowline's aims were admirable, including decorating rooms in the homes of elderly and incapacitated people. The membership was extremely diverse in age from teenagers to university students, and reflected the religious mix of Hampstead. There were Jews and Christians (no Muslims were around in the 1960s) and black and white. Richard was always welcome and was seen as a sort of elder brother. We never felt he was 'policing' us – though he probably was. Some of the older generation viewed our club with great suspicion and distaste.

Harries also initiated 'Out of Doubt', a series of groups for some of the many agnostic young people in Hampstead, during the holidays.

A parish research group, run under Harries' increasingly commodious umbrella, had been considering the very high suicide rate in Hampstead – three times the national average. Harries was in touch with Chad Varah, guild vicar of St Stephen's Walbrook in the City and the founder of the Samaritans. It was decided that Hampstead should have a Befriending Group where individuals, properly trained, would offer friendship in time of need, not professional advice. One hundred and ten people offered Harries their assistance and were interviewed by Chad Varah's staff. In this way the Samaritans established a befriending group in Hampstead.

St John's had its formidable folk. Mrs Black-Hawkins, wife of the headmaster of University College School, was in charge of numerous parochial activities. The community was divided between those she approved of and those she did not. The goodlooking, charming and energetic young curate was top of her approved list. This swayed the parish 'ladies' in Harries' direction. There were other formidable, potentially divisive, corporate bodies at St John's. One of them was the choir! If half the congregation went to hear Joseph McCulloch when he was preaching, the other half went to listen to the music. The regular congregation of 200–250 was swollen at festivals and high days to 800, and half of these came to hear the choir and music of professional standard under the direction of a widely respected and renowned organist and choirmaster, Martindale Sidwall. He was also professor of organ at the Royal Academy of Music and director and founder and conductor of the London Bach Orchestra. Harries appreciated the music as an aid and uplift in worship to the glory of God, but not as simply the pre-eminent reason for church attendance.

St John's was traditional Church of England with the main Sunday services of sung Matins and very-sung Evensong! A Sung Eucharist, minus the choir, was celebrated at 9.30 am. The *Book of Common Prayer* was an ancillary article of faith and there were many who intended keeping it that way including Ele Hall's predecessor. Younger people and a sprinkling of older parishioners without clout were keen for what they regarded as modern language in the new experimental services and to have the parish Eucharist as the focus of worship. With a preponderance of articulate people on the parochial church council, annual meetings were forums of heated debate on either side.

John Willmer, parishioner and server of long duration, regards Harries as someone who recognized both points of view and acted to some extent as a bridge between them, exercising a mollifying influence:

The team of servers presented another problem. Ele Hall was less in the Catholic tradition than Alan Rogers. Many of the servers were in (the former) tradition but the younger ones wanted to move with the changes in the wider Church which led to a not entirely happy relationship with the vicar. Richard was charged with the responsibility of the training and practice of the servers and liaised with the vicar over any problems. This avoided any outright conflict or resignations. Thus smooth working in the sanctuary was continued.

Harries was most 'at home' and influential amidst the artistic community, those on the borderlands to whom he was drawn as iron filings to a magnet. His already wide knowledge of the arts, particularly literature, sat well in Hampstead. Ernest Raymond (a major writer of his time) and Diana, his wife, a novelist, are examples, as Diana Raymond explains:

> Richard's arrival in Hampstead coincided with that time in my life when I returned to the Church after a long absence – indeed since I left school . . . Dante wrote 'In the middle of the way of life I found myself in a dark wood'. It is a common part of the journey, and it was of mine. I did not at first take Communion; I sat at the back, more or less anonymously . . . I saw Richard from the point of view of a novice and learner. But it does mean that stepping somewhat apprehensively into new territory, I was extremely lucky that he was one of those who (all unknowing) helped me on the way.
>
> Richard was a good and affectionate friend to my late husband, Ernest Raymond, who was then in his later seventies. Ernest's relationship with the Church was an ambivalent one. He was ordained deacon in the summer of 1914. Three weeks later Gavrilo Princip fired his shot in Sarajevo. He was posted to the Middle East and took part in the landings on Gallipoli, which gave rise to his first novel, *Tell England* (1922). After the war Ernest found himself at odds with his chosen path of priest. He always had trouble with the harsher sayings of Christ, in contrast to the other side of compassion and love. In the end he resigned his Orders and became a full-time novelist, though never losing a deep love and fascination with the Church. He used to talk to Richard at length particularly when Ernest was in hospital for a cancer operation, and found him a sensitive and helpful companion. I feel sure these conversations played their part in bringing Ernest back to the Church. 'Not,' he said, 'as a teaching priest but as a learning layman.' I remember Richard talking to Ernest about one of Ernest's books *Good Morning, Good People* (1970). Richard said how much he liked Ernest's writing of a midnight Mass one Christmas at St John's. Ernest held that though people talked much of the diminishing of Church attendance, this full and fervent congregation made a statement. Perhaps only one statement but, as he wrote 'A day is a day and a victory is victory'.
>
> Ernest died on 14 May 1974. A memorial service was held at St John's a few weeks later. I approached the church with son, step-daughter and step-son, and other members of the family. On the open space I saw a tall, familiar figure moving idly as those waiting alone do. He was then vicar of Fulham. I had not expected to see him. But as I did I felt a deep spring of comfort in a harsh time, knowing how glad Ernest would be to see him there.

For his last three years at Hampstead, Harries combined his curacy with being chaplain of Westfield College in the University of London. He was appointed by the new principal, Dr Bryan Thwaites, a mathematician and technologist, most recently professor of theoretical mechanics at Southampton University. There was no natural meeting of minds between principal and chaplain and this extended to religion. Thwaites was traditional, formal and conservative in his views. It was a strange time for Harries who thought he would be allowed to inject imagination and freshness into chapel life. Instead, he was expected to take morning prayers twice a week attended by very few students. Harries had intended working ecumenically, getting Christians to offer intelligent joint witness in the college. Instead they huddled in their denominational groups. The majority of Anglican students were absentees, seeing their prime loyalty to the central chaplaincy at Bloomsbury. Harries realized he was unable to make much impact, in part because he was seen as something of a plant by the principal. But he made a number of friends amongst the more radical younger lecturers.

If there was no impetus or encouragement for Harries in the strictly chapel aspect of his work, he looked elsewhere to make an impact. Anxious to bring a Christian component into an arts festival, he organized the showing of Passolini's Marxist interpretation of Jesus, *The Gospel according to St Matthew*, in his view the one good film about Jesus that had been made. There were technical problems with the showing of the film but it was important that an attempt had been made. An embarrassing low point was the public meeting he organized for Canon John Collins, then at the height of his powers through CND, to speak about his Christian faith. It was widely advertised in the college but very few attended. Harries, relatively apolitical before Hampstead, became absorbed in and by Christian–Marxist dialogue which led him to study a number of revolutionaries and liberation theology. At Westfield he organized successful seminars, one with Father Laurence Bright, a Dominican and founder of the Slant Group of Catholic Marxists. Nonetheless, Hampstead was so enjoyable and animated that Westfield seemed harder work and duller by contrast. Harries' inventive ideas were constant but lacked support, hardly auspicious for him and not worth further strenuous mental and organizing effort.

Towards the end of his time in Hampstead, Harries began writing for a wider public. It happened through chance. He was so irritated – angered – by the colonels who took over Greece in what they called the name of Christianity that he was catapulted into writing an article on the relationship between Christianity and power, much influenced by Simone Weil. Thus another characteristic is revealed. When Harries is provoked by what he regards as immorality or evil he becomes a man of action unacquainted with doubt. He sent his article to the one newspaper which has always claimed his loyalty, *The Guardian*, whose features editor, Christopher Driver, said he much liked it but it was not written out of personal experience of Greece. Of course, it wasn't. Then he sent it to the recently founded *New Christian* which published it. Thereafter Trevor Beeson, the editor, asked him to write or review on a reasonably regular basis.

Thus began an overwhelming love of writing. A vocation?

In *Prayer and the Pursuit of Happiness* Harries provides two recollections of Hampstead:

I remember setting out one afternoon to do some visits and suddenly being aware that I was in fact going out to look for someone more miserable than myself to comfort. I continued on my way but the awareness that in visiting I was meeting my own needs as well as those of others did, I think, make the eventual encounters more satisfactory.

'Are you happy?' was a question put directly to Harries by an American lady who was unhappy:

Faced with that full-frontal question I shifted uneasily in a way that could be regarded as characteristic of the English, and then said 'Yes' without thinking about it; or only thinking about it to the extent that if I said 'No' I knew I would be involved in talking about myself in a way I did not wish to do. In fact it wasn't the kind of question I agonized over. I got on with the job and with living. A very healthy attitude some will say . . . (but) for some people the subject is inescapable for they feel the shadow of their own unhappiness.

Such memories camouflage Jo and Richard's personal suffering. Ele's widow, Patricia Hall, was aware of the agony: 'For a short time all went well and Jo was expecting a baby. When the baby boy arrived she became extremely worried and upset and Richard was the helpful, loving husband and Jo got better.' This was the first hint of an affliction in Jo, later diagnosed as suffering from bipolar disorder, and an intermittent lifetime's suffering for both of them, often, not always, disguised from others.

Six years is a long time for a curacy. Ele Hall regarded Harries' ministry as 'tireless, able and inspired'. There is ample evidence of a host of people helped by Harries, who gave them sustenance on their journey, often resulting in a change of direction. He used signposts, never prescribing what particular route should be followed. Peter Raymond speaks for many:

I was a confirmation candidate as a 22-year-old in the mid-Sixties when Richard was a curate. I always remember his very practical view of Christianity. He was keen to show how evil and pain can be turned to good; how people come together in adversity; learn from the mistakes that led through a perverse cause and effect, and above all, make the distinction between the evil doer and the evil done, condemning the latter and forgiving the former. He was also able to accommodate doubts into faith; doubt not being a denial but a questioning. The question 'what is the meaning of pain?' is a philosophical one but Richard made it clear that pain was not an evil in itself, and could actually be a cleansing factor in our ongoing relationship with God.

Richard worked well with Joseph McCulloch and took part in discussions with Joseph from the pulpit at Hampstead. As an artist myself, I always appreciated their recognition of the role of artists and creativity in general in Christian faith. The painter and composer have at once a universal language and a personal statement of faith which Joseph took to new depths of under-standing at one meditation for Good Friday, comparing the seven sayings from the Cross with the seven lamps of art. I am sure Richard would have approved! Richard, I think, did not say that we needed all the answers to the mystery of faith, for the artist's role is more an expression of the wonder, a posing of questions for the watcher, reader or listener in a contract whereby they make their own judgements. In all Richard gave me a very thoughtful introduction to the Christian faith, which was not taught at all at my school, King Alfred in Hampstead.

There was a moment when it was likely that Harries would move to be vicar of Christ Church, Hampstead, but he was rejected by the trustees. It was time to move. He informed the Bishop of London, Robert Stopford, what kind of parish he wanted and what he wanted to avoid. 'I did not want an inner-city church, where the congregation would be eclectic. Nor on the other hand did I want to worship what E. M. Forster called "the great suburban Jehovah". I wanted to be vicar of a parish in a kind of middle city area which was still mainly residential.' The bishop may have admired the clarity of a young priest's assumptions about his future, but indicated that nothing was available. Harries, feeling cast-out, quickly changed direction, seeking and finding a position as lecturer and tutor at Wells Theological College.

Chapter Four
Breaking Forth

Theological college tutors are not on the whole a distinguished clerical caste. Many arrive from relative obscurity, stay for a short period and return whence they came. Those who dedicate their ministerial lives to theological teaching, similar in kind and length to their university equivalents, are remembered.

Thirty-three-year-old Harries arrived at Wells eager to enlarge his experience. Intellectually he was nothing special except in already having an extraordinary power to assimilate what he heard and read. He had, and still has, a great curiosity, an engaging manner, no introspective chaos or obvious bricked-up ambition. He made friendships with ease, though not necessarily deep ones.

Wells was the third oldest theological college, founded in 1840. It was never in the first division marked by Cuddesdon and Westcott House, Cambridge (1851). The majority of theological colleges were party colleges, catering for either Evangelical or Anglo-Catholic students. The more unaligned were Wells, Queen's College, Birmingham (1828), Lichfield (1857) and Lincoln (1874), with Ripon Hall, Oxford (1898) having established an identity with Modernism.

Wells had two 'revivals', or shifts in emphasis, following the Second World War. The first came under Kenneth Haworth, principal 1947–1960, who was unfearful of appointing staff who would polarize debate, including John Robinson and Kenneth Skelton. One feature of the college provided a healthy tension: students arriving direct from universities mingling with a more knowing, more mature set, from a harsher background – the experience of war. It was a period of reform in the Church of England, liturgically focused on the parish Communion. Many names associated with this movement were immensely, often intensely, radical in putting ideas into practice without necessarily pursuing or swallowing whole the 'new theology' which was both behind and in front of their radicalism.

When Kenneth Haworth left in 1960 to be Dean of Salisbury, Wells needed another revival. Tom Baker, sub-warden of Lincoln Theological College, was appointed. Professor Dennis Nineham describes Baker's approach with precision: 'Without being an exact scholar in the technical sense, he has always kept abreast of current theological thinking and has an enviable gift for expounding the gist of it in a way that makes this thinking clear to all and does justice to the insights of it without obscuring either the defects or the difficulties to which it gives rise.'

By this time there was some debate as to whether bringing men together in semi-monastic groups in the depths of the country was the best way to train them for the kind of ministry which many of them would exercise. Working in uncongenial places amidst dirt, squalor and monotony, with the absence of mental stimulus or with the ambitions of suburbia, could be, and often was, destructive of the intellectual, pastoral and spiritual qualities which should be the marks of priesthood and of any minister of the Gospel.

Tom Baker picked an intentionally varied staff who were able to equip people for the chasmic turbulences of the 1960s. Harries was chosen to lecture on 'Doctrine, God, Christ and Man, and Ethics' – admitting 'the Church and Sacraments have never been a fundamental concern of mine'. It was essential for him to study what was being written by theologians whose names and theses were new to him. As for ethics, he began more or less from scratch because ethics had been so inadequately addressed during his years in theological college and not at all during his time at university. Thus ill-equipped, the lecturer set to work to teach and guide students with hastily acquired knowledge of hitherto unexplored territories.

Any lecturer in theology should remember that it is a science with its own specialized vocabulary. Those determined to translate everything into a language that can be understood by 'the people' finish up with battered words and meaningless clichés. Self-motivated and largely self-taught, Harries was drawn to theologians who supported or substantiated his own developing predilections. It was to be a feature of his own approach as he avoided the stiff joints of the academic and never acquired the hardened arteries of the theological hack. This was equally invigorating for both lecturer and student. There was an able staff each with their own distinctiveness: 'Tom Baker, David Mealand (later of Edinburgh University) and Tony Barnard (a future chancellor of Lichfield Cathedral) had all been influenced by Rudolf Bultmann. This was the first time I had really come across, at close quarters, the influence of a much more radical form of religious belief. My own New Testament studies at Cambridge had been primarily linguistic and there was also the influence of Donald MacKinnon. Intellectual contact with these three at Wells made me realize I was a theological conservative. For example, when we mounted a conference on the Resurrection I was the one put in to defend a traditional account, which I did drawing on the work of Pannenberg.

'Another crucial influence from my time at Wells was having to lecture week in week out. This laid the foundation for a great deal of work I have done since. As far as doctrine is concerned, I had the opportunity to assess the range of extraordinary theologians who took the future seriously – Pannenberg and above all Moltmann. They took seriously all the questions posed by the Death of God theologians, process theologians and so on, but came up with an answer which was much closer to the New Testament, more orthodox and which gave an impetus to Christian action in the world.'

Wolfhart Pannenberg, born in 1928, was a German Protestant and a professor at the universities of Mainz and Munich. He set out to respond to the atheist critique of religion by seeking common ground in a theory of knowledge which did not itself require religious faith. He advanced a concept of reality which could be described as both genuinely Christian and yet also intellectually acceptable to non-Christians. You can almost feel Harries' foundations being strengthened. More powerful cement came from another heavyweight German, post-Barthian theologian Jürgen Moltmann, born 1926, who held a chair at Tübingen. He became a Christian believer while a prisoner-of-war in Scotland and England, and a Christian activist when he was released in 1948 to take part in the reconstruction of his ruined homeland.

Harries' curiosity meant he always left his mind on the latch so new thinking entered his domain without difficulty. Moltmann's notable trilogy *The Crucified God*, *The Theology of Hope* and *The Church in the Power of the Spirit* pierced Harries' mind and soul. The first book was a meditation around Bonhoeffer's words from prison, 'only a suffering God can help'; the second (which had the greatest influence on Harries) was a dialogue with the Marxist, Ernst Bloch; the third rejected the Heidelberg Catechism's definition of the Church as 'the community of the elect destined for eternal life' which 'the Son of God gathers out of the whole human race'. For Moltmann the Church is not essentially a stabilizing force in society, or a source of psychological reassurance in crisis, or a means of personal escape from the wicked world. He taught that theology made it obligatory on the Christian to sponsor social change, even to the point of revolution. The Church must identify itself with human suffering and 'the true Church is the song of thanksgiving of those who have been liberated'. Moltmann had some influence over the development of liberation theology in the Church in Latin America.

In some surviving lecture notes, Harries draws attention to one aspect of 'Hope', a theme which repeatedly recurs in his published writing: 'Hope must transform all our thinking and acting – *spes quaerens intellectum* – *spero, ut intelligam*. Our thought will be anticipatory and provisional – we will not be content with a fixed scheme in either thought or society (i.e. Marxist Utopia). Hope is a continuing revolution. This view clearly does justice to affirmation of the world and man's responsibility in it. We have a mission to the world to inject it with hope and save it.'

In the scales of Harries' mind, world affirmation weighs down world renunciation. Is this a consequence of these early theological explorations having been incarnational rather than soteriological? This does not mean he was so naive as to be a perfectionist or an Utopian or a 'secular' Christian. Indeed, we will discover his awareness – a Platonic awareness – of the reality of the 'other world', the eternal, even if he does not go as far as to embrace the view that the criterion of any religion lies in what it has to tell us of death! But the kinds of activist preoccupation which tempt and absorb a person may lead them to forget (in Archbishop Leighton's words) that 'the fashion of this world passeth away as a pageant or show in a street, going thro' and quickly out of sight'.

Wells was another formative period of Harries' life. The emphasis on group work in the college was new to him. The students lived in separate houses in the Cathedral Close and each staff member was assigned to a particular house. Once a week the staff spent an evening in these 'cells' which could be confrontational and disturbing for both parties. That there was growth as a result of this multi-cellular structure was the result of Harold Wilson, principal of Salisbury Theological

College, who was a leading expert on group work and a close friend of Wells. Then there was the style of worship which was special for Harries:

> It was ordered without being fussy; aesthetically pleasing without being ornate; simple yet with substance. Of course we had marvellous surroundings, the undercroft of the cathedral with its central altar and ancient stone: but it was more than that. At its best the worship captured Taizé's talent for drawing on the riches of the whole Christian tradition without being heavy or archaic. It was at once traditional and contemporary. It was worship that came into its own at the Easter Vigil, when the college took over the Cathedral as a whole for services which were unforgettable. Many former Wells students must have tried, as I did later at Fulham, to kindle that magic elsewhere. Of course there were other qualities that Tom (Baker) brought to the college, not least his theological seriousness and his pastoral sensitivity, but it is that sense of living and praying as a community, sharply contemporary yet at one with the Church down the ages, that I celebrate.

Hope, joy, optimism and confidence are already irreversible aspects of Harries' character and deeply ingrained, but it is easy to confuse their meaning for him. He always has an apposite quotation to support any view he holds and often uses one to express something with a clarity or feeling that he finds difficult in his own words. In this way he illuminates what he describes. In a sermon on 'Divine Gladness' in preparation for Christmas 1971 and for the ordination to the diaconate of Jim Harris, he quotes Owen Chadwick on Robert Browning – introducing the subject in this way:

> Sometimes, where argument has been indecisive, the atmosphere which fills the air at Christmas has worked the miracle, and brought about such utter confidence. The carols, the giving and receiving, the active remembering of the lonely, the excitement of children, the slipping away of old grievances, the lights and the laughter – such things can seep through the senses into the core of our personality, and transform a grudge against life into gladness; can make resentment give place to rejoicing. On Christmas Eve 1849 just such an experience happened to the poet Robert Browning. 'At this time', Owen Chadwick has written, 'Browning found an optimism about the world which was never to leave him . . . Browning became an optimist, but a Christian optimist; that is one who sees the world as it is, as often soiled, and often criminal; a child with the promise of eternity lying in hay which would not be clean . . . Browning himself was fascinated, almost obsessed by the wickedness of the world. See the vice, and the folly, and the tawdriness, and the transitoriness and the pretence of the world – and then have hope . . .'

And Harries would become adept at recognizing the truth about the present rather than staring at the tea-leaves and predicting the future. This brings us to his

41

introduction to a prophet who was a decisive influence. It came in the form of a book – *Moral Man and Immoral Society* by Reinhold Niebuhr (1892–1971). 'I can still feel the thrill of intellectual recognition and insight as I read it on the train going to London. Niebuhr's approach to political questions has remained with me ever since.' Niebuhr was an American Protestant theologian best known for his writings that seek to relate Christian social teachings to contemporary political and social issues. He showed Harries that it was possible for a theologian to speak about what was happening in the contemporary world without merely moralizing or emitting pious platitudes. For he had a power that was novel then, and is rare now, of analysing movements and events and political crises and of discovering more in them than was imagined by the professors of secular creeds and ideologies. Current affairs, as he commented on them, were seen not only to be more complex than appeared at first sight, but also to have an uncanny light cast upon them by different aspects of the Christian faith. He had, as was well said, an 'extraordinary perception of the complexity of human motives and of the relation between morality and interest and power in society'. He was both radical and realistic. He punctured illusions, especially Utopian and perfectionist illusions, but he never encouraged fatalism or disengagement. And he was as much at home in the pages of *Time, Life, The Atlantic Monthly* as in the specialized journals of theology.

Niebuhr's thought was without boundaries though there were Protestant principles articulated by him, including:

- sin remains persistent even in the life of the redeemed
- in the political world, the only attainable goal is justice, not love
- political and economic conflict is inevitable.

In *Moral Man and Immoral Society* he stressed that collective behaviour of necessity differs radically from individual conduct. 'Every effort to transfer a pure morality of disinterestedness to group relations has resulted in failure.' He did find a place for pacifism in the Church. Niebuhr upheld the view that religious pacifism, as a symbolic portrayal of love absolutism in a sinful world, has its own value and justification. A Church which does not generate it is the poorer for its lack.

Harries found Niebuhr's writing trenchant, disturbing and prophetic. He was in good company. When reviewing a biography of Niebuhr in 1988 he quoted William Temple, who once said, 'At last I have found the troubler of my soul.'

Niebuhr had his critics, who charged him with going too far to compromise with existing social systems. For Harries he was the template for so many future areas of interest. Niebuhr provides no catchpenny answer as this is not necessarily a sign of grace. A surfeit of religion may mean a paucity of Christianity. Or again, on the relations of Christians and Jews in Western Christendom, seldom has someone been able to mark with such penetration how much Jews and Christians have in common and where their faiths diverge.

Niebuhr's Gifford Lectures of 1939 – 'The Nature and Destiny of Man' – were criticized for lacking a doctrine of the Resurrection, the Church and of the relation of the common life in the body of Christ to human destiny. Throughout Niebuhr's thought is an exposure of the ecclesiasticism, arrogance and intolerance of Churches. He touched many raw nerves by his nimble intellect, high intelligence and continuously flowing pen, but he could distort the position of his foes.

In September 1984 a conference was held at King's College, London under Harries' auspices: 150 people attended from Europe and North America. A subsequent book, though provoked by the conference, was not simply a product of it. Harries edited and introduced *Reinhold Niebuhr and the Issues of our Time* (1986). In addition he contributed *Reinhold Niebuhr and his Pacifist Critics*. Other contributors included established Niebuhrian thinkers from America and, from England, Ronald Preston, Keith Ward and Daphne Hampson. Harries drew attention to Hampson's contribution:

> Fundamental to Niebuhr's outlook is his account of sin as pride. But is this a peculiarly male way of looking at the world? In a stimulating chapter Daphne Hampson suggests that it might be, and that, as a result, his understanding of human nature can be inappropriate for women. She also affirms that 'a woman's different view of the world and way of inter-relating may help to cure the human situation which Niebuhr depicts'.

The Bishop of Chelmsford, John Gladwin, has known Harries over a lengthy period and worked with him as secretary or member of many working parties. He summarizes Harries' method in dealing with ethical issues:

> Niebuhr's method in seeking languages that would act as a bridge between the realities of our secular, social and personal lives and the wonder and mystery of the Gospel have been attractive to Richard. It's meant that he has been able to listen in a relaxed way to what the secular world is saying and to try to perceive the objective truth of the wider human community without compromising a deep spiritual commitment to the Christian faith. So his ethical and theological method is always on the borders between the Church and the wider community. That's made him a really good performer in the public forum on some of the troubled issues of our time.

As Harries' life in thought and action unfolds there will be recurrent thank offerings to Niebuhr, who, for the moment, has the penultimate word:

> Love may have to live in history as suffering love because the power of sin makes a simple triumph of love impossible. But if this were the ultimate situation it would be necessary either to worship the power of sin as the final power in the world, or to regard it as a kind of second God, not able to triumph, but also strong enough to avoid defeat.
>
> The vindication of Christ and his triumphant return is therefore an expression of faith in the sufficiency of God's sovereignty over the world and history,

and in the final supremacy of love over all forces of self-love which defy, for the moment, the inclusive harmony of all things under the will of God.

Harries was already being widely noticed and praised for his ability not simply to regurgitate what he had studied, but to summarize sympathetically and, where necessary, critically, with a discriminating judgement. He was regarded as a new bright light in the theological firmament. With this went an ease of manner and an efficient way of matching promise by performance. Deadlines were met. Is it any wonder that he was already entering those pastures where thinkers graze and produce reports? He was a member of a working party of the Advisory Council for the Church's Ministry (ACCM) in 1972. Its chairman was Sydney Evans, dean of King's College, London; and its members were Gordon Dunstan, professor of moral and social theology at King's; Margaret Kane, theological consultant on industrial and social affairs to Ian Ramsey, Bishop of Durham; Helen Oppenheimer, writer on moral and philosophical theology; Ronald Preston, professor of social and pastoral theology, University of Manchester; Keith Ward, lecturer in the philosophy of religion at King's, and Harries. Ronald Coppin of ACCM acted as secretary. Harries felt privileged to be part of this group whose published findings *Teaching Christian Ethics* was a syllabus for teaching Christian ethics in theological colleges – something which had dropped out of the curriculum altogether. Harries wrote the sections on 'Towards a Christian Social Ethic' dealing with Augustine, Luther, Calvin, Aquinas and the Catholic view, Reinhold Niebuhr, and Liberation Ethics. The publication was a handbook for teachers of Christian ethics and was not superseded for some time.

At Wells, Harries started work on a PhD on the Just War tradition, supervised by Gordon Dunstan of King's, in particular the principles of proportion and discrimination which are the key moral criteria for nuclear debate. 'I did a great deal of work on the thesis but eventually the pressure of too many things in London led me to drop it.' Harries could have prefixed the London commitments with the words 'stimulating' and 'exciting'. On one level it appears he could fulfil his obligations to Wells Theological College with alacrity and thoroughness, leaving time to pursue his accelerating outside interests. On another level, was it insufficiently satisfying work being a theological college tutor? In a television feature on ordination training while he was at Wells, Harries had a memorable phrase: 'Within every priest there needs to be a certain sort of inner bloody-mindedness'. Did he prefer and need the stimulus that London provided? How far did his absences limit his impact on students at Wells? His time there was brief and though there is little evidence of personal impact he was regarded as successful. But London was ever more tempting. In 1972 a letter arrived from Robert Stopford, Bishop of London, inviting Harries to be vicar of All Saints, Fulham. 'This was the one job in my life I knew quite clearly I wanted to do.'

Chapter Five
Golden Years

Wells Theological College had been an unscripted, though not an unfruitful, pause in Harries' life. At the end of his Hampstead curacy in 1969, his dearest wish was to be a parish priest in London. Retrospectively he muses: 'If I ever considered what I thought I would do, I saw myself knocking on the doors of some depressed northern industrial town in the rain and bringing light and comfort to the inhabitants. That's how I originally envisaged my vocation when it first came to me in the army. A very paternalistic image, and a very, very conventional image too. And of course the reality was very different. But my early notion of it was clearly linked to my strong sense, which I have always had, about the truth of a Christian view of existence, which was that people would be a great deal *happier* – in the proper, profound sense of that word – if they believed in God and made God a part of their life. And that wasn't simply about going to have tea with people: it was about trying to help people to discover what I believe is the meaning and the purpose of all our lives.'

These thoughts are highly coloured and do not easily cohere with most people's opinions of Harries. They omit an important ingredient in his character, one which he acknowledges. As it explains, if only partially, future complexes, contradictions and paradoxes, it is well to consider it at this juncture. 'I'm not a very introspective person,' he says. He is propelled by what he feels to be right courses of action, by what he thinks God is calling him to do, by ways in which his natural gifts and developed skills can be used. Sometimes this has meant responding to other people's views of his talents, by effectively proffering what they propose. Fulham was a constant cascade of initiatives. He admits, 'that there are all sorts of reasons why I've ended up doing what I have done. It's always possible to find psychological, sociological and no doubt biological explanations for everything we believe and do, and I believe that the "religious" explanation for things works in conjunction with these other explanations, and not as alternatives to them'. We will discover a rigorous intellect, an analytical mind capable of a scythe-like destruction of false or pretentious ideas and propositions, and a fearlessness in discovering and exposing hypocrisies and deceit in the institutional Church and in the policies of governments. These were not implanted by his background or education, which is why it is essential to probe a personality which does not probe itself.

By 1972 the suffragan bishops of London were in all but name area bishops, and Fulham fell within the jurisdiction of the Bishop of Kensington, Ronald

Goodchild, who warned the churchwardens of All Saints that there would be considerable changes if Harries were appointed. When they met Harries they found it difficult to decide who was interviewing whom! However, they accepted him with alacrity and nervousness, for they were only too aware of the parish's recent history.

What was Harries' inheritance? There were 15 Anglican churches in Fulham and, with a single exception, they were of nineteenth-century origin. The exception was All Saints, population 9,000. It stood next to Fulham Palace, the historic home of the bishops of London, although Stopford was to be the last bishop to live there. All Saints could trace its history on that site to 1242: an ancient church, seared and scarred by the centuries, whose fabric, austere and challenging, attested the changing fortunes of the generations which had lived and rejoiced, and toiled and played, and sinned and suffered around it. All Saints was an eloquent symbol of eternity, proclaiming year in and year out, amid the babel of the world's voices, that men and women's source and destiny were not earth-born and earthbound, but spiritual and undying. Deep in the hearts of the people, in spite of their apparent irreligion, and frequent neglect of the ordinances of Christianity, was a treasury of reverence and affection for their parish church, which no other building could create or secure. The history was not lost on Harries, who constantly commended the change and continuity of the Church of England as witness and strength. In 1972 Fulham was largely occupied by people in the uneasy middle of the middle classes, but this was changing rapidly with young professional families moving into the area. The consequent danger was the alienation of local people who were being priced out of the market.

There had been two postwar incumbents. Prebendary A. H. G. Hawes was vicar from 1946 to 1965. Following war damage, the building had required renovation and the congregation needed rejuvenating. This was achieved with energy and speed. In Hawes' early years, All Saints flourished. His work amongst children was conspicuously successful. Unfortunately, in later years he was ill and his behaviour became exceedingly strange. Most clergy have their band of loyal supporters and the Hawes' defenders excused his habits as being those of an eccentric, which was not the case. Relations between vicar and curates were strained and the method of communication was by written notes rather than conversation. Hawes became increasingly reclusive. Those were the days when clergy did not receive professional care, whether medical, psychological or social, when needed. Bishops stopped short of the scrutiny that would have enabled the emergence of a diagnosis and consequent appropriate care and treatment. By the time Hawes died in 1965 the parish was again in dire need of revitalization.

Bishop Stopford had been translated from Peterborough to London in 1961 and had brought a well-trusted priest from his former diocese to All Saints – Canon Donald Andrews, vicar of Kingsthorpe since 1946 and later rural dean of Northampton and a proctor in convocation. It was a well-meaning appointment, but an unfortunate and mistaken one. On the surface it appeared the sound exercise of the bishop's patronage. Andrews was a priest of acknowledged ability and experience, well respected by Kingsthorpe parishioners and fellow clergy. Whether through lack of inquisitiveness on Andrews' part or through concealment by All Saints, he was unprepared for what he encountered when he arrived. During the long incumbency of Hawes there had developed a group of good and strong laity who had subsequently become strident and vociferous – 'the awkward squad'. They held that the vicar should confine himself to 'spiritual' matters and they would look after everything else. Andrews was faced with parochial church council meetings which developed into battlegrounds where confrontation and rancour were commonplace. The introduction of Christian stewardship was one of many time-bombs which exploded in the vicar's face. At one meeting the vicar used the phrase 'd'you see?' only to be met with 'Don't you "d'you see" me!!' Many of the confronters were still at All Saints when Harries arrived.

At so many turns Andrews encountered a solid wall of obstruction, although it was not all lack of progress or failure. He was conservative in his theology and churchmanship, and perhaps too obviously authoritarian in his approach – only to be expected in a priest ordained in 1928. In many ways he was representative of the prevailing tempo and outlook of the Peterborough diocese, which tended to be against most of the reforming policies of the Church of England in the 1960s. Andrews moved too late in his ministry from a sphere of influence to London where he was inconspicuous. A corrosive sense of bitterness seemed to envelop him. Arriving in 1965 it was not long before he was smitten by that debilitating clerical disease known as 'When I was . . . When I was in Kingsthorpe . . .' It was there he had had status (which was important to him) and a fulfilling ministry of which many people were its beneficial recipients. He announced his resignation from All Saints in 1971.

In the 1920s and '30s All Saints had been decidedly Anglo-Catholic. Although the candle power had flickered somewhat, it was still, when Harries arrived, a church of Catholic tradition, with incense, colourful processions, ecclesiastical haberdashery, daily Eucharist, reservation of the Blessed Sacrament, Confessions – but without the lace and tat found in many such churches. Harries was fortunate. He was not succeeding a success. The parish desperately needed a jolt. He was half the age of his predecessor and described as 'tall and handsome, in a military sort of way, slim bordering on thin with regular features and good skin'. He was married to Jo, a doctor, and they had two young children, Mark and Clare. When they moved into the vicarage, a beautiful house hidden behind a block of flats and the church hall, next to Putney Bridge, they were instantly hospitable. Previous vicars had been addressed as 'Father'; Harries was 'Richard'.

The Fulham years were ones where Harries' personality was both revealed and elusive. There were many constants and a few paradoxes which will become clearer as his life and ministry further unfold. There was no strain of the populist in him, and to say he was popular in the usual meaning of the word is not an accurate assessment. He was uncamouflaged yet not easy to read; charming and relaxed, yet to a degree distant and aloof; reserved not ebullient; encouraging rather than enthusing; intellectual rather than academic. He had the ability of a skilled communicator but did not use it to sway a crowd. He was approachable yet kept his personal and family

47

life to himself. He had a sharp and wide range of intelligence, intuitive sympathy and interest in people. There was no mateyness or false bonhomie about him. His circle of intimate friendships was small, close and rewarding. Although his range of acquaintances was exceedingly large and always changing and growing as his interests multiplied, he was not guilty of cultivating people for his own ends. He was trusted.

Ideas and people filled his ministerial life. All Saints wanted a vicar who would listen to, care for and uplift them. He has a good memory for faces and the people behind them, and he is not easily forgotten. Breaking for a drink at the nearest pub during the arrangements for his Institution service, he was at once recognized by the barmaid, a Confirmation candidate from Hampstead. Immediately he broke off to renew contact with her. If stopped in the street he would engage in conversation with someone, giving no impression that he was on his way to a meeting. The transformation of the parish began with his positive attitude to people. He was invariably appreciative and encouraged people to use their gifts and take on responsibilities.

The resurgence began immediately. In the parish magazine for December 1972, two and a half months after his Institution, he wrote: 'I am conscious the whole time of how much there is to be done, and how much could be done by us in the service of Christ – and how short a thing a lifetime is'. Most people like getting their own way and Harries was no exception. He had a rather smooth grit about him, a determination which was never steel-like in substance, but sustained through careful planning. His reasoning and persuasive powers were keen. His intellect was used in argument but not in demolishing an opponent. He quickly transformed All Saints, and many of its hitherto stubborn stick-in-the-muds, who adhered to the view that the best times in the parish had been the day before yesterday, were soon convinced of the need for reform. Harries' first task was visiting the diehards and disaffected.

There is no false modesty or mock humility about Harries. Neither is he power seeking, or in the mould of 'Father knows best' – although he usually did. Authority was a different matter. Many priests want authority for themselves but resent being under authority and are, therefore, unable to exercise it when necessary. London had far too many priests who genuflected to their bishop but were also a law unto themselves – and to everyone else in their parishes. There are many confusions and conflicts between authority and authoritarianism and Harries was exemplary at affirming the former and avoiding being trapped in the latter. The clergy of the 1960s and '70s needed to believe in and train the laity to be human resources. People are God's choice for accomplishing his purposes. As part of this training, clergy needed help to distinguish between symptoms and causes: an elementary distinction, yet many clergy could not make it. They had to learn how to read symptoms and to recognize that people not only have problems, but resources as well and that clergy benefit people best by helping them to use their resources in relation to their problems; that they should never do for others what they can do for themselves; that people change slowly, and with difficulty; that resistance and resentment need not be signs of failure, but signs that real learning is taking place. At Fulham, when individuals with a problem or anxiety saw Harries, he did not solve it for them but assisted them in discovering solutions within themselves. This was a strength. Priests also need to look for, recognize and respond to God's activity in the world, independent as it may be of Church auspices! It can be hard for them to accept that God may instruct the Church through the world as well as the world through the Church. We know that Harries' future reveals ample testimony of embracing the world without being seduced by it. At Fulham he showed a freedom to risk, to act, and let the actions go; to speak a word and let it go. This meant that he was not swamped by those bouts of self-doubt and stress evident in priests who desire to hold onto things, to qualify their thoughts, to speak but to hold onto the words, to act tentatively so as to prevent their action from having its way.

Worship is the primary function of the Church from which everything else either flows or stagnates. The services at All Saints were in need of radical revision. Elsewhere, but by no means everywhere, it was an exhilarating if traumatic time for the Church of England. The *Book of Common Prayer* was receding towards antiquity but was yet far from oblivion. Harries was convinced that a good liturgy is both historic and contemporary. It should accurately reflect a New Testament view of the Church and its ministry, not a view belonging to a particular society and a moment in history. A danger of the *Book of Common Prayer* was that the beauty of the prose could become, not a vessel for prayer, but a formula which imprisoned prayer and even presumed to imprison God. It was recognized that in one way Thomas Cranmer was deficient. The great Consecration prayer at the Eucharist was atonement centred. The sixteenth century was a period of guilt and the liturgy reflected this. In some of its prayers the Prayer Book is guilt, not love, orientated. It reflects a stern, authoritative view of divinity, whereas the true Christian perspective revolves around love. The various new 'Series' of services – and Series One had reached All Saints – moved away from too much guilt towards more love. Harries has always been watchful of the language used in worship. That it should be right for its purpose was more important than that it should be relevant. It should be the best that can be found and that 'best' extended to the buildings in which worship was offered – stone, wood, metal, glass, music, poetry, art.

Harries was usually in the vanguard of reform. But he was never an uncritical enthusiast for all elements in the new services. Within two months of arriving in Fulham he called a special meeting of the parochial church council to discuss worship. If there was wary anticipation by the congregation, the results were frankly amazing, as recorded in the Minutes: 'After a celebration of Holy Communion according to the new Series Three form at 8 pm in church, the Council commented on and discussed this rite. A proposal that the church should adopt this form of service was carried unanimously.' For an experimental period of two months from 1 January 1973 the new Series would be used with the celebrant facing the people, selected lay people leading the prayers, an offertory procession, people recommended to stand for the 'Thanksgiving' but 'free to adopt any other posture they prefer', and places for silence. In a sermon Harries said: 'Worship can be a marvellous, rich, thrilling, deeply satisfying experience.' For him and the congregation, the liturgy was not primarily something that was said or sung but something done, an action in which everyone participated, not a solo but a full orchestral performance. In March 1973 Harries invited Canon Ronald Jasper of Westminster Abbey, chairman of the Church's Liturgical Commission, to visit All Saints for a question and answer session and then a booklet was issued covering all aspects of Series Three.

However, Harries later became critical. Writing in *Theology* on 'Alternative Services – The Test of Practice' he observed:

> When *An Order for Holy Communion Series Three* was first produced I welcomed it as an improvement on what had gone before. At Fulham, in a mixed parish, it has been used at all Communion services for over three years. The feeling of many people, clergy and lay, is that the service in its present form does not stand the test of time. With use it develops a wooden quality that is very difficult to counteract. Given that Series Three is here to stay it is of the utmost importance that there is more freedom at certain points in the service: for example, in the words said before the Confession. At the moment the minister has to say either one of the comfortable words or the two paragraphs of liturgical commission prose. What he actually wants to do at this point is either say something very simple such as 'Let us humbly confess our sins to Almighty God' or something slightly expanded that takes up the theme of the readings and sermon, giving it a penitential dimension. The Roman Missal is an admirable guide here as elsewhere. The rubric reads, 'The priest invites the people to call their sins to mind and to repent of them. He may use the following, or similar words.' The words which follow are, 'My brothers and sisters, to prepare ourselves for the sacred mysteries, let us call to mind our sins.'

Harries' critique of all the Series Three services – actual and proposed – focused on the language and methods of the commission. He pointed out that 'the language is best characterized as unbiblical biblicalism. Those who wrote it apparently believed you express biblical truth by highly selective quotation out of context or by jamming together a number of biblical phrases. The result is often unmelodious, meaningless and unbiblical'. Here, and always, he was concerned with language. The poverty of Christian language disturbed him. It is the symptom of a deep-seated disease, a malaise of the imaginative and intellectual life of the Church. People frequently pray for what they do not have: they simply repeat the formulae taught them and their devotion skates on the surface of words. Harries would have liked to have written an experimental eucharistic service.

In his planning and initiatives Harries was not working alone. When he was appointed to Fulham the bishop decided he should have a deacon. Harries, still at Wells, first met Peter Kaye (curate 1972–1974), in the tearoom on St Pancras Station, an unlikely venue for an interview. Peter Kaye's memories catch the spirit of All Saints:

Staff meetings were often a time to draw out some of the new ideas and developments we had been individually mulling over. Often it was not quite clear whose idea something was, only that one thought it worth a try, and I have never been sure whether that was because we 'made a good team' or were thinking along the same lines, or whether it was a subtle management technique on Richard's part. For instance, jointly, we wanted to address the difficulty that there were numbers of parents who would drop their children off for Sunday school but not stay for church themselves. The Family Service was born: at 11.15 am after the main Eucharist – deliberately only half an hour – with its own service book, a variety of carefully written modern responses, a three-paragraph creed illustrated by an internationally known artist, and a selection of modern and fun hymns. The service was based on the premise that it was quite possible to retain the interest of both the adults and the children if we were patronizing to neither. Services contained moments of fun and laughter. I seem to recall on one occasion Richard and myself wrestling on the floor of the chancel as part of a sketch . . . readings from Scripture and non-biblical sources and, not surprisingly, poetry, all fitting together to make a theme which had depth and simplicity.

This approach created a whole new constituency at All Saints, bright, youngish professionals with children. This was after all Fulham in the throes of 'gentrification'. Richard was keen that we know our parishioners, so we did house-to-house visiting and knew precisely who lived where, and whether they might be persuaded through our church doors. Quite poor households were only minutes from the mansion flats of Hurlingham Gardens and we visited everybody. Richard had the knack, sadly lacked by me, of remembering names and faces seemingly without effort. He did not leave all the visiting to me and at Evensong we would mention new contacts to one another and offer them in prayer.

There were remarkable personalities in the parish – local families with connections going back generations, and some who had moved into the suburbs who came each week like clockwork. The 'Social Club' was a key institution in the parish – not a licensed establishment, but one of the parish organizations, harking back to pre-war days when social life centred on the church hall and its activities. Richard offered proper supervision, making me accountable for undertaking regularly the sick-visiting and the house-calls to regular parishioners as well as the house-to-house visiting, which was all part of the task, so that I did feel that I was being 'trained', but this was combined with a great deal of encouragement to 'do my own thing'. With Richard's encouragement I was able to undertake regular psychotherapy training which I was just beginning then, to undertake work as assistant chaplain to the Charing Cross Hospital Medical School, take part in city-wide planning for an ecumenical festival (That's the Spirit), set up a prayer circle for healing, and so on. He was happy to delegate and almost on arrival handed to me the responsibility to develop a strong choir. Mr Sims the organist reluctantly agreed to our plan to coax lads into the choir by holding a club for them in the hall after practice! It worked and the choir grew, nearly all the boys going on to Confirmation. Mr Sims was a strange, somewhat stubborn man, with his own style of humour. During the run of one of our pantomimes he managed to incorporate the song *What I want is a proper cup of coffee* into the voluntary as we were solemnly processing into church. These were happy and positive times. Richard set up a parish conference where amongst other things some of us learnt the moves of Tai Chi Ch'uan – 'Taking the tiger to the mountain' as it was explained.

The Bishop must have thought highly of Harries as a trainer of curates as there was a constant flow of them: Peter Wheatley (1973–1978), now Bishop of Edmonton; Christopher Moody (1975–1979); and Stephen Wilson (1979–1982). David Tann had been a curate when Donald Andrews was vicar. He left for secular employment in teaching but returned as an honorary curate when Harries arrived and stayed until he left, whilst being head of religious education at Green School, Isleworth.

Christopher Moody has recollections which complement those of Peter Kaye:

I was very young and unsure of myself and he managed to guide me and give me confidence without in any way being over-directive and heavy-handed. For a time there were three of us on the staff. Staff meetings happened on a Monday morning and included theological discussion and long-term planning as well as diary checking and a pastoral review of who was in the congregation, who was ill etc. The congregation continued to grow the whole time I was there and there was sometimes an explosive mixture of old-style Londoners and very middle-class people who were beginning to find Fulham an attractive location. There was a full range of services with a sung Eucharist with incense, a Family Service as well as an 8 am and 12 noon Communion service and a traditional sung Evensong, which meant that everybody was able to find a niche somewhere. The Family Service was perhaps the most creative act of worship, involving all sorts of material – poetry, drama, music, silence – and the gifts of an extraordinary range of lay people.

One of the things Richard insisted on was that all the clergy attended all the services, whether you were doing anything or not, which meant that you were able to learn critically from each other and to get to know all the congregation(s). We also had the privilege of listening to a wide range of visiting preachers. It meant that I was introduced to a wide variety of worship and a lot of experiment early on – including liturgical dance! – within what was a liberal High Church tradition, and that breadth of churchmanship within a clear theological perspective has remained foundational. There was plenty of tension and disagreement, but church was never boring and there were momentous occasions like the full Easter vigil liturgy in a packed church, which have stayed with me ever since. Richard was very generous, both in his time and his hospitality, and very supportive of the gifts of others. He encouraged me, for example, to write a passion play which was performed in churches throughout the deanery with actors and musicians all drawn from the congregation, and was quite happy to allow the time taken from other duties.

We met daily for Holy Communion and Evensong and a lot of ground was covered in the slow walks back from the church to the vicarage. So we became a team who knew each other very well and sparked off each other all the time. We had house groups in the parish as well, and what I remember about these is the breadth of opinion that was expressed. There wasn't the fear of rocking the boat that seems to dominate churches today. We were still in open dialogue with agnostics and people of other faiths. I remember that a significant number of adults were baptized and confirmed while I was there and I date my own 'birth' as a pastor from when I was responsible for the preparation of 12 of them drawn from all ages and social backgrounds. I still remember them in my prayers even now. Richard was a very tolerant colleague. I wasn't very well organized. I forgot things and overslept, wore my hair long with a beard and rolled my own cigarettes. There must have been some criticism. But I was never patronized or made to conform by Richard or anyone else. Richard was always very interested in other people's fields of work and he had a humorous but challenging manner which allowed people to be themselves. He wasn't at all churchy.

Christopher Moody has put his finger on a single vital characteristic of Richard Harries: 'He wasn't at all churchy'. This made him attractive to casual visitors and all newcomers. He was alert and attentive, welcoming people as people and not as potential pew-fodder. It is not easy to combine deep seriousness, rich humanity and discernment with what may be called an uncomplicated lightness of touch. Earnestness in the right cause is good; humour and love are usually better. Even when he was sought out by Christians, they encountered a down-to-earth, up-to-heaven approach. One further set of recollections come from parishioner Mrs Sandra Gee. Her story is personal but replicated, with variations, by others:

I first met Richard Harries in 1974. Philip and I wanted to get married and were looking for a suitable church. (I had not been to church for about two years, following a rather nasty division within the Congregational church I had attended as a child.) I used to listen to Richard's *Prayer for the Day* on the radio and decided he was exactly the sort of clergyman I wanted to conduct the wedding. A friend of ours went to All Saints Church in Fulham and took us along. We enjoyed the services, got married there in 1975, were confirmed in 1976 and have been active members ever since.

Richard made us very welcome at All Saints and managed to get us on a Parish Weekend very soon after joining. He was very cunning – he told us that there would be several young couples just like us going; he told the elderly ladies that there would be several elderly ladies there; he told the young, single people that the weekend was ideal for them and so on – with the result that there was an excellent cross-section of the parish present, some of whom would never have dared go by themselves! I remember that first Parish Weekend was somewhat on the intellectual side with some of the speakers better suited to third-year theological students. It was interesting that, during a walk on the Saturday afternoon, several of us gradually admitted that we hadn't understood a word of the morning's events. However, it was noticeable that subsequent weekends were pitched at a more general level – Richard Harries was even seen to be doing liturgical dancing on one occasion (not a born dancer!).

Today there is much talk about Marriage Preparation classes – and I now play an active part in the courses held at All Saints – but it is interesting that Richard organized courses back in the Seventies: he would take one session on the actual marriage service, and a couple of marriage guidance counsellors would take the next two sessions. They were excellent and we felt that a real interest was being taken in our wedding and future life together.

Richard's sermons were always full of literary quotes – particularly from T. S. Eliot and, when I worked for him some years later when he became dean of King's College, London, I discovered that he had an excellent card-index system of quotations and references. He had a good sense of humour and there was one particularly funny sketch at the parish concert, when Richard and his two curates (one was very musical with a lovely singing voice, and the other was also musical and particularly good at prayers) had fallen on hard times and were busking on the London Underground. One sang and was selling psalms, the other selling prayers, and Richard was selling T. S. Eliot quotes.

One of the churchwardens, Christopher Day, a master at King's School, Wimbledon, recalls Harries enjoying performing at parish concerts. 'He could be hilariously funny in a rather Peter Cook style – and he gave a good impression of T. E. Lawrence as Doubting Thomas in one rather antique Passion play. He was a lively member of the Social Club and usually led the way to the nearest hostelry on outings.'

Giving and generosity were recurring themes. Archbishop Michael Ramsey of Canterbury's take on Romans 14.8 contains the arresting words: 'A church which lives to itself will die by itself'. All Saints responded to this dictum through its giving which was a consequence of faith. It supported St Mary's Mission, Ovamboland (on the Namibia/Angola border) followed by other specific places and causes in the world. Christian Aid was a great beneficiary. In addition, at least ten per cent of the regular parish income went overseas. Of more than 300 parishes of the 25 deaneries of the London diocese which contributed to the United Society for the Propagation of the Gospel (USPG), All Saints was the highest individual parochial contributor.

Although there was a tradition of sacramental Confession according to the best Church of England formula – 'All may, some should, none must' – during Harries' time there was a steady, constant and ever-growing stream of people, young and old, who availed themselves of this sacrament of reconciliation. There were no boxes into which people disappeared but a small crucifix on the wall in the Lady Chapel, which was given in thanksgiving at this time, marked the place where people knelt.

That Harries genuinely knew individual members of the congregation is attested whenever one of them was ill or died. At funerals he used language which was unmistakably related to the person. Martin Wimbush says, 'It was this capacity to capture the essence of a person that made him special. When my father died in 1977 he wrote to me of my mother Evelyn: "After Roger's death I doubt she ever slept really well. In those long nights she experienced both anger and reassurance; darkness and mystical illumination". In 1984 Harries returned to Fulham to give the address at Evelyn Wimbush's funeral, at the end quoting Gerard Manley Hopkins: *That Nature is a Heraclitean Fire and of the comfort of the Resurrection* (Poems 1918).

> In a flash, at a trumpet crash.
> I am all at once what Christ is, since he was what I am, and
> This Jack, joke, poor potsherd, patch, matchwood, immortal diamond,
> Is immortal diamond.

'On behalf of us all, I thank God for the facets of Evelyn's diamond that glinted, gleamed and flashed before us and I praise Him that she is now, immortal diamond.'

Within the wider community of Fulham, Harries relished and took full advantage of any ex-officio membership which came his way and was never a mere name adorning notepaper. The two most important were his chairmanship of the Sir William Powell Alms Houses and the Lygon Alms Houses. As a result of government legislation, alms houses were able to register as housing associations. This made them eligible for government grants, so with a chairman's persuasive push and shove, the Sir William Powell Alms Houses were refurbished and the Lygon ones pulled down and rebuilt as self-contained, warden-assisted accommodation of a high standard. They were opened by the Queen Mother in 1980. Harries was also chairman of two Church of England schools in the parish, a primary school and a large comprehensive. Each had problems requiring negotiating skills with prickly educational authorities, teachers and parents.

It should not be minimized that Harries' preaching was a magnet drawing enquirers and those on the perimeter, to sample All Saints. It should not be assumed that he was one of London's outstanding preachers. He was not! But he was widely known through his broadcasting and journalism. His discipline and working methods in the parish enabled him to achieve more outside than seemed possible without neglecting his work as parish priest.

We have already observed how Harries' pithy journalism began and grew at Hampstead. He wanted to air his views and be known to and by a wider audience. If he was opinionated it was never a strident voice seeking the limelight for its own sake. He was more interested, and certainly effective, in contributing to contemporary issues. He was not obsessed with single issues. In 1973 Harries' name and voice became nationally recognizable. He was invited to present *Prayer for the Day* on BBC Radio. He did this every Friday at 6.50 am for 11 years without a break, then less regularly and intermittently until 2006. He said, 'It was in fact a *Thought for the Day*, followed by a very brief prayer. It was a lovely spot to have, as people at that time of the morning seem more receptive than later. When I started doing it, it was pre-recorded, but feeling the need of a new challenge, I started doing it live and so every Friday I would drive or be driven into the studios at Broadcasting House early in the morning to do this. Obviously the media exposure helped one's ministry in the parish.' It was the kind of discipline which more clergy could do with experiencing. He had one sentence – two at the most – to grasp and hold listeners' attention. The broadcasts produced a mountain of letters which received individual responses. Two collections of his radio talks in the Fulham years were published: *Prayers of Hope* (1975); and *Prayers of Grief and Glory* (1979). In addition, Harries had a weekly devotional spot in the *Church Times*. Another book, *Turning to Prayer* (1978) was written to offer practical suggestions on how to pray, making it a more natural and real part of people's lives. In 1983 *Praying Round the Clock* was dedicated: 'For the congregation of All Saints' Fulham from whom I received so much in the years 1972–1981'.

When, in September 1981, a single edition newspaper – *Not the Church Times* – was printed, scurrilous and satirical relief was brought to the Church of England. By this time Harries was well known and a devotional article was included – 'The Clarity of Ambiguity' by one Dick Harries. It was, of course, a parody, highlighting several of his foibles and fancies, most noticeably his apparent lust for quotations. He was right to defend himself: 'First, if I have come across something good, a line of a poem or a paragraph in a novel, I want to share it with others. Second, a poem may be the distilled experience of years of feeling, thinking and struggling for the right words.'

For Harries, whose activism was excessive, and he himself admits to being a workaholic, prayer was an essential stabilizer, keeping his spiritual life earthed. In the parish, the unrelenting hectic pace of life was always *vivace*, very occasionally *rallentando*, never *adagio*. The danger was justification by perspiration. Busyness has to do with self and the need to prove things about self. A lively, thriving church may mean a too talkative one where people become victims of the activity alibi. Fortunately, Harries recognized the need in himself for pause. That is why quiet days and retreats became part of the tempo of parish life. Keeping the church open during the week was a Harries' imperative so that passers-by could slip in to sit, rest, contemplate or pray. It had been a serious issue when, in 1973, there was a series of church fires started by arsonists in south and central London. St Mary's, Putney, across the Thames from All Saints, was destroyed. In the spirit of Dunkirk, a rota of church-watchers was formed at All Saints. Every night they would take turns to sleep in the church until a fire-detector system was installed. Determined that it would open daily from 10 to 5 at least, a roster of willing church-minders was introduced.

Harries' book *Being a Christian* (1981) was written at Fulham. It emanated from his adult confirmation classes. In 1973 23 adults were confirmed. He thought 'mature adulthood is arguably the best time to take so important a step'. Each session started with an introductory talk, for example, How do we know God is Real?; Who is Jesus?; The Meaning of the Eucharist; Love and Politics. In the book, as in the classes, Harries displayed a gift for taking hard nuts, cracking them and turning them into succulent fruits without neutralizing the difficulties of Christian belief in a secular world. His discursive informality helped the listener, as it helped the reader, to begin a personal pilgrimage. He did not provide a plateful of answers. Instead he encouraged people to think for themselves but would always be sensitive to those who needed mental crutches to help them over the stiles of doubt leading to faith. A doubt was an idea that was still alive.

In 1981 Harries had been at All Saints for nine years. He was ready for – needed – new challenges and stimulae. He notes: 'I was 36 when I became vicar of Fulham, with a young family. In some ways the years from 35 to 45 are the ones when one has most to give in terms of a combination of energy and experience. One always wants to achieve things. So it was a demanding nine years, mainly concentrated on building up the congregation and on what I could in the wider community.' There is evident in Harries a wholeheartedness in service. He has not surrendered himself to the squalid ambition of place-hunting. He recognizes that confidence is a plant of slow growth. It is also indispensable to spiritual influence. Congregations are quick to discern a restless priest who yearns for a touch of purple. They find him out. Wherever a parish priest cares for the souls of those he serves, he gains a rich recompense in their trust and love.

Harries has never been a clergyman's clergyman. His home, with its amazing hospitality provided by Jo, was ever-welcoming to non-churchgoers, a sanctuary too. A night at the theatre with Jo and friends was better than a yawn-inducing day spent in an ecclesiastical assembly. Ambitious clergy like to know bishops and those dignitaries who they think may help them climb to greater heights. Not Harries. He has always been interested in how power is exercised in parliamentary corridors and places where decisions are made, but has shunned involvement in the stifling passages of persuasion in Church House, Westminster. At Fulham he was only involved in clergy gatherings when necessary. He has always been dismissive of the calculated and concentrated energy of organized minorities of clergy and laity who huddle in partisan shelters. This said, he could not be ignored by the hierarchy who made him responsible for post-ordination training in the Kensington jurisdiction of the diocese of London.

Although he was not eaten up with ambition, it is simplistic and inaccurate to assert that he was not concerned about his own future. Yet he was neither fearful nor careful with his incursions into public controversy. Some of his writings, including his letters to *The Times* and *The Guardian* when vicar of All Saints, were not likely to endear him to the Church's leaders of the time. Following Michael Ramsey's retirement as Archbishop of Canterbury in 1974, the hierarchy of the Church of England went into limbo with Donald Coggan at Canterbury, Stuart Blanch at York and Gerald Ellison at London. Harries was sparked to respond to some of the archiepiscopal initiatives. One example will suffice to indicate Harries' many interventions. In 1975 the Archbishops of Canterbury and York issued a Pastoral Letter about the moral crisis facing the country. It was an appeal to the nation to turn from material to spiritual values. Archbishop Donald Coggan, whose integrity was beyond reproach, was simplistic in summing up his message as 'God first, neighbour second, self last'. In a pluralistic nation this was simply not to take unbelief seriously. But for a challenging, if misguided, denunciation by Mervyn Stockwood, Bishop of Southwark, in the Communist *Morning Star*, Coggan's squib would have remained damp. Instead, for two months, there was a fierce correspondence in the secular and Church press, questions in Parliament and much pulpit and podium comment.

Chancellor E. Garth Moore wrote to *The Times* (6 November 1975) stating: 'A political programme . . . is largely a matter of expediency and must rely on compulsion for its implementation. Christian morality by contrast is unconcerned with expediency and relies, not on compulsion, but on the voluntary acceptance of obligations by individuals.' Harries was stung into responding, which he did in a letter to *The Times* (11 November 1975). His short, veracious and sane reply is worth quoting as it includes principles which have remained with him:

(Garth Moore's) statement is untrue in at least three aspects:
1. Political programmes are not largely matters of expediency. They nearly always express an idea or vision of the kind of society that is held to be desirable and this for most people is a matter of moral choice.
2. Political programmes depend very heavily on consent, both for their acceptance and their implementation. Hannah Arendt showed this to be so even in the case of dictatorship. It is certainly true in our kind of democracy.
3. Christian morality ought to be concerned with expediency as well as with goals and virtues. That is, moral decision-making includes assessing the consequences of a proposed action and weighing the gain in one value against the loss in another.

Much of Harries' future will concern practical applications of these principles in Church and State alike. Fundamentals about religion and private morality rarely lend themselves to crisp discussion before a national audience. The media was not conceived to encompass philosophies: God and the cosmology do not cramp easily into half a column or a five-minute slot. It is one of Harries' abiding achievements, sown and grown at Fulham, that he could speak and write of verities in few words, attract an audience and make people think. He was attentive and listened to the widest variety of opinion but in the end he thought for himself.

In 1979 he was one of the speakers at the triennial conference for clergy of the diocese of St Albans, held at the University of Kent during Robert Runcie's episcopate. The speakers, well known for stimulating audiences, included Lady Oppenheimer, W. H. Vanstone, Richard Holloway, Eric Abbott and Eric James.

The speeches were included in *Stewards of the Mysteries of God* (1979). Harries' talk was on True Belief, prompted and undergirded by the work of Samuel Beckett and Albert Camus. He concluded that a credible Christian view of existence was not simply an intellectual problem.

> It's the moral passion and power of 'true unbelief' that has to be reckoned with. Christians have not on the whole comprehended the fact that there are strong moral arguments against their position. They tend to assume that if Christianity isn't true, at least it is the most moral view of the world going. But this can be disputed. Alec Vidler has pointed out that it was not the rise of science or biblical criticism that turned people like George Eliot away from Christian faith. Rather, 'What is called upon them to believe, with such confidence of its superiority, struck them as morally inferior to their own ethical ideals and standards.' The question then is this. Having really listened to and felt the force of voices of people like Camus and Beckett, how can the Christian faith be stated in such a way as to come across as a morally convincing, morally compelling alternative? Before human suffering, faced with a person whose anger leads him not just to protest but to commit himself to the alleviation of this suffering, a person who, despite everything, is determined to live and live with courage, what can be said?'

These were questions which were already and always in Harries' mind. Could he make a contribution towards some solutions? If so, it would have to be in a different arena, outside a parochial setting. But, as one curate of All Saints asserts, 'I knew at the time that these were golden years for me.' And for Richard Harries too!

Chapter Six
Nothing is Value Free

In 1980 an advertisement appeared for the appointment of a new dean of King's College, London. The college was founded in 1828 to provide, in the words of the Charter, 'for the general education of youth in the various branches of literature and science, and in the doctrines and duties of Christianity'.

Long before the college moved into the noble new building in The Strand it had become a mighty academic institution with departments of chemistry, physics, history, philosophy, medicine, modern languages, English and war studies as well as theology.

The changing role of the dean is reflected in Harries' three post-war predecessors. Eric Abbott, 1945–1955, was dean of the whole college whilst in charge of the theological faculty and warden of the hostel in Vincent Square, Westminster. He was already an influential figure which would come to final fruition as Dean of Westminster Abbey. He provided, guided and cajoled King's. He gave himself wholly and generously to those studying theology who would proceed to ordination. He loved generously and particularly. He was one of the Church's great spiritual directors and counsellors, a strange mixture of being utterly confidential, as one would expect in such a priest, with also a love of gossip. There was an aura about this sartorially elegant and correct priest He bound people to himself so that many were recognizable as 'Eric's boys'. Unfortunately he suffered his first heart attack at King's and was not helped by his great sense of doing his duty by overworking.

Abbott was succeeded in 1956 by Sydney Evans, one of the Church's neglected servants. No finer tribute to his life and work could be expressed than in the words of John Baker, then Bishop of Salisbury, in the service of thanksgiving in Salisbury Cathedral in 1988. Some extracts follow as there are a number of similar characteristics and interests to those of Harries, even if their personalities widely diverged:

> There was his breadth of culture. Nowadays most of us have what might be called a *Readers' Digest* acquaintance with a good many topics. Sydney's culture was not of that sort. When he was seized of some special interest, he had to pursue it widely and seriously, whether it was art, literature, history, music, the theatre, or the ancient Mediterranean world on which he lectured to such appreciative audiences on his regular Hellenic cruises. Nor did those loves stop at the theoretic or spectator level. He enjoyed painting. His sensitive but unforced reading of poetry drew out the best of all responses – it made you

want to read the poet for yourself. He was himself an artist in words. During his three years as Public Orator in London University he both gave and received much delight . . . King's, however, reminds me of another side to Sydney's complex and versatile character.

Sydney was never afraid of power. On the contrary, he enjoyed it. He was a very political creature, who understood well that 'politics is the art of the possible', but who relished the challenge of pushing the frontiers of that possible further out than anyone else thought they would go. Perhaps the most remarkable example of his persistence and diplomatic skill was his achievement in persuading a secularist University of London to found and fund no fewer than two chairs of Christian theology.

It has to be said that you do not get results like that by a wholehearted devotion to open government. Meetings, for Sydney, were opportunities to guide others into the right way. But there are costs to be paid for such a style; one of them is loneliness. It is a theme to which he often turned in his addresses; and without doubt he was wrestling with a personal problem. The remedy he suggested for the anguish of loneliness was to face and accept the unpalatable truth of the solitude of others.

Sydney Evans was not a saint, at least in the way the Church conventionally uses that word. But he showed to many the secret of what he once called 'a holy humanness'.

Professor John Barron was dean of the faculty of arts at King's and professor of Greek language and literature in the University in the mid-Seventies when financial pressure on theological colleges led to mergers and closures. It also led to the withdrawal of support for the department at King's on the part of certain bishops on whom it depended for the funding of ordination training. No longer viable as an independent institution, the department was forced to reunite with University of London King's College, as a publicly funded and therefore non-denominational department of theology on the same footing as law and French. Professor Barron explains:

There was, therefore, no longer a theological college to administer, and the dean became stranded as a kind of super-chaplain. For an ambitious individual of marked skill and inclination towards leadership, the downgrading implicit in the new arrangement would be barely tolerable. Sydney Evans wisely concluded that a move was essential both to himself and to the college. At King's, always hobbled by its church-mouse level of endowment, there was a real question-mark over his replacement, which would not, of course, attract public funding. The college did, after all, have a recently appointed Anglican chaplain, Colin Slee (now Dean of Southwark), a graduate of the college and something of an Evans-clone: why did we need a dean as well?'

The position of dean was retained with a distinctly different flavour. Initially, in September 1977 a good Anglican English pragmatic compromise was made with the appointment of one of the professors, who would have no administrative burdens, as dean. The appointment was only superficially imaginative. Sixty-four-year-old Ulrich Simon was professor of Christian literature. He was a Jewish refugee from Hitler's Germany – his father was murdered at Auschwitz. Simon came to England in 1933, became a Christian and was ordained in 1938. He was a stimulating teacher but his prophetic approach to the Bible was out of sympathy with the times. He was also opposed to liberal trends in postwar Christian theology and ethics. One of his books, *A Theology of Auschwitz* (1967), remains important.

In the event, Simon's position as dean was merely transitional. A new charter and statutes changed the nature of the office. Once again, in 1980, the position of dean was queried. It was fortunate that the principal of King's was Sir Neil Cameron, a former marshall of the Royal Air Force and Chief of the Defence Staff. Cameron was an evangelical Christian with a simple, profound, uncomplicated faith. The Victorian Byzantine chapel was almost opposite his office. It was his custom, on his way into work, to kneel quietly for a minute or two, commending the day and its many decisions into the hands of God. Harries recalls Neil Cameron's faith as 'all of a piece with the rest of his personality and it therefore took on all his directness, naturalness and charm. Because his faith was so integrated with his whole being, he was able to relate easily to people from different backgrounds of belief and non-belief and to respect practising Christians of other traditions'.

Cameron was also a man of vision and recognized that having a dean could be the basis for a much wider-ranging contribution to secular as well as Church affairs. Simon stepped down in 1980. Several people approached Harries at Fulham and informed him of the vacancy at King's. He evinced little interest. It was only when John Houlden, professor of theology at King's, pressed Harries that he seriously considered responding to the advertisement. He did so and found that King's wanted a new-style dean who would not have or want power in the college, but would have a prestigious position with a high public profile which could help the name of the college outside. Harries had the potential to fill these requirements and his appointment was announced in January 1981. His installation by Sir Neil Cameron took place on 19 May 1987. Bishop Kenneth Woollcombe, an assistant Bishop of London and a former Bishop of Oxford, licensed him. Lord Annan, vice-chancellor of the university and Lord Jellicoe, chairman of the college council, were there to support Harries and the large congregation included a sad but proud contingent from Fulham.

Harries, looking younger than his 44 years, was received with acclaim. His combination of charm, unaffected faith and intellectual curiosity won him wide sympathy and immediate friends. He showed very clearly that, whereas the chaplain ministered primarily to the students, there was also a spiritual and pastoral role to be filled among the academic staff. One professor exclaimed, 'We did need a dean.' John Houlden is of the view that 'Richard had the luxury of an extended sabbatical. He could do whatever he liked (within limits, I suppose). Ironically, his very public weekly appearance on *Thought for the Day* made him a well-known figure within the college, to students and especially staff.'

Being dean of King's was a position of leadership. But of what kind? His route to the position was an unusual one. Professional success so often and largely depends on personal influence. Ambitious parents, more prudent than high-minded, choose a public school for their boys, where schoolboy friendships will have a practical value in later life by easing entry into positions of authority and leadership. Harries' parents were oblivious of their son's vocation to the priesthood.

Such success, gained by influence in the absence of merit, is not what is meant by leadership, though it may carry its possessor into the leader's place. Harries was unusual in being a clergyman who was expected by others to ascend the ecclesiastical ladder. Unlike many clergy he never employed himself in studying clerical vacancies. Clerical assemblies with their churchy gossip were already places he shunned. His achievements were his own. A mixture of *gravitas* – serious, never solemn or pretentious – and *merita* – achieved by hard mental graft – were already characteristics. He would exercise an unusual kind of leadership at King's and later at Oxford. We know of his experience, but what were the qualities he brought to his new position as dean? Were there limitations as well as strengths?

First, his intellect! Once ordained, many clergy are swept into the distractions and fatigues of parochial work and find reading, study and all mental effort difficult and perhaps also distasteful. A bishop visiting a priest will glance at the books in his study and draw conclusions from what he sees and what he does not see. Mandell Creighton's well-known *mot*, 'The English people hate knowledge for its own sake', points to a bitter truth. Harries had long since formed the habit of using his mind to justify his convictions and beliefs. He had seized every opportunity to gain entrance into the ranks of thinking, cultured, informed and learned people from a wide range of disciplines. Of course, intellect is not enough. Intellect is not light: it is only the wick which must be fed constantly with the oil of compassion and service to others. Harries does not dazzle, but illuminates the darkness or throws a white beam ahead of a heavy-laden and far-journeying humanity on the road which leads to a better order of things.

Second, he has vision, which includes both foresight and insight. This requires wisdom, the faculty of making the best use of knowledge and is a combination of discernment, judgement and sagacity. Wisdom has been defined as 90 per cent being wise before, rather than after, the event. Vision also includes optimism and hope, traits already embedded in Harries which would be both strengths and vulnerabilities in the future. He is an optimist. The pessimist always sees difficulties before possibilities and tends to hold back. The man of vision sees possibilities even when there are difficulties and always looks ahead with great hope.

Third, Harries was highly intelligent, extremely well-informed with a well-stocked mind. He was self-contained, self-sufficient, unpretentious and detached. He is an honest man, of a piece, provokingly conscientious. His passion for liberty and justice is deep and genuine and his heart beats firmly on the left. He is rarely obscure or far-fetched and his judgements are not the slave of his resentments.

Fourth, he had developed an amazing versatility. Dangers attach to this commendable quality. Versatile people are usually very bright and are attracted to like-minded people. They may be tempted to pride – the pride of intellectual scorn, the pride of knowledge, provoked by the ignorance, stupidity and obstinacy of others. Versatility is often shadowed by suspicion, and pursued by calumny. The fanatical, the entrenched bigot, the cynical, as well as the merely 'traditional', will all, from their different standpoints, misunderstand versatile people. Their intellectual range will offend them, as will their sympathy with and their indifference to many conventions and their ready acceptance to comprehend and accept change. Versatility has its dangers but its strengths outweigh them. Harries is not an opportunist, neither is he frivolous nor intellectually flighty. He is subtle and consistent. Does it stem from his Christian convictions? It may not be quite claiming with St Paul that Harries' versatility has its roots and its limits in discipleship: 'I am become all things to all men, that I may by all means save some. And I do all things for the Gospel's sake.' There must be something of this as he proceeds to pursue and act on his convictions where, self-evidently, no personal advantage can be claimed. By his actions he demonstrates that versatility, an essential ingredient in his personality, can be gracious and elevating when used not for one's own satisfaction but in the service of others.

Fifth, and more difficult to define! What of a Christian leader at King's? All leaders need and seek prominence, publicity and a measure of popularity for propagating their views. They also need courage. Harries was not lacking in enjoying, perhaps seeking, the limelight even if it was subdued. Yet a priest must seek to humble himself before God. Self-effacement, not self-advancement and advertisement, was Christ's definition of leadership. Courage is that quality of mind which enables a person to encounter difficulty or danger with firmness and without fear of depression of spirit. Courage is demonstrated in a willingness to face unpleasant and even devastating situations and conditions with equanimity and act with firmness. A courageous leader will take the necessary action even though it means incurring personal unpopularity. This would be more difficult for Harries.

Finally, Harries is extraordinarily unwilling or unable to say anything to others about his deepest feelings. It may be that they are so deep as to have become subliminal; but is it repression that has made them so? The dislike of emotional expression is especially seen in a reluctance to talk about religious feelings, interior conflicts and personal crises, or of realizing some of them consciously. An unnatural veil is pulled down over the heart. This was not a problem at King's but would resurface at Oxford.

These are some of the characteristics of the new dean. In 1985 Neil Cameron was succeeded as principal by Stewart Sutherland (now Lord Sutherland of Houndwood), dean of the faculty of theology and religious studies. Fruitful relations continued. For Harries it was as if the soil had been fertilized and his own growth was immediate and massive. According to the new principal, Harries was very good at identifying opportunities to provide new, wider contributions to the affairs of both the college and the wider community. Changes continued throughout the 1980s. A new college was designed, which included the merging of King's School of Medicine and Industry, Queen Elizabeth College in Kensington and Chelsea College of Science and Technology. Sutherland had been Cameron's vice-principal and they worked together in planning these imaginative developments, and he recalls Harries' contribution:

> Throughout, Richard Harries was a helpful commentator who would stand aside from the inevitable political academic arguments which took place. The merger process was controversial, almost inevitably so. But in the long run it has worked and I've no doubt that Richard's presence in informal chats and councils with Neil Cameron was as helpful to Neil as they became to me. Practically everyone else in the college (indeed in the colleges) in question was an interested party. Richard could stand above all this.
>
> One of the consequences of the new structure was that an Associateship of King's College (AKC) course was offered to non-theologians. To the amazement of many, this voluntary course, which consisted of a weekly lecture and an exam at the end of each year, turned out to be very successful. Certainly in my last year of contributing to that course towards the end of the 1980s, there were no fewer than 800 students enrolled across the full range of faculties. Richard's contributions to these lectures were always popular, well targeted and worth hearing. Again the opportunity to lecture to such a wide-ranging group of students was doubtless, for him as it was for me, more the challenge and a major opportunity.
>
> The atmosphere in King's at that time was one of major change and upheaval. This included the position of the Anglican Church within the college. I was surprised on going to King's how prominent the position of the chapel was and its place in the wider community. Many academics had little to do with that side of the college, but a significant number from a wide range of faculties did see the chapel and therefore the dean as important in the pattern of college life. It no longer had the formal position of previous years, but it was part of what defined a distinctive tradition of King's. I took particular delight in teasing Richard from time to time with agnostic and heretical ideas. He took this in good part.

Before turning to the many facets of Harries' thought with action launched from King's, another recollection of John Houlden is pertinent:

> Early in his time, he announced that he would give an inaugural lecture, an innovation as far as the dean was concerned and normally confined to new professors. I confess that at the time I thought this somewhat forward on his part, and my suspicion of foolhardy ambition was encouraged when I saw that his subject was, as I recall, something in the area of biochemical ethics!

However, I attended the full-house occasion and was cheered on the way out to hear biochemists praising what they had heard. So very much 'one up' for Richard. But the occasion did exemplify the assurance which leads him to take up subject after subject and dare to write (and speak) about it when he can hardly claim to be an authority. He has the journalist's talent to get a subject up and deal with it with sufficient expertise and in an attractive way, which lifelong experts can fail miserably to do. This capacity – and courage – continues to be shown.

Everything Harries did at King's and Oxford was conditioned by a single dominant all-embracing belief: 'I argued then, as I argue now, that nothing in this life is value free. Every institution and every course of study is in fact imbued with certain values, a particular perspective. The idea that there is a neutral zone is an illusion.'

Chapter Seven
Uncompromising Obedience

In 1972 Harries wrote an article *Are Non-Revolutionaries Living in Mortal Sin?* Ten years later he published a book with an equally arresting title *Should a Christian Support Guerrillas?* They did not come from the favouring hand of a crypto-Communist, closet terrorist or someone puzzled or appalled that the reply could be anything other than self-evident for a Church of England priest, a resounding 'no'! But Harries had studied Marxism and wondered if there could be such a thing as a 'Just Revolution'. In order to arrive at his own position he also studied liberation theology and its impact in Central and South America, and then considered its relevance for South Africa, Russia and other countries where 'revolution' or reorientation was necessary.

There were many components melting in the crucible. In *New Fire*, the journal of the Society of St John the Evangelist (Cowley), Harries highlights the '*Revolutionary Priest*' and sociologist, Camillo Torres of Columbia. Torres believed that 'the duty of every Catholic is to be a revolutionary', and shared with Che Guevara the conviction that 'the duty of every revolutionary is to make the revolution'. Such a statement stirred Harries: 'A man who started off with a simple desire "to be more useful socially", and was led by his experience of God and the conditions in Columbia to take up arms against the government because he believed that revolution was, as he put it, "the only effective and far-reaching way to make the love of all people a reality", puts a question mark against many traditional assumptions. In the words of Peter Levi, the poet and literary critic, "there was a headlong straightness about him; it is part of his religious victory that no religious man today would dare to be sure that God was not closer to Camillo Torres than to most of us".' Harries, whose clarity of mind does not lead him into 'headlong straightness' on this issue asked, 'Is he indeed the authentic Christian of our time?'

Light shone from an unexpected place, namely the institutional Church. In 1968 at Medellin in Columbia, the Roman Catholic Latin American Bishops' Conference (CELAM) proclaimed a message which gave a new dimension, not only to that region but, through a series of global impulses, to the universal Church. It came in the wake of Pope Paul VI's *Populorum Progressio*, on development among the world's poor nations (March 1967). Solidarity and subsidiarity are the twin pillars of Catholic social teaching – the first, that we are all responsible in some way for one another; the second, the idea that political and social decisions should be taken at the lowest level possible, consonant with good government. At best they are held together by a constant quavering tension: at worst they separate.

Medellin was a charter for liberation theology: the system of thought which plucked the Church once and for all, or so it then appeared, from the sidelines and committed it to an active role in creating a new society. The crux of the argument was whether, in the face of a social order rightly described as 'institutional sin', where the Kingdom could have no roots, the Church should resign itself to the inevitable and try to curb its worst excesses from within, or whether it should seek to liberate all people from it and pave the way for authentic human development. Many of the 'liberators' were seeking a third way in political and economic terms: an alternative to the two great impersonal influences, namely the party in Communist countries, and multinational capitalism elsewhere. They were looking for a way to be Christian in the social order. Some pinned the flag to state socialism, especially where there seemed to be no other way, but many talked about 'autogestion', the cooperative system in which business enterprise is owned and controlled, not by the state, but by those who work in it. But at Medellin, the bishops looked at the poor. At the meeting of CELAM at Puebla, Mexico in 1979 the Church's lens moved to focus on the message the Church should portray.

Peace and justice became inextricably hyphenated. Harries found inspiration in Hélder Câmara (1909–1999), the diminutive, barely five-foot tall, Archbishop of Olinda and Recife in Brazil. His constant message was of justice, which was heard with little response by the authorities. By fighting, Câmara did not mean using arms. Harries always stressed that pacifism is not to be equated with passivity. Non-violent agitation was Câmara's means of achieving an end. He was friendly with Giovanni Montini, later Pope Paul VI, and his own contacts in Rome helped him to open the Church to the needs of the modern world. He abandoned his palace for the aptly-named 'church of the frontiers' tucked away behind the city's inner ring road, having his supper at a taxi-driver's stall across the road and hitching lifts around the city instead of running an official car. These were not mere gestures. He gave Church land away for the landless, set up a credit union and relinquished much of his administrative authority to clergy and lay people. Resigning, aged 75, in 1985, Câmara lived to see the 'Church of the Poor' dismantled by his successor, a dour canon lawyer, large and healthy who wore ornate purple attire with a huge gold cross. Furthermore, the papacy of John Paul II had arrived.

It is already possible to contemplate areas of convergence and divergence between Harries and Catholic social teaching, for he does not swallow whole any aspect of political, economic or social teaching and philosophy, and he is wary of dogma everywhere. He asked, which is more Christian: to refuse to take up arms and trust that patiently borne suffering will eventually win – or to take up arms to stop powerless people suffering at the hands of oppressors? To support those who have everything to lose – or those who have everything to gain?

In finding his own route in this forest, inhabited by ideologues, Harries always avoided the narrow path which leads to single definitions and solutions. He would never be the author of political programmes or manifestos. Neither would he be cornered by adversaries and put up against a wall. That is not to say his reasoning was equivocal or academic. The wrestling took place off-stage, behind the scenes.

The moment one thinks he is off to man the barricades, or confront the enemy with slogans, he comes armed with Christian principles and arrows of reasonableness. In his postscript to *Should a Christian Support Guerrillas?* Harries muses:

> A philosopher once remarked that all ethics is a training in sympathy. One might have expected a philosopher to stress other qualities. But it indicates that a reasonable approach, far from being cold, as has sometimes been pictured, is in fact rooted in the capacity to enter into other people's situations. The reasonable person tries to look at the question from the standpoint of everyone concerned, to weigh up all the factors.
>
> A reasonable approach also involves the attempt to liberate oneself from personal prejudice. This is of course the reverse side of trying to enter into the situations of other people. Unless we do this we simply reflect the views of our upbringing, social milieu, class or country. But to make the effort to transcend our own limited point of view is not only an attempt to think straight, it is an expression of Christian love.
>
> A further feature of a reasonable approach is the attempt to be consistent. On many ethical questions there can be no final agreement because people make different assumptions and it is not usually possible, from a neutral point of view, to show that one set of assumptions is correct and the other false. But what we can ask of ourselves and others is consistency . . . Consistency sounds a dry idea, but it has a close connection with the Christian faith. God, we say, is faithful. We ourselves seek to be faithful in return. What is consistency but faithfulness in the realm of thought?

Latin America was outside Harries' experience at this time. His concern was with South Africa. He joined the massive and campaigning throng who regarded apartheid as a heinous evil. He supported sanctions as a way of bringing economic pressure to bear. He supported the World Council of Churches' campaign to combat racism, which gave grants for non-military purposes to the African National Congress (ANC) and other anti-government groups. He believed that a case could be made out in principle for a just revolution, but what separated him from many other opponents of the regime was his criterion, a proviso – was there a reasonable chance of success? In *Should a Christian Support Guerrillas?* he argued and applied his Christian yardstick to the nature of the tyranny in South Africa. 'Is it long-standing and manifest? Have every peaceful means of exchange been explored? Second . . . is a revolutionary force with the potential to stay in existence long enough for the political battle to be won?'

Harries' theoretical convictions did not modify or melt, but solidified in 1982 when he was invited to give five lunchtime talks, from 9–13 August, at the multi-racial Cathedral of St Mary the Virgin, Johannesburg. The publicity leaflet promised listeners they would 'have the opportunity of hearing thoughtful religious addresses clothed in the modern manner where erudition and academic knowledge is combined with the successful communication required today'. The format comprised a simple service, with special regard to businessmen, with prayers, hymns and then the talk. The five topics were Searches for Happiness; for Fulfilment; for Peace of Mind; for Love; for Success. At a glance these topics suggest they were more likely to satisfy participants at a current day Alpha Course than a multiracial audience in South Africa.

Harries recalls a moment when the message may not have reached any audience:

When I presented my passport at Johannesburg airport I was asked for my work permit. 'I was told by your Embassy in London I didn't need one,' I said. 'I've been invited over to do some preaching.' I showed the lady my letter of invitation and she took it, together with my passport, to someone else, who in turn took it to someone else. Meanwhile I waited. After about 20 minutes a man came up to me and said, 'We are allowing you in this country for seven days only and you are not allowed to speak at any meetings.' 'But I've been invited to preach!' I said. 'You will have to get permission from the Minister in Pretoria.' So, the person who had invited me had to ring up the Leader of the Opposition, who rang up the Minister – and eventually after a lot more fuss I was given permission to preach! For me this was just a pinprick, but it is a sign of the rigid control the Government of South Africa exercises over every area of life.

It was a wonderful opportunity for Harries to meet prominent opponents of apartheid and to witness the malefic consequences of the South African Government's legislation. No Anglican visiting South Africa at that time need be ashamed of their Church's witness. No other Church came near it by comparison. Long before a mitre was placed on Desmond Tutu's head, the names of Trevor Huddleston, Michael Scott, Ambrose Reeves, Joost de Blank, Edward Crowther, Kenneth Skelton, Colin Winter and Gonville ffrench-Beytagh resonated as heroic – and not only in the black townships. Many potential black African leaders had Christian roots, among them Oliver Tambo, Walter Sisulu, Nelson Mandela, Z. K. Matthews, Albert Lutuli, Robert Sobukwe. All these had a common pursuit, even when detained or deported, heeding the words of Camus: 'Real generosity towards the future lies in giving all to the present'.

Harries was typical of visitors in wishing to meet as many 'marvellous' people as possible, listening with his mind as well as with his ears. He met Beyers Naudé, Nadine Gordimer, Helen Joseph, Alan Paton, Sheena Duncan, Denis Hurley and Desmond Tutu.

Harries met Beyers Naudé at his home in Johannesburg where he was living as a banned person. The visit had a lasting impact on Harries. Naudé was born into the heart of Afrikanerdom and his father was one of the founding members of the Broederbond, the Freemason-style secret society which still controlled life in South Africa in 1982. Like his father, Beyers became a minister of the Dutch Reformed Church (DRC) which preached the separation of the races. Gradually he was rethinking his position, so when the Sharpeville Massacre occurred in 1960, he was ready to move against the Government and his own Church! What did Harries learn from his meeting with Naudé?

I was very conscious of the strength of the forces keeping a DRC minister to his traditional ways. First, there is the sense of divine vocation which the Afrikaners share with the Israelites, that God has made a covenant with them and that if they are faithful to him, he will give them the land in perpetuity.

Then there is the fact that a minister of the DRC is chosen by the congregation, paid for by them – and can be sacked by them. The minister then has to find a new job, which after a long theological training and perhaps years in the ministry of the Church, with a wife and family, is not easy to do. Recently, there has been a great stirring in the DRC and 136 ministers have come out openly against apartheid. But talking to Beyers brought out the strength of the forces that condition us. It seemed that only a person of his massive, almost myth-like integrity could make the break. I say 'condition us' meaning all of us. It is easy to congratulate Beyers Naudé from a safe distance with a kind of patrician liberalism. From our superior vantage point we think it's nice that someone sees things as we do. But men of God challenge all of us. Beyers Naudé called into question the basic outlook and assumptions of the society in which he was born and nurtured, as did our Lord in his time. They found them at cross purposes with the Gospel. The question they pose to me is: 'What assumptions of the society which conditions me, which I am likely to take for granted, are at odds with the Gospel?' O God, grant us the light to see as clearly as he saw.

The second point about Beyers is that the fundamental motivation for all that he does is obedience to Christ. A good example comes from his farewell sermon to his congregation in 1963. He took as his text Acts 5.29: 'We must obey God rather than men'. After dealing with his own decision to leave, he turns to the congregation, 'You also are called to choose, to make a decision . . . is his Word, the highest authority, the final word for you? If so, do you obey his Word? Do you live according to his Word? . . . Oh, my Church, I call this morning, in all sincerity from my soul – awake before it is too late. There is still time, but the time is very short, very short.'

Yet the Naudés shunned by their own people, have made this rejection a source of great blessing. He told me that it has enabled both himself and his wife to experience the grace of God as at no other time in their lives. And it has brought them into the wider supportive fellowship of the Church as a whole, which they value. Through the stream of visitors who come to see him (he is only allowed to see one at a time) he exercises a remarkable ministry. He is a man in the mould of Dietrich Bonhoeffer, with a passionate, intelligent, Bible-based obedience. So much English Christianity, however sensible and sound it may be, gives the impression of being rather pragmatic. Beyers Naudé points us to a discipleship in the political order, in which we all inescapably dwell, based on uncompromising obedience to Christ.

On his visit to South Africa, Harries had a real opportunity to enter into life in Soweto and the struggle against apartheid there, with the Black Sash and with women's organizations in Durban and elsewhere. On his return to England Harries published his impressions in *Church Times* and *The Times* which were subsequently printed together by the Christian Institute.

There was another influence, that of his host, Simeon Nkoane, the Dean of Johannesburg, who, shortly after Harries' visit, became Bishop of the Eastern side of the Johannesburg diocese. Nkoane was a professed member of the Community of the Resurrection, Mirfield. Harries is wary of using the word 'holy' or 'saintly' about anyone still living and not often about the deceased, but he did so of this Mirfield father, whom the South African Government did not want in their midst any more than they wanted Trevor Huddleston – although in this case Nkoane was a black South African. What was it that Harries saw and felt? What most people recognized in Nkoane was articulated by Fr Crispin Harrison CR on hearing of Simeon's death:

> Simeon laughing. Simeon praying and Simeon surrounded by his people. Joy bubbled up in him constantly. He was self-forgetful, living in others not through them, yet he could be impatient, unreasonable, assertive, even aggressive, especially if his authority were challenged. Though seriously ill he did not welcome the death he knew was coming. During the last week before his passing or transformation he said, 'It's important to think big. It's wonderful if it comes off.' And a little later, 'What will they think of my vision?'
>
> Desmond Tutu's farewell was *Hamba Kable, Qhawe* (Go well, brave man) but Simeon Nkoane was smiling when the solemn words of the final commendation, 'Go forth Christian soul on your journey from this world' were read. He struggled to get up as if ready to go to God.

The aftermath of his visit, the articles he wrote and the broadcasts and talks he gave, made Harries a target for a campaigning organization, not as adversary but as potential leader. He was asked to become chairman of End Loans to Southern Africa (ELTSA). This was new and unnatural territory for Harries as it involved attending the annual general meetings of some banks and companies and asking questions about their South African policy. Instead of a loud, provocative, interrupting voice, company directors found a modest, penetrating one, no less determined to elicit a response. Not for the last time Harries' natural demeanour and smart appearance were a positive aid. This chairmanship made him more aware of the hard professional and commercial realities facing company directors. Unbeknown at the time he was preparing for the future when he would ask the question, 'How far can Christian Gospel principles provide a basis for formulating ethical investment standards?'

In 1984 Harries encountered a different kind of tyranny. In April the Archbishop of Canterbury, Robert Runcie, asked him to be his representative at a conference in Moscow, called by the Russian Orthodox Church for world religious leaders, on the subject of weapons in space. The purpose of the gathering was to elicit from those attending the strongest possible condemnation of the actions of the United States which, willy-nilly, was forging ahead, deaf to all opposition. It gave Harries the opportunity of gaining an instructed interest in the Space Defence Initiative (SDI) and the role of anti-ballistic missiles. He needed no conversion, but his total opposition to the SDI was reinforced, first because he was convinced that no shield in space could defend a country from an incoming flight of nuclear missiles; second, he believed it would de-stabilize the nuclear balance in which he did believe!

The visit to Moscow was his first entrée into the world of the Russian Orthodox Church which stood for a clear and undiluted sense of order both within and beyond this world. The Orthodox Churches engaged the world with gusto, albeit with some restrictions, while practising a transcendent, luminous spirituality. He imbibed an emotionally seductive, intellectually majestic and liturgically magnificent Church which was not meant to make him feel comfortable. Orthodoxy is not apprehended or appreciated in that way. Yet the awesomeness of God is earthy too, not easy for Western consumption.

A few weeks later, in September 1984, Harries was in Moscow again, this time the result of an initiative by Canon Paul Oestreicher and at the invitation of the Soviet Peace Committee, a government-sponsored organization. The word 'peace' was a mantra on everyone's lips. This distracted rather than impressed Harries. 'Wherever we went the theme was hammered. Outside the big pioneer palace there was a vast banner: "Peace and friendship to all the children of the planet".' Peace education was an important agent of internal cohesion. Harries was not deceived by the rhetoric, for it was also the vehicle for carrying the historical burden of Marxism.

Such trips achieve no tangible results, though they help mutual understanding and, for Harries, above all else, provide rewarding occasions for meeting people. Occasionally meetings were more like 'audiences'. When they met the magnificent Metropolitan Philaret 'we asked how he felt about the restrictions on religious literature. A young theological graduate answered first. He said he had been brought up in an atheistic household – but that Marxism could not embrace every aspect of life. In the arts, in music and literature, the religious imprint, as he called it, had been left. He had been drawn into the Church through these. Secondly, the official works of atheism quote great passages from religious philosophers in order to refute them. So it is possible to read about the Christian faith there. Then Philaret himself spoke. He said that when someone came to him he lent them his own prayer book. They copied it out by hand. They valued it then. "We do not believe", he said, "that the road to Golgotha should be made easy".'

On another occasion when Harries said he was disturbed by the level of fear of nuclear war in the Soviet Union, and that everyone who thinks about these things knows that deterrence is pretty robust, one member of the Soviet Peace Committee said to him, quite without a blush, 'It's only on the basis of fear that we are able to mobilize people'. After Moscow the group went to Georgia where the Peace Committee was like a government-inspired Rotary club. It was to be the first of numerous visits to that country.

There was an established Anglican–Orthodox International Doctrinal Commis-sion which tried the patience of any Anglican. The Orthodox Church had little understanding of how the Anglican Communion works. The reverse was equally true. Discussions were difficult because the Orthodox regarded everything as set-tled. What therefore was there to discuss? How could the Orthodox be expected to comprehend a Church that claimed to be Catholic and worldwide when several parts of it reached diametrically opposing decisions? How could the Orthodox have much interest in a Church that appeared to think worship was for the sake of the worshippers? Any progress appeared to go nowhere slowly. However, the Arch-bishop of Canterbury thought there was a possibility of slight movement with the Russian, as opposed to the Greek and other Orthodox Churches. He decided to set up a liaison group between the Church of England and the Russian Orthodox Church with the hope of fostering practical cooperation. Harries was asked to chair the group and there were meetings in London and Moscow. But it was not Harries' shot of vodka. He admits, 'it was a frustrating experience. Although a number of valuable suggestions were made about how the Church of England could help the Russian Orthodox Church take best advantage of the many opportunities now opening up before it, internal dissension in that Church and lack of resources meant that they failed to take of advantage of these. Furthermore, when the Church of England decided to ordain women, a great frost set in.' One liaison group meeting was so unsatisfactory that Harries gave up both his chairmanship and membership. The former passed to someone who had the looks, empathy and sanctified patience for the post – Richard Chartres, Bishop of London.

Harries brought his experiences into his *Thought for the Day* as, for example, in 1991 following a meeting of the liaison group in Estonia. He was effective at catch-ing the attention of listeners by evoking a single incident or contrasting memories. The group stayed in a convent set in the countryside, dedicated to prayer and work, mostly farm labour done by hand. The Sisters worked hard from five in the morn-ing until ten at night. That was realism, but there was romanticizing too:

> Our sense of enchantment was at its highest during Church services. The haunting Orthodox music sung by two choirs, flickering candles amid the icons and reverent worshippers. Amongst the worshippers I could not help noticing a rather restless, mentally handicapped boy being looked after by his mother. They were there again for the Sunday morning liturgy. The child, now calm, came up to receive Communion, arms devoutly crossed, held by his mother. In a flash I seemed to see the whole life of that mother, the disbelief and pain when she first discovered that her child was handicapped, the disap-pointments, all the difficulties and struggles. Yet above all I saw that mother's love: her arms, firmly but gently round her son, guiding him to Communion . . . That mother revealed something else also; the transforming power of human care. The truth in human romanticizing is the possibility of things being different, better, more beautiful – and this is real, not just escapism, for it is a true insight into the transfiguring possibilities of love; which is capable

of turning the ordinary into the wondrous; human anguish into the material of eternity.

In 1993 the Archbishop of Canterbury, now George Carey, was making an official visit to Russia, Armenia and Georgia. There was all the panoply of such events with receptions for national and local dignitaries. In Moscow, as a result of the Church of England ordaining women to the priesthood, the visit had slipped down several grades. Patriarch Alexis II had been imprisoned by the Communists, and was now a powerful figure, physically, mentally and spiritually. He met the English party at Danilovsky Monastery and was not mealy-mouthed in his condemnation of the ordination of women, and would brook no interference in Russia by the Roman Catholic Church or American evangelical missionaries. By contrast, the reception in Armenia was warm and friendly. Harries was taken aback when a local dignitary said to him: 'Everything connected with Mrs Thatcher is holy.' (The then British Prime Minister had made a huge impression when she opened the Lord Byron School, a building for 1,000 pupils financed by British aid.) Here Harries saw an example of what the status of the Archbishop of Canterbury means as a worldwide religious leader. Armenian archbishops from Los Angeles, London, Istanbul, Canada and Australia had flown in to greet him. If the English contingent expected results from the visit they were disappointed.

Then there was Georgia which made the visit so very worthwhile. There was a long session with the President, Eduard Shevardnadze, a practising Christian, who was having a bad time with two civil wars going on, a precarious political base and virtually no control of the army. Patriarch Illya II, a warm and intelligent man, with a huge entourage, met the visitors and made them welcome. Language was always a problem on such visits but more so in Georgia, with its own alphabet and language. Russian is their second language. It is also the oldest Christian nation in the world. Christianity became the state religion in the beginning of the fourth century. As a country it is surrounded by Muslim nations and has suffered much in order to maintain its own identity and distinctive culture.

However, for Harries, it was conversations with the Evangelical Baptist Church of Georgia which were to change his perspective and make a permanent link and friend. This Church was founded in 1867 as a result of an indigenous Protestant movement. Tbilisi, the capital of Georgia, became a cradle for the Baptist movement in the former Russian Empire, from where it spread to Russia and other regions. It is quite unlike the Baptist Church in the United Kingdom, and should be considered as a Reformed Orthodox Church. It is committed to the great Reformation principles of Europe, but retains its Orthodox legacy, strong Orthodox Trinitarian faith, two natures of Christ, balanced Christology, Orthodox liturgical traditions, iconography and Christian art and music. Its Presiding Bishop is Malkhaz Songulashvili. He first met Harries during the 1993 visit. He was not then ordained and worked for the Tbilisi State University and acted as interpreter during discussions. The two met again on several occasions in Georgia and Oxford. In 1995 Bishop Malkhaz came to study in Oxford and was invited to stay at Bishop's

House. He recollects being left in charge of the house – and the cat – whilst Harries and his wife Jo were away in the Middle East. It was while staying in Oxford that religious violence broke out in Georgia and he was forced to return home immediately.

In 1997 Harries made his third visit to Georgia, this time with Jo and Dr Arthur Peacocke, who was to deliver some theological lectures at Tbilisi University on science and religion. Harries gave lectures on Christianity and the visual arts. Richard and Jo travelled throughout Georgia visiting churches, cathedrals, museums and making many friends. During the course of the visit the Georgian Orthodox Church decided to withdraw from the World Council of Churches, and the Patriarch, who was friendly towards Harries, who had hosted him in Oxford when he visited England, refused to see him. Bishop Malkhaz feels he has been affirmed in his ministry by Harries in numerous ways:

> Bishop Richard was most supportive in the time of religious violence in Georgia. He wrote letters to various people about it in Britain and beyond. Jo and Richard have been like parents in Christ, who always worried about my well-being and that of my people. The Bishop has always been supportive of the social ministries for the poor and destitute and he is very appreciative of the work our Church has undertaken to serve the wider society in Georgia. Owing to his support there is a Diocese of Oxford Room at the Betheli Centre in Tbilisi which is the only ecumenical project in Georgia. He has been supportive and encouraging of the school of iconography which is very new, not only for the Baptist Church of Georgia, but for the Orthodox culture as well. The school is developing a modern approach towards the centuries-old tradition of icon painting in Georgia. Bishop Richard believes in education, therefore it was no surprise that he agreed to be associated with a School of Elijah in Georgia, as a board member of the project which trains both men and women for Christian ministry.

Russia is never more than a book away from Harries. If he were incarcerated on a desert island he would have with him Dostoyevsky's *The Brothers Karamazov*. This book has had the most effect on his life. 'It wrestles, as no other book does, with the fundamental issue of evil and suffering and how, if at all, they can be reconciled with a belief in a loving God. It set an agenda which is still with us.' One week after returning from Moscow in 1984 Harries was preaching his 'Opening of Term' sermon at King's:

> Religion, said someone, is giving freely without any strings. It is the God who gives himself freely to us without any strings who is revealed in Jesus Christ. In *The Brothers Karamazov* there is a remarkable scene when Christ returns to earth and confronts the Grand Inquisitor in Seville. The Grand Inquisitor, far from being penitent for the atrocities carried out in the name of religion, accuses Christ of having too high an estimate of man, of treating him as free,

when he could not cope with freedom. The Church has had to correct your great work, he says to Christ, and once more men rejoice that they are led like sheep. Dostoevsky had a true feel for Christ. Christ gives God to us, freely without strings. The Church has always found this difficult to live with, has tried to coerce people and still tries to do so in more subtle ways – through stirring up the wrong kind of guilt, through making people feel small and mean and dirty and then offering Christ as a salvation from these feelings. I discover in myself sometimes the tendency to make people feel guilty.

Chapter Eight
Et Alia

The accumulation and breadth of Harries' activities and achievements at King's is immense, suggesting hyperactivity on a dangerous scale. Whereas some contemporaries were manufacturing crutches for lame excuses on a range of ill thought-out policies with few results, he ran a forge manufacturing irons in the fire. An observer may deduce that he snatched at any passing opportunity and claimed it for himself. That is slander. He knew what he wanted to do and why.

What had this to do with King's? And where would it lead? One hoped not in death as it did with another over-active person, one of the great glories of the Church of England, Ian Ramsey, Bishop of Durham. On one occasion Alec Hamilton, his Bishop Suffragan of Jarrow, gave Ramsey candid advice, that his first duty was to do the work he was paid for and only then to undertake additional tasks. The difference was that Harries was paid to do almost anything he liked, and the times were right for him to pluck fruit from whatever trees suited his taste. With this nourishment, in a new environment. King's and the Church would not be the only bodies to be enriched.

Major themes of the King's years abide and merit separate treatment. There are other topics, however, both fleeting and permanent, which should not be neglected as they affect his future life and ministry.

There are opposing views on Harries' preaching. He finds preaching difficult, never routine or easy. The ministry of the Word was, to the preachers of the sixteenth and seventeenth centuries, an awful and exacting service, into which they poured their learning and zeal. Today the sermon has shrivelled in length and diminished in importance. The Church of England balances Word and Sacrament. To the validity of sacraments, of course, a priest can add nothing by his virtues and efforts, and from such validity his failings and negligences can withdraw nothing. That 'the unworthiness of the minister hinders not the effect of the Sacrament' is the indispensable postulate of sound Anglican teaching, and has been vehemently insisted upon by the Church against countless heretics. As soon, however, as the priest leaves the altar or the confessional, and enters the pulpit, the situation changes. Much turns there on preachers' personal fitness for their work, and on the conception they have formed of it. Their personal sincerity, their known convictions, their acquired knowledge, their natural ability, even their reputation, appearance, manner and voice, will all have a bearing on their preaching, and affect its fortunes. The truth of their message, of course, is independent of the particular form in which they may present it, but its power to attract people, secure their audience, and affect their minds will be to a very considerable degree contingent on the individual through whom it was delivered. Albeit the fortunes of the divine seed are strangely determined by the state of the human soil into which it is cast; and any results are rarely completely known to the sower. Harries is well aware of the mysteriousness in divine action which eludes observation and defies analysis.

Although Harries was influenced by a few great preachers he, sensibly, did not attempt to translate their methods into his own. At Fulham, unlike Hampstead, he occupied the pulpit on a frequent basis. Appreciated by a regular congregation he was able to use the pulpit for sustained teaching. The sermon was one of the instruments of didactic and pastoral duty. Pastoral preaching is not primary intellectual, but devotional and practical. It reflects the knowledge and insight of the parish priest and is directed to the actual circumstances of the persons to whom it is addressed. The congregation at Fulham had got to know their vicar's personal idiosyncrasies of expression and his use of quotations.

At King's he was not required to preach frequently to the ever-changing congregation. He found subjects which alerted and stimulated. In view of subsequent observations from Oxford days, it is well to record a King's view, from Dame Averil Cameron who was professor of ancient history, now warden of Keble College, Oxford. 'As dean, it was left to the incumbent to make of it what he could by personal impact. This Richard did extremely well. His presence, his humane vision and his knowledge of literature and art made him a good preacher and gave the chapel a splendid feel. His voice had something to do with that too. There is a very special quality about Richard's voice and the way he puts things in the pulpit (and in his broadcasts) which were evident when I knew him as dean of King's. It is definitely part of his gifts.'

In 1982 Harries gave the Drawbridge Memorial Lecture on 'Astride of a grave' – Samuel Beckett and Christian Hope. These lectures were a tribute to a former secretary of the Christian Evidence Society which was founded in 1870 by Anglicans and Nonconformists with the object of tackling the problem of unbelief in Victorian society. Although not in the society's original Memorandum of Association, open-air speaking and lecturing became one of its main activities with the twofold purpose of reaching the working-class population, and countering the outdoor secularist speakers, notably at Speaker's Corner, Hyde Park. Tracts and books supplemented this activity. Over a long period the society was successful, but the two decades leading to 1980 were ones of decline. In 1982 the Bishop of Peterborough, Cyril Eastaugh, resigned as chairman through illness.

Following his Drawbridge lecture, Harries was invited to join the board of the Christian Evidence Society and in July 1983 he was elected chairman. A year later St Paul's Cathedral was full to hear another Drawbridge lecture, this time by Bishop Desmond Tutu on Christian Witness in South Africa. Revival of the society's fortunes was swift under Harries. New trustees came from publishing and broadcasting. He strengthened the sense of belonging and commitment, especially by sharing meals together. He engaged well-known people to lecture –

Dr Sheila Cassidy, Professor John Polkinghorne, Irina Ratushinskya and Bishop John Baker – and pressed forward with personal initiatives – pure Harriesesque – with two conferences at Cumberland Lodge in Windsor Great Park, the home of St Catherine's Foundation: one in 1968 to consider The Soap Opera: Mirror or Shaper of Society featuring such programmes as *EastEnders*, *Coronation Street* and *Neighbours*. Scriptwriters, producers, authors, actors, academics, researchers, journalists and clergy required little persuading to make the journey to hear Dorothy Hobson, Piers Plowright, Julia Smith, Melvyn Bragg, Alan Plater and Katharine Whitehorn. Although the conference was an exhilarating talking-shop and reported in national newspapers, its outcome was disappointing for Harries who bewailed a 'strange shyness, amounting at times to recalcitrance even to discuss questions of moral values'.

Four years later Richard and Jo Harries hosted the second conference on 'The Reawakening of Religion?'. On this occasion a diverse range of people attended, including Jews and Muslims, sharing their opinions and beliefs, but again there was more intellectual stimulus than practical results. However, by 1992, when Harries resigned as chairman, the society was alive and breathing healthily and continues to do so. Harries has always been a keen, good and successful debater against adversaries on religion. In 1999 he spoke at the Oxford Union against the motion 'This House No Longer Believes in God' which was proposed by Denis Cobell, head of the National Secular Society. The motion was soundly defeated – Ayes 202, Noes 478.

Although Harries at this time usually avoided close involvement in internal Anglican controversies, he could not escape the ordination of women to the priesthood. In the October and November 1985 Bishop's Newsletter, the Bishop of London, Graham Leonard, wrote on this issue, his principle motive being to encourage serious discussion in an ever-increasingly intemperate atmosphere. Harries responded with an Open Letter made public in January 1986 which was reproduced in *The Tablet* on 8 February 1986. The Bishop treated Harries' contribution seriously and gave it wings by generously agreeing for it to go out with the London diocesan mailing. Harries' format was to quote some of the Bishop's objections, taken directly from his newsletter, and answer each of them. The Bishop's objections were familiar, that Christ chose only men as his Apostles; that God made us male and female, which entails real differences in our psychosexual being and in our personal identity – we are to be saved in our masculinity and femininity, not from them; that God chose to become incarnate as male. And, 'In human life the masculine is associated with giving and the female with receiving. God is pre-eminently the giver, who takes the initiative for our salvation. A male priesthood symbolizes the initiative, as well as the authority, of God. Mary, on the other hand, symbolizes the receptive, obedient response which is due from mankind.'

Most of Harries' answers were likewise familiar and well-rehearsed, although two of his extended points were less frequently propounded by supporters of the ordination of women:

Bishop: Christ challenged the outlook of his time on earth when it conflicted with a clear will of God e.g. on Sabbath observance.

Harries: (Christ) challenged it [the outlook of his time] by his treatment of women and by according them a share in his ministry. Should he have challenged it even more directly by making women apostles? The apostles were called by Christ to leave their homes and to go out and about the countryside calling men to repent before the imminent rule of God in human affairs. Given the position of women in society at that time, would it have been sensible to do this? Or even a real option to do so?

Harries was forceful in answering the Bishop's objection that 'In human life the masculine is associated with giving and the female with receiving':

It seems dangerous to associate a giving and receiving type of love exclusively with either masculinity or femininity. For many, if not most, people the giving of love *par excellence* is known in the love of a mother. God is indeed the one who takes the initiative and the Son of God was born as a man. But it would of course be circular to argue from this that only masculine love should be associated with taking the initiative. Within the blessed Trinity there is perfect mutual giving and receiving between the Father and Son. It was this eternal relationship that was disclosed in human terms. In the Gospels the Son owes all that he has, and receives all that he is and does, from the Father whom he seeks to be perfectly responsive. The picture we have at the baptism of Christ is the truth of the whole incarnate story and this is the story in time of what happens endlessly in the Godhead. It is not therefore simply Mary who is a symbol of human responsiveness to the Father but Christ himself. Indeed, ontologically, her responsiveness is grounded in and derived from the perfect filial response of Christ to his Father. For Christ is the exemplar and symbol of receiving (as well as giving) love. This, too, should be symbolized by those who share in his priesthood. The priesthood represents not only the initiative and authority of God but the receptivity and obedience of mankind. As Christ, the true priest, unites in himself both giving and receiving, so those who partake of his priesthood symbolize both aspects of the love of the Godhead. It is no more tenable to argue for an all female one. Symbols are certainly important and the ordination of women to the priesthood would have a profoundly positive effect. It would bring home the truth that in Christ 'there is neither male nor female' (Galatians 3.28), or to put it another way, that God includes within himself the fullness of masculinity and femininity. Further, it would help to communicate more of this feminine side of divine love.

Harries' concluding reasoning was that 'many women feel an *internum testimonium Spiritus Sancti* leading them to offer themselves for ordination. The Church should now test this, in individual cases, as it does for men. If there is no theological reason

81

why women should not be ordained, as has been argued, the present failure to test women's vocation is an act of basic injustice at the heart of the Church's ministry.' The difficulty, even danger, is that when the argument appears to veer away from the heights and depths of theology and doctrine, to the plateau of simple justice, a new set of arguments and principles emerge.

The Open Letter was prefaced by five names from different Churches and traditions expressing support for the ordination of women. They were Alan Webster, dean of St Paul's, a leading campaigner; Bishop Kenneth Woollcombe, an active sympathizer; Michael Sayward, a leading evangelical voice; and two Jesuits, Robert Butterworth SJ (Roehampton Institute) and Robert Murray SJ (Heythrop College). Bishop Graham Leonard was not alone in regretting that Harries had invoked support of the Jesuits. 'I can appreciate the argument on the basis of your standpoint, that the Roman Catholic Church might benefit from the experience of seeing women ordained in the Church of England, but I find it distressing and offensive to seek support from members of that Church where it is not permitted.' *The Tablet* surprisingly appeared to stoke the fire of division or, at least, make mischief, in an editorial introduction which stated that the Bishop had 'threatened to lead a schism if such a development occurs' which the Bishop denied.

Over the years Harries gave strong support to Christian Action, which was founded in 1946 to stimulate Christians and all people of goodwill to action in public affairs in accordance with Christian insights. Its president was Canon L. John Collins and Harries was vice-chairman of the council from 1979 to 1987. Canon Eric James was a superb director and knew better than most how to bring it into the public arena on the most commanding issues of the time, for example, Faith in the City, Homosexuality, Christian Education and Human Rights.

In 1984 Harries was a member of a sturdily independent working party on Human Rights and Responsibilities in Britain and Ireland: A Christian Perspective chaired by Sydney D. Bailey. Its members and consultants included Roman Catholics and Protestants from England, Wales, Scotland and both parts of Ireland and Harries shared insights with people who were less prominent then than they would later become – David Trimble, then a lecturer in law at the Queen's University, Belfast; Mary Robinson, a member of the Senate of the Republic of Ireland; Enda McDonagh, priest and professor at the Pontifical University of Maynooth; James Whyte, a minister of the Church of Scotland and Sean Farren, a lecturer in education at the University of Ulster. Already established names were Sir James Fawcett, chairman of the British Institute of Human Rights; Anthony Lester, QC, who specialized in constitutional and international law; Ben Whitaker, former MP for Hampstead, then executive director of the Minority Rights Group and Paul Siegart, barrister and author. They did not bow their differences into a corner. On some crucial matters, there remained differences of judgement and this was reflected in the final report. Harries' input is recognizable in a section on 'Rights and Responsibilities in Christian Ethics'. If human rights are a reflection of the justice which God requires in all human societies, Christians can have no release from the constant endeavour to see justice upheld. 'But the concept of responsibility implies more than this. Its basic and most ancient meaning is *accountability*: to be responsible is to be accountable to someone else for what one does.' That a sense of responsibility is a highly esteemed moral quality will feature in Harries' own works.

During the King's years Harries was a member of the Home Office Policy Advisory Committee on Sexual Offences. It was a representative committee chaired by Lord Justice Waller whose members included lawyers, a consultant psychiatrist, social worker, headmistress, sociologist, justice of the peace, probation officer, journalist and a police officer. The committee, working closely with the Criminal Law Revision Committee (lawyers only), was concerned with a range of issues, one of them prostitution. Suggestions ranged from legalizing prostitution on the one hand to prosecuting the punters on the other. In the end the committee's emphasis fell on making it an offence for a man to use a motor vehicle for the purpose of soliciting a woman for prostitution. This was significantly modified in the House of Lords.

Harries noticed how the committee was more libertarian than otherwise in its approach, regarding the law as morally neutral. Members thought that the alternative was to regard the law as an instrument for enforcing morals. Harries' own approach was different from either of these two. 'I believe that the law inescapably reflects moral values and assumptions and that it is right that it should. But I also believe that it is fundamental to a democratic society that there should be the maximum respect for the liberty of conscience of each individual citizen.'

Harries was at one with Thomas Aquinas that law is ultimately grounded in natural law. The issue came to a head for Harries when the committee discussed the question of bestiality. They all agreed that the then life sentence for someone convicted was far too harsh. Should it be an offence at all, and if so on what grounds? Some members argued there need be no offence because someone guilty of such an act could be convicted for cruelty to animals. But suppose there was no cruelty and that the animal enjoyed it? 'I argued that there was something fundamentally unnatural about the act, in the sense that it was a violation of the dignity of a human being and that it was quite right for the law to support a sense of human dignity by having such an offence. The law could reflect an important moral principle which was valid whether or not pain or pleasure was caused to the animal in question.'

Another chairmanship was that of the Southwark Ordination Course, which celebrated its twenty-fifth anniversary in 1984. Its genesis had been the initiative of the Bishop of Southwark, Mervyn Stockwood, who wanted to train men for the ordained ministry while they were still in secular employment and to encourage some to remain in their employment after ordination. The bench of bishops was unenthusiastic but, unexpectedly, the Archbishop of Canterbury, Geoffrey Fisher, gave his guarded support and urged Stockwood to go ahead. Stockwood regarded the Archbishop as basically a liberal traditionalist who, like Gamaliel, took the line that if the movement were merely human it would collapse of its own accord. But if it were of God it could not be defeated.

The driving force was the Bishop of Woolwich, John Robinson, and Canon Stanley Evans, a former Communist, was the course's first principal. Nothing was allowed to be second-rate about the course. Students, studying part-time, took the same exams as their contemporaries at traditional theological colleges. The first students were ordained in 1963. Harries began to appreciate what non-stipendiary ministry could offer. By 1984 several hundred men and women were trained in this way – solicitors, bankers, engineers, teachers, drivers, conductors, social workers, barristers, accountants, nurses, clerks and policemen. When Harries questioned students he was struck by the dual nature of their experience. First, they felt that training in this way stopped theology becoming remote and ensured that the Church kept close to the reality of the world. Second, and even more emphatic, was the value that they placed on the insights and support of each other. The course embraced both Evangelical and Catholic extremes as well as all shades in between. There was no factionalism. Like all pioneering organizations, Southwark had its imitators in different dioceses. Later, Harries, as an enthusiastic supporter of this kind of ministry, would see the Oxford (now the St Albans and Oxford) Ministry Course forge ahead.

Harries' introduction to the worldwide Anglican Communion was in 1984. Admittedly it was entrance through a side-door as he had no official, synodical or other institutional 'ecclesiastical' credentials. However, the Anglican Consultative Council decided to form the Anglican Peace and Justice Network (APJN) in that year. Its purpose was to gather together those already at work in their own provinces to share concerns and expertise so their work may be more effective, and to stimulate further thought, awareness and action within the Anglican Communion. Behind this bland officialese was a determination to sting individual provinces to awareness of what was happening elsewhere in the world, to rethink their assumptions and act! The blend of thought and action appealed to Harries who was a founding member of APJN, the only member of the network from England.

In 1985, the network was asked to prepare a study document to enable a Communion-wide discussion on peace and justice, which would assist bishops preparing for the 1988 Lambeth Conference. Harries wrote the largest section on *Human Rights and Responsibilities: The Christian Basis of Human Rights*. There were portions on Christians in Palestine; the Poor in Brazil (a country in which Harries was to have a special interest); and the Oppression of Women.

APJN met in Jerusalem in 1986. It was a salutary experience for Harries. Until then the lens of his usually wide and acute vision did not extend to encompass the Anglican Communion. He was not even aware there was an Anglican Church in the Philippines until he met Bishop Robert Longid of the Northern Philippines whose godfather was President Marcos. Marcos had also been an official witness at Bishop Longid's wedding; but the Bishop later spent his life fighting the President. Harries reported on the gathering in the *Church Times*, 5 September 1986:

> We tend to pride ourselves in the Church of England that, though we may not be very heroic or saintly, we are at least 'sound'; our judgements are balanced; we are mature. But in Jerusalem it was, above all, the African bishops who

seemed to bring the charism of wisdom to our group: Jonathan Onyemelukwe, the Bishop of the Niger, and Peter Hatendi, the Bishop of Harare, Zimbabwe. Their sagacity, balance and fairness, their maturity and foresightedness were the very model of episcopal guardianship. The week brought home to us how many terrible conflicts there are in the world today, but also how Anglicans are in the work of reconciliation. Bishop Andrew Kumarage explained to us the background of the wretched killings in Sri Lanka between Tamils and Singhalese. Bishop Charles Albertyn brought us up-to-date on South Africa, as did others for Kenya and Tanzania. Lest those from Britain felt superior, David Bleakley kept the reality of Ireland before us. We understood something of the work going on for Maoris in New Zealand and for the Aborigines in Australia, and of the struggle to prevent Pacific Island peoples suffering from nuclear testing.

Harries was proud to belong to this worldwide Communion. He attended further meetings of APJN in London; Singapore (1987); Harare; Zimbabwe (1989); and Porte Alegre, Brazil (1991). It was in Singapore that he was alerted to the crucial importance of Third World Debt as a burning issue, one which is still alight. Porte Alegre was painful: 20 million people lived in inhumane conditions in Brazil's cities. Harries was at one with Luis Prado, Anglican Bishop of Pelota who wrote: 'The facts of debt are the facts of death. So, as Christians, we believe that the debt crisis is not just an economic issue but a theological and pastoral one. The poor countries' debt is paid with hunger and death. So the debt is a sin because it means a rejection of God and His Kingdom of Life. God's purpose is rejected. Mammon and all its consequences – injustice, violence, despair and death – are affirmed.'

Bishop Luis Prado says Harries had 'a role and significance to our Communion. He is indeed a very special gift to all who have the privilege of sharing his life and work'. Harries and Prado developed a lasting friendship and Prado speaks with deep appreciation of the hospitality he has received over the years from the Harries family. He is impressed too by Harries' skill as a communicator: 'His theological approach is always pastoral and that pastoral or Eucharistic style of life and thinking puts him alongside the best of our Anglican theological traditions. Talking to him, listening to him and reading his writings, we see a man of many tools. The priest, the professor, the bishop, the citizen, the educator, and altogether it is possible to hear his silent voice as a writer . . . He trusts the present time as a promise of God for a beautiful tomorrow . . . As a priest, Richard knows the human soul. He knows how to talk to our emotions, our memories and our hopes. As an educator, he sees our minds and hearts. As a writer, he raises an inspiring wish for growth through prayer.'

APJN constantly monitored the Palestinian/Israeli conflict; human rights violations in Kenya; the division of North/South Korea; and other tensions and conflicts throughout the world. The question arose as to how Church life could be transformed at provincial and local level in such a way that the concerns of justice, peace, reconciliation and creation would be at the centre of their work and witness.

With all this frenetic activity from someone who appeared to others as 'relaxed', were there any brakes or checks on him? In A *Dictionary of Christian Spirituality* Harries has an entry on penitence – 'an indispensable pre-condition for the communion with God for which man is destined. Psychoanalysis has both confused and enriched Christian teaching on penitence. On the one hand Christians have been forced to question sometimes simplistic views of good and right and wrong. On the other hand they have often been led, particularly with the help of a wise counsellor, to a deeper understanding of the springs of behaviour.'

Auricular Confession remains a point of controversy in the Church of England, even by those who uphold the supremacy of the *Book of Common Prayer* in which it is unostentatiously enshrined. The Exhortation ends with a phrase which became so familiar that its purport could be misconceived:

> If there be any of you who by this means (i.e. self-examination, confession to God and where necessary, reconciliation with one's neighbour) cannot quiet his own conscience herein, but requireth further comfort or counsel, let him come to me, or some other discreet and learned Minister of God's Word, and open his grief; that by the ministry of God's holy Word he may receive the benefit of absolution, together with ghostly counsel and advice, to the quieting of his own conscience, and avoiding of all scruples and doubtfulness.

It seems quite plain and undeniable: the action is to be voluntary – it must not be imposed as a condition of Communion; the action is individual – one person comes to one minister; the minister is to give 'ghostly counsel and advice', which implies confidential communication and, if necessary, interrogation; the minister by 'the ministry of God's holy Word' is to impart 'the benefit of absolution'; which phrase, however much *more* it may legitimately be taken to mean, cannot mean less than that, by expounding the promise of Scripture, the minister is to help the person to realize that he or she is forgiven by God and can have the grace to amend, if he or she truly repents. That is sacramental Confession when God forgives and the priest forgets. Harries knows the value of this practice.

There is not the same controversy about spiritual direction. To have a spiritual director is valuable in times of health; and it may be invaluable in times of spiritual trial. For such trial has its own uniqueness, its own antecedent history, its relation to one's general spiritual condition. A wise director, male or female, may be a person of consolation at a difficult time, a veritable agent of the Divine Comforter, but also capable of stripping someone spiritually naked as a raw nerve. One of Harries' closest friends, Rabbi Julia Neuberger, knows that 'Richard is a deeply spiritual man, to many people's surprise. He likes/needs spiritual direction, and has often, informally, been a sort of spiritual director for me. But Jewish spirituality is so different that he feels chary of going too far.' The Oxford years will reveal numerous examples of people who turned to their bishop for moral, spiritual and pastoral guidance. Priests and bishops are not necessarily aware at the time of how God works through them and how their counsel and advice leads to enduring changes in individuals.

Harries is an admirer of the English mystic, Julian of Norwich. Contributing to *Julian, Woman of our Day* by Robert Llewelyn, he underlines her central theme: 'First, everything that happens, even sin, is known and allowed by God; sin is of course not directly willed by God but nothing that happens, happens outside the knowledge and tolerance of God. Secondly, our sin does not prevent God's goodness from working and bringing from it some compensating good. Julian writes, "Were I to do nothing but sin my sin would still not prevent his goodness from working." Thirdly, not only does God work, but the good he brings out of the evil does in the end more than compensate for it: "just as every sin has its compensating penalty because God is true, so the same soul can know every sin to have its corresponding blessing because God is love".'

Harries appreciates 'the wisdom and treasures of God are unplumbable. It is part of what makes him God. He shows us what is appropriate and what we are ready to receive at a particular stage of our development. The knowledge we need is the knowledge to do his will. This is the knowledge that leads to salvation.' Those who are able to reflect on Julian's visions are better able to delve and encounter the mysteries of faith and especially on the love of God.

Chapter Nine
The Conscience of a Multilateralist

We know that Harries is thoroughly Niebuhrian, and this includes his approach to the nuclear issue. Writing to the Archbishop of Canterbury, Rowan Williams, in 2005 Harries reiterated what he perceives as the continuing relevance of Niebuhr to contemporary issues. By this he means:

1. Being aware of and taking seriously the power relationships in human existence, particularly those between groups.
2. Being aware of the human capacity for self-deception, mutual deception and illusion, together with our tendency to justify what we do in moral terms, not only at an individual but at a corporate level.
3. A recognition that in the world as it is, in order to get any kind of proximate justice, attention needs to be paid to where power lies, particularly economic power, and what countervailing forces there might be.
4. The ethic of the Kingdom bears upon the totality of human existence even though under the conditions of finite, sinful existence it can only be enacted in a very partial way.

As far as points one and two are concerned your own writings are thoroughly Niebuhrian even though I know you have reservations about points three and four . . . I would want to argue that even if some of the foundational theology can be criticized, Niebuhr's analysis of the world is distinctively Christian and that no other faith or outlook could achieve the kind of balance that he does. Without the Christian faith, hard-headed realism quickly slips into brutal realism or cynicism. Other faiths, and the Christian faith in some forms, quickly turn into individualism or escapism. And without the Christian faith, all forms of optimism are likely to experience bitter disillusion.

Niebuhr guides Harries' thinking on the nuclear issue and can be found in many of his published contributions to the debate. These include *The Morality of Nuclear Deterrence* (1982); *Conventional Killing or Nuclear Statement?* (1983); *Power, Coercion and Morality* (1983); *The Strange Mercy of Deterrence* (1985); and in many reviews of books on the subject.

What did Harries contend were the key ethical concepts of discrimination and proportion for the deployment of nuclear weapons?

First, proportionality as a principle, if accepted, clearly rules out any policy which rests on wholesale, indiscriminate extermination of the enemy, any policy of massive retaliation or any policy of deliberate frightfulness which aims only at displaying the power and ruthlessness of the attacking party. Taken seriously it would rule out all major thermo-nuclear war, since no conceivable legitimate political aim could justify the mass destruction and appalling after-effects which attend the general and indiscriminate use of nuclear weapons. This is the fundamental objection which lies at the root not only of pacifist protests, but of all Christian and humanitarian protests against nuclear war. The only moral justification (so to call it) for the possession of nuclear weapons at all is as an insurance against their being used first by some other party. The principle of proportionality regained acceptance when the two great nuclear powers – America and Russia – came to realize not only each other's power but the reality of the consequences of nuclear war. It also lay behind the American doctrine of 'controlled response'.

Second, the principle of discrimination has suffered more than any other in the development of modern war, partly because of the increasing involvement of all sections of the nation in the war effort; partly through the increased use of weapons or methods of attack (the mass bombing raid, land and sea mines, etc.) which do not permit of discrimination; and partly through the growth of irregular warfare. Here again policies of massive retaliation or deliberate terror have been ruled out. Further, some attempt has to be made to re-establish the distinction between combatants, regular and irregular, and non-combatants and the human rights of the populations of occupied countries, interned civilians and prisoners of war. Again, if this principle is accepted, clearly mass attacks on cities, as conducted by both sides in the Second World War, must be considered impermissible, even on the excuse that drastic and spectacular action of this kind in the end shortens the war.

A third principle, that of reprisals, is more ambiguous. It cannot be denied that the threat of equal or even greater destruction has been an element in preventing the outbreak of war. To this extent the preventive possession of nuclear arms can be given some appearance of moral justification, though a precarious one. The real moral dilemma lies in the intention to use them. On the one hand, to intend action which one knows would be wrong if one were to take it, is in itself immoral; on the other hand, to threaten drastic action with the assurance that, if pushed to the extreme, one will not take it, is futile. In the crude circumstances of international power politics, these may appear philosophers' riddles, unlikely to affect the actions of governments. They represent, nevertheless, a real moral problem, felt by individuals, if not by governments. To be manifestly capable of drastic action without using the threat of it as an instrument of national advancement, and maintaining an ambiguous silence about its possible use, seems to be the most any major power can manage to achieve by way of a moral posture.

King's was the context in which Harries became prominently absorbed in the issue of nuclear weapons. Groups sprouted as if from nowhere and many unlikely liaisons were formed of those who pursued a line of multilateral as opposed to unilateral disarmament. Harries was very prominent in groups, either as a member or, more likely, as chair. It was not in his nature to be passive in any organization he joined. Neither was he satisfied with the passing of resolutions, not even as a prelude to responding to crucial issues of the time. His interest was in the centres of decision-making, both politically and militarily and ultimately in the nature and structures of power. He was beguiled by those who moved in the passages of persuasion and in the corridors of power.

From the outset Harries studied and pondered on the nature of the advice proffered to government ministers. In the 1960s and 1970s there was a tendency for the advice, particularly on the part of the military specialists, to be given from too narrow a standpoint. That is to say, the advice given was the best technical advice the professional expert was able to give; but, while he may well have felt personally concerned at the implications of his conclusions, he regarded it as being no part of his function or brief to refer officially to the moral considerations. But a laudable hesitation in venturing moral judgements may end in their being omitted altogether. This was the root of the trouble. It was important that all advisers in making recommendations should consider and draw attention to any moral aspects which may deserve consideration. The ideal was that all those concerned with the formulation of policy should regard it as a proper part of their duty, not merely as soldiers or as administrators, but as human beings, to take into account the moral dimension and its implications. This did not mean that every adviser had to offer a personal, moral judgement on the points at issue. It did mean that they would have to be ready – and able – to perceive where moral implications were inherent in the policy recommendations, and to indicate their nature and offer some assessment of their significance. This was Harries terrain!

Harries may have abandoned his earlier intention to pursue a PhD on the Just War tradition but the subject had been constantly on his mind at Fulham where two articles were published in *Theology*: in 1972 *'The Tygers of Wrath are Wiser than the Horses of Instruction' An Alternative to Christian Pacifism* and in 1975 *The Criterion of Success for a Just Revolution*. In the first article Harries had already concluded that:

> Absolute pacifism can have the effect of obliterating the distinction between a limited and proportional use of force and indiscriminately destructive violence. It tends, also, to blur the differences in the causes for which armed force may be used. For if the use of force is the supreme evil, even the attempts to assassinate Hitler, and Hitler's destruction of millions of Jews, come into the same category. Similarly the bombing of an arms factory and the obliteration of Hiroshima or Dresden are not distinguished very clearly. This point is made by Professor Anscombe: 'Pacifism teaches people to make no distinction between the shedding of innocent blood and the shedding of any human blood. And in this way pacifism has corrupted enormous numbers of people who will not act according to its tenets. They become convinced that a number of things are wicked which are not; hence, seeing no way of avoiding "wickedness", they set no limits to it.'

We live in a world where groups within nations, and nations themselves,

have different, often conflicting, interests. This is an inescapable concomi-
tant of finite existence. It is not in itself the result of sin, nor is it an unmiti-
gated evil. Some of the conflict so engendered can have its poison drawn
through a process of ritualization, or institutionalization; that is, the conflict
can be expressed within the stylized forum of a law-court or the United
Nations Assembly. However, at the moment, a great deal of conflict cannot
be so tamed, and in order that some kind of *pax-ordo-justitia* may be maintained, overweening national pride, aggressive imperialism and brutal repression need to be brought up short by seeing teeth bared, and a glint of menace
in the faces of the threatened. This is not a happy situation, and upon it falls
the absolute demand of love on whose light we see it to be so far fallen. The
same claim of love beckons us on to negotiate, legislate and weigh actions
carefully, so that it may correspond more nearly, even marginally, to the
divine purpose. So long, however, as finite existence lasts, we cannot presume
to do more than approximate to what is required, and situations will continue
to occur when 'The tygers of wrath are wiser than the horses of instruction'
(William Blake). Our hope must be that, in all conflict situations but particularly those involving nuclear powers, men will sense the wrath arising from
afar and examine their actions from the standpoint of the threatened group;
that they will act carefully, negotiate, compromise and continue to believe
that partial agreement is better than no agreement at all.

Historically, the most marked disagreement had been between Christian pacifists
and those who would not consider war as the greatest of all evils in all circumstances. There was a shift and modified positions due to the manufacture of nuclear
weapons. So far as the Church of England – and the Anglican Communion – was
concerned, the convictions of the pacifist appeared to be reaffirmed by Lambeth
Conference statements in 1930 and 1948: 'war as a method of settling international
disputes is incompatible with the teaching and example of our Lord Jesus Christ'.
This statement may be unexceptionable in itself. But it starts off the nuclear debate
on the wrong lines, because it starts people thinking in terms of the traditional
debate between pacifists and non-pacifists. And since most Christians are not traditional pacifists, they are thereby conditioned against nuclear pacifism before the
discussion has properly begun.

From the 1960s onwards there were signs, not yet clearly delineated, of other
ways forward. Could an approach be found to the whole subject which would be
recognized as a way towards the objectives which Christians shared, however much
they may differ as pacifists, unilateralists, multilateralists, passive resisters, reluctant
participators or in other ways? The Lambeth Conferences of 1958 and 1968
repeated the 1930 statement, although in 1958 it also called for governments 'to
work for the control and abolition of all weapons of indiscriminate destructive
power, atomic, biological, and chemical, as a condition of human survival' and
'Nothing less than the abolition of war itself should be the goal of the nations, their
leaders, and all citizens'. In 1968, at the precise moment that the bishops were

framing their statements on war and peace, Russian troops marched on Czechoslovakia. A few bishops opposed the resolution, some wanting it sharpening and strengthening, others cautioning against running into the danger of an absolute ethic in one area of life, war and peace, and not in others! But the desire for comprehensive unanimity cloaked the resolution in a certain anonymity.

Already Harries was mixing with activists from all sides of the nuclear argument who explained and clarified their positions and sought ways to influence the influencers, and even the Government itself. He was already a reliable reviewer of books on the subject, with genuine appreciation of their contents combined with an intelligent and critical appraisal. Reviewing *The Ethics of War* by Barrie Paskins and Michael Dockrill (1980), Harries examines Paskins' 'pacifism of scruple':

> Paskins balances the case for pacifism by a strong argument in favour of fighting, even when the cause looks hopeless. The argument has three main strands. (a) As human beings we have a sense of gratitude to our own people and if they were fighting for survival this would lead us to want to share their situation with them. (b) Death itself is not the worst that can happen. Death is part of life and all life is tragic. The worst that can happen is a meaningless death. Those who choose to fight for their people risk death but it is a meaningful death. (c) There is something appalling about people submitting meekly to extermination. When people rise up and fight, we recognize in their action a last flicker of humanity. This is an unusual argument of great interest, which certainly balances a pacifism of scruple. In the end, Paskins thinks, we are all faced with an existential, that is, a criterionless choice, between these two options.

With such a scattering of seeds there was no more fertile academic orchard in England where they could grow and multiply to greater maturation than King's College, London. Why there and how? It is the setting for one man's advent.

King's has a department of war studies. There was a professorship of war studies, held with distinction by Sir Michael Howard from 1963 to 1968, who was subsequently Chichele professor of the history of war at Oxford, later Regius professor of modern history. He was succeeded by Sir Laurence Martin. The staff included Brian Bond and Wolf Mendl, both readers; and Michael Dockrill and Barrie Paskins, both lecturers. Mendl was head of the department and a Quaker. Paskins, by training a philosopher, was a member of the working party which led to *The Church and the Bomb* report. The others were historians. When Laurence Martin left to be vice-chancellor of the University of Newcastle-upon-Tyne in 1977 the post was left vacant. Sir Lawrence Freedman takes up the story:

> When Neil Cameron became principal it was clear that the department of war studies, which to the extent it was contributing to the national nuclear debate, was doing so from a pacifist viewpoint. Now I think that was unfair to both Paskins and Mendl who were both deeply serious and far from

sentimental in their assessments of international affairs. Nonetheless I know this influenced Neil's judgement. I think this was why he was keen to see the Chair in war studies filled – it had been vacant since 1978. I was very lucky in the timing. The nuclear debate was raging and I had written extensively on the topic – a book on *Britain and Nuclear Weapons* (1980), regular appearances in the press, and my big book *The Evolution of Nuclear Strategy* (1981) appeared just before the job interview. I'd been at Chatham House, with time to write and no teaching. So I had an unfair advantage over the others. About a year or so before the job was advertised, when he'd just been appointed to King's, Neil came to see me at Chatham House and told me that he intended to have the Chair filled and that he wanted me to apply. Because of the bad state of universities at the time, with funding being cut, there was a general view that King's couldn't afford a new professor and so his plans would have to be abandoned. But Neil was popular, his right-hand man, the bursar, Myles Tempany, could make anything happen and this was something that mattered to him. So the Chair was advertised in the summer and I was appointed that November, aged 33. In April 1982 I started.

So did the Falklands War. This led me to my first contacts with Richard because we organized a debate. Soon the nuclear issue took over again. I was personally uncomfortable with this. First, the Falklands had made me realize how little I understood about conventional war. Second, I wanted King's to be an academic rather than a campaigning department, yet the nuclear issue was polarizing. Because I didn't agree with CND (the Campaign for Nuclear Disarmament) or END (European Nuclear Disarmament) – I got put on the other side of the debate as if I agreed with all government policies (which I didn't) and had no worries about nuclear weapons (which I did). Part of my problem was that CND et al. made claims about policy which I knew to be incorrect, but in seeking to explain the origins of, for example, NATO's cruise missiles, I was bound to be contradicting alternative explanations forwarded by CND. This included notions about American motives and the automaticity of escalation once any fighting began.

This became apparent to me not long after I arrived when I was an 'expert witness' in a TV debate between Bruce Kent and Keith Ward, then a profes-sor in the theology department at KCL, and another 'muscular' Christian' on these matters (it was a joke at KCL that war studies contained the doves while theology had the hawks). Paul Rodgers from Bradford 'peace studies' was on the other side. One newspaper report wrote something along the lines of a 'Professor of War Studies versus a Professor of Peace Studies. Symbolic. Frightening. Fascinating'. I suspect that Richard, like me, found this context difficult. One was trying to sort out positions on difficult issues, yet was read-ily pigeon-holed as pro-CND or pro-government.

Perhaps the other point to note about me is that I am Jewish. The fact that so much of the debate at King's and elsewhere involved Christians, including the clergy, I found intriguing rather than bothersome, especially when I was asked to join in. Richard was well aware of this, as he had a fondness for Jewish jokes. There were a number of bodies around that tried to find a 'middle way', normally around the idea of arms control, and he and I would often be there together.

After the mid–1980s and Reagan/Gorbachev summits the nuclear debate died down and it was possible to move on to other issues. Arms control now was much more flavour of the month and so those organizations that claimed to be promoting it got more time than the quality of the work might have deserved. Incidentally my work as adviser to the House of Commons Select Committee on Defence, which I really enjoyed, was about the second and third issues of policy, and teasing out what the Ministry of Defence was really up to, rather than the big first order issues with which Richard was most engaged, although of course you can't in the end address one set of issues without the other. The FCO's (Foreign and Commonwealth Office) advisory committee met irregularly and was very much a talking shop. I don't think it ever came close to exercising real influence. To the extent I had any, which was and is impossible to measure, is that, at least at the start of the 1980s, there were very few academic specialists on these issues around, and in London, and so I was part of a rather small group of people, including officials, who would meet and talk about policy questions.

The components in the cauldron came to boiling point as the result of an initiative by the Church of England. Its Board for Social Responsibility produced a report, *Christians in a Violent World*, on the general subject of war and disarmament. In response to a resolution of the General Synod in July 1979, a working party of the Board was set up primarily to study the implications for Christian discipleship of the acceptance by the major military powers of a role for thermo-nuclear weapons in their strategy; and secondly, to consider the bearing of this on the adequacy of past Christian teaching and ethical analysis regarding the conduct of war. Its members were: John Austin Baker, Bishop of Salisbury (chairman); Sydney D. Bailey, chairman of the Council on Christian Approaches to Defence and Disarmament and a former chairman of the Division of International Affairs of the British Council of Churches; the Revd Dr John Elford, lecturer in social and pastoral theology in the University of Manchester; the Revd Paul Oestreicher, Canon of Southwark, member of the General Synod and secretary of the Division of International Affairs of the British Council of Churches; Dr Barrie Paskins, lecturer in war studies at King's College, London; and the Revd Dr Brendan Soane, lecturer in moral theology, Allen Hall, Roman Catholic archdiocese of Westminster.

The working party deliberated from 1980 to 1982 and the result was the much leaked and controversial report *The Church and the Bomb: Nuclear Weapons and Christian Conscience* (1982). It would lead to a ferocious national debate. In essence the report's controversial conclusions and recommendations sought to persuade the Church that it had a duty to withdraw from the establishment consensus which had hitherto backed Britain's nuclear weapons policy. It proceeded from an analysis of the morality of nuclear war to an analysis of the morality of nuclear deterrence, and appeared to lean heavily towards an anti-deterrence conclusion. 'We regard it as proven beyond reasonable doubt that the Just War theory rules out the use of nuclear weapons (damage to non-combatants and neutrals, environmental and genetic damage, combine to make nuclear weapons indiscriminate and nuclear war almost inevitably disproportionate). The evils caused by nuclear war are greater than any conceivable evil which the war intended to prevent.' Thus nuclear weapons can never be used except immorally. As for deterrence, 'for its supporters, (it) is the safest way of ensuring that nuclear weapons will never be used. Those in government who support this policy are not maniacs who do not care whether they incinerate the world. And it seems a matter of commonsense that a potential aggressor will hold back if the cost of attack is likely to be too heavy. We feel the force of these arguments and recognize the formative effect on British policy now of our weakness towards Hitler 50 years ago. The validity of deterrence depends on nuclear weapons being as horrible as their opponents claim . . . If the deterrent is to work, you have to convince an enemy that you are willing to use it; but if you have to use it, it has failed . . . We believe that the nuclear element in deterrence is no longer a reliable or morally acceptable approach to the future of the world, and that it is not sufficiently compelling to outweigh the huge moral imperatives against using nuclear weapons at all . . . There are no risk-free options on nuclear weapons. You may either decide for a nuclear component in deterrence, and risk nuclear war, or decide against it and risk the political and human consequences of blackmail and defeat by someone with fewer moral inhibitions. We conclude that a Christian must take the second of these risks.'

Harries was quick to respond by a letter to *The Times* (21 October) and in an assessment in the *Church Times* (22 October). In his letter he drew attention to two, amongst many, defects in the report:

First there is no discussion of the role of power in human affairs and no theology of power. In the world in which we actually live the establishment of some kind of rough and ready justice is bound up with the achievement of right power relationships between groups, nations and alliances.

This insensitivity to the power factor affects the judgements of the report at certain crucial points. For example, the authors claim that Soviet intentions are relatively benign. Yet most major powers have an incipient expansionist tendency rooted in a defensive/aggressive mentality and the crucial question is how, in such a world, a war is to be averted. For some Christians morality in the international order must primarily be about the management of power to achieve peace, order and justice. The instinctive bias of this report seems to be towards the renunciation of power rather than its control. Secondly, the presupposition of the report is that a world in which nuclear weapons were dismantled – they cannot of course be disinvented – would be safer than our present one. This is highly questionable. Martin Luther stated that he would rather have as ruler a bad man who was prudent than a good man who was imprudent. No words can do justice to the horrifying nature of nuclear weapons but they force rulers to be prudent as never before.

The big televised debate at General Synod on 10 February 1983 matched its advance billing. The three major participants were the Bishops of London (Graham Leonard), Salisbury (John Baker) and Birmingham (Hugh Montefiore) but major and influential speeches came from the Archbishops of Canterbury (Robert Runcie) and York (Stuart Blanch). Graham Leonard was also chairman of the Board for Social Responsibility and when the Board had discussed the report it decided to distance itself from the most controversial conclusion, that Britain must renounce the possession of nuclear weapons. In moving his motion Leonard pleaded for realism as it would be lacking in Christian responsibility to urge courses of action upon people which they knew, in effect, were not practical possibilities for them. John Baker who, incidentally, was making his maiden speech as Bishop of Salisbury – he had been rector of St Margaret's, Westminster and chaplain to the Speaker of the House of Commons when chairing the working party – moved his amendment which reflected the unilateralist approach: 'phased disengagement of the United Kingdom from active association with any form of nuclear weaponry'. It was substantially defeated by 338 to 100. Hugh Montefiore's amendment upheld that there was a moral obligation on all countries, including NATO members, publicly to forswear the first use of nuclear weapons in any form, even on a small scale, because of the high risk of all-out nuclear war as a result. This was carried by 275 to 222 and the whole motion incorporating it was carried by 387 to 49. Even the Prime Minister, Margaret Thatcher, thought it was 'a marvellous debate – the quality should be a lesson to anyone'. Harries was uneasy that the General Synod 'sought to talk morality not high-minded strategy'.

John Baker has a reflection on the nuclear controversy 24 years after the publication of The Church and the Bomb: 'It was a great solace to the Establishment. Graham Leonard was determined to redeem the Church of England from the stigma of infantile and sentimental unworldliness. But, as it turned out, after the collapse of Communism, it was The Church and the Bomb which had read the signs of the times aright, i.e. about what was going on in the minds of the Kremlin. The basic ethical dilemma had, of course, never been settled: does having nuclear weapons mean you have to use them? The conclusions of The Church and the Bomb read more like a NATO position paper than a serious attempt to wrestle with the Gospel in the modern world.'

During his King's years, Harries was constantly and continuously working in groups to educate the public and seek to influence government policies. He was also adamant that theological reflection was needed: 'The Church of England desperately needs a coherent and consistent theological perspective from which to approach these vital matters . . . we oscillate between the natural law tradition and a religiously tinged situationalism. It is often said that one of the great defects of the Church in this country is the lack of any systematic theology. An even greater defect is the lack of any systematic ethics.'

What did Harries do in pursuing a line of multilateral as opposed to unilateral disarmament? His position at King's gave him opportunities of meeting people from all sides of the debate, both those who had a working knowledge of the subject as well as academics. He was also closely involved, often responsible for, the burgeoning organizations.

The Council for Arms Control was launched in 1981. Harries was a vice-chairman and regarded it as the most important organization to which he belonged. Members included Lord Gilbert of Dudley (ex-Labour minister in the Ministry of Defence – MoD); Sir Ronald Mason (ex-chief scientific adviser – MoD); John Edmonds, who led the UK Delegation to Comprehensive Test Ban Treaty Negotiations in Geneva; the legendary Leonard Cheshire; General Sir Hugh Beach, member of the Security Commission, warden of St George's House, Windsor and director of the council from 1986 to 1989. The Bishops of Durham and Birmingham, John Habgood and Hugh Montefiore, were also members.

The council's intention was to lay before the public what it saw as the central territory that existed between unilateral disarmament and increased military spending. It examined and publicized the progress of negotiations towards the whole range of arms control and disarmament agreements, giving wider coverage to the outcomes of such talks than was given by the media. It planned to penetrate the propaganda battle by reaching young people in particular with a bi-monthly free bulletin distributed to schools, colleges, churches and youth clubs. Harries' persistent endeavour was to reconcile differences of opinion rather than exaggerate them. 'Its appeal to me was that it was not simply a right-wing organization, it was mainly made up of people who were centre-Left in politics but who took a fairly hard-headed view of international relations.' The council ran out of money and closed in 1991.

Shalom, chaired by Harries, was formed in 1983. This specifically Christian group brought together 19 people who believed that the Church's debate about nuclear weapons had been too shallow. Shalom, under its director Alan Booth, produced material for schools and study groups, with a range of pamphlets with such titles as 'Living with the Bomb' and 'Christian Education in an Armed World'. The thrust of their argument was Niebuhrian, in Harries' words, 'that relationships between powerful groups were more complex than CND suggested and that faithful Christian discipleship did not mean they automatically had to become unilateralist'.

The Pembroke Group, in which Harries was conspicuous, was formed on the initiative of Michael Quinlan, a senior civil servant at the MoD, and Malcolm McCall, a not very senior chaplain. It was an entirely informal outfit – not an 'organization' – set up with no sort of official clearance from the Ministry of Defence. Senior civil servants, theologians and chaplains of the armed services were roped in, unsystematically; all folk concerned with the ethics of the issues but not holders of the absolutist anti-nuclear view. There were quite significantly diverse opinions with the group; for example Hugh Beach and, less vocally, Arthur Hockaday, a senior civil servant at the MoD, who were very sceptical of the case for UK possession of nuclear weapons. Pembroke sought to explore and test ethical reasoning on a range of awkward questions in a gathering of people whose starting-points were broadly similar enough to avoid the risk of simply descending into argumentative confrontation. Eventually the group produced *Morality and Deterrence into the Twenty-First Century* (1990) to which Harries wrote an introduction.

The most long-lasting organization, and still extant, is the Council for Christian Approaches to Defence and Disarmament (CCADD) with Harries as president. Once again senior civil servants such as Michael Quinlan, Arthur Hockaday and David Fisher were members. How was their membership regarded by the Government? Harries contends that Michael Quinlan was 'the guru for our thinking behind all the groups – a Roman Catholic, with a razor sharp mind who was the architect of British nuclear policy and who refined all our thinking about the morality of deterrence'. How far was their work government inspired, to counter CND propaganda?

Michael Quinlan provides perspective:

The Government did indeed, under Michael Heseltine (who became Secretary of State for Defence at the end of 1982), set up some systematic arrangements for countering the anti-nuclear movements; I believe these mainly took the form of establishing a small division of civil servants, under an assistant secretary, to work on the matter. (I myself had ceased to work in the Ministry of Defence as Deputy Under-Secretary of State (Policy) in July 1982, and did not return to the defence field until becoming Permanent Under-Secretary of State in April 1988, though by my own choice I maintained a degree of personal interest in the issues meanwhile.) But it is absolutely not the case that the activities of people like Arthur Hockaday, David Fisher and me, in any of the groups or elsewhere, were in any way ordered or prompted by 'the Government', whether in ministerial or any other guise. Our motivation came from within ourselves, with a certain amount of stimulus from the concerns of the Churches and from the challenges – sometimes spiced with insinuations that we could not be in entirely good faith – levelled at us by folk like Bruce Kent. The ethical problems surrounding nuclear weapons were evident to us, and a series of practical policy issues highlighted them from the late 1970s onwards after a period of nearly 15 years in which the UK had not had to face big nuclear decisions. We recognized that Christian morality was not something to be left outside, like hanging up an outdoor coat, when we came into the office, and we faced up to the problems accordingly as a matter of personal imperative.

The 'authorities' were in fact distinctly wary of at least my own public involvement in the ethical debate, especially as major aspects of UK nuclear policy became in the 1980s – as they had not been in the 1970s – matters of contention between the Government and Opposition front benches. I recall for instance that in 1982 somewhat heavy weather was made of letting me reply to a rather personalized attack in *The Tablet* by Fr Roger Ruston OP; soon afterwards I was discouraged from publishing other pieces I had written;

and Michael Heseltine personally vetoed the prompt publication (which Margaret Thatcher had herself favoured) of *The Ethics of Nuclear Deterrence: A Critical Comment on the Pastoral Letter of the U.S. Catholic Bishops.* I managed to get it in *Theological Studies* only later in 1987, when Heseltine's successor was rather relishing reversing some of his predecessor's rulings.

Nuclear Weapons and Preventing War was a short 'anonymous' essay by Quinlan, which appeared initially in the '1981 Statement on the Defence Estimates'. It became widely known that he had written it. A talk he gave in 1982 in the Head-master's Lecture series at Ampleforth College was published in *The Ampleforth Jour-nal* in 1982; and *The Ethics of Nuclear Weapons* is a more recent contribution to a monograph *Thinking About Nuclear Weapons* (1997) by the Royal United Services Institute for Defence Studies. Michael Quinlan's is not an isolated civil servant voice in print. Arthur Hockaday and David Fisher have many books to their nuclear credit.

Harries benefited from knowing many former senior military people who had served in and survived the conflict of war. They knew the meaning of war, its terrible cruelty, its frightful wastefulness, its almost conceivable horror. They had returned from countries where formerly prosperous cities had been transformed into smouldering cinder-heaps. Harries was not cheated by the pageantry and rhetoric of war. It forced him to consider weapons of mass destruction and the threat of all-out war. The authors of *The Church and the Bomb* had argued on the basis of the Just War criterion, that a policy of deterrence based upon the possession of nuclear arms is totally immoral. For Harries that moral argument did not stand up to analysis. When he had gathered his thinking into an overall consideration of the Christian approach to war, he wrote his book on *Christianity and War in a Nuclear Age* (1986):

> How far will we be able to go down the road towards general and complete disarmament? In one sense we must go right to the end of the road, for the King-dom of God is characterized by general and complete disarmament. Nothing less than that must satisfy us. But we can neither say that the vision of that society will be realized on this earth, nor deny that it will be. It remains as the absolute standard, hovering over every moment, and will do so to the end of time. It beckons to us to realize it within time, but we will never be in a position to pre-dict when and how it will be realized, any more than Jesus himself was in that position. This vision of a society lived in total trust on God and with complete openness to one another is not a Utopia. Utopias are either fantasies that have no basis in reality or else dreams that people think can be made realities if all the ordinary features of life are ignored. The Kingdom of God differs from Utopias both in being grounded in reality, indeed in being the ultimate reality, and also by living in tension with, rather than ignoring, political realities . . .
>
> The nuclear threat hangs over us as a warning of the cost of going to war. In this is a divine judgement forcing states to be prudent and cautious; to find ways, other than war, of resolving their disputes. So there is a strange mercy in nuclear deterrence, but it lives in tension with the hope of the Kingdom of

God, that perfect society in which neither war nor deterrence will be any more. That society has its origins and destiny beyond space and time but it has to be built up, worked for and worked towards within time and space.

There was one final task which overlapped King's and Oxford. In 1986 Harries was asked to chair a working party of the General Synod's Board for Social Responsibility on 'Peacemaking in a Nuclear Age', the title of the report published in 1988. Its concern was with the political rather than the military, with theology rather than ethics. Some of the usual names were recruited – Hugh Beach, Keith Ward, Michael Howard. New recruits to the established sanctum were Joanna James of the Centre for Defence and Security Analysis, University of Lancaster; Mary Kaldor, senior fellow, Science Policy Research Unit, University of Sussex; Alan Brooke Turner, formerly British Ambassador to Finland and minister at the British Embassy in Moscow; and Rowan Williams, then professor of divinity, University of Oxford. John Gladwin was secretary. Thus a medley of expertise – historical, diplomatic, strategic, military, economic, theological, ethical – was brought together. Harries loves working in this kind of diverse milieu where agreement is not a foregone conclusion. It was not anticipated that the report would be unanimous. By now Harries' customary and unusual skill in the chair enabled people to accept and agree with the thrust and urgency of the arguments, whilst accepting differing judgements on specific areas. In this way he achieved nuanced unanimity.

This major report examined the Christian traditions of peace, hope and patriotism in the setting of the search for peace in the world. It found deep connections between these Christian themes and the present situation. It looked at the history of East–West relations especially over the previous 40 years and at the prospects for the future. It examined the need for detente and the hope of reconciliation and considered the need to approach and manage conflict in the world. It also considered the meaning of deterrence for arms control and reduction, and concluded with a challenge to the Churches about their continuing role in peacemaking in a nuclear age.

On 9 March 1988 Harries gave a lecture at St Anthony's College, Oxford, on *Shalom and Pax: Christian Concepts of Peace* which provided the basis for the first chapter in 'Peacemaking in a Nuclear Age'. It is important in understanding the foundation of Harries' thinking on this subject so a few extracts follow, without the lengthy scriptural references:

SHALOM: the peace in which everything flourishes. This is a peace which envelops the whole of human life. It is not just the peace of solitary individuals but the peace of the whole community. It is not only an inward state but an outward condition. It embraces life in its totality, inward and outward; personal, social, political, economic and environmental. The root meaning of the word Shalom is 'whole' and it indicates well-being in its fullness, spiritual harmony and physical health; material prosperity untouched by violence or misfortune. Two particular aspects of Shalom can be noted. First, Shalom includes all that we mean by justice. In this life peace and justice often seem to be in tension. Sometimes we are offered the choice of striving for one or the other and it is not possible to have both at once. Again, in this life, different understandings of justice are often in conflict. But where there is Shalom, all that is indicated by true justice is present. So it can be said that where God's justice is present, Shalom will also be present.

Secondly, the realization of Shalom in its fullness belongs to the realm of hope. Throughout the Hebrew scriptures there is a yearning for the time of Shalom, expressed in unforgettable images. In these scriptures peace is sometimes envisaged as the abolition of war and the rule over the nations by Israel's messianic king and sometimes as a paradisal existence in which all forms of strife will have been removed. But both sets of images assume that Shalom in its fullness belongs to the eschaton, the final age, when God's just rule will transform and suffuse all things. Shalom is a longed-for peace. Can we hope for its appearance on earth? Or is it a peace that lies beyond the spatio-temporal order? Is it a peace that can be achieved in history or does its realization lie beyond history? What we can affirm is that Shalom is that state of affairs when God will be all in all, towards which the created order is being led; a vision which one day (within time or beyond time or both beyond and within) will be a reality.

PAX: when war is absent but coercion may be implicit or latent. Shalom is such a heady notion it is easy for theologians to overlook the vital need for Pax. Any country that has known war on its own soil, or which has been beset by civil strife, knows the great blessing of a simple cessation of hostilities . . . It is difficult to find an adequate one-line definition of Pax because a state of affairs where war is absent can also be one where coercion, in one form or another, is present. This coercion may be basic to keeping war at bay, as in a system of mutual deterrence, or its impact may be minimal. There is no war going on between the USA and the USSR but coercion, in the form of mutual deterrence, is fundamental to their present relationship, and, many would argue, to the absence of war. Societies are held together by a mixture of coercion and consent. Neither, by itself, provides a strong enough adhesive. If income tax were purely voluntary who would pay it? The minimal essential conditions for any kind of properly human life depend in part on the ability of the Government to enforce its policies, whether or not everyone entirely agrees with them. This means in specific terms, the presence of a police force, courts of law and the army . . .

Coercion, overt or implicit, is a permanent feature of sinful human existence. Individuals, groups and nations have an ineluctable tendency to pursue their own interests without taking the interests of others into account. Worse still, they can deliberately negate the interests of others . . .

INNER PEACE. The longing for an inner peace or serenity, what Wordsworth called a 'Central peace, subsisting at the heart of endless agitation' is widespread. It has also been disparaged as a luxury of the bourgeois class, the expression of an inner discontent that can be afforded only by those with an outer content in more than their fair share of this world's goods. From a Christian perspective this is only a portion of the truth. For the Christian, faith offers an inner peace which is not to be accounted for wholly in sociological or psychological terms. This inner peace can be grasped even in the midst of turmoil and conflict. For it is a peace that nothing can destroy. But it is not an alternative to Shalom or an attempt to escape the obligation to bring Shalom to bear on the whole of human existence . . . Inner peace is a foretaste of what one day will include the whole of social, economic and political existence; and inner peace carries with it an obligation to work for the whole of which it is part.

The General Synod debated 'Peacemaking in a Nuclear Age' on 9 November 1988 and resolved:

a) that this Synod, welcoming the more hopeful relationship between East and West, urges Her Majesty's Government to take the initiatives necessary to achieve major reductions in nuclear and conventional armaments; including: i) working for agreement between the nuclear nations on a Comprehensive Test Ban Treaty; and ii) using what influence it may have to encourage both superpowers to disengage from programmes leading to Strategic Defence Initiatives and the general militarization of space;

b) that this Synod calls on Her Majesty's Government to make moral rather than commercial criteria the primary factors in determining policy for the sale and transfer of arms especially to areas of Third World conflict, and to renew efforts to secure a worldwide ban on weapons of chemical warfare, including international agreement on effective measures against those countries which use them . . .

What is the sum of Harries' exhausting, but not exhaustive, commitment to the nuclear issue? How did his convictions arise, develop and influence people? Few people thought more, dissected arguments more and worked harder. To what end? Is there a legacy? During the Cold War he supported 'with some moral fear and spiritual trembling', a policy of nuclear deterrence by the NATO powers. He did this for three reasons. First, while he hesitated to say that Soviet Communism at the time was a unique evil, it was certainly a serious one. It was not simply just another tyranny or regime in which there were severe human rights abuses; it was not that it was expansionist or even that it was atheistic: Soviet Communism, he thought, was like Nazi Germany; no longer the state described in Romans 13 which was to be obeyed, but the state of Revelation 13 which had usurped the function of God and become demonic. It therefore had no more claim on us. It was a very serious evil that, in other terms, one might describe as based on the great lie. All tyrants and despots use lies from time to time but lying was fundamental to Soviet Communism because it was based on a false understanding of the nature of human beings and human society, in which the state played the part of God.

Second, Harries supported a policy of nuclear deterrence because he believed that it was essentially stable. There was always the possibility of accident or miscalculation, but the Soviet authorities were rational. They calculated what was in their interest and for the first time in human history it could not conceivably have been in the interest of either the Soviet Union or NATO to engage in all-out war. Despite a great deal of scaremongering in some quarters the system was fundamentally stable. There was a nuclear stalemate.

Third, Harries did not think that every possible use of nuclear weapons was essentially indiscriminate and disproportionate. Although there was always the possibility of escalation from a low level exchange to one which was disproportionate and indiscriminate, the fear of escalation was one of the factors making for a stable deterrent system and that possibility and fear could not be regarded as intrinsically immoral.

When the Cold War ended, Harries turned to other issues by choice and necessity alike. He was by this time Bishop of Oxford! Later we will see his return to the subject of Just Wars in the House of Lords and elsewhere. The world is different now, as is the nature of the threat Britain faces. There is no regime or threat comparable to Soviet Communism. This does not mean to say that nuclear weapons in some places are not a stabilizing factor. They are. It may also be that the possession of massive nuclear capability by the United States is a sobering fact which some countries, such as North Korea and Iran, must certainly take into account.

But from a strategic point of view there is for the foreseeable future no serious threat to the United Kingdom from a nuclear weapons state, or a state that might conceivably obtain nuclear weapons. Harries' more recent studies conclude that the main threat the world faces is from terrorists, and nuclear weapons are not an appropriate or possible weapon to use against terrorist groups, who as likely as not will be embedded in civilian populations. There is a, just conceivable, theoretical threat in the future, were the United Kingdom to be decoupled for defensive purposes from the United States and face a nuclear nation whose regime operates on the basis of rational calculation, and wishes to threaten our fundamental interests. Or there may be a threat by being coupled with the all-powerful United States! The Government of the United Kingdom is right to think about such possibilities. It is charged with the responsibility for protecting its citizens and it needs to take every possible circumstance into account. Yet there are some risks which perhaps ought to be taken, even by governments. At this point Harries looks for a New Testament perspective.

Christians in the New Testament were conscious of living between the times, between the time of Christ's Resurrection and his coming again in glory. During this interim period, in which we still live, it is necessary for human institutions, such as the state and government, to continue, because there can be no viable or meaningful human life without some degree of order, both nationally and internationally, and in a fallen world this depends on a degree of coercion. So long as God wills human life to continue, he wills those human institutions to continue. Yet they will come to an end, as will all human coercion. Christians have resolved the tension between what is necessary to survive now and that ultimate state of affairs brought into existence by Jesus in various ways. Harries believes that it is a mistake to dissolve the tension, either by assuming that the Kingdom of God can be acted out in its fullness here and now, without any kind of qualification of compromise, which leads to principled pacifism, or to the idea that the ethic of the Kingdom has no bearing upon present power realities. They have to be taken into account. We need government and we need sometimes to use force in the international sphere. But the ethic of the Kingdom bears upon these realities, and we should look for and work for signs and anticipations of what will one day be here in its totality and perfection. This has a bearing on how we weigh different kinds of risk.

There is another factor derived from the New Testament which is important in Harries' thought, namely that we are to 'fear not'. Human life will never be risk-free and we cannot anticipate and guard against every possible kind of risk. The attempt to do so, to make ourselves or our nation absolutely secure and invulnerable, is hubristic folly. So there are occasions when a Christian, without being irresponsible, will want to act on the basis of trust and goodwill, even in a world where there is still malicious mistrust and ill will. Governments themselves can give a moral lead, as the United Kingdom has sought to do over issues such as debt relief for the poorest countries in the world, overseas aid and trade justice. No doubt politicians who are committed to such causes will argue that they are in Britain's best long-term interests and so they might be. Nevertheless, the moral passion behind such causes is one that goes beyond prudential calculations about what is in the national interest.

In a world of notorious uncertainty, with the possibility of an as yet unknown threat arising, Harries proposes that a prudent government will argue in favour of keeping a nuclear deterrent, for the future is unknown, unsafe and unpredictable. A Christian can argue firstly, that we can never make ourselves absolutely secure and safe, and the attempt to do is misconceived. There are risks whatever decision is made. Secondly, one kind of risk, which Harries thinks is not always considered, is the moral risk of actually having to use nuclear weapons in a way that would be indiscriminate and disproportionate. Thirdly, if we believe in non-proliferation, the credibility of nuclear weapons is a major factor in both the strategic and moral equation. Fourthly, without being reckless, if there is a balance to be struck, a government may be right on occasions to act on the assumption that trust rather than mistrust, good will rather than ill will, persuasion rather than coercion are the values of the Kingdom. Since these will ultimately prevail they can be anticipated in some way, in however fragmentary and partial a fashion, even here and now.

For Harries, moral principles and political judgements are inextricably intertwined. Political and military judgements are also moral judgements and moral judgements cannot be separated from an assessment of the consequences of any proposed course of action. Harries' task – like those of the Churches – has been to put forward and press these criteria, probing and testing whether or not they might be met. At all times his moral seriousness has been evident. He has the conscience of a multilateralist, is an idealist without illusions, motivated by his Christian faith. It is a remarkable and continuing contribution!

Chapter Ten

Cornerstone

The dean on paper remained number two in King's College, after the principal, and was on the college council. Harries was also responsible for running the AKC (Associate of King's College, London) course. The original AKC, a full-time theological qualification for Church of England clergy who did not want to do the Bachelor of Divinity (BD), had been abolished. What remained were theological lectures for non-theological students and lectures on non-theological subjects for theological students. This was much to Harries' taste. The AKC is a remarkable phenomenon, originating in the fact that King's is, historically, an Anglican foundation. 10 am every Monday was sacrosanct for the AKC lecture. No department was allowed to timetable anything else for that hour. Harries organized lectures on a range of theological subjects including New Testament, ethics and the philosophy of religion. The course consisted of one lecture each week with an examination at the end of every year. Because the AKC lecture was built into the college timetable, it was part of its life, supported by heads of department and attracting large numbers of students. It was important that the dean was on good terms with the heads of departments, so that they encouraged their new students at the beginning of every academic year to consider seriously doing the AKC course, in addition to their degree. From the outset Harries absorbed himself in this role and set out to acquaint himself with these influential 'heads', not least those who were either non-religious or antipathetic towards the 'Church'! Because he showed more than a fleeting interest in the range of disciplines, he was successful in attracting scientists in the college to think more widely than their own subject. In his time between 800 and 900 students acquired the AKC. For the first time, Harries' administrative capacities were tested and stretched and he was not found wanting. He created his own effective systems which were administered by a first-rate secretariat.

In addition, there were the lectures on non-theological subjects for the theological students. This awakened the itch of cupidity in him, providing wonderful scope for inaugurating and organizing courses on such subjects as classical civilization, religion and literature, and the development of theatre in the West. He contributed occasional lectures to each course. The dean also had the responsibility of fostering the vocation of ordinands, although King's no longer trained them. Harries did this by hosting informal gatherings and was always available to see individuals if they wished. He also chaired the student welfare committee.

Harries developed his own views on the subject of higher education. Giving the 1986 Mary Roberts Memorial Lecture in Wales on 'Bias, Commitment and Value in Education', he summarized his values:

> First, a respect for the freedom of the taught. Second, an awareness that what we teach will be impregnated with values. Third, an awareness that fearful of our finitude we tend to absolutize our own standpoint and give ourselves in effect a pretended God's-eye view. Fourth, a love which enables us to enter into and feel the appeal of religious and political traditions other than our own and fifth, a critical scrutiny of our own position so that it is open to emendation, change and development.

The enlarged constituency of King's was accompanied by a substantial increase in students. Harries used his independence as dean to the full. He was astute and adept at establishing and conveying his own views without treading on the toes of separate individual disciplines. His presence was never imposed but always 'felt'. Just as he was not a weather vane responsive to every variation of popular whim, so students were helped to distinguish the essential from the accidental. He had the highest aspirations for King's which he was determined should provide opportunities for students to think, to love truth for its own sake, to reverence knowledge, and to avoid or despise mental cowardice and indolence. Liberty and enlarged vision were goals for students and experienced by Harries himself as if heeding Lord Acton's advice: 'Resist your time – take a foothold outside it'.

Harries initiated interdisciplinary seminars for members of staff. One of these was on religion and literature which was also the subject of the Hockerill Lecture in 1982 which featured C. S. Lewis, Stevie Smith, R. S. Thomas and D. H. Lawrence.

Following publication of the Conservative Government's Green Paper of May 1985 on *The Development of Higher Education into the 1990s* the Labour, Liberal and SDP parties produced their own reports. There was a common theme, that the country's economic performance depended on a higher educated and qualified workforce. King's held a conference at Cumberland Lodge, Windsor Great Park, in November 1986 on *Influences on Higher Education: Teaching, Research and Society*, chaired by the principal of King's, Professor Stewart Sunderland and addressed by Sir Monty Finniston, former chairman of the British Steel Corporation; Dr Edwin Kerr, former chief officer, CNAA; Sir Denys Wilkinson, vice-chancellor, University of Sussex; Shirley Williams MP, president of the Social Democratic Party and Harries, who had prepared a paper on *Ethical Imperatives or Market Forces?*. Once again he referred to the university or college as 'a community of teaching and learning in which each teacher is influenced by his/her colleagues and, as a result, keeps his/her own subject in perspective in relation to the others'. Harries had already patterned himself in this way. He exuded a libertarian approach, ever wary of legalism. His experience at King's was that life is so rich in novel situations, human nature so fertile in surprises, that the attempt to conduct by casuistic decisions is bound to fail sooner or later.

Harries used Newman's *The Idea of a University* as both a foundation and a step-ping-stone. One extract is important:

> If a practical end must be assigned to a university course, I say it is that of training good members of society. Its art is the art of social life, and its end is fitness for the world . . . It teaches him to see things as they are, to go right to the point, to disentangle a skein of thought, to detect what is sophistical, and to discard what is irrelevant. It prepares him to fill any post with credit, and to master any subject with facility. It shows him how to accommodate himself to others, how to throw himself into their state of mind, how to bring before them his own, how to influence them, how to come to an understanding with them, how to bear with them. He is at home in any society, he has common ground with every class; he knows when to speak and when to be silent; he is able to converse, he is able to listen; he can ask a question pertinently, and gain a lesson seasonably, when he has nothing to impart himself; he is ever ready, yet never in the way; he is a pleasant companion, and a comrade you can depend on; he knows when to be serious and when to trifle, and he has a sure tact which enables him to trifle with gracefulness and to be serious with effect. He has the repose of a mind which lives in itself, while it lives in the world, and which has resources for its happiness at home when it cannot go abroad . . . The art which tends to make a man all this, is in the object which it pursues as useful as the art of wealth or the art of health, though it is less sus-ceptible of method, and less tangible, less certain, less complete in its result.

Here, in a nutshell, is a description of a prime ingredient in Harries' personality. It is this, perhaps more than his deeds and successes, which will project and commend him to those searching for leaders in the Church of England. It should not be underestimated how Fulham and King's had shaped him. In each place the human-ity of the person was complemented by the Christian faith which undergirded and projected his thinking. Preaching *The Mulligan Sermon* at Gray's Inn in 1983 he concluded:

> Not simply in our personal life but behind the structures of our institutional life, is a human face that we meet as one limited, vulnerable, weak human being to another. And behind that face is a Lord, at once divine and human, who questions us, consoles us and summons us to personal responsibility before the claims of love and life, claims which can never be fully met, and who therefore holds out forgiveness and the grace for new resolve.

One has to pinch oneself to realize that in 1987 Harries had been at King's for only six years. He had spread himself deeply and broadly, seemingly extravagantly, with-out an untoward effect on his input and output. There was still a freshness about him. Endlessly self-motivated and open to the seductive offers which presented themselves, he remained well content with his lot. He and Jo had rich hinterlands and their own house in Barnes made London accessible for theatre, music, art and friendships. It was a rich life.

Although by now widely known, Harries did not particularly contemplate his future. He was not troubled with constant offers of advancement – so called! Preferment is a contagious disease in the Church of England. Once caught it is not easily cured. It nips away at the interior self. Each week the ecclesiastical newspapers provide possibilities and hope: bishops retire, die or are translated to other sees; archdeacons advance to mitred status; deans resign or die.

There was a time when, in William Cowper's words, 'The parson knows enough who knows a duke' (Tirocinium 1795). Today the temptation is for elevation-addicts in clerical collars to meet the 'right' people, especially those who are deemed to have influence in high places. 'Networking' is the latest preoccupation and extravagance. Fortunately, the majority of faithful priests accept St Peter's words to the presbyters of the Asiatic Churches: 'Feed the flock of God which is among you, taking the oversight thereof, not by constraint but willingly; nor for filthy lucre but of a ready mind; neither being lords over God's heritage but being examples to the flock' (1 Peter 5.2–3). Such work combines energetic striving and mental effort, back-breaking and heart-rending ministry, coping with success and failure in the parishes, of finding souls and losing them, of endeavouring to be holy and good. Such is the lot of many of the ablest priests in the Church of England. They have a high indifference to personal fortune which is an attribute of the highest kind of leader. Incorruptibility is ever honoured and its absence is rarely pardoned.

There were many people who had desires and anticipations for Harries' future. Some, for example, suggested he would make a superb dean of St Paul's or of Westminster. The rhythm of daily liturgical life may have appealed but it induces a smile to contemplate him planning interminable services for endless national occasions and taking his place, dutifully coped, at the end of lengthy processions.

Harries had no desire to leave King's and his wife certainly did not wish to leave their private existence and home for a more public role. Indeed he was oblivious to episcopal vacancies. In 1987 there were four, each prompted by retirement – Bath and Wells, Birmingham, Lincoln and Oxford. Patrick Campbell Rodger, Bishop of Oxford, had announced his retirement in 1986 to take effect the following year. Harries has a memory:

> The only hint, in retrospect, was that the first weekend of October 1986 there was the usual gathering of new students from King's College, London at Cumberland Lodge, over which I presided. One of the parents who brought their son to that gathering, Richard Kingsbury, the vicar of St Peter's Caversham in the Oxford diocese, said to me when we met, 'You're going to be the next Bishop of Oxford'. As I didn't even know of the vacancy and such an appointment had never crossed my mind, and for other reasons, it all seemed totally unlikely and I simply dismissed the remark out of hand. It only came back when a letter arrived from the Prime Minister, Margaret Thatcher.

Canon Richard Kingsbury observes, 'It was a hunch, no more, but RH credits me with some insider-information (quite mistakenly). His reaction was a visible blanching of utter surprise. That's the only time I've seen RH lost for words.'

The envelope arrived with its unexpected content from the Prime Minister asking whether he would allow his name to go to the Queen for nomination to the See of Oxford. He read the letter and showed it to Jo. 'It just seemed so obvious it was the kind of thing one couldn't refuse.' He did not need to consult anyone for advice: 'It was simply a question of resigning oneself to what was clearly a duty, and an opportunity to be stretched and fulfilled in various ways that only that kind of job makes possible. I remember saying to my wife, as it were by consolation, 'Well, at least we'll be living at Cuddesdon'. We both love the location. It was only later that I found out in fact the previous bishop had moved the house into Oxford itself.'

Was he even aware that he had accepted oversight of one of the largest dioceses in the Church of England? The geographical size of the diocese had not much changed during the twentieth century – Oxfordshire, Berkshire and Buckinghamshire. But whereas the population in 1901 was 633,393, it increased to 794,309 by 1936, to 1,836,000 in 1985 and to 2,058,000 by 1987. The waxing population was served by a waning number of clergy and benefices. In 1936 there were 760 stipendiary clergy and 627 benefices. By 1987 the numbers had shrunk to 425 and 334 respectively. Although the population of the diocese was exceeded by London, Chelmsford and Southwark, the number of parishes (631) and churches (816) was the largest in the Church of England.

Was Donald MacKinnon giving the future Bishop of Oxford advice and a warning in a 1967 broadcast:

> We have this treasure in earthen vessels; and these earthen vessels include historical institutions. But those who help to maintain and operate them must always remember just how much these institutions are the products less of divine Providence than of the grisly complexities and accidents of human history. To serve them, no doubt, is a psychologically satisfying role for those called to exercise office and administration in them; it may indeed become so satisfying a role that it inhibits all power to criticize, all power to recognize the need for radical renewal, even for that kind of transformation which can only be described in terms of death and Resurrection.

Someone at King's referred to Harries as a cornerstone – an indefinable constant and solid presence. We know at one level the range of his interests, activities and achievements. At another level he was, in common with R. S. Thomas, using a 'serene chisel' to interpret faith.

Chapter Eleven
+ Richard Oxon:

How far will Harries heed the advice and strictures given by his hero, Austin Farrer, when he preached at the consecration of Robert Cecil Mortimer as Bishop of Exeter on 25 April 1949?

> A bishop is given to his people; he is no more his own. His business is to make men Christians and to keep them Christians, that is the beginning and end of his task: and against this standard he must constantly be measuring the multifarious workings of his diocese, and the use he makes of his own time. The responsibility is his, and he takes it. That does not mean that he is auto-cratic. It is easy to be autocratic, and to refuse responsibility: the two faults go excellently together. The autocrat is too weak to face the painful claims and the complicated needs of mankind: he shuts himself up in the fortress of his own opinion: he is neither exposed to men nor at the disposal of men: if they are to be saved at all, they are to be saved his way. This is no shouldering of responsibility; it is the evasion of it. The bishop's responsibility is for the needs of men as they are, and he must feel the full impact of them: he must hear every opinion, by meeting it on equal ground; he must give to others' wisdom or experience the weight it really has; he must dare to be distressed by a heart-breaking world, and distracted by an untidy world: and he must dare to act. This is responsibility, but it is not autocracy . . .

There is a lot of general fantasy about what it means to become a bishop. It is com-monly thought, not invariably assumed, that outstanding service as a parish priest is an essential, certainly more than adequate preparation for episcopal ministry. In reality, observation and common sense suggest instead that the transition to the episcopate contributes a substantial break in vocational life. It would be better if the emphasis were less on occupying an office and more on exercising an apostolic vocation. Nomination as a bishop marks a radical and often costly change in a man's life, though not always perceived as such by him or by the Church. Minis-terial abilities in the episcopate are different from those of the priesthood. Many old skills fade, even fall into disuse; new skills must be learned. Hitherto unknown, unexplored or unheeded gifts are needed.

How many former parish priests, now bishops, miss the pastoral care and coun-selling of individual people; offering the sacrament of reconciliation; baptizing;

preparing young people for confirmation; solemnizing marriage; ministering to the sick and the dying; conducting funerals? How many former tutors, lecturers, professors and deans – even a dean of King's College, London – miss the academic stimulus; the pastoral opportunities which present themselves with students and staff; the freedom to discover new ways of developing and exercising ministry and influencing people and institutions alike?

As a bishop, new skills are required – making judgements about people, planning, decision-making, presiding at large gatherings, chairing committees. In his role as president of the Eucharist – and confirming and ordaining – new demands will be made on his liturgical presence and knowledge. He will miss the close, regular contact with one set of parishioners or the more fleeting succession of students and the opportunities of fruitful relations with academic staff. Instead he will have major responsibilities for all the parishes and clergy in a diocese. He is no longer a 'priest among others' but rather one who has legitimate authority and informal power over other deacons and priests. These facts have ramifications for the bishop's professional life and for many aspects of his personal life as well.

'Elevation' is a poor description of what happens in consecration or episcopal ordination; the stratified hierarchical image no longer serves, although it remains visible in particular places. Episcopal ministry is not the 'top' of ministry, but rather the means for incorporation of all in ministry, and the bishop is the resource for lay, diaconal and priestly ministries. This is a different vocation from that which is given and granted in ordination to the priesthood. The role of servant to the servants is a function which a person enters at the time of acceptance and consecration.

A bishop is faced with the constant giving of self. Only a sense of vocation and grace will save him from pursuing his own ends for their own sake. Self-fulfilment is a particular absorption and temptation of the age. The teaching of the Gospel is quite plain: those who seek to look after their lives will lose them. True fulfilment for Christians is found through acceptance of whatever God puts in their way. The crosses and contradictions that are good for bishops are the ones God actually gives them. In de Caussade's words: 'There is no moment at which God does not present himself under the guise of some suffering, some consolation, or some duty. At every occurrence we should find a gift from God.'

No new bishop should be unaware of his inheritance. The diocese of Oxford was created in 1542 out of the diocese of Lincoln. Its succession of bishops does not compare, outside the archbishoprics, with London, Durham and Winchester of the same period. Two bishops, John Potter and Thomas Secker, passed through on their journey to Canterbury. Henry Compton was translated to London and, as an archbishop manqué, was rejected on two occasions for Canterbury. In the past 150 years three bishops of stature and distinction merit recording.

To Samuel Wilberforce (1845–1869) may be traced the genesis of today's demented activism. When he arrived in Oxford, the year of Newman's secession to Rome, he found the area of his jurisdiction poorly equipped in plant. He added no fewer than 200 to the churches of the diocese, and he was responsible for the

111

foundation of 250 elementary schools. It has been pointed out with justice that he revolutionized episcopal administration. In place of *otium cum dignitate* (leisure with dignity), the scholarly or merely aristocratic seclusion that had characterized the prelates of the eighteenth century, the Church awoke to the vision of a busy and bustling organizer to whom every detail of clerical life and work was a matter of immediate personal concern. In the administration of confirmation and ordination, the change was most clearly seen. Candidates for the former were no longer blessed in a haphazard manner when the bishop happened to be in the neighbourhood. A rota of regular and reverent services was arranged with sufficient notice for candidates to be thoroughly prepared. Similarly ordination was made as public as possible and was preceded by a retreat in the bishop's own private chapel. The fact that these measures have become part of normal ecclesiastical practice is a sufficient indication of Wilberforce's success.

At a national level his influence was equally conspicuous. The old-fashioned archbishops were over-shadowed by the brilliance of their junior colleague. Wilberforce was able, on occasion, to galvanize them into some semblance of activity, and reforms were effected. The most important was the revival of Convocation, which had not met for the transaction of business since 1718.

Great as was his work, the man himself was greater. His versatility was considerable. He was no scholar: he had neither the learning nor the pedantry of Pusey and Newman. But he had the skill to see the essential elements in their position and he had the statesman's gift of realizing what was practicable. As things were, he did not possess sufficient science or philosophy to put him on the right side of the Darwinian controversy, but he had enough of both to make him the most noteworthy opponent of the new views. He managed to keep closely in touch with intellectual developments in spite of having little time for reading. Over all other characteristics towers Wilberforce's amazing capacity for work. He had an abounding energy and vitality that outlasted and exhausted all who were with him for long.

What of Wilberforce's personal piety? He was charged with worldliness. How far ambition and capacity for negotiation are compatible with Christian love and humility may or may not be questionable, but if he manifested the first two traits he also gave evidence of the second. He never lost the flavour or the vocabulary of that evangelical piety in which he had been brought up, but he combined them with love for the Church and its sacraments which was strengthened by his contacts and even his conflicts with Keble and Pusey. His whole life was steeped in a passionate devotion to Christ and to the souls for whom he died. Of lasting impact was the preservation of the central core of Anglican churchmanship and he changed the popular conception of a bishop.

The second bishop with a permanent place in history is William Stubbs (1889–1901). Gladstone was responsible for his earlier appointment to Chester in 1884. Stubbs had been vicar of Navestock in the Chelmsford diocese for 16 years where he combined parochial pastoring with academic pursuits. He was also a Regius professor of modern history at Oxford, and his volumes on *The Constitutional History of England* and his Rolls series are permanent legacies. The qualities he brought to the bench of bishops were pressed home in a letter from another distinguished scholar, Mandell Creighton, himself to be a great Bishop of Peterborough, then of London:

> Frankly, I have been somewhat alarmed lately at the thought of the want of wisdom in the Bench. There is zeal, earnestness, practical ability, eloquence enough – but wisdom! . . . I think that your accession to the Bench will bring strength everywhere it is needed. Your large knowledge of everything concerned with the history, position, and principles of the Church will be of invaluable usefulness. Your statesmanlike views and your experience of affairs will secure universal attention.

The third name is Charles Gore (1911–1919). Formerly Bishop of Worcester, then a commanding figure as the first Bishop of Birmingham, it needed the persuasion of Prime Minister H. H. Asquith, the Archbishop of Canterbury, Randall Davidson, and close friends to lever him out of Birmingham. It was probably a mistake. When he died in 1932 Dean W. R. Inge wrote of Gore's huge output of written works that, 'they exhibit extreme honesty of purpose, fearless acceptance of Christ's teaching honestly interpreted, scorn of unreality and empty words, and a determination never to allow preaching to be divorced from practice'. The prophetic flavour he brought to Oxford was disturbing to many. It was the essentials alone for which he really cared. It is vital to grasp two dominant elements in his life. First, he had no serious doubts of the intrinsic doctrines of Christianity. Secondly, he loved and believed in the Church as seen in the historical process. In a similar way to Harries he was bothered and bored by details of ceremonial, yet he was always ready to champion the oppressed, though he might find the things they did difficult to defend. Sometimes as a bishop he laid down the limits of his toleration. On one occasion, being about to take part in what he expected to be a somewhat elaborate service, he told the vicar, 'You can do anything else you like with me, but I won't be kissed'.

Gore, founder of the Christian Social Union and the Community of the Resurrection, Mirfield, combined spiritual and intellectual power to a remarkable and very unusual degree; he was an aristocrat, reserved, fastidious, detached; few, even of his closest friends, could quite banish a kind of awe they felt in his presence. He loved beautiful things, though his own home was always austere. He could be indignant and could arouse anger in others. He was an enthralling human paradox, great yet gentle; witty; ruthless yet tender; brilliant and yet completely humble; of high and unbending principle, yet sensitive. He became critical of those Anglo-Catholic tendencies which were inconsistent with loyalty to Anglican principles. It was Gore who, more completely than anyone else, exploded the 'High Church and Tory' myth. Of the other seven bishops of the twentieth century, only one had had any parochial experience and that was in the Scottish Episcopal Church. Francis Paget (1901–1911) and Thomas Banks Strong (1925–1937) had spent between them 70 years at Christ Church; Hubert Murray Burge (1919–1925) represented a different world and a diminishing path to episcopal office, that of a public school headmaster; Kenneth Escott Kirk (1937–1954) was an Anglo-Catholic and notable moral theologian (Regius professor of moral and pastoral theology and canon of Christ Church).

Only three crosiers distant from Harries was Harry James Carpenter (1955–1970), for 28 years at Keble College, first as tutor, then as warden. Diligent, pedantic, nervous, without physical presence, taking no measures to project his voice or himself on platform or in pulpit, yet he had no 'side' and, despite shyness, was content in meeting people where he found them. There was an ordinariness about him that was not unattractive. Initiatives were few but sustained once hatched. Much personal good was done by stealth. His reliability led to time-consuming outside work, notably proposals for Anglican-Methodist unity. He was overwhelmed by the burden of incessant labour. Although diocesan administration was no stranger to this former warden, he was not naturally equipped for 'being a bishop'. His theological base was sound and firm and his piety was evident.

When Carpenter resigned in 1970 there was a feeling that Oxford needed a bishop who could comprehend a vastly changed world and a reluctantly changing Church – a 'new' man in all senses of the word – for one of the most complex dioceses in the Church of England. The unexpected appointment in 1971 provided anticipated satisfaction. Kenneth John Woollcombe, aged 46, principal of Edinburgh Theological College, married to Gwenda, with three children, was appointed. Except for a curacy in Grimsby he had no parochial experience but was familiar with the university having been for seven years fellow, chaplain and lecturer at St John's College.

Woollcombe, tall, composed and attentive, was an excellent and attractive presence in any pulpit. His appointment to Oxford heralded great change, not because of new policies, but because the imperative of Christ would bring changes in direction, focus and perspective. He wanted Christians to be explorers. There were no trumpets – triumphalism belonged to a fast receding past. He had the clarity and directness of a good teacher, quick on the draw with words. He moved his office to Diocesan Church House as Cuddesdon Palace was ten miles out of Oxford, well off the bus route and secluded. The clergy were not bombarded with documents, which is why occasional pastoral letters or visitation charges were welcomed, as were his teaching weeks. He arrived early for services so he could meet and converse with people before rather than simply shaking hands afterwards.

Woollcombe's agreeable personality was such that, although he was authentically radical and liberal on many of the rising ecclesiastical controversies, he did not cause great offence by the use of provocative language. Yet it was a mistake to think that smoking a pipe suggested sweet reasonableness! He was dynamic and could be volatile. Like Wilberforce, he was convinced that secularity was the great danger and weakness of the Church of England. The Church of England generally warmed to Woollcombe and the religious affairs correspondents of newspapers thought of him as a possible future archbishop. On emerging issues his position was clear. He was president of the Anglican Group for the Ordination of Women to the Priesthood. He advocated either more provinces than the existing two (Canterbury and York) or else fewer and larger dioceses. He was prepared to confirm children from the age of seven when they would continue to receive regular instruction. He was chairman of the Churches' Council for Covenanting. He calculated that after absences – General Synod, House of Lords, Church Commissioners, his commitments with SPCK and the World Council of Churches, miscellaneous absences and holidays – for something like 34 weeks of the year he was not at the disposal of the people he had been consecrated to serve.

In February 1976 Gwenda died of cancer. The Bishop of Ely, a former bishop suffragan of Dorchester, Peter Walker, wrote movingly: 'She surrendered her life with deeply Christian trust and simplicity, her family close to her; and there was a depth of quietness, the tangibility of many prayers, in the room of Churchill Hospital on that evening of the Transfiguration. Thinking of Gwenda then, one can think only of something by God's grace triumphantly accomplished.'

Kenneth was all her concern and such was their dependency that with her death, 'I began to realize that one pair of hands and eyes could not do justice to the work which the incumbent of the see of Oxford has to do'. That was his message to the clergy in October 1977 when he announced his intention to resign effective from 31 March 1978. His last year was difficult. He was weary, disappointed, had lost his sparkle and said that in another life he would opt to be a Buddhist. Resignation brought relief and his friend, Bishop Gerald Ellison of London, found a niche for him in the diocese, then a canonry of St Paul's, and to the joy of his friends he eventually remarried, to Juliet Dearmer, now a priest.

Oxford was offered to Robert Runcie, Bishop of St Albans since 1970, but he declined. Again there was another surprising appointment, the translation of Patrick Rodger from Manchester. A Scotsman, Rodger had held various appointments in the Scottish Episcopal Church but his abiding interest was in ecumenical relations. There was much embarrassment in 1965 when he was chosen by the executive committee of the World Council of Churches to succeed Dr Visser't Hooft, a decision which was overturned by its central committee. Great capacity and integrity, breadth of outlook and a transparent personality were strengths. A weakness was that he did not have the cutting edge for bold initiatives or the ruthless energy needed in such a role: not one to make waves or introduce disturbing personalities. This mixture of traits was noticeable in Manchester where he lacked the hardened toughness for work in that urban environment. But what he said and wrote was always worth hearing and reading – and heeding. He was impatient at the Church's increasing bureaucratization and lust for legalism as if emulating the State. There was zeal found in his ecumenical vision which also embraced other faiths. He left Cuddesdon Palace for a house in Oxford.

There were merits in Rodger's style of gentle, quiet, low-key leadership. He was trusted and his major achievement was the establishment of the episcopal area system which Kenneth Woollcombe had initiated. He set a style for his successor in consciously distancing himself from day-to-day episcopal oversight, leaving that to the area bishops, although he kept himself always available with his finger on the diocesan pulse. He was also a sensitive pastor. Nationally, he initiated the Partners-in-Mission Consultation which resulted in a wide appraisal of the life and work of the diocese. Canon T. R. Milford, Master of the Temple, preached at Rodger's consecration in 1970 and referred to 'an uncovenanted charisma, of which the bearer himself may be quite unconscious. This gift is not the same as an attractive personality; in fact the man's own personality may get in the way. It is a sort of transparency, and as far as I can make out, the way to receive it is not to try for it directly, but just to be yourself; and the best way to be yourself is because you are in love with your people'. On his retirement Rodger returned to Scotland where he could be most himself.

The vacancy-in-see committee met to prepare a 'Statement of the Needs of the Diocese' for the Crown Appointments Commission. The committee asked that the forty-second bishop of Oxford should not interfere with, but would encourage positively, the settlement and development of the area scheme. He should be able to lead a team of bishops and archdeacons, oversee diocesan planning and policy and head the central administration at Diocesan Church House. He would have his own episcopal area, the deaneries of Oxford and Cowley. Unless already familiar with Church life in the geographically small area of central Oxford, he would be unaware that it was something of a poisoned chalice. One matter was already effectively settled. The division of this large diocese had long been deliberated. As recently as 1968 a working party had been set up by the Diocesan Conference. It reported in 1970. It was not a unanimous report. The opinion was that division of the diocese at that time, whether with or without shared administration, 'might well result in the hampering rather than the advancing of the work of the Church in this part of the country'. In effect any proposal for dividing the diocese in the future was dead. Oxford adopted an ideal area system which, unlike London with its area synods, remained a unity. It was a deliberate decision not to have separate administrative offices in the areas.

The area system enabled the new diocesan bishop to be free of shackles and it was hoped someone would be appointed who would fulfil a national role. Previous episcopal experience was not a crucial factor. Only five out of 18 bishops of Oxford since 1800 were bishops before they were appointed to Oxford. Proven creative orthodoxy would be an admirable theological position and was likely to overflow into churchmanship. Harries seemed a near perfect fit for Oxford. And there was a bonus. Unlike any of his twentieth-century predecessors, Harries had 15 years of proven parochial experience at Hampstead and Fulham. That counted! In addition, his broadcasting and writing commended him to those on the vacancy-in-see committee even if they had little personal knowledge of him.

The public announcement of Harries' appointment was made on 26 November 1986 but, as with many such appointments, he was a long time arriving! His consecration as bishop was at St Paul's Cathedral on the Feast of the Ascension, 28 May 1987. It was where he had been made deacon and ordained priest. Although he was the only bishop being consecrated, St Paul's was packed. The Archbishop of Canterbury, Robert Runcie, was, in Harries' words, 'On his very best form, warm and humane. We virtually danced down the aisle together after the consecration'. A friend of Harries', Patrick Gowers, composed a special anthem for the occasion, *Viri Galilei*, an ambitious piece for two organs, which has since become well known when sung by major choirs. The selection of preacher is the privilege of the conse- crand and Harries chose Canon Eric James, preacher at Gray's Inn, director of Christian Action, and chaplain to the Queen. Eric James excels on such occasions, matching his theme with the occasion. Also, like Harries, he knows he must capture a congregation's attention in a single sentence and then continue to hold them there! 'Only connect . . .' was his two-word lure. The epigraph was set by E. M. Forster at the front of *Howards End*. Eric James thought it articulated and expressed the role of a bishop. He was candid. 'When we connect "connecting" with the atonement itself, we begin to see the pain and the price of connecting: that no bland Anglican sleight of hand will do. At-one-ment is achieved often only at cost and with costly confrontation.' He singled out one or two features:

> 'Only connect . . .' The University of Oxford, they tell me, tends to keep its bishops at arm's length; but Oxford remains one of the great symbols and centres of scholarship and research. It will be no mean achievement, Richard, if you can strengthen the connection between scholarship and the Church, not least in the pulpits and pews of your diocese . . . 'Only connect . . .' What reso- nances of that phrase throb through the Church and the world today! I wonder, Richard, how you will help the rich Oxford commuters to connect with the poor of, say, Cowley; and the decision-makers of the Chilterns to connect with those whose destinies they control in the North East and North West; how you will help the employed of Oxford to connect with the unemployed: the white people to worship with the black, and to grow in understanding the Sikhs, Hindus and Muslims, in, say, Slough . . . 'Only connect . . .' Church and State. Your own appointment, Richard, is – for better, for worse – part and parcel with that connection. But in your time as bishop, it is urgent that a connection between Church and State be forged and fashioned afresh that better reflects the realities of the religious and social situation of England today – and of the Church of England – and above all the priorities of the Gospel . . .
>
> 'Only connect . . .' Recognize the masculinity and femininity in yourself, and you will want to see that masculinity and femininity in yourself recog- nized by the Church in the women and men who present themselves to you for ministry in Christ's Church.

Harries' enthronement took place on 30 June 1987 at Christ Church, the smallest and the most hidden of all the English cathedrals. The see of Oxford was combined with the college, which was reconstituted as Ecclesia Christi Cathedralis Oxon, by Henry VIII in 1546, the year before his death. Christ Church is the most imposing ecclesiastical building in Oxford, standing on the site of a Saxon nunnery and chapel founded by St Frideswide who died about 735. A priory of Augustinian canons was later established and it was they who began to build the present church about 1160. St Frideswide is the patron saint of city and university and her shrine and burial place are still venerated. Christ Church was never intended as the setting for grand occasions; 950 people may be squeezed, like sardines in a tin, at a Christmas carol service, but fewer than half that number can be accommodated in places where they can see as well as hear. If the congregation at the enthronement was expecting clues for Harries' episcopate in the form of packets of initiatives or blueprints they were disappointed. Yet reading his sermon afterwards in the *Oxford Diocesan Magazine* it was possible to discover his foundations, his motivations, his passions and his will. In forecasting for the next decade the 'exciting and encouraging' future for the Church, he was over-optimistic. Another forecast was only too real:

> The growth of intolerant extremism in Christianity, Islam and Judaism, is a grave danger to humanity and the cause of true religion . . . The opportunity we have before us is to share with those many contemporaries who have lost a passionate sense of the dignity and glory of being human, a vision which springs from the Holy One who has made us in the image of his own eternity. It remains true for us, as it was for Yeats, that:
>
> > everywhere
> > The ceremony of innocence is drowned;
> > The best lack all conviction, while the worst
> > Are full of passionate intensity.
> > *The Second Coming*, 1921

The problem, and the opportunity, before us, is to combine strong conviction with deep respect for those who do not share our convictions; to love God with a passionate intensity whilst at the same time showing a true understanding of those who find such belief impossible. (The) diocese of Oxford has a particularly awesome responsibility within the Body of Christ. The ability, the talent, the resources and influence of people in the diocese are striking. Church people are helping to make decisions that vitally affect the lives of those in our inner cities, in our national life as a whole and in the developing world. Inevitably the words of the old prayer come to mind: from those to whom much has been given, much will be expected. It is not that the diocese is in a lordly position to give from on high, for within the Body of Christ we are receivers one of another; and we have more to receive than we know from our fellow-believers suffering oppression or poverty. But as we have much to receive from those to whom our Lord said the Kingdom belonged, so we have much to give.

Harries' future is one of giving and belonging.

Chapter Twelve
Unremitting in Repose

For the next 19 years there was to be incessant activity. How Harries managed to pedal so constantly and furiously without the chains coming off his mental and physical bicycle is almost unfathomable. Was there a need to expand his already over-large commitments now joined by meetings of the House of Bishops and General Synod, and soon the House of Lords beckoned, together with extra-diocesan speaking and preaching engagements – all clamouring for time and attention? In 1987 he could not foresee the massive and complex developments in such areas as social morality and medical ethics, which he would be keen – or driven – to pursue, well beyond the need of normal curiosity. It is only a discerning and perhaps loving eye which can comprehend the changes in Harries, whilst acknowledging that he remained essentially the same. There are paradoxes. Many people want to understand – and judge – him according to their own lights rather than accepting that they do not engage with him beyond a pedestrian level. He is not as compartmentable as some people think him to be. In other spheres they laud unity in diversity. Why not in their bishop?

A repeated description of Harries as a diocesan bishop is that he is 'laid-back'. Thus classified and docketed, admirers and antagonists alike use it for their own purposes to laud or criticize their bishop's personality and actions. 'Laid-back' has become one of those generally overused fuzzy couplets with mixed meanings. Of Harries, it is a deficient description which neither captures nor explains him.

Most people's previous experience of their new bishop had been through the intimate medium of the radio, where to listen to him on *Thought for the Day* was rather like having him in the same room. Even reading his published books, articles in periodicals or frequent appearances in newspapers, leads people to think they know him. They were to find that there was a disparity between such encounters and the person they first met as bishop. 'Bishop's Home', 27 Linton Road, Oxford, would be a more accurate description than Bishop's House, for to enter it was to be enveloped in unfussy, comfortable, homely and convivial surroundings. At the shared centre of it was his wife Jo, who carries more letters after her name – MA, MB, BChir, and DCH – than does her husband! In the appointment and making of bishops there is someone who is often overlooked. Some provinces of the Anglican Communion take a special interest in and care for the domestic circumstances of bishops-elect. They consider wives and children as participants, not hyphenated adjuncts to their husbands and fathers. It is genuine rather than interfering, patronizing care. The word of the new bishop is insufficient. The electors want to know the truth. After all, his wife may be ecstatic, lukewarm or antagonistic of the step he is to take. She may well have her own profession. She may not be a conspicuous churchgoer. She may not be an Anglican. She may not even be a person of faith. Until comparatively recently, the Church of England had no credible record in recognizing that wives of bishops are more than wives of bishops! They are persons with individual interests, histories, opinions and convictions, with independent outlooks. Her mental agility and academic achievements may exceed those of her husband. For any bishop's wife there is sacrifice and there is a price. She will observe that for her husband being a bishop is over-demanding of energy and pressurized but he is happy, fulfilled and satisfied. It is good for him – he is growing, developing new skills, widening his interests and responding to new challenges. His wife may wish to be as closely involved as is practicable with her husband's ministry – or she may not so wish. She may find her own distinctive place in the diocese, separately from her husband, although that is rather less likely. Or she may be like the dutiful wife of a chief executive of a major company who has breakfast on her own (he has already left for the office at an unnecessarily early hour) and is there to greet him during the evening when he returns, tired but exhilarated, more interested in relating 'his' day than listening to his wife's 'day'. Jo Harries is as elusive of labelling as Richard. Her original intention was to be a medical missionary working with Muslim women. Then she met Richard, with an equally compelling calling, though not one which would extend to being an Anglican priest-mullah in an Islamic country. Marriage is a shared vocation and Jo's commitment is complete.

From the outset Harries' domestic and diocesan arrangements for working were admirable. He had his study and library at Bishop's House. Richard and Jo immediately installed a chapel in one of the upstairs rooms. It was a functional oasis, surrounded not by palm trees, but by a range of pictures and a beautiful icon. This, falsely, created a cluttered impression but each was part of a past and continuing ministry. Muted inspiration and calm were evident in a place you know was well-seasoned with prayer. His official working office was at Diocesan Church House, North Hinksey Lane, where his staff were also based. They comprised a domestic chaplain, a personal assistant, an administrative assistant and a communications officer. It provided a good working environment, for most diocesan officials were no more than a corridor away. However, Church House had a certain life and logic of its own, and sometimes ambiguities and resentments arose from this around the diocese.

Harries' chaplains were close and detached at the same time and this opaque relationship extended to his senior colleagues. Each chaplain came from a parochial curacy. The word 'domestic' is a misnomer as the chaplains lived in a house in Marsh Lane, Oxford. A bishop's chaplain may be immensely trusted as a confidante, the repository of secrets and the beneficiary of much wisdom, sometimes regarded as an 'adopted son'. On the whole that close relationship did not obtain with Harries although he did regard them as good friends. The chaplain's day began with morning prayer at Bishop's House and then straight to Diocesan

Harries' parents, Brigadier Bill Harries
and Greta Harries

Harries as a young soldier

Harries (left) ice-skating on a pond in Gerards Cross with mother and brother Charles

Consecration as Bishop of Oxford, Ascension Day 1987,
by Archbishop Robert Runcie with the Bishop of Rochester,
Dr David Say, in the background. Harries is being presented with a
cross by Metropolitan Philaret of Minsk and Bylorussia

In Singapore in 1987 for an Anglican Peace and Justice meeting with Archbishop Robert
Runcie and Luiz Prado, Bishop of Pelotas in Brazil, who remains a good friend

In Kimberly, South Africa, with the Bishop of the Diocese, Njongonkulu Winston Ndungane, later Archbishop of Cape Town, and his wife Nomahlubi

Harries with Rabbi Lionel Blue in Oxford making a film for television

Harries on a pastoral visit

Harries on a Swan Hellenic cruise, giving a site
talk at Nicaea in Turkey, where the council was
held in 325 which formulated the Nicene Creed

Harries holding a Kalashnikov as part of the campaign against the arms trade

Members of the Royal Commission on the reform of the House of Lords.
Standing (l–r): Baroness Dean, Lord Butler, Professor Dawn Oliver, Kenneth Munro,
Professor Anthony King, Ann Benyon, Richard Harries,
Bill Morris, Sir Michael Wheeler Booth.
Seated (l–r): Gerald Kaufman MP, Lord Wakeham and Lord Hurd

On a solidarity march during the Iraq war through Oxford with Jewish, Muslim and other church leaders, from the Synagogue to the Mosque, via the University Church

Walking in the Chilterns with Anthony, Julia and Harriet Neuberger and Harries' wife Jo

With the family. Standing: Harries and daughter Clare. Seated (l–r): grandson Luke with son Mark, wife Jo with baby grandson Ben, grandson Toby with daughter-in-law Cilla

A residential staff meeting walk in April 1997.
From the front: Dominic Walker, Bishop of Reading, later Bishop of Monmouth; Colin Bennetts, Bishop of Buckingham, later Bishop of Coventry; Frank Weston, Archdeacon of Berkshire, later Bishop of Knaresborough; Andrew Cain, chaplain; Mike Hill, Archdeacon of Berkshire, later Bishop of Buckingham then Bristol; Anthony Russell, Bishop of Dorchester, later Bishop of Ely; Terry Landsbert, Secretary of the Diocesan Board of Finance

Harries with his wife Jo, on the occasion of his re-introduction into the House of Lords on 25 July 2006

Church House for normal office hours. In addition there were regular daytime and evening visits throughout the diocese. Facilitating and minute taking at collegial and congenial staff and residential meetings was important. Their task was to provide administrative support for Harries. They also acted as chauffeur in the official Rover (later a Toyota Prius) though Harries normally drove himself to places close to Oxford and used the coach to go to London. The chaplain's post was two-thirds time, enabling the holder to pursue postgraduate studies or additional pastoral work with the other third.

Harries describes his overall method of working and the emphases he placed on aspects of it. 'I am well organized, and use every scrap of time. This means looking ahead and seeing what engagements need preparing for and using spare spaces of time, i.e. coach journeys to London, or half an hour after breakfast, to do this. When I'm writing something I will try to get up early to do an hour before breakfast and then perhaps keep an hour or so clear in the morning before going into the office. The only real time though for writing anything has been in the summer for part of August and a bit of September. Obviously, in a lot of my writing I have been able to use things I have written before. I also have wonderful support in the office. This means that I can dictate everything and have it typed out for me. For difficult sentences or paragraphs I scribble something out very roughly by hand and then dictate. Although I can type and use a word processor and do so as a last resort, in fact this method of producing what I do is much quicker and, as some people have found, it's not always easy to think clearly whilst one is typing or using a word processor. As an example of the support I get: I might scribble out my *Thought for the Day* on a pad going up to London on the coach. When I get there I'd ring it through to the office and Christine (Lodge, my personal assistant) would take it down in shorthand. She would type it out and fax it through to the House of Lords. Another aspect of my work pattern is that I try to put my intellectual energy into what I judge to be a priority of what really matters. So I avoid getting bogged down in detail on those areas that I think can either be properly delegated or which I know other people will do far better than I do. So for example, although I've had some interest obviously in what used to come under the heading of Doctrine II, Church, Ministry and Sacraments, I know there are plenty of other members of the House of Bishops who will read all the papers very thoroughly and have strong views about all these issues. That's not where I put my energy – I put it into what was Doctrine I, God, Christ and Humanity, and, following from this, ethical issues. I seek to operate on the borderlands between the Christian faith and the world and that's where I try to focus the energy I have, rather than dissipating it on a lot of Church-related issues. I do of course have to do some of those, being responsible for running the diocese of Oxford and being a member of the House of Bishops, responsible for the Church of England and I hope I do that side of things moderately effectively but it's not where I try to make my major contribution. Another feature I suppose is that I find I really only have intellectual energy for a few hours' serious work in a day, and that's in the morning, so if I have any serious thinking or writing to do that's when I do it. I would use the time for the rest of the day in things

121

which may be important but they don't require quite so much concentrated focus.'

Harries appointed five chaplains during his time at Oxford. Did first impressions endure? They are certainly revealing of the person who would be their 'boss'. Martin Gorick was chaplain 1991–1994. Educated at Selwyn College, Cambridge and Ripon Hall, Cuddesdon he was curate of Birtley in the Durham diocese when invited for interview with his wife Katherine on the way back from a camping holiday:

> Katherine was looking slim and tanned in shorts and T-shirt and Richard used to joke that that's what got me the job. No written job description in those days. We had a chat in his book-lined study. My job was to 'run the diocese' while he got on with everything else! The chaplain had to hold the office and all the administration together, do some research for him and be his chauffeur and companion on trips outside Oxford. I remember having a meal in the kitchen that first evening with Richard and Jo. Very relaxed, friendly and jolly at the end of his day off. The next morning we came down for breakfast and it felt as though he'd never met me before. He was ready for work, formal and distracted, and that's how it could be. It could be confusing. Many people saw just the 'work' focused side and could find him cold. Others would see both sides and wonder what they'd done wrong as I did that first morning! But it was just how he was.

This 'first impression' is shared by many. Gorick's subsequent affection and respect for Harries grew into 'a real love for someone who had been an outstanding apologist for the Christian faith'.

Andrew Cain, chaplain from 1994 to 1998, was educated at Aberdeen University and Ripon College, Cuddesdon and was curate of St John's, Walworth in the Southwark diocese. He was interviewed in the garden at Linton Road on a summer day and found the process awkward. His first impression was that Harries was a deeply reserved and cautious person but, like Gorick, he soon came to appreciate his 'deep integrity, sincere prayer and faith, and profoundly thoughtful life'. He points out how difficult it must have been for the family not to have been able to attend a place of worship together regularly in peace. Cain looked back on this time as one of the happiest of his life.

Soon after his arrival, Harries established a diocesan communications committee and in 1989 appointed Richard Thomas, who came from a similar position in Winchester, as diocesan communications officer. Oxford was not unknown territory, for his curacy had been at Abingdon. He recalls Harries saying: 'My job as a bishop is to let good things happen.' These words echoed throughout his episcopate and formed his last message to the diocese.

At this juncture it is timely to refer to the hiddenness and openness of Richard Harries. He is not the sum of his parts. It is the complex whole of a single character that fascinates, puzzles and surprises. On one level the contradictions, not many layers beneath the surface, are not easily understood. Paradoxically, on another level he is precisely as he appears. Canon Martin Peirce, former diocesan director of ordinands, writes for many and is persuasive:

> He catches so many things spot on, which everyone recognizes as spot on. This may indicate, a funny thing to say about so complex a man, that there is a certain simplicity in Richard. Much of him really is as he appears to very many people – we know his shyness, his quickness and his breadth of mind, his tremendous application, his courage, his trusting you to do your job, and so on. We know what kind of thing we'll get, when he appears in front of the TV cameras, or gets up to preach, or comes into the church hall after a service. And yet, how little do we know, we also feel.

Most correspondents emphasize that Harries is a very private person. Is this because he has much to be private about, to conceal, or is it that he has deliberately developed a public persona to hide vulnerabilities? Dame Suzi Leather, former chair of the Human Fertilization and Embryology Authority, is used to being on the receiving end of maleficent assaults. Harries said, 'My dear, you must grow a carapace.' Had he followed his own advice? Many people from childhood set to work to build themselves a fortress, a shell, against the alarms and disappointments of a cruel and dangerous world. He could not foresee that before leaving Oxford he would need a strong shield against the battering of critics and the venomous-tipped arrows of ecclesiastical barbarians!

'Many men', observed the great Bishop Joseph Butler of Durham, 'seem perfect strangers to their own character.' Is this true of Harries? He is not self-analytical and thus not self-critical. There is nobody else, except a wise spiritual director, who can be trusted to do the work of criticism faithfully. Wives and best friends are only partially equipped for this task. There are haphazard perceptions – glimpses – of Harries in, for example, his appreciation of works of art, and what he chooses to reveal in speech and writing. We have noted a finely organized observer, not in the sense of brooding and burrowing, but in that of seeing and elaborating that which he has absorbed. He has a tolerant view of life, yet is not blind to its amazing and persistent hypocrisies, and he feels the pathos of the human lot. There are constants – his passion for liberty is deep and genuine and he has never trimmed his liberal roots and instincts. There is ambition, though he deftly avoids making his reputation his god. He is no plaster saint. He can experience flashes of anger, along with a sense of the dramatic and has a range of human foibles.

Harries is not isolated from his contemporaries. His many interests and social life counter any such suggestion. Yet he is exempt from the kind of salutary criticism which is involved in association with one's equals. A bishop is flattered by his inferiors, and the publicity in which he lives exposes him in unusual measure to the chronic disease of passion for eulogy, for giving and receiving compliments, although a certain caution prevents him from being too free with the former or applying afterglow to the latter.

At many turns there are contrasts and divergencies. Harries has the courage to face situations frankly, to think clearly and to act resolutely. He also evades conflict until forced upon him as a last resort, when action in the first resort would have prevented painful encounters and confrontations. If he sidetracks some unpalatable issues by delegating them to others he is also capable of taking a principled, unwavering stand on others, mindful of Shakespeare:

> Thus conscience does make cowards of us all;
> And thus the native hue of resolution
> Is sicklied o'er with the pale cast of thought
> And enterprises of great pith and moment
> With this regard their currents turn awry,
> And lose the name of action.
>
> (*Hamlet*, Act 3 scene 1)

A kindly disposition, generous temperament and sanguine outlook is evident and paramount. This is a strength. Its correspondent weakness is accepting people's estimate of themselves without due enquiry, which would lead to some erstwhile friends mutating into wolves in sheep's clothing. If there is unruffled patience with the problems of individuals and the cross-purposes of committees, there is also, in the phrase of Baroness Perry of Southwark, an 'air of detached and slightly weary cynicism about him'.

Harries is a carnivore of work, with a mind to leave a footprint, a legacy. It is too soon to know what that will be, but there will be one. Is he reminded of Robert Browning's 'Paracelsus' where Aprile is made to say:

> Knowing ourselves, our world, our task so great,
> Our time so brief, 'tis clear if we refuse
> The means so limited, the tools so rude
> To execute our purpose, life will fleet
> And we shall fade and leave our task undone.

There was one forum, a treasury of frankness and fellowship, where a few brother bishops were committed to the same difficult venture, and confronted by similar trials and problems. An 'episcopal cell' was formed in 1987, composed of recently consecrated diocesan bishops. The idea was that of Harries and Robert Hardy of Lincoln. Invited to join were bishops of different views and personalities, with a mix of churchmanship and regions: George Carey of Bath and Wells; Simon Barrington-Ward of Coventry; David Hope of Wakefield; and, though not yet a diocesan bishop, Tom Butler of Willesden. A little later John Taylor of St Albans joined the cell. A pattern emerged of meeting in January at the Convent of the Incarnation, Fairacres, Oxford, and before the July General Synod in York, then either at Lincoln or at Bishopthorpe when David Hope was translated to York in 1995. These were good occasions for shared confidences, genuine mutual support, sounding-boards for looming controversies and time for relaxed conviviality, banter, prayer and worship. David Hope remembers Harries 'ensuring that when we went to Fairacres we had plenty of booze with the evening meal. What the nuns thought of it I am not so sure though latterly when they came to clear up they too would be encouraged to a glass!!' Yet even in the safety of the cell there was a 'holding back'. Lord (George) Carey's view is:

> I have not met anyone who really knows Richard or can be regarded as an intimate friend. Even in our cell he revealed little of his background and never revealed his private emotions, cares and fears. He remains a serious man. Sometimes this serious side gave the impression of detachment and even aloofness. It was my wife, Eileen, who cajoled Richard into giving the wives a greater role with respect to our cell. (The custom was for the women to meet separately at Jo's house.) He simply assumed that the wives would meet up together while the men did serious thinking. This did not please Eileen and some of the others. Then, usually at the end of the meeting we would all gather, men and women, at Jo and Richard's home for lunch prior to our departure. Jo had a wonderful gift of hospitality, and it was always a joy to come to their warm home. She is a very intelligent, attractive woman who has supported Richard's ministry through thick and thin, but unlike Eileen, is not at the heart of it. She has maintained her own independence.

Even less frequently mentioned are the inner springs of Harries' life 'hid with Christ in God'. This is plainly fundamental to an understanding of his life and work. His early collections of contributions to *Prayer for the Day* still have resonance. His selection of readings through the Christian year – *Seasons of the Spirit* (1984) – with (Roman Catholic) George Every and (Orthodox) Kallistos Ware, and *Praying the Eucharist* (2004), are more than aids to praying. They draw people into prayer and encourage them to continue. Harries draws adroitly and evocatively on poets and novelists, saints and sages, who have spoken to him from their felt experience. No one is better at enlarging prayer: 'God wants us to act through the whole of what we are, not just our conscious minds and driving wills.' A host of people express gratitude to Harries for giving them a divine nudge, helping them to use their minds as well as their hearts in praying. Prayer is conversation with God. Only too often churches make it a monologue, and do not provide opportunities for God to get a word in edgeways.

We are still searching for Richard Harries. He has already made a wide and varied range of friends and found acceptance in circles generally antipathetic to priests and bishops. It is among these other people and places where he may be more truly found. In *The Time of my Life* Denis Healey says: 'Politics has never been the whole of my life. Some of my friends complain that I possess the opposite shortcoming from Mrs Thatcher's – I have too much hinterland. My wife and family have always meant more to me than the House of Commons. I once told an interviewer that I did not need the love of the people because I had the love of my wife. He thought it a somewhat chilling remark; I do not find it so. Nothing is more dangerous than the politician who uses politics as a surrogate for an unsatisfactory personal life.' In Harries the word 'politics' can be replaced by 'Church'.

A rippling stream of consciousness from Baroness Julia Neuberger is close to the kernel:

Richard is one of my closest friends – surprisingly, really, as at first I would have said we were very different. He needs desperately to reach warmth, and I think he finds it in some of us Jews he has met, and found something that he does not feel his particular brand of Christianity gives him. He is someone of immense integrity, combined with a great sense of humour. But he finds it hard to be really close to many people. When bad things happen – as they do to all of us – he is completely wonderful to others, but finds it hard to accept comfort himself. One of the things I have learned over the years is that he finds it easier to face things head on. If life is bloody in some way, his faith will let him accept it and deal with it, but human beings need to be able to talk to him without being mealy-mouthed or shilly-shallying.

Recollections: When the AIDS crisis first hit, Richard using humour and the power of common sense, alongside a truly Christian version of acceptance and tolerance, to pour cold water on those who wished to incarcerate or label those who were carrying the HIV virus – I recall hearing him being very strong and firm and very funny about sharing a Communion chalice at King's College all those years ago. And teasing me because I had turned up to speak at that same conference with bags and bags of vegetables for a dinner party that night, which I put in his office. He has always thought I am obsessed by eating vegetables . . . folk memory of scurvy? But he enjoyed the seriousness of the debate combined with the absurdity of my massive shopping. 'How many leeks do you need for ten people?' was the kind of remark . . . Richard at Passover Seder in our house, knowing more Hebrew than many of the Jews present, and able to add in his scholarly knowledge about the Christian links to some of what we read, but being shy about doing it, because it is not 'his' festival . . . Us encouraging him . . . Richard at Jo's party, being uncharacteristically beamish and quiet, enjoying Jo being so fêted, and loved, by us all – not normally very demonstrative to her in public, he was immensely so that day . . . Richard needing to be hugged when he is feeling angry or let down . . . Richard grey round the gills with pain after surgery on his first hip – then telling us to come to lunch as it will distract him. How do you distract someone in great pain? You tell him Jewish jokes. They aren't funny, but he appreciates the effort . . . Richard walking in the Chilterns, carrying a map and refusing to let anyone else see it. He likes to be group leader . . . Richard and Anthony, my husband, vying for who will be toughest on a walk. Jo and I lagging behind. Richard, Jo, Shirley Williams and I walking together . . . Richard, Shirley and Anthony talking politics, Jo and I talking food. Then swapping around, and Richard and I talking politics, and Jo, Shirley and Anthony talking pensions . . . Richard and Jo staying with us in Ireland, and it being a perfect, peaceful, funny time, but also one where we went to see many early Christian monuments we would never otherwise have visited. Learning a lot from them both whilst they stayed. Loving picnicking and pottering with them . . . a perfect time of even-tempered joy.

I think Richard is very emotional, but a bit strangulated in expressing it. I suspect that has more to do with his upbringing than his intellectual temperament. He doesn't throw himself into the passing fashions. But when convinced on an issue, e.g. homosexuality and the need for equal rights for gay men in the Church – he acts and argues bravely and fearlessly, and with great passion. He was partly convinced of this by my daughter Harriet, herself a gay young woman, who once – on a walk – argued him fiercely into a bush about it all! Is Richard self-analytical? Absolutely not. He and I share that. He wants to be known and loved – and not judged. He finds it hard in public life to be truly open – as we all do. But I think he is very open to his real needs. I think he is shy, and has overcome with a formal carapace. Underneath, he is immensely warm, longing to be known more, afraid of expressing pain but sometimes needing to. Adjectives that come to mind – brave, fearless, warm, tough on himself, great integrity, emotionally needier than he thinks he is, extremely clever, agile physically and mentally, versatile in his talents and interests, spiritually very aware.

It is impossible to know what makes Harries 'tick', as they say, without recourse to the rich sources from which he gains strength, explanations and directions – poetry, art and theatre. Spiritually, year by year, the tree of knowledge sheds the season's leaves through which he draws substance; it may need some of its season's outgrowth to be pruned; but the roots which give it anchorage and irrigation are still securely planted in the ground. This being said, there is nothing static about Harries' convictions. But are they really rock-like, or do they coincide with T. S. Eliot's, who, in a discussion with Hugh Sykes Davies about Marxists said, 'They seem so certain of what they believe. My own beliefs are held with a scepticism which I never even hope to get rid of.'

And in an essay on Pascal (1931), the religious thinker whom Eliot found congenial above all others:

For every man who thinks and lives by thought must have his own scepticism, that which stops at the question, that which ends in denial, or that which leads to faith and which is somehow integrated into the faith which transcends it. And Pascal, as the type of one kind of religious believer, which is rightly passionate and ardent, but passionate only through a powerful and regulated intellect, is in the first sections of his unfinished Apology for Christianity facing unflinchingly the demon of doubt which is inseparable from the spirit of belief.

Or again, in a letter to his American friend Paul Elmer More about hell, Eliot retorted:

> To me religion has brought at least the perception of something above morals, and is therefore extremely terrifying; it has brought me not happiness but a sense of something above happiness and therefore more terrifying than ordinary pain and misery; the very dark night and the desert. To me, the phrase 'to be damned for the glory of God' is sense and not paradox; I had far rather walk, as I do, in daily terror of eternity, than feel that this was only a children's game in which all the contestants would get equally worthless prizes in the end.

Reading Harries' voluminous output of writing, there is little resonance of Eliot from this last paragraph. Harries prefers 'happiness' to 'terror'. Yet it is easy to see why Harries places Eliot on a pinnacle. His poetry and prose portray powerful feelings, almost passion. His style is compact, evocative, ironic, paradoxical. His enormous influence rests in his unexpectedness. Those who seek him find he was a revolutionary force because he was a traditionalist. Progressives do not start a new direction; they go faster along the same old grooves. Eliot, the unbeliever turned churchwarden, handled the deepest religious themes without the usual conventional, religious language. It was persistent internal haggling that pushed him to examine more closely the claims of Christianity, especially those doctrines held and embodied in the oddest Church in Christendom, the Church of England.

The contrasts in Harries are to be found in two of his books on art: *A Gallery of Reflections: The Nativity of Christ* (1995) and *The Passion in Art* (2004).

Chapter Thirteen
Seer and Overseer

Christian communities without a spiritual hierarchy lie at the mercy of their spiritual aristocrats. An eminent thinker, gifted leader or outstanding preacher is apt to carry all before him in a tide of unmodulated enthusiasm. This cannot happen easily in an episcopally led and synodically governed Church where most, if not quite all, decisions have to win acceptance from a general body of capable and responsible, but by no means necessarily personally distinguished, men and women, whose minds revolve in a constant plane and like a gyroscopic compass serve to keep the community on a level course. It needs a strong convulsion to make them revise their prejudices, as even St Paul found when he attempted to introduce what the apostles and elders thought were innovations.

Harries already knew that the Church of England has a kind of built-in obsolescence and can be stubborn, even unbudgeable, when confronted with reforms not to the taste of a complacent majority – the lump in the leaven – or of highly motivated organized minorities. Whatever qualities accompanied Harries to Oxford, a trinity of functions were new to him, those of guardian, governor and guide. It was 'governorship' which came least naturally to him.

When Harries became a bishop everything was new to him. He had not even been a member of General Synod. He was not dewy-eyed about institutional religion. The dangers of duplication and unduly centralized administration are clear. Yet for any live Christianity, some institutional form is a necessity in order to preserve for each unit the sense of belonging to a larger whole, to develop that spirit which takes the vision beyond the individual, to the parish, to the diocese, to the world. The dangers of institutionalism are real: but so are the dangers of individualism.

The diocese of Oxford is divided into three archdeaconries – Oxford, Berkshire and Buckinghamshire. Except for the deaneries of Oxford and Cowley, over which Harries had oversight, the Oxford archdeaconry is under the jurisdiction of the Bishop of Dorchester. Berkshire and Buckinghamshire come under the bishops of Reading and Buckingham respectively. Each of these separate areas comprises more parishes than in the dioceses of Birmingham, Bradford, Bristol, Coventry, Guildford, Newcastle, Portsmouth, Ripon and Leeds, or Sheffield, and each has a greater population than Carlisle, Ely, Gloucester, Hereford, St Edmundsbury and Ipswich or Truro dioceses.

The diocesan bishop is the personal symbol of continuity and unity for the

Church and leader in apostolic ministry and the teaching of the faith. The tension between these two dimensions of episcopacy is not easy, either for the individual bishop or for the diocese he serves. Unlike several large dioceses, Oxford had moved from dominant and autocratic leadership. There had been a shift of authority from a single, central figure, a kind of 'solo hero', to a dispersed authority where the key word is collegiality.

From the outset Harries exercised episcopacy in his particular and individualistic way which attracted great praise and satisfaction with sporadic outbursts of dissent and blame. Doctrines (like the imminent end of the world or the resurrection of the flesh) once sanctified by universal or almost universal acceptance, lose their authority when later experience or clearer knowledge deprives them of the wellnigh universal assent they had earlier possessed. Tradition is thus continually being re-fashioned by experience. Some traditional doctrines are abandoned altogether; others become secondary rather than primary, unessential rather than essential. The authority of the Church, if it is true to Christ and the leading of the Spirit, is never static. Harries will be an exemplar of holding and conveying this truth. It is the duty of the Church to drive out heresy, to preserve and proclaim the truth. But, as is well known, the heterodoxy of today is often the orthodoxy of tomorrow. Thought looks after itself when it is free by producing more thinking and fresh investigation. Harries is a careful interpreter of the ever-changing movement of thought and has insights of his own to offer.

Incoming diocesan bishops may be pleased or otherwise with their inherited hierarchy. It can be many years before resignation or death provides the opportunity for making a new appointment. Harries was fortunate. Kenneth Woollcombe had made some good appointments: Peter Walker to Dorchester (translated to Ely), Eric Wild to Reading and Simon Burrows to Buckingham.

Simon Hedley Burrows, aged 45, was appointed to Buckingham in 1974 by Kenneth Woollcombe who told him, 'There's no point in being an area bishop, unless you enjoy it'. He quickly established himself with the clergy and people of his area inculcating a sense of belonging, helped by his generous hospitality, together with his wife, at their house in Great Missenden. His experience in establishing a team ministry at Fareham (Portsmouth) meant he matched necessity with opportunity in forming team and group ministries in Buckinghamshire. Although he was always 'The Bishop' he did not break the first episcopal commandment, 'Thou shalt not take thyself too seriously', taking comfort in Staggers' (St Stephen's House) Law that 'the higher the doctrine of episcopacy, the lower the opinion of the bishops'. He was a priest and pastor mindful of Owen Chadwick's words in a sermon preached at his consecration: 'If you are exceeding busy, over-busy, time is full of jingle-jangle – overwork – hullabaloo – tares everywhere choking seed, you are deaf to momentous words that speak profound in your Soul.' A bishop needs 'to be *still*; to have open ears; to keep close to the source of all the strength that comes to the soul – you cannot bully men into faith, or argue them into faith, or cajole them into faith or even surprise them into faith. They might start to have faith if you have faith – real faith, trust, not just a formula of the lips'. Simon Burrows admitted confusion about the basic philosophy of episcopacy. 'At the moment there are two ideas co-existing uneasily. The first is the traditional concept of the bishop as Father-in-God, which in psychological reality frequently means Mother-in-God. The second is the idea of the bishop as primarily exercising a management role. This produces particular confusion in the context of "the pastoral care of the clergy". What do we actually mean by that phrase?'

In Harries' 19 years as bishop he appointed eight area bishops and eight arch-deacons. We catch the unusual flavour of his personality and the substance of his judgement when monitoring his choice of bishops. The method of appointing them substantially changed during his period of office. He explains:

I can indicate the nature of the present process by contrasting what happened with my first nomination. The then Archbishop of Canterbury, Robert Runcie, wrote me a letter during a General Synod meeting which he passed over to me. This letter strongly recommended a particular person. I arranged to meet this person. We went for a walk together, neither of us being able to indicate why we were meeting, yet both knowing. He was nominated and was an extremely valuable member of the senior staff and area bishop for a number of years before going off to be a diocesan. The present system could not be in starker contrast. In 2003, for example, the two area bishoprics of Reading and Buckingham became vacant. There was an extensive consultation in order to draw up a job description for each of them, which was approved by the Bishop's Council. I encouraged anybody who wanted to, to send me in names and I consulted the Archbishops' Patronage secretary in order to get names from him in the light of the then agreed job descriptions. In the end I had more than 90 names. I had appointed an advisory group which consisted of the chair of the House of Laity, the chair of the House of Clergy and a lay person very experienced in Church appointments, together with each rele-vant archdeacon. The difficult task was short-listing but in the end we focused on four names. There was a round of preliminary one-to-one interviews, with each of the archdeacons and myself. There was then a full interview with the advisory group at which each of the candidates had to make a presentation on how they saw the role of a bishop in relation to one of the two areas, in the light of the job description. The advisory group offered invaluable advice. That said, I would emphasize strongly the importance of this decision being that of the diocesan. It's vital that the diocesan has a team with whom he can work closely and one of the aspects being Bishop of Oxford, for which I am profoundly grateful, is that I've had 18 years of an extremely happy senior staff team, who have had a lot of fun together as well as doing some serious work. That said, it is no less vital that the diocesan bishop plays fair in terms of bal-ancing the different traditions in the Church of England. One of the area bishops has always been an evangelical and of the eight nominations I have made, three have been evangelical and five various shades of Catholic. In view of the increasing strength of the evangelical tradition in the Church of

England at the moment, I would expect that balance to change over the next few decades. I've always sought to nominate the best person for the job and striving to achieve a balance in terms of churchmanship has not, in any way, detracted from that principle.

Omitting for the moment the present bishops of Dorchester, Reading and Buckingham, it is relevant to glance at the first five appointments. The first was Anthony John Russell, aged 44, to Dorchester. He was incumbent of three rural parishes in Warwickshire, director of the Arthur Rank Centre within the National Agricultural Centre, and canon theologian of Coventry Cathedral. He was already the most conspicuous, much published and best informed authority on rural affairs in the Church of England. His family had farmed in Oxfordshire for several generations and were involved in setting up Banbury cattle market. He holds strong opinions on agriculture and the countryside which he expresses with modest forcefulness. That is why he is trusted as an effective spokesman. Unlike faith in urban Britain, in rural areas 'only the Church is capable of knitting together the frayed ends into a fabric beneath which we can all shelter'. In Church affairs he was content to 'call myself conservative with a small "c" – prayer book Catholic is about right.' Russell speaks of Harries' outstanding leadership, clear vision and ability to enthuse and motivate his senior colleagues: 'All this could only be done by somebody who has his spirituality firmly rooted and this can be clearly seen as we join him for the Eucharist before staff meetings.' Russell also points out the strong contribution Harries made to the life of the national Church and adds the interesting reflection that, 'I never heard voices from inside the diocese who saw this as anything other than appropriate for an extremely gifted and able man'.

John Frank Ewan Bone spent 26 years in Buckinghamshire, including 12 as archdeacon. He was 59 in 1989 when, to his complete surprise, Harries invited him to be Bishop of Reading. He was known to be solid and steady though behind his slight physique and quiet demeanour was a great strength of purpose. Reading was not an easy prospect as some clergy looked to a previous era for inspiration, that of Lancashire-born Eric Wild who arrived in Berkshire and proceeded to have a love affair with the royal county, first as archdeacon then as bishop (1972–1982). Patrick Rodger described him as 'a big man, in jovial mood looking like a Friar Tuck and in disapproval pretty formidable. This size, however was apt to disguise a sensitive spirit, that of a man who could feel keenly the joys and sorrows of life and to whom therefore his faith was a deep necessity'. He was a familiar figure throughout the county and ecclesiastically was an arch decentralizer who would not have been happy in Harries' episcopate.

Harries was aware of John Bone's interest in 'social responsibility' issues and special knowledge of education. A more urgent imperative was the need for a bishop with Catholic credentials who would love, care for and enable the clergy who felt neglected. Bone was bespoke for this work. When he retired in 1997, Reading was a happy area aided by his invincible sense of humour. Bishop Bone has these reflections on Harries:

An apparently confident man with a strange lack of self-assurance. I only really got to know him when we began as a staff team to work on a scheme of peer-appraisal. I was partnered with him, and we would work together on various aspects of our professional lives. Although this was intended to help one's personal and professional development, it was interesting how the openness and frankness of the exchanges helped enormously the feeling of collegiality. It was as if a mask had dropped and one was with the real man.

One matter which concerned Richard was that the clergy needed to be loved and cared for by their bishop; it had been neglected. Richard was content to leave all clergy appointments to me; all institutions and licensings; all the confirmations except a handful; the pastoral care and discipline of the clergy. I cannot recall any occasion on which he acted in any way which undermined my position or authority as area bishop. He always upheld the principle that clergy or laity in the archdeaconry should first of all approach their area bishop, and he meticulously referred correspondence addressed directly to him back to me to deal with. On the very rare occasions (I think only once) when he decided to deal pastorally with a priest, he did so only after consulting me, and for the good reason that he had known the man and his wife before he came to the diocese. Big matters of diocesan policy were very often initiated and driven through by Richard. I recall the process of setting out the statement of 'Vision and Priorities' for the diocese. This was his project, and much of it was written by him, and his energy took it through all its consultative stages. It was unusual for him to work in such a detailed way on anything which touched on diocesan administration; with that he appeared to be bored and quite ready to leave to others.

The range of responsibilities of an area bishop stretch far wider than those for a suffragan bishop. There is both temptation and danger that area bishops may be so preoccupied with leading their mini-dioceses that the essential pastoral episcopal ministry ranks lower in their thoughts, plans and diaries.

It is easy to succeed someone who has made a failure of their job. The task of picking up pieces may be wearing. It is also rewarding and applauded. The appointment of a new bishop of Reading in 1997 had none of these advantages, for he would follow John Bone, a priest-pastor wearing a mitre who was diligent, loved and trusted. Harries' choice was imaginative and personable. Edward William Murray – 'Dominic' – Walker, aged 49, knew what was expected of a bishop. No one who had been Mervyn Stockwood of Southwark's domestic chaplain for three years could not know! It was a double-edged experience. Bishops, such as Stockwood, who attract and like courtiers, were at the far end of the episcopal spectrum to Harries. Perhaps there was a tincture of Stockwood in Dominic Walker's one time Alfa Romeo, rather less his known attendances at dog races. But Dominic – a member and one-time superior of the Oratory of the Good Shepherd (OGS) – had his feet firmly on the ground.

As a teenager he had joined the Community of the Glorious Ascension. Serving the weak, the vulnerable, the homeless and the dispossessed was the outer clothing of a rich inner and disciplined spiritual faith. As team rector of Brighton for 11 years, his vicarage was shared with others, at one time with four who all had psychiatric or support needs. He had studied both theology and psychology. He was already used to juggling demands on his time with serenity and good humour. Words of W.W. Wiersbe were used in the parish magazine when he left Brighton: 'What I am is God's gift to me; what I do with it is my gift to Him.' A fellow member of OGS, Lindsay Urwin, Bishop of Horsham, described Dominic as 'a priest of considerable wisdom and stamina, spiritual depth and security in the faith he believes'. Although Anglo-Catholic, Dominic accepted the decision of the Church to ordain women as priests. He was known as the leading authority on exorcism in the Church of England. Was one bishop prescient when writing to him on his appointment to Reading, 'What is it coming to? The House of Bishops needs a resident exorcist?'

Dominic Walker was consecrated on the day of the 1997 General Election. The result was to his satisfaction as he was a lifelong member of the Labour Party and chaired the Brighton and Hove branch of the Christian Socialist Movement. In 2003 he was elected Bishop of Monmouth in succession to Rowan Williams. The bishops of Oxford, Dorchester and Buckingham were at the 'Welcome and Installation' of this servant, shepherd and presbyter whom Reading loved as he had loved them.

Colin James Bennetts was an evangelical, with a curacy at St Aldate's, Oxford; chaplain of the Oxford Pastorate; and for ten years vicar of St Andrew's, Oxford. He is forthright with his conviction that the power of the Gospel is needed to disperse the negativity found in the Church and the spiritual wimpishness of some of its adherents. He is sufficiently bold to believe and assert that 'The Church of Christ (and that's not synonymous with the Church of England) is still the primary agent for the preaching of the Gospel and for the revealing, the uncovering, of God's Kingdom'.

As Harries' choice for Buckingham in 1994, his experience increased to cover such matters as interracial issues in Slough and ecumenical ventures in Milton Keynes. He became a national face when he co-chaired Springboard, the Archbishops' Initiative for Evangelism. It was good that one area had a pastor evangelist as bishop. All too soon Colin Bennetts was installed as Bishop of Coventry on Palm Sunday, 1998, where he informed the congregation, 'During the four years that I was Bishop of Buckingham I found myself licensing or initiating a large number of new parish priests. The advice I often gave to the "receiving" congregation was this: take a good look at the faces of the "sending" congregation, those who had, so to speak, come to say goodbye. If they left the church sad or downcast, then we were probably on to a winner. If, on the other hand, they went out grinning from ear to ear, then it almost certainly wasn't good news.' The contingent from Oxford at the Installation was not bubbling with laughter.

Harries did not have far to look for an inspired appointment for Buckingham in 1998. He had already appointed Michael Arthur Hill as Archdeacon of Berkshire in 1992 and, now 49 years old, Mike (as he was known) Hill was to be an area bishop. Again his qualities were in great contrast to Harries'. Born in the North-West, he would have liked to have been a professional footballer but instead, when he left school, he embarked on a business career where entrepreneurship would bring lots of money. He had no religion when, aged 19, he was 'conned' into going to a Christian party at Scargill House in the Yorkshire Dales. There, two encounters changed his life, one with Christ, the other when he worked at Scargill for a year with Anthea, who became his wife. Motivated by discipleship and people, this evangelical Christian worked in the printing industry until he was 25 when he entered Ridley Hall for ordination training. From the outset of his ministry, arriving in Oxford in 1981, he developed, motivated and inspired other people. Ever aware of less committed and occasional Christians, he asked, 'What is it about the Christian story that we've made irrelevant, uncompelling and marginal?' His outward-looking and enthusiastic vitality for the Gospel led to seeking ways of *Reaching the Unchurched* (the title of his book) which opens with the sentence: 'It's not the Church of God which has a mission, it's the God of mission who has a Church.' From the dead hand of maintenance to the living reality of mission is the thought that impels his episcopate.

Peter Judd, a former Berkshire priest and Provost of Chelmsford, preached at Hill's consecration, in Southwark Cathedral on the Feast of St Joseph of Nazareth, 1988. He told of attending a circus at the Royal Albert Hall when a young boy. The circus had been composed of clowns, jugglers and acrobats – no animals – and had opened with the clowns skilfully changing places with the front row of the audience, leaving them stranded in the arena. The 'traditional' idea of a circus had been transformed by modern dance, classical ballet, gymnastics accompanied by a variety of music – jazz, popular, ethnic. The costumes were amazing and the whole experience was stunning. 'Clearly they had reinvented the circus by going back to its roots and building on the essential, whilst discarding what was no longer appropriate . . . at the same time they had plugged into contemporary culture – in music and presentation – to produce something deeply traditional and vibrantly modern . . .' Peter Judd likened this experience to the ideas in Mike Hill's book where 'he talks about digging out the rubble that gets in the way of the task of mission. And he talks about Churches which understand the need to engage with our culture including the culture of the young. The alternative is to choose to live in a world of our own.'

For two mitred views on the areas and on Harries I turn to two former area bishops. First, Colin Bennetts:

When I returned to the Oxford diocese in 1971, I had just done a four-year stint as canon residentiary and director of ordinands in the Chester diocese. The contrast in the ethos of the two dioceses was considerable. Chester was considerably more conservative, both theologically and culturally, and so in a number of respects it felt good to be able to breathe an atmosphere that was more relaxed and less defensive. This is no doubt due, in part, to the presence of the university right at the heart of the diocese, but one should not underestimate the freedom of spirit that Richard himself exhibits and therefore encourages in others, not least his close colleagues. Many people refer to him as 'laid back'. This is undoubtedly true but I believe it also demonstrates a characteristic of Richard's that I find particularly refreshing, namely his willingness to trust those whom he works with simply to get on with the job. Let me illustrate. At the end of my first year in Buckingham I asked Richard for some feedback on my ministry. He was genuinely perplexed by the request and saw little point in doing anything like a formal review. This was typical of his general attitude which assumed that things were going well unless I chose to tell him that they were not, in which case he was more than ready to listen and advise . . . There was a general acceptance, indeed a willing acceptance, that his gifts were best used on the national level both through his writings and broadcasting as well as his increasing involvement in the House of Lords . . . One practical drawback to this rather disconnected style of working was that we were frequently left in ignorance about Richard's activities. It was not at all unusual for the local press to phone up asking me for a comment on one of his recent pronouncements, only for me to ask what exactly he had been saying.

So far as Richard the person is concerned, it is slightly more difficult. In one sense he is a very private person. Private he may be, but he is undoubtedly a man of many passions. These manifest themselves in private conversations as well as in his more public communications. In particular I would highlight his commitment to social justice and his lifelong defence of the Christian tradition of the Just War. For those who get close to him Richard is great fun to be with. He has a ready sense of humour which is not always appreciated by those who do not know him well, some of whom find him aloof and non-communicative. The truth is that he has little in the way of small talk, preferring intellectual rather than personal interactions.

Second, Dominic Walker:

The invitation to consider being Bishop of Reading came out of the blue. I had met Richard only once before, but he had met with a small group to consider names and I received a 'phone call from his chaplain asking me to meet up with him. When we met it was clear that he had an overall view of the diocese, but not a detailed knowledge of the areas and that the area bishops were given a free hand. This proved to be the case. My immediate impression was to see the variety of people who formed the senior staff, who were all very able but also different and using their gifts and insights. Richard seemed to be good at picking his team and using their gifts, and whilst in theory he knew the importance of team building, it didn't really happen! From time to time, he would say that we needed to do some 'peer reviews' but during my time it didn't happen. When however, it was decided to put all the clergy through leadership training, which began with a 360-degree appraisal, the senior staff went first. He was friendly towards us, but his style was laid back. He didn't 'manage' us so we never knew if we were doing a good or a bad job, although occasionally we would hear of complimentary comments he had made to others about us. The team-building happened through trust and friendship, and the annual residential staff meeting which included an energetic walk with Richard in his walking boots striding ahead. On reflection it was an effective and enjoyable team even if the modern models of line management, targets, benchmarks and cascading were missing. Richard invited me to lunch after I had been in post a few months to ask how things were going. After that he just let me get on with it and never interfered or tried to stop any personal initiatives. The real partnership was between the area bishop and his archdeacon. I suspect that like many bishops, Richard prefers the old way of doing things . . .

He gave us areas of diocesan responsibility. I chaired the Liturgical Committee and the Ordained Local Ministry group and forged the link with the diocese of Vaxjo in Sweden. At meetings, Richard would drive the agenda and get through business. He has a low boredom-threshold and we soon learned to know when he was getting bored either with the whole meeting or with particular speakers. His good brain enabled him to chair meetings with efficiency and good humour (unless he was bored). And yet I have never known him to be intellectually arrogant. He is more interested in outcomes than process, so personal interviews were scheduled for 30 minutes (which in effect is 20 minutes after coffee, introductions and farewells) because he is more focused in dealing with what the person wants and how to respond, than he is in giving them time to feel heard, valued and worthy of a bishop's time. This means that some people see Richard as somewhat aloof and cool and even lacking pastoral care, but I think that is to misjudge him and was certainly not my own personal experience of him.

What does this reveal about Anglican Harries? Most evidently he desires to uphold the comprehensiveness of the Church of England. During his time as bishop, the broad constraints and balances lamentably changed, to the Church's detriment. Until recent times, the Church housed three denominations under one roof, each bringing riches to the building. Evangelicals, once known as 'Low Church', brought into Anglicanism a strongly positive wave of enthusiasm for the Gospel, tinged with Lutheran pietism. They kept a burning love for the conversion of souls and for the winning of the world for Christ. The Anglo-Catholic, Tractarian or 'High Church' movement contributed a revived sacramentalism, a sense of liturgy, and an emphasis on personal discipline of life on the lines of strict churchmanship. The modernist, liberal or broad Church movement was as much intellectual as religious, sitting loose both to dogma and to ecclesiasticism. Modern thought was brought into the range of the Church's sight in order that the intellect could be used in the presentation of Christian faith.

The evangelical Archdeacon of Berkshire, Norman Russell, notes convincingly that, 'Liberal bishops tend to be divided between those who are genuinely inclusive of all traditions across the spectrum and those whose liberalism is largely expressed in tending to appoint those who are clones of themselves. Bishop Richard has always been a person of wide sympathies and generosity of spirit, and although they would not always agree with his views, I think it would be fair to say that almost everyone across the spectrum from Reform to Forward in Faith has appreciated his willingness to allow them space within the diocese.'

A former Dean of Westminster, Michael Mayne, counselled two men on the day of their consecration as bishops in 1979, with words which should reverberate in Oxfordshire, Berkshire and Buckinghamshire:

If you forget you are first and foremost a seer and an overseer, that is to say a contemplative, you will be tempted to justify your existence by working yourself to death. And that you have no right to do. As Father Herbert Kelly, founder of Kelham, used to say: 'I wish the clergy would do ten times less and think ten times more. What we want of the prophet is not work, but vision, sight and prayer.' More than anything else it is that serenity, that space at the heart of you, that will clear your vision and allow you to be an effective pastor to the many who look to you as a reconciler and interpreter: one who points men to Jesus as their true centre and to the Spirit of God active in their midst. And finally, lest the thought of the gravity of your office overwhelms you, I beg you to retain the gift of laughter. To sit light to yourself: to take neither yourself nor your office with a seriousness it does not deserve . . . to care passionately that we sing the Lord's song in a strange land; to care passionately for people and for the Kingdom; but still to be able to laugh at yourself with that laughter which is healing and redemptive, for it means viewing yourself with a sort of loving forgiveness which is an echo of God's loving forgiveness of you.

Chapter Fourteen
The Success of Failure

This chapter delineates, measures and considers the consequences of the success of a failure. Where to start this particular story?

Following the Sharpeville massacre on 21 March 1960 there were financial consequences for South Africa. One was the economy. The withdrawal of foreign investment produced an economic crisis and a slump that were not easily overcome. But the labyrinth of economic ties to other countries, not least Britain, was neither penetrated nor spoiled. Within South Africa the Government acted swiftly, readily gaining the cooperation of South African business leaders and, in view of the crisis, stabilized the situation with remarkable speed. The draining away of foreign investment was gradually reversed. The financial lungs of capitalism recovered to full breathing health and the propensity for making money resumed.

Throughout the Christian centuries thought has been directed to responsibility in the sphere of finance. A Church has its moral and religious imperatives which should be paramount. How is it able to keep its spiritual and ethical concerns untainted by the mundane and practical elements of the counting house? Does the creation of wealth add to the Church's treasure? The ministry of the clergy of the Church of England – the most subsidized and mollycoddled in the Anglican Communion – would be demoralized and decimated without the Church Commissioners for England!

The Church Commissioners was formed in 1948 by joining together two charitable bodies: Queen Anne's Bounty, established in 1704 to improve clergy incomes and housing in areas of need, and the Ecclesiastical Commissioners, who in 1840 were empowered by Parliament to redistribute some of the Church's historic resources. This newly created body had the merits and blemishes of a quasi-government department. The Commissioners' main responsibilities are:

To obtain the best possible long-term return from a diversified investment portfolio in order
  – to meet our pension commitments;
  – to provide the maximum sustainable funding for our other purposes such as support for the work of bishops, cathedral and parish ministry.
In doing so, to pay particular regard to making 'additional provision for the cure of souls in parishes where such assistance is most required'.
To administer the legal framework for pastoral reorganization and settling the future of redundant churches.

Managing assets requires financial dexterity and refined judgement in a notoriously fluid and unpredictable market. The Church Commissioners are, like a department of State, run by senior civil servants with ministerial authority. They are part of the centralizing and bureaucratic postwar Church, which the advent of synodical government has done little to decrease or allay. The opinion has grown, perhaps mistakenly, that there are two Churches of England, one organizational, anonymous and administrative, the other evangelistic, personal and spiritual.

Although the Commissioners have precise aims and terms of reference, they function behind closed doors similar to any other financial institution. Greater transparency in their affairs is a forlorn hope. Their annual reports are not dissimilar to those of public companies, self-congratulatory if possible, always self-justified.

The three principal officers of the Commissioners are the First, Second and Third Church Estates Commissioners. The First is in effect the full-time chief executive; the Second is a Member of the House of Commons: both are appointed by the Queen; the Third is appointed by the Archbishop of Canterbury. The Church is one of the biggest property- and landowners in the country. The portfolio of the Commissioners is likewise large and the responsibilities of the First Church Estates Commissioner no less enormous. The person holding this position from 1969 was Sir Ronald Harris, a rector's son, educated at Harrow and Trinity College, Oxford, who came up through the Treasury. At the time of his appointment, Britain had a billion pounds invested in the Republic of South Africa and the Church of England had an investment in this. Under his guidance the Commissioners purported not to invest in companies operating wholly or mainly in South Africa, but according to Sir Ronald:

1. they accept that an investment of their size cannot but hold investments entailing some degree of involvement, direct or indirect, in South Africa, and where they hold such investments, they do what they can to promote enlightened policies by the companies concerned;
2. they use their influence to prevent direct and unconditional lending to the South African Government by companies in which they hold an investment.

He referred to this in an unpublished document 'South Africa: A Personal Assessment' following a sabbatical journey to South Africa in January/February 1978 where he met people of all races. As he was also a director of the insurance company 'General Accident' he had easy access to bankers and leaders of industry.

In the English Churches, there were intermittent pleadings for the withdrawal of investments, or at least against new ones. The grounds for opposing such pleas encompassed a spectrum of opinion: that it was the non-whites who would suffer first and most heavily; that stable and indeed increasing foreign investment was essential to the growth of the economy; and that this alone would progressively improve the lot of the non-whites and increase the opportunities for them to rise to positions of greater responsibility and influence in industry and commerce and help prepare them for exercising political power in due time. Recent history attests that was an illusion seen through rose-coloured spectacles.

Whilst liberal Western democracies wished to see the end of a demonstrably illiberal and unjust system of apartheid, the way to achieve this was unclear. Violent confrontation from outside may simply drive Afrikanerdom back into a defensive 'laager'; and outside intervention on the side of the oppressed may result in massive African casualties in loss of work and in the mortuaries.

Sir Ronald Harris pointed 'to a need not for "heroic" attitudes or actions on the part of South Africa's well-wishers from outside, but rather for intelligent and caring concern and active support for any practical measures, whether by industry and commerce, by the Churches, or by any other form of organization, which are aimed at loosening the shackles of apartheid and ameliorating its effects in prac-tice'. This smooth diplomatic language was a palliative to avoid starker realities.

In the Commissioners' annual report for 1972, a list of proscribed investments was included – 'directly in companies operating wholly or mainly in certain trades – armaments, gambling, breweries and distilleries, tobacco, newspapers, publishing and broadcasting, and theatre and films – or in Southern Africa'. In his book *Number One Millbank* (1997) Terry Lovell noted:

> The reference to South Africa had a particular significance. It was designed to ease the concerns of those who were becoming increasingly alarmed by a growing international human rights problem – the South African white minority government's policy of apartheid which for many years had permit-ted social and economic discrimination against and exploitation of millions of black workers.

There was one of those rare moments at General Synod in November 1973 when members rose, and the chamber reverberated with applause. Fr Hugh Bishop, superior of the Community of the Resurrection, Mirfield, always capable of raising the emotional temperature of any gathering, made a plea that Synod should recog-nize the Christian Institute of South Africa and its director, Dr Beyers Naudé, shortly to be put on trial for refusing to testify before a Government commission. It was in the context of a debate initiated by the Revd Paul Oestreicher, a quiet, calm but no less persuasive advocate of his cause, who described South Africa as 'a nation in agony despite a deceptive façade'.

The Church of England was not allowed to sideline this issue or omit it from synodical discussion. A British Council of Churches report – 'Political Change in South Africa: Britain's Responsibility' – in 1979 recommended disengagement and investment sanctions against South Africa, as the way of opposing, and eventually defeating, apartheid. When the General Synod debated the report in November 1979 it encouraged 'widespread consideration . . . for economic disengagement in support of efforts to secure a more just society in South Africa'.

In July 1980 a working paper – 'The Ethical Use of Investment Funds' – from the Church of England's Board of Social Responsibility, was published. The

Commissioners could not use their funds 'purely to promote socially desirable ends if this conflicts with their prime duty', but admitted that lists of banned investment categories were of limited usefulness. The interests of multinational companies were often difficult to trace and onerous to attempt to change.

In July 1982 the General Synod called for the progressive disengagement of all investments in South Africa. The commercial secrecy moved no further than 'constructive engagement'. Under Sir Ronald Harris' regime the Commissioners did not wear earplugs and to an extent, if with a cautious tread, moved in recognizing the rising clamour of critical voices. No more than that. General Synod repeatedly called on the Commissioners to disinvest from companies with a stake in the South African economy, but they consistently replied that they were only able to disinvest from companies whose main business was there.

By the mid-1980s dispassionate observers contended that financial pressure was one of the keys being used to dislodge some of the foundations of the bank vaults which may lead to the end of apartheid. In particular the refusal of the City Bank in New York and others to reschedule South Africa's loans, was a turning point.

Harries was not part of that body of protesting agitators who unreasonably overlooked the fact that the Commissioners had a legal duty to maximize their profits and could not afford only to invest in a smaller section of the market. A general tightening of resolve came after 1983 when Sir Douglas Lovelock succeeded Sir Ronald Harris as First Church Estates Commissioner. Lovelock was a government civil servant for 34 years and he surfaced at No. 1 Millbank (the Commissioners' headquarters) as supremely self-confident, highly capable and overbearing. Unlike his predecessor he was not over-concerned with hostile criticisms, and the bleatings of General Synod underwhelmed him. However, the vocal opposition to South African investments was beginning to be exercised in some dioceses; for example, Oxford was politically aware before Harries became bishop in 1987. It was monitoring its own financial portfolio and withdrew its investments from the Church of England Central Board of Finance because of the Board's failure to meet criteria over South Africa.

Throughout his ministry Harries' own position was plain and never varied:

> Christians in Great Britain are almost 100 per cent united in their detestation of apartheid. But how can we bring it to an end? One way would be to help ship guns and ammunition to those who are engaged in the armed struggle. This is not a path that all Christians feel they can support. There is of course always the power of loving persuasion. However, the White regime in South Africa has ignored all calls for it to change its way for 70 years now. The brutal question that history teaches us, is that no ruling elite ever willingly shares power with other groups. The white regime in South Africa is yet another example of this sad reluctance. Is there no course of action open to us other than armed struggle or talk?

A miscellany of movements, organizations, reports and debates kept South Africa in the news. *The Future of South Africa* (1965); *Facing the Facts* (1972); *Political Change in South Africa: Britain's Responsibility* (1979); *The Ethical Use of Investment Funds* (1980) were among the publications flowing from the Church of England and the British Council of Churches. Each made its trumpeted entrance, achieved a few headlines in the Church press, seldom in the secular media, bowed and left the stage. More compelling, because more permanent with persistent pressure, was a flurry of organizations, four of which Harries was involved with directly or indirectly.

Christian Concern for Southern Africa, supported by most of the major Christian denominations in Britain, was primarily concerned to share information, publishing regular news-sheets and penetrating analyses. Its executive secretary, the Revd R. Elliott Kendall, was also a member of the management committee of the Ethical Investment Research and Information Service (EIRIS), established in 1983 to provide information to help concerned investors apply positive or negative ethical and social criteria to investment, and to promote a wider understanding on corporate responsibility issues.

The Christian Ethical Investment Group (CEIG) was founded as a voluntary pressure group in 1988 to promote a stronger ethical investment policy in the Church of England – 'being an ethical investor means using your money not only for profit but also for improving the world we live in'. Initially its patrons were the Bishops of Bath and Wells, James Thompson; Coventry, Simon Barrington-Ward; Liverpool, David Sheppard; Manchester, Stanley Booth-Clibborn; Oxford, Richard Harries; Ripon, David Young; and Croydon, Wilfrid Wood. The chairman was the Archdeacon of Bedford, Michael Bourke, and the secretary was the Revd Bill Whiffen, a priest in the Oxford diocese and member of the General Synod.

The Ecumenical Council for Corporate Responsibility (ECCR) was set up in 1989 to study and research the corporate responsibility of the Church's investments and the companies in which those investments were held with special reference to transnational corporations. In addition there was a South African Group in General Synod and a British/South African Bishops Link Group in which Harries was prominent.

In a factual memorandum on South Africa (January 1986) the Commissioners put forward four main arguments as to why they continued to ignore the July 1982 General Synod resolution calling for progressive disengagement from the economy of South Africa:

1. That the Commissioners' investments in companies operating in South Africa are 'very small'.
2. The disinvestment in companies operating in South Africa 'would risk seriously damaging the long-term interests of our beneficiaries'.
3. That the Commissioners 'seek to ensure that these companies follow enlightened employment and social policies in South Africa' and
4. That the Commissioners cannot legally disinvest in companies

operating in South Africa as 'financial considerations must be a major factor in all investment matters and this has been underlined by a recent legal ruling on the responsibilities of Trustees and the management of charitable funds'.

For a debate at General Synod in York, July 1986, Frank Field MP issued a counter-brief for members of Synod. He commissioned EIRIS to undertake a special analysis for the debate. Their main conclusions shattered much of the Commissioners' argument for involvement in South Africa, chiefly concluding:

1. That the Commissioners' involvement in the South African economy is far larger than their public statements suggest.
2. The EIRIS brief also casts doubt on the Commissioners' claim that legally they are unable to cease holding shares in companies operating in South Africa and that it is impossible for them to construct a portfolio without any South African involvement. This is an argument which the Commissioners ought to find difficult to sustain . . . What is their legal defence for excluding investment in companies with major interests in armaments, gambling, brewing and distilleries, tobacco and newspapers when we are told – in connection with South Africa – that financial considerations must be 'the major consideration'?

Frenetic discussion and argument at this level may cloud the issue. More critical is to ask how far were the vast number of Church of England pew-dwellers concerned and convinced by frequent debates at General Synod or in their dioceses on the subject of South Africa? How far were the contents of the avalanche of reports digested? How far were consciences deeply troubled over white South African rule and the plight of the black majority in that country? They prayed for the ending of apartheid but did their minds connect when it came to the means of doing so? Should the Commissioners give due consideration to the wants and circumstances of the parishes from which their rental income is derived?

Harries attended a private meeting in July 1985 at Church House, Westminster, prompted by the Bishop of Manchester, Stanley Booth-Clibborn. Others present included the dean of St Paul's Cathedral, Alan Webster – himself a Board member of the Commissioners; Bill Whiffen; the Revd Peter Wheatley, vicar of St James West Hampstead, chair of Christian Concern for Southern Africa, a General Synod member, member of the Board for Social Responsibility International Affairs Committee, and Harries' former curate; and Peter Webster, executive secretary of EIRIS, who had prepared papers for the gathering. They recognized that the Commissioners were dab hands at protracting conversations. Whatever irritation was felt they responded to all queries with apparent patience and thoroughness. They had all the attributes of *Yes Minister*. But their critics knew they were unlikely to effect changes without outside propulsion. If Harries was convinced of the cause he was even-minded in his approach. If there was no substantial investment in South

Africa, could it be reasonably argued that any change would be merely cosmetic? A cool appraisal of the position came from the Archbishop of York, John Habgood: 'If an alternative analysis can be made to stand up then this may convince some of those who, like myself, do not at the moment believe that any further disinvestment will make much sense.'

Was it unrealistic to ask the Commissioners to shift their portfolio by over £70 million? But could they make a significant gesture to have a moral effect in this direction by selectively disinvesting? Yet for all the noise that was made, the clergy of the Church of England needed to be asked squarely whether they would be prepared to face a reduction of their income and their pension should the Commissioners move their investments from South Africa. At the July 1986 Synod a member of the Commissioners' staff was reported as mischievously and untruthfully spreading a story that there would be an alleged cut of £2,000 a year to each clergyman's salary if the policy of disinvestment proceeded. Not so many takers now!

Dean Webster pressed Lovelock on the legal questions, 'suggesting that we would be acting in some way against the law if we divested still further' (Letter, 8 September 1986). The Commissioners relied on the judgment in the case of the Miners' Pension Fund Cowen v Scargill (1985. Ch 270) in which Sir Robert Megarry, presiding, said:

> In considering what investments to make trustees must put on one side their own personal interests and views. Trustees may have strongly held social or political views. They may be firmly opposed to any investment in South Africa or other countries, or they may object to any form of investment in companies concerned with alcohol, tobacco, armaments or many other things. In the conduct of their own affairs, of course, they are free to abstain from making any such investments. Yet under a trust, if investments of this type would be more beneficial to the beneficiaries than other investments, the trustees must not refrain from making the investments by reasons of the views that they hold.

Lovelock's response to Webster (Letter, 18 September 1986):

> Could anything be clearer than that? Though myself no lawyer, it seems to me that the law is here discharging one of its historic and most important roles, that is to say protecting the position of those unable to speak for themselves. The return on the capital entrusted to the Commissioners will be used to pay pensions to clergy not yet retired; widows not yet widowed; and dependents not yet orphaned. These people may be in receipt of payments for very long periods ahead and their position has to be protected on this long-term basis.

In October 1986, Christian Concern for Southern Africa instructed Andrew Phillips, senior partner of the solicitors Bates, Wells and Braithwaite, to advise on the impact of charity law on the investment policy of the Commissioners with regard to South Africa. The advice which came was that trustees cannot go against the charitable purposes of which they are guardians. A religious charity cannot take the view that the 'end justifies the means' and has to ask whether an investment is wholly consistent with the Christian purposes for which the charity exists. Investment is not a neutral, but a positive, act and will be seen as lending approval to the company invested in. A charity which exists for the cure of Christian souls should not lend support to anything inconsistent with that purpose.

Over the succeeding months the difference of views and interpretation proceeded apace in private and in public. In November 1986, Andrew Phillips, Douglas Lovelock and Frank Field appeared in a BBC broadcast. It was clear that some of the Commissioners wanted to be able to shelter or hide behind legal inhibitions. The spectacle of the Church militant here on earth seeking excuses for not applying Christian precepts and insights to the whole of its life and actions was not an edifying sight.

In March 1987, Alan Webster wrote a paper 'Ethics of Investing in South Africa Today' which he submitted to the Commissioners for consideration. He was blunt about the way forward:

> The inaction in regard to investment and apartheid, which has obtained for many years, should speedily be brought to an end. The main purpose of the Christian faith, in terms of the Kingdom of God, is to extend through love, the freedom, justice and peace of mankind, or in a biblical word 'righteousness'. It is inconceivable that, where those aims are being grossly denied or defeated, Church investment should cooperate with the oppression to secure income. Every possible step should be taken to cease such Church involvement. It is idle to argue that absolute separation of funds from South Africa is illegal and impracticable. Moral responsibility consists of doing what is possible, and considerable disinvestment, done publicly, is possible and called for without further delay.

At the board of governors' meeting on 26 March 1987 there were clear and stark divisions. There were those who thought that the Megarry argument should be left to rust in favour of a polished, amoral investment policy. Less time should be spent in qualifying and evading the issue of disinvestment and more thrust be put into finding and isolating a few specific companies whose shares could be sold as a signal of intent to South Africa. On the other hand, individual members of the board spoke strongly against disinvesting – 'Stick to the Law' was the bunker in which they hid. 'Use discretion skilfully' was countered by 'the law limits our discretion', which was itself countered by 'in Church matters, we ought to consider the Gospel. We are not simply bound by the law'. The outcome was, predictably, no change.

In the hope that the disagreement could be resolved without resort to litigation, a meeting was arranged on 5 May 1987 between the Commissioners (Douglas Lovelock; James Shelley, secretary to the Commissioners; Lord Churchill, the Central Board of Finance's investment manager; Wills, their official solicitor) and Alan

Webster; Andrew Phillips; Bill Whiffen and Michael O'Connor, vicar of Rainham, Rochester, who was concerned with the issue of investment in South Africa and also a member of the standing committee of General Synod. By this time the Commissioners had received the response of their Counsel, Owen Swingland QC, also a Church Commissioner from 1982–1990. The result of the meeting was Lovelock's determination to advise his fellow Commissioners against seeking the guidance of the court as to the correct construction to be put upon their statutory functions.

From mid-1987 the focus changed. A small group met in July to consider bringing a declaratory summons against the Commissioners if sufficient funding could be found. Harries preferred that they should concentrate on efforts to persuade the Commissioners to disinvest from Shell, where their holding was £24.7 million.

On 5 November 1987 representatives of Christian Concern for Southern Africa met with the Commissioners to consider the EIRIS report 'Ethical Investment Dilemmas: the Church of England as a Case Study'. Despite an open and friendly atmosphere, and mutual recognition of their Christian responsibilities, there was a continuing complete impasse on two fundamental issues: what are the objects of the Commissioners and what are the constraints on their powers of investment?

Harries continued to be actively in touch with Lovelock, the Central Board of Finance and other bishops. In September 1988 the newly formed Christian Ethical Investment Group moved to centre stage. In addition a number of legal opinions was obtained about the exact nature of the Commissioners' responsibilities. One by Timothy Lloyd QC (28 July 1988), an expert in charity law, reaffirmed that the paramount duty of the Commissioners was not simply to maximize income to pay the clergy: 'They can and should also bear in mind . . . that the support of the clergy is only a means to the higher end of the promotion of the Christian faith, through the Anglican Church, and is only one (albeit the major one) of the means by which they are permitted to achieve that end.' This was in contrast to the legal opinion of Owen Swingland QC (2 February 1987) that the sole purpose of the Commissioners is the financial support of the clergy. Responding to Timothy Lloyd's opinion, Owen Swingland said (20 October 1988), in relation to his earlier opinion supported by the Commissioners: 'I do not think that Mr Lloyd differs very much from what I there say', but then goes on to say, 'I have emphasized that the duty of the Commissioners is to invest their funds for the benefit of the clergy.'

This advice seemed to Harries to be self-contradictory and therefore incoherent. In a paper on 'Bishops as Church Commissioners' (January 1989) he contended:

First, there is a very clear difference, which is fundamental, between the traditional picture of the Church Commissioners and the opinion of Timothy Lloyd QC. Secondly, the Commissioners do already, quite rightly, take into account moral considerations in their investment policy. They do not, for example, invest in tobacco, alcohol or arms. So although they invest for the benefit of the clergy they do not do this simply for the highest possible return. In short, the policy of the Commissioners on this matter does seem extremely confused.

The actual position in relation to investments is that the Commissioners say that they have sold their shares in companies that have more than ten per cent of their business in South Africa. The point is, however, that even ten per cent or less of the business of a major international company like Shell or ICI in South Africa is a very substantial stake. According to recent figures the Commissioners have £90 million invested in eight major companies with 70,000 employees in South Africa. This is a clear denial of what the House of Bishops in Synod voted for.

There are, then, three points. First, a major matter of fact and principle. As bishops we do have power to ensure that the Commissioners follow policies in accord with our recommendations. Secondly, the present position of the Church Commissioners on the relations of morality and investment is confused. Thirdly, the fact that the Commissioners still have and are seen to have a substantial stake in the economy of South Africa. Recently, bishops of the Church of the Province of South Africa have called unanimously for sanctions and economic pressure of all kinds.

Harries never veered from his conviction that clarity and action were needed and were unlikely to be achieved except through a legal declaration. During 1989 he was beginning to be an isolated episcopal voice. Even sympathetic bishops were wavering in their support for action in the courts, notably, Stanley Booth-Clibborn and David Sheppard. Others like the Bishop of Worcester, Philip Goodrich, preferred to exercise influence through the Commissioners, and Simon Barrington-Ward, within the House of Bishops. David Sheppard consulted the small informal group of urban bishops but they were unenthusiastic. When Harries reaffirmed his readiness to go ahead with a case, the bishops of Manchester and Liverpool said they were not prepared to be joint plaintiffs. There developed an extraordinary 'doctrine of unripe time'.

Harries and CEIG knew that there would be significant expense in bringing and defending court proceedings. They were advised that resolution of the legal matters could be dealt with without the need for oral testimony. The award of costs is in the discretion of the judge, and in these particular proceedings it was possible that the court would feel that it was equitable that costs should be borne out of the assets of the Church Commissioners, given the issues involved and absence of any self-interest on the part of those bringing the proceedings. Harries wrote to Lovelock asking if the Commissioners would agree to bearing the costs of the proceedings. As a lesser consideration, but still of considerable importance, the Commissioners could agree not to seek costs against those bringing the proceedings in the event that the costs were awarded against the latter.

Forty-five members attended a CEIG meeting chaired by the Bishop of Manchester on 21 February 1990. A decision was taken that a case should be brought with the co-plaintiffs – Harries, Michael Bourke, Archdeacon of Bedford and William Whiffen. Harries said that guarantees for £25,000 were needed before proceedings could commence.

On 6 March Harries wrote to his fellow Commissioners advising them of the position and was still hoping that an agreement over costs could be reached, although intimating that other guarantees would be necessary. On 26 March there was a press conference. In May the Commissioners issued a press release, having decided not to meet the legal costs of Harries and CEIG. The Commissioners' decision was endorsed unanimously by the board of governors. In a press release they said, 'The inevitable result if the bishop achieved his objective would be a reduction in the income available to meet the commitments placed upon them by statute,' and ended, 'As he (Harries) already knows we should welcome a full discussion with the bishop and his colleagues at any time.' Such a statement was for public consumption alone, the bleating of an injured party. It was as insincere as it was absurd.

Harries' involvement had begun when he was dean of King's. Reflecting on this tortuous journey he muses: 'A number of discussions have taken place over the years between myself, wearing various hats, and Sir Douglas Lovelock, wearing various hats. Sir Douglas stayed in my house last year (1989) for 24 hours, during which time we discussed various aspects of the Church Commissioners' investment policy. Together with members of the Oxford Diocesan Board of Finance, I had a meeting at the Commissioners' with Sir Douglas in relation to Central Board of Finance funds, but on the same issue. The Bishop of Manchester, one of a number of bishops who are patrons of the CEIG, discussed various aspects of the matter with the Assets Committee. I have a very full correspondence with Sir Douglas, in which he has always attempted to meet the points I made in some detail. I have had two meetings with John Lyttle (the Archbishop of Canterbury's secretary for public affairs) at Lambeth Palace, and one with the Archbishop of Canterbury specifically on this issue in order to fully appraise him of what was going on and in order to ensure that he is not embarrassed. In the light of the above, I was astounded to read in the minutes of the board of governors for 17 May that "the Board thought it a pity that the First Commissioner's invitations to discuss the concerns of the Christian Ethical Investment Group had not been taken up"'.

Archbishop Robert Runcie had pressure both from the Commissioners and his own advisers. In *Number One Millbank*, Terry Lovell refers to Harries believing he was the victim of a 'dirty tricks' campaign at Millbank , particularly over the costs: 'Douglas Lovelock wanted to turn public opinion against me by the idea that I was really wasting the Church's money on something which could have been resolved in another way.'

There was another 'dirty trick' which Harries claimed. He also received a letter from Dr Robert Runcie asking him to call off his legal action. The Archbishop was in 'a difficult position as chairman of the Church Commissioners . . . and pressure was put on him to write me an official letter asking me to withdraw, which, of course, he had to do in his official capacity as chairman.' But Runcie, 'a good friend then and now . . . rang me up to say that it was coming'. He claimed: 'The pressure to write the letter was put to Runcie by Sir Douglas Lovelock', adding that it was leaked to the media before he had received it. It was all part of 'a very carefully orchestrated campaign to prejudice Church opinion against me and the action'.

For Harries this was one of those occasions where it was better to grapple with the principles involved, rather than pragmatically shuffling round them, which is often the wiser and more comfortable course. It is likely that the archbishop did not share Harries' view that this was a real and vital issue. It seems that the notorious remarks of Canon Gareth Bennett in the Preface to *Crockford's Clerical Directory 1987–88* are only too accurate: '(Runcie) has the disadvantage of the intelligent pragmatist: the desire to put off all questions until someone else makes a decision. One recalls the lapidary phrase of Mr Frank Field that the archbishop is usually to be found nailing his colours to the fence. All this makes Dr Runcie peculiarly vulnerable to pressure groups.'

By July 1990, £23,000 (which increased to £30,000) had been received in guarantees and donations to enable the court case to go ahead. Unlikely guarantors surfaced and expected donors began to make excuse. Thus Harries became CH.1990.H No 6450 in The High Court of Justice Chancery Division:

Plaintiffs
(1) The Right Revd Richard Douglas Harries, Lord Bishop of Oxford
(2) The Venerable Michael Bourke, Archdeacon of Bedford
(3) The Reverend William Whiffen
Defendants
(1) The Church Commissioners for England
(2) Her Majesty's Attorney-General

At the end of 1990 the Church Commissioners' holdings of land were valued at about £1.7 billion, their mortgages and loans at about £165 million, and their stock exchange investments at about £780 million. In 1990 these items yielded altogether an investment income of £164 million. The Commissioners' income also included some £66 million derived principally from parish and diocesan contributions to clergy stipends. Their total income in 1990 was £230 million, 85 per cent of which provided almost one-half of the costs of the stipends of the Church of England clergy, much of their housing costs and almost all their pension costs.

The Plaintiffs claimed two declarations: that the Commissioners . . . are obliged to have regard to the object of promoting the Christian faith through the established Church of England; and that (they) may not act in a manner which would be incompatible with that object.

The case came before Sir Donald Nicholls, the vice-chancellor, on 7 and 8 October 1991. Neither the Plaintiffs nor the Defendants were required to appear in person. The forest of papers before the vice-chancellor included sworn affidavits by Harries (36 pages) and Lovelock (22 pages), a statement by the Archdeacon of Bedford on 'The Cure of Souls' and further affidavits by Harries responding to

Lovelock's. The Church Commissioners continued to compound hypocrisy by making a vice of their supposed virtue by shedding crocodile tears in their 28-page summary of their argument – 'The Church Commissioners approach this case with sorrow. They recognize the sincerity of the Plaintiffs' position but they believe it to be profoundly mistaken. They consider that these proceedings should never have been brought.'

Sir Donald Nicholls delivered his written complex judgment on 25 October and concluded:

> The fundamental difficulty I have with these declarations is their ambiguity. The objects of a charity can be stated at different levels of generality. Stated at one level of generality, the object which the financial payments made by the Commissioners seek to achieve is the promotion of the Christian faith through the established Church of England. That is not in dispute. And it is clear that in managing their investments the Commissioners do have regard to that object. That is shown by their ethical investment policy. Thus there is no need for the court to make the first declaration. But the matter goes further. The first declaration is not merely unnecessary. 'Have regard to the object' is a loose phrase, and there is a real danger it will mean all things to all men. Such a declaration should not be made. Likewise with the second declaration. The phrase I have used above when considering the position of charity trustees is 'conflict with'. In the course of argument many other phrases, synonymous to a greater or lesser extent, were canvassed before me: directly contrary to, inimical to, inconsistent with, undermine, defeat, incompatible with. Each of these phrases has its own shades of meaning. I certainly do not claim that 'conflict with' is superior to all others. There may be circumstances where other phrases would be more helpful and apt. But it seems to me that, in general, this phrase encapsulates as well as any other, and better than some, the principle which is involved. Even so, and even if this change were made to the wording of the second declaration, I do not think such a declaration would be of assistance to the Commissioners. In particular, it would not deal with how the Commissioners should proceed when confronted with differing views on whether, on moral grounds, a proper investment is in conflict with the objects the Commissioners are seeking to promote.
>
> I shall therefore not make either declaration.
>
> I add only this. In bringing these proceedings the Bishop of Oxford and his colleagues are actuated by the highest moral concern. But, as I have sought to show, the approach they wish the Commissioners to adopt to investment decisions would involve a departure by the Commissioners from their legal obligations. Whether such a departure would or would not be desirable is, of course, not an issue in these proceedings. That is a matter to be pursued, if at all, elsewhere than in this court.

The resulting publicity and comment in the secular and Church press was almost uniformly critical, even hostile, towards Harries. There were a number of appealable points. The lack of relationship in the judgment between the argument that the self-constraint of the Commissioners in terms of their existing ethical policy, meant that there was no error of law (which entirely begged the point of the proceedings); the whole of the argument in the judgment about South Africa, when the Plaintiffs and their lawyers had studiously avoided dealing in specifics; the assumption by the vice-chancellor that, if they had correctly informed themselves as to their duties along the lines they indicated, the Commissioners would have come to the same conclusions vis-à-vis investments as they had hitherto. There were striking omissions, particularly in terms of the policy of the Commissioners in the property speculation of the 1980s and 1990s, which was the more striking given the discussion of the contemporary planning laws and the impropriety of the Church taking account of any views other than those expressed via the planning procedures.

However, Harries' lawyers concluded that they had no confidence of winning an appeal or indeed in getting the Court of Appeal to grant leave to appeal. The danger persisted that the court would consider the claims too academic or theoretical, against the existing ethical policies of the Commissioners, buttressed by a general anxiety (apparent from the judgment of the vice-chancellor) as to just where things might lead if they reached any other decision than the pragmatic one already reached.

Each side in the case was responsible for paying their own costs. Although the Plaintiffs' costs far exceeded the sum guaranteed, the lawyers generously waived any sum beyond the £30,000 raised. The Commissioners were quick to state that their costs would have to be met out of the money allocated to stipends, which could mean about £9 less for every serving clergyman, whose stipends averaged £11,400.

On 15 November Harries issued a news release that the Plaintiffs would not be appealing. The case was a landmark one vis-à-vis the charity sector and the investment powers and duties of trustees. The Plaintiffs may have failed to persuade the High Court to grant the relief they sought, but Harries believed that the judgment had highlighted a number of issues that the Church of England should not ignore. They had been defeated in battle, but the war was far from lost. There was success in the failure. The nature of this success was twofold. The vice-chancellor conceded a number of important points. It is right and proper for trustees to take ethical considerations into account, provided this does not lead to any financial detriment. More strongly, it is right for them not to invest in companies that clearly contradict their core purpose, even if doing so is financially less than the best that could be achieved. The standard example is that it would be clearly wrong for a cancer research charity to invest in tobacco companies. Since the High Court judgment, although trustees of charities have regard to the financial aspect, they have been much more open to the ethical dimensions as stated in the vice-chancellor's summing up.

The other area of success was the way the case jolted the Church Commissioners into taking the ethical dimension more seriously. Sir Michael Coleman, the then new Church Estates Commissioner, was keen to do this. A special committee, the Ethical Investment Advisory Group (EIAG) was set up to consider this aspect of all the Church's investments. This does not mean that it makes unanimous or harmonious decisions – *vide* the overturning in 2006 of the General Synod vote on the 'Caterpillar' case, where the issues were complex and not conducive to a simplistic approach. (Synod urged that the EIAG hold intensive discussions with Caterpillar, 'with a view to its withdrawing from supplying or maintaining either equipment or parts for use by the state of Israel in demolishing Palestinian homes'.) But at least there is now a committee with very seriously-minded members, treating the issues with knowledge and intelligence. Is not this a result of Harries' action in the High Court?

By 1994 the Church of England was in financial crisis. Clergy and laity alike were ostriches. There was – and probably still is – a woeful ignorance of where the money goes and where the money comes from. In an article in *The Times* (16 February 1994) Harries explained how the clergy of the diocese of Oxford were financed.

> Oxford has a budget of £11.1 million for 1994. We will receive £1.3 million from the Church Commissioners, a mere 12 per cent (although to be fair there are hidden subsidies in the form of episcopal costs, National Insurance and pension contributions) – Overall the Church contributed £63 million to stipends. But donations raise the substantial sum of £250 million. The big cuts predicted over the next few years are the culmination, albeit a drastic one, of a process.
>
> In this diocese, we agreed some time ago that rather than be overwhelmed by forces beyond our control, we needed to manage change. (Roughly speaking, it will be necessary to find £20,000 per member of the stipendiary clergy.)

On 25 April a report of the House of Commons' Social Security Committee was published ('The Operation of Pensions Funds: The Church Commissioners and Church of England Pensions'). Its chairman was Frank Field MP. It was an indictment on the leadership of the Commissioners from the mid-1980s to 1992. Although the Commissioners increased their assets between 1984 and 1989 from £1.7 billion to over £2.9 billion, the continuation of high-risk activity, principally property speculation, deep into the recession brought about the decline in assets to £2.1 billion by December 1992. The report did not spare by name Sir Douglas Lovelock and James Shelley, respectively first estate commissioner and secretary. 'It was these two individuals who were architects of the momentous decisions both to invest in speculative property developments and also to borrow large sums to help finance those developments.' It was a mixture of naivety, recklessness and/or arrogance. Traditional prudence was vanquished. The leadership of the Commissioners:

- failed to comply with normal accounting practices, thereby creating a misleading impression of the true state of the Church's finances;
- established a series of development companies into which major injections of funds were made without due diligence;
- allowed the Archbishop of Canterbury (George Carey) only to learn fully of the financial losses by reading the *Financial Times*;
- foolishly speculated without proper expertise or advice in property developments using borrowed money; irreparably damaged the income flow to the Church;
- published misleading information in their annual reports;
- has in all likelihood done more than any other single act to destroy the parish system of the national Church;
- failed to assess and to meet greatly increased pension obligations.

The mandarin officials were fortunate that a Black Maria did not arrive at their doors.

There is a footnote and an epilogue. On 25 March 1990 Robert Runcie announced that he was resigning as Archbishop of Canterbury to take effect on 31 January 1991. At the height of speculation about his successor Ladbrokes had Robert Eames, Archbishop of Armagh 2–1 favourite; Richard Harries second favourite at 5–2; David Sheppard at 6–1; John Taylor of St Albans and Mark Santer of Birmingham at 8–1 and John Habgood, Archbishop of York, was put at 2–1. George Carey was not even in the paddock. Many people hoped that Harries would move to one of the archbishoprics, but thought his chances had been dashed by the High Court case. Would he have achieved more at Canterbury or York? Would he have liked to be Cantuar or Ebor? Would he have made a good or a great archbishop? He was offered and declined the bishopric of Winchester in 1995 to succeed Colin James.

Chapter Fifteen
Advances and Limits

Jews are traditionally religious people. Their worship is all-embracing. Worship in the synagogue centres on the Law of Moses, contained in the Pentateuch (Genesis to Deuteronomy). These, written in unpointed Hebrew on parchment scrolls in traditional manner, are read over the Sabbaths and festivals of the year. They are called *Sepher Torah* or Scrolls of the Law – *Torah* being the Hebrew for 'law' in the sense of 'teaching'. They are housed in an Ark, an ornate cupboard symbolizing the Temple.

Jewish worship is not confined to the synagogue. The Sabbath is greeted by a ceremony called *Kiddush* or Sanctification, which takes place in the home on Friday evenings. Candles are lit and a blessing said over them by the housewife, and, too, over bread and wine which is then divided and shared among the family and guests. At the close of the Sabbath (which lasts from sundown on Fridays to sundown on Saturdays) there is a ceremony called *Havdalah* which marks the conclusion of the Sabbath joy. During this, a spice-box is passed from hand to hand by which the sweetness of the Sabbath is remembered. There is something attractive and mesmerizing about this natural form of piety. It is likewise a reprimand to vanished practices of Christianity in England.

When Harries was at Cuddesdon as a student, Christian–Jewish relations were no more than a side-shoot. A lecture by Dr James William Parkes hardly touched Harries. Later Parkes' publications acted as a powerful fertilizer to Harries' thought. Parkes was a Christian writer under the pen-name of John Hadham, adopted when he wrote *Good God* (1940) and did not want to get his controversies mixed. He had a worldwide reputation for solid, objective scholarship on Judaism and was also concerned, with Richard Acland, for the promotion of Common Wealth, a new political party; he was chairman of its national committee. Parkes' ordained life started in 1925 at St Stephen's, Hampstead, and the wardenship of Student Movement House. Work with universities in Europe sparked his interest in Jewish questions. His first book *The Jew and His Neighbour* appeared in 1930. Five years later the Nazis reached the conclusion that his thinking and knowledge were dangerous, and an attempt on his life was made in Geneva.

Membership of what was named the Manor House Group enveloped Harries in a genuinely life-enhancing experience, the impact of which has endured. It changed his perspective and direction. The prime launchers were a rabbi and a priest. Rabbi Tony Bayfield was director of the Manor House, East Finchley, renamed the Sternberg Centre for Judaism in 1983. Marcus Braybrooke was director of training in the diocese of Bath and Wells and shortly to be executive director of the Council of Christians and Jews. They were already exploring interfaith subjects and wanted to establish a new, small and committed group of people who shared assumptions about the value of dialogue and critical thought.

The members from 1984 were Rabbis Albert H. Friedlander of the Westminster Synagogue and dean of Leo Baeck College; Jonathan Magonet and Hyam Maccoby, principal and librarian respectively of Leo Baeck; Julia Neuberger of South London Liberal Synagogue; Colin Eimer of Southgate Reform Synagogue, intellectually and emotionally involved with Shoah (the holocaust, time of desolation); Norman Solomon, Orthodox rabbi to congregations in Manchester, Liverpool and London. The Christians were Harries; John Bowden, priest and director of the SCM Press; Anthony Phillips, lecturer at St John's College, Oxford; Kenneth Cragg, a former assistant bishop in Jerusalem; Alan Race, director of studies on the Southwark Ordination Course; and Margaret Shepherd, a member of the Roman Catholic congregation of the Sisters of Sion.

The group met twice a year for a whole day and once a year residentially at Charney Manor, Oxfordshire. At Charney Manor, a typical Harries boot-trek, politely called 'a guided ramble', was an essential feature, though some of the urban rabbis conveniently forgot to bring suitable footwear and were more likely to be found searching the shelves in Blackwells bookshop. Rabbi Tony Bayfield has memories of 'Richard leading us on a walk in the Oxfordshire countryside and taking us to the White Horse – which was covered with snow. He announced that it was indeed there and we should take his word for it. I suggested that this was not untypical of Anglican theology relating to God and we have long enjoyed the joke'.

'Dialogue with a Difference' was a precise description of the Manor House devotees. We are not here concerned with details of the dialogue, but only with its effect. Harries spotted a fascinating difference between the Jewish and Christian approach to discussion. Christians listen politely, never interrupt each other and tear each other to shreds afterwards. Jews interrupt endlessly, and never get as far as tearing each other to shreds as the speaker never gets to the end anyway. Unlike Christians, Jews argue with God. Harries was seen by some Jewish members as passionate about what moved him, not what should move them. That was characteristic, believing that the best dialogue comes from understanding what moves the other, not by trying to force it on the other. Harries has the ability of being both an observable and discreet presence, always alert, never imposing himself on a group of which he is an equal among equals. He knows how to listen without intent. In so many Church groups one realizes that everyone is talking for their own interest, not listening – or only with impatience – waiting for their turn to report to their own advantage the things that are of concern to them, or the things that have happened to them. It was an important constituent in his expanding chairmanships.

One Jewish member says, 'We learned from Richard's disciplined spirituality.' Another Jewish perception is, 'What we discovered was that Richard was a liberal Christian, open to the other, self-critical yet robust – very much the child of his military background.' And another captures his open-mindedness, 'ready and eager to learn about other religions'. There was something else about close encounters with Jews. A character in J.B. Priestley's *Saturn Over the Water* (1961) had this to say about Jews: 'I like them. They don't, as so many of the English do, quietly die while still moving around and talking. Jewish zombies are hard to find. While they're living, they're alive. I don't mind people being tough and aggressive, if at the same time they're intelligent and warm hearted.'

For Harries, 'Manor House' was not heart or head, but head first, then making room for heart to move in. The growth in appreciation was evident. A shared intellectual approach and impatience with waffle was a bond. He admitted to being conscious of how much he had needed to be re-educated. A book, *Dialogue with a Difference: Manor House Group Experience*, was published in 1992. It comprised essays covering the substance of their discussions: 'Making Theological Space for Each Other'; 'Text, Tradition and Historical Criticism'; 'Shoah, Suffering and Theodicy' and 'Religion and the Transformation of Society'. Harries' contribution was 'Theodicy Will Not Go Away'. The issue was the implications of the Shoah. He parted company with Braybrooke who asserted that questions of theodicy are basically irrelevant. For Harries:

> From a Christian point of view it needs to be asserted that memory of the Shoah needs to be kept alive and thought of as a crucial event in human history. We need to be continually reminded, until the end of the ages, of the depths of depravity to which human beings can sink unless they take steps to guard against it, and in particular we need to be aware of the terrible consequences of certain tendencies within Christianity unless positive action to counteract them is taken. The Shoah may or may not pose any new questions for theodicy. But it ensures that the old questions, in particular the old question of Christianity's relation to Judaism, and the consequences of this, continue to be faced.
>
> Because of his aim of creating free beings, God does not always succeed in preventing evil. But he is ceaselessly at work bringing good out of evil through the willing cooperation of those striving to do his will. A new relationship with Judaism is one urgent good that the Church needs to wrest, through the grace of God, from the sorry story of the past.

Harries returns to this subject time and time again. His lectures, reviews and conversations on Jewish–Christian relations brought his name to the attention of Anglican worthies. It is an example of his deep delving analysis and ability to communicate in speech and writing that, as if from hardly anywhere, he was suddenly recognized as a specialist of this subject – and on many others which he mastered. There was criticism from academics and others who questioned, not his dexterity and innate ability, but his authority. But Harries did not set himself up as an authority. It was his wish to share his knowledge with others as against the unskilfulness of academics who kept their thoughts within the restricted boundaries of quad or court, emerging only in the pages of esoteric academic journals – dust to dust!

The Church of England has a discontinuous record of relations with Judaism. Progress in the twentieth century began in 1927 with the formation of the London Society of Jews and Christians, 'to promote fellowship and understanding between Jews and Christians'. Charles Raven, W.R. Matthews and B.H. Streeter were active in this. In the Thirties, as the Nazis took power, Bishop George Bell of Chichester was the determined champion of the Jews and Non-Aryan-Christians against Hitler's persecution. After the Second World War, James Parkes made an important contribution in the field of anti-Semitism. In 1942 the Council of Christians and Jews was formed, 'to combat all forms of religious and racial intolerance, to promote mutual understanding between Jews and Christians and to foster co-operation in social and community service'. Later the Archbishops of Canterbury and York had a number of Anglican-Jewish consultants. Canon Peter Schneider was one of them and with Rabbi Norman Solomon arranged the first Anglican–Jewish Consultation in 1980 on the theme 'Law and Religion in Contemporary Society'. The Chief Rabbi, Immanuel Jakobovits, asked Solomon to act on his behalf as Jewish co-convenor of a further consultation. Unfortunately Schneider died, which caused a hiatus. Then, Anthony Phillips, steeped in the Old Testament, with many rabbinic friends, was appointed in 1984. Harries is of the view that the position was not one which meant much to the archbishops, but it was welcomed by the Jewish community because it gave them a person to whom they could relate directly, thinking he would have the ear of the two archbishops. In 1986 Phillips resigned on his move to be headmaster of King's School, Canterbury. Harries was asked to succeed him. If they thought this would be an undemanding honorary position they were mistaken. Harries does not skim the surface but dives deep. Any position accepted by him raises the profile of the organization.

Without delay, Harries and Solomon co-convened a second international consultation at Shallowford House, Staffordshire, in 1987 on social and moral concerns under the joint chairmanship of the Archbishop of York (John Habgood) and the Chief Rabbi (Jakobovits). Shortly afterwards, and in the year of his nomination to the see of Oxford in 1987, Harries attended the seventh meeting of the Anglican Consultative Council in Singapore as secretary to Section II (Dogmatic and Pastoral). Here the Council was persuaded to draw up a set of guidelines on Jewish–Christian relations for the Lambeth Conference. In the Singapore report 'Many Gifts One Spirit' it was clear that this was not a relished opportunity, though a necessary one.

> There are two reasons why Jewish–Christian relations need to be handled with special care and sensitivity. Firstly, Judaism and Christianity are both hewn from the same rock, the people of God of the Hebrew Scriptures; and both communities appeal to those Scriptures to discern the mind and will of God; secondly, because of the tragic history of past relationships, culminating in the Holocaust, a history poisoned by much anti-Jewish feeling.

The timing of Harries' appointment was fortuitous as a Lambeth Conference was looming and he himself had added extra weight as Bishop of Oxford. He was invited to chair a small group to produce some 'Jewish–Christian guidelines for the Anglican Communion'. He assembled a few people, friends from the Manor House, with the additional name of Michael Nazir-Ali, then the co-ordinator of studies and editor for the Lambeth Conference, also director-in-residence at the Oxford Centre for Mission Studies. They wrote some guidelines which they hoped that the Lambeth Conference 1988 would endorse. In clarifying why Jewish–Christian relations are special the draft guidelines were succinct:

> Judaism is a religion, a people and a civilization. It is a religion, because at its heart is the belief in the one God, creator of heaven and earth, who has revealed his will to us. It is a people, because Jews know and define themselves as Jews even if they do not fully share the religious beliefs of Judaism. It is a civilization, because Jewish language, culture, art and philosophy have not only woven themselves into other cultures, but they are significant in their own right. It is to a living religion, people and civilization which we seek to relate.
>
> For Christians, Judaism can never be one religion amongst others. It has a special bond and affinity with Christianity. Jesus was a Jew and the Scriptures which informed and guided his life were the books of the Hebrew Bible. These still form part of the Christian Scriptures. The God in whom Jesus believed, to whom he totally gave himself, and in whom we believe is 'the God of Abraham, Isaac and Jacob'. A right understanding of the relationship with Judaism is, therefore, fundamental to Christianity's own self-under-standing . . . A wrong understanding of our relationship with Judaism means a wrong understanding of ourselves.
>
> There is a further, tragic, reason why Jewish–Christian relations are special. The Christian Church, in establishing its identity, has often engaged in a fierce polemic against Judaism, with terrible consequences. Even today, Christians, including some scholars, sometimes seek to exalt Jesus by misleading pictures of the Judaism of his time. Repentance and a resolve to purify the Christian faith of negative attitudes towards Judaism is vital. A close relationship among Jews and Christians, which for so long has been spoiled, must be restored. As the Archbishop of Canterbury (Robert Runcie) has said recently, 'Christians have a continuing need to purge all anti-Jewish teaching, which has caused untold suffering in the past'. Finally, both Christians and Jews, with their passionate belief in the one God and their firm hold on to the infinite worth and dignity of every human person, need to unite in their witness to a world characterized by godlessness and inhumanity. There is much that Christians and Jews should be doing together, that God's name might be honoured and his will obeyed.

Harries decided not to release the guidelines before Lambeth nor have a press conference, though he did have a preliminary chat with Clifford Longley, the then religious affairs correspondent of *The Times*. This was unwise as, unknown to Harries who does not take *The Times*, Longley divulged the contents. The eruption was immediate and came with volcanic force from Hugh Montefiore, Bishop of Birmingham until 1987. Distressed by the newspaper report he wrote to Harries (11 July 1988):

> 51 years ago I became a Christian, a fulfilled Jew; and I have to admit that in all that time I have never felt really at home in a massively Gentile Church, seemingly full of Gentile assumptions. From the excerpt it seems that I should not be in the Church at all, but that Christians should pray that I should be 'faithful to the Torah'. Although it is no business of mine, I do wonder whether you consulted with any Jewish Christian before agreeing your guidelines? They seem to put us out in the cold. Of course Judaism is a living faith, and faithful Jews are very close to the heart of God. But how can I not pray that my brothers and sisters after the flesh will find that more excellent way than the Torah that God has shown me?

Harries was aware that the group had not sufficiently, or at all, considered the position of Christians from a Jewish background. Although mistaken, the group's reasons were understandable, because of an instinctive reaction against (a) the fundamentalism of a number of Jewish Christians and (b) the uncritical support of the State of Israel of some others. Harries sent the draft guidelines to Montefiore, inviting his comments.

Montefiore's Jewishness was an essential part of his being. He became a Christian at Rugby School as 'a fulfilled Jew'. His faith in Christ was neither a consequence nor a corollary of faith in God. Passionate in his defence of Jews, he was critical of the ways in which they had been treated by the Christian Church. There were many times he found it hard to be at home in the contemporary Church, whereas the early Church comprised both Jew and Gentile, and both were essential to its well-being. As a Christian he retained his Jewish sense of 'chosenness'. In responding to the draft guidelines he urged the removal of passages which seemed to imply that the Jewish religion was a parallel religion and that Christians should pray that Jews should remain faithful to the Torah. He pointed out that the Torah was not of as much relevance to liberal Jews as to the Orthodox. The overall impression left on Montefiore about the guidelines was that the differences between Christians and Jews had been minimized in such a way that Christianity had been diluted to Judaism rather than Judaism made more like Christianity. Never minimizing the differences between Christians and Jews, he held:

(a) Jews are offended by the doctrine of the Trinity, which they believe is incompatible with the Unity of God.

(b) Christians believe that God was incarnate in Jesus Christ which Jews believe offends against the Second of the Ten Commandments.

(c)   Christians believe that through Christ they have free access to the Father: Jews claim this as their birthright.

(d)   Christians believe that the law is no longer binding upon them while Jews (Orthodox ones at any rate) believe that all those who are Jewish, together with proselytes, should keep it.

The New Testament indicates two roads by which people come to Christ. There is the road of the Jew, the road of history, by which disciples of Moses moved out of their ancestral theism into Christianity, finding in the Incarnate the climax of divine self-revelation, the key of Israel's history, the fulfilment of prophecy; and there is the road of the Gentiles, the road of the conscience, which led the victims of polytheism through spiritual bankruptcy and moral despair, to the feet of the Redeemer, in whom was proclaimed the remission of sins and who brought life and mortality through the Gospel.

In the Lambeth Conferences of 1988 and 1998 Harries showed his mettle and proved his distinctive gifts. *Alice in Wonderland*'s 'Everybody has won and all shall have prizes' has been a reasonably accurate description of the worldwide Anglican Communion during the twentieth century. It enabled the umbrella of comprehensiveness to cover all manner of doctrinal storms, theological squalls and organizational showers. Whenever the possibility of a tornado threatened, it was stopped in its terrifyingly destructive progress by forms of words. Find the formula and stop the tornado! And the size of the umbrella increased until it seemed as if any and all were welcome to shelter under it.

But in 1988 it did not appear that Harries would be successful. Amendments were made to the guidelines. After massaging they were not as forceful or effective as Harries' original draft. When they came before the conference itself there was further fury from two directions, one of which should have been predictable, the other less so. Evangelical bishops were opposed because the guidelines excluded the idea of mission to the Jews. The other opposition came from Middle-Eastern bishops: why no reference to Islam? Harries put his effort and soul into dialogue leading to reconciliation. This reveals something very important about Harries, applied to most other areas of his life. He is primarily a facilitator, and a very good one too!

If the guidelines had been restricted to Jews, Harries' task would have been merely half-difficult. Islam was different and for most bishops was a great unknown. 'Dialogue' held a positive meaning for Westerners. It was perceived and received very differently by bishops from the 'Third World', for example, parts of Africa, where increasingly militant Islam was seen as a threat to the very existence of Christian communities. In the Middle East, the Bishop in Jerusalem and President Bishop, Samir Kafity, was born in Palestine; the Bishop in Egypt, Ghai Abdel Malik, was Egyptian; the Bishop in Iran, Hassan Barnaba Dehqani-Tafti, had a Christian mother and Muslim father and was baptized when he was 18. They did not simply have knowledge of Islam, they 'felt' it. Suddenly, and with little time, Harries, in addition to recasting the original guidelines, was faced with the enormously difficult challenge of including Muslims. Rarely had he had to work under such pressure to produce a document.

Another arch-reconciler was instrumental in bringing bishops into agreement. The Archbishop of Melbourne, David John Penman, was ideal as he had nine years' experience as a Church Missionary Society missionary in Pakistan and the Middle East. Harries says, 'With a great deal of political footwork and extreme anxiety I got our document rewritten'. Result – Resolution 21 at the conference was passed unanimously: no vote against and no abstentions. The full text 'Jews, Christians and Muslims: The Way of Dialogue' appeared as an Appendix to the official Lambeth Conference 1988 report 'The Truth Shall Make You Free'. It contained signs and omens for a troubled future:

In understanding Islam it is necessary for Christians to grasp the central place of Islamic law in Muslim life. Islamic law, *Sharîa*, is based on the belief that God has, as a gracious act of mercy, revealed to humanity basic guidelines to live both individually and in society. Whereas Christians today tend to think of Christian faith as a personal commitment which can be expressed quite happily in a secular society, seeking to influence society but not seeking to impose a 'Christian' system on it.

Many Muslims believe that God has revealed his will on how the whole of society is to be ordered, from details of banking to matters of public health. Although based on the Qur'an, the sources of Islamic law are much wider. The picture becomes even more complex if one attempts to include the Shi'ites who are the majority in Iran and form significant minorities in many parts of the Muslim world. A long development independent from the majority Muslim community (Sunni) has resulted in a very different ethos and theology, making blanket statements about Islam almost impossible when Iranian and other Shi'ite thinkers are taken into account. Some non-Muslim communities living under Islamic rule experience the application of *Sharîa* law as oppressive and inhumane. Another aspect of *Sharîa* law which causes some distress is the treatment of women. We note that in some respects Islamic law has pioneered the rights of women in certain parts of the world. For example, under Islamic law, married women had the right to own property and conduct business in their own names thirteen centuries before these rights were granted in many Western countries. It is hoped that Christians and Muslims may search together for ways in which the position of women may continue to be improved for the benefit of society as a whole. We also need to remember that classical Islamic law provides safeguards for the rights of religious minorities which are not actually being enforced today. Further, in judging, we must always be careful to compare like with like. We must compare the highest and most humane ideals of Islam with the highest and most humane ideals of Christianity and the misuse of power at the hands of Muslims with the misuse of power at the hands of those who call themselves Christians. It is also worth noting that there is a long and distinguished tradition within Islam which seeks to interpret the *Sharîa* in the light of contemporary conditions. There are many able exponents of this tradition today, and Christians need to affirm their work, particularly in view of the religious fundamentalism ascendant in so many parts of the world.

The Lambeth Conference recommended that the Anglican Consultative Council, through an interfaith committee, set up working parties to draw up detailed guidelines. But once the fever had passed and bishops returned to their diocesan responsibilities, the impetus for action waned. However the Churches' Commission for Interfaith Relations was formed to respond ecumenically to the Lambeth Resolution. Harries chaired a working party of Christians and Jews which produced in 1994 'Christians and Jews: A New Way of Thinking'. There was a missed opportunity and a disappointment. The principal authors of the publication were, with one exception, the same people who had been at Manor House and in the pre-Lambeth group. Would it not have been better to open up to other influences? Nonetheless the booklet itself was brilliantly concise and published at a time when anti-Semitism was once again resurfacing. It included advice to Christians about relationships with Jews, with practical steps which could be taken. Harries admits 'the follow-up to this has been disappointing. My hope was that every Church in the British Isles would endorse this but a lack of energy in the bureaucracy has resulted in little happening.' In 2006 the situation remains comparatively unchanged.

There was – and is – another factor! The proselytizing wing of the Church of England was at work at General Synod 1996, when a question was asked: what plans had the Board of Mission to express support for members of the Church who saw themselves as both Jewish and Christian, and wished to share the good news of the Messiah with fellow Jews? Reports continued to be written and decanted on people who appeared unconvinced of their importance or even relevance.

Harries was asked to chair the Interfaith Committee for the Rights of Jews, Christians and Muslims in the Soviet Union. For years the group endeavoured to visit the Soviet Union but their visa applications were repeatedly blocked. When the Cold War ended the need for that committee also ended.

In 1992 the Runnymede Trust formed a commission to examine the nature, causes and consequences of current anti-Semitism in Britain, and to make policy recommendations as appropriate. Harries was invited to chair it and the quality of its membership guaranteed success for a rigorous examination of the subject and conclusions lucidly expressed. Members were Professor Akbar Ahmed (University of Cambridge); Professor Geoffrey Atkinson (Royal Holloway, University of London); Paul Boateng MP; Professor Ivor Crewe (University of Essex); Tony Howard (journalist); Anthony Lerman (Institute of Jewish Affairs); Neville Nagler (Board of Deputies of British Jews); Rabbi Julia Neuberger (Runnymede Trust); the Baroness Perry (House of Lords); and Ms Nasreen Rehman (Runnymede Trust). The director of the Trust, Robin Richardson, was secretary. The report, taking its title from a comment by Conor Cruise O'Brien: 'A Very Light Sleeper: the persistence and dangers of anti-Semitism', was published in January 1994 (reprinted in

November 1997) and was commendably short (63 pages). Key distinctions were made between anti-Judaism, anti-Semitic racism and anti-Zionism and, important for the future, action was urged against anti-Semitism and integrated with action against other forms of racism.

Among the broad sweep of recommendations, the media, which affect opinion by providing many of the images and stereotypes people use to understand current events, were encouraged to 'develop and publish codes of practice on how they would report matters relating to Jewish communities'. Further points made were that: care should be taken to avoid stereotyping by cartoons and sensationalizing anti-Semitic incidents devoid of context; the Secretary of State for Education should examine how the place of the Jewish community in British life is taught. The importance of liberal democracy and cultural pluralism as part of the curriculum was recognized and welcomed. Perhaps consideration of the United States' experience of teaching citizenship should be given. The commission was wary of increasing Government legislation, but European legislation to protect ethnic and religious minorities was urged. The Public Order Act should be reviewed and the possibility of a Racial Violence and Harassment Bill should be considered. 'The Christian Churches should strengthen their educational programme for more sensitive presentation of Christianity in relation to Judaism.' Interfaith groups should be encouraged to bring people together of different faiths. Public figures should influence the general climate of public opinion. 'It is salutary in this regard to recall that senior politicians, industrialists and Church leaders in some parts of the Continent have a rather better record in this matter recently than their counterparts in Britain.'

In 1989 Harries was involved in the major international conference at Oxford on the Holocaust – 'Remembering the Future' and contributed an important paper 'Theological Responses to the Holocaust'. Not for the first time Harries' approach was from a 'rather different place from other writers on this subject'. And neither for the last time was he moved by an experience. When he went to the Holocaust exhibition at the National War Museum he was, like most visitors, reduced to silence, horror, anger and fear. But he ventured a criticism: there was no section dealing with what Judaism calls 'Righteous Gentiles'. Sir Martin Gilbert wrote a heart-rending book *The Righteous: the Unsung Heroes of the Holocaust* (2002). Tens of thousands of Jews survived because of Gentile help. The terrifying risks that were taken, usually for love of mankind and decency, occasionally for money, by individual Christians, was heroically immense. Harries comments, 'For all the books that have been written by philosophers and theologians there is in the end a simple capacity in every human being to distinguish good from evil.'

No words can convey the unspeakable horror of the suffering and evil of the Shoah – a word preferred and more accurately used by scholars and writers. Harries often quotes Elie Wiesel:

> For us today –
> 'How is one to speak of it?
> How is one not to speak of it?'

Is there a sense in which Harries follows Wiesel, that in the depths of our questioning we are most likely to discover God? Indeed, is this subtlety near to the heart of his own faith? In his autobiography *Night* (1981) Wiesel moves from youthful belief to disillusionment. As a young boy Wiesel haunted the Hasidic synagogue in Sighet. The beadle, Moshe, was a mystic. He explained to the young Elie that every question possessed a power that does not lie in the answer:

> 'Man raises himself toward God by the questions he asks him.'
>
> He was fond of repeating, 'That is the true dialogue. Man questions God and God answers. For we don't understand his answers. We can't understand them. Because they come from the depth of the soul, and they stay there until death. You will find the true answers, Elie, only within yourself!' 'And why do you pray, Moshe,' I asked him. 'I pray to God within me that he will give me the strength to ask him the right questions.'

Harries has felt deeply, thought sharply and written conspicuously about Christianity and Judaism. Already there is one magnificent legacy: *After the Evil: Christianity and Judaism in the Shadow of the Holocaust* (2003) which traces his journey and encapsulates his thought. He was chairman of the Council of Christians and Jews from 1992 to 2001. When asked to comment on Harries, Lord Jakobovits, Chief Rabbi of the United Hebrew Congregations of the British Commonwealth 1967 to 1991, was typically forthright and exact:

> I have written few approbations with greater pleasure and deeper conviction. Richard Harries has brought a new rigour and depth into Jewish/Christian relations, and Britain owes him an enduring debt for this valuable enrichment of interfaith amity and understanding. Having myself much enjoyed his friendship over the years, I can personally testify to his charm in cultivating fraternal feelings transcending religious differences, and to his statesmanship in guiding vital aspects in the cultivation of mutual understanding and shared efforts in fields of great complexity and challenge.

This view is shared by the president and doyen of the Movement for Reform Judaism and founder of the Three Faiths Forum, Sir Sigmund Sternberg, who unites with Rabbi Tony Bayfield, head of the Movement for Reform Judaism:

> Richard held the position of chair of the Council with characteristic seriousness and made a truly significant contribution. He won universal trust and his commitment was unswerving. He has embodied the Anglican Church's desire for a healing of the relationship between Christians and Jews and recognised the need for sibling understanding and respect based upon separate theological space.
>
> Many of us were late to hope that he would be appointed Archbishop of Canterbury and were sad that his liberalism and questions to the Church

Commissioners about ethical investment seemed to handicap his candidacy. We were very fond of George Carey but Richard would have been our choice (if you will forgive that indiscretion and presumption) – for his courage, clarity and convictions.

Major initiatives had not diminished when Harries arrived in Oxford. Indeed they expanded, as even more opportunities were possible. It was likely, and confirmed by experience, that he would not be tempted, if invited, by Church of England synodical overtures to move up narrow and exclusive blind alleys. Instead, 'It seemed an opportune moment to initiate a similar group (to Manor House), this time including Muslims; and the presence in the city of the Oxford Centre for Islamic Studies was a great help in this regard. So the Oxford Abrahamic Group has been meeting ever since: usually twice a year, but sometimes three times, for the best part of a day at my house in north Oxford. At each meeting, three short papers are given on an agreed subject, one from each of the three Abrahamic faiths, followed by extensive discussion. It has usually been possible to take two subjects in a day, one in the morning and one in the afternoon. Initially, the intention was for the group to number 12 scholars, four from each faith, though in practice the overall membership has been larger in order that around a dozen scholars might be available to attend each (or any one) meeting.'

The Abrahamic Group included: (Muslim) Tim J. Winter; Dr Annabel Keeler who worked in the field of Islamic mysticism and Qur'anic hermeneutics as a junior research fellow at Wolfson College, University of Cambridge; Professor Yaha Michot, a fellow of the Oxford Centre for Islamic Studies and lecturer in the faculty of theology, University of Oxford; Dr Lufti Radwan, environmentalist, lecturer and organic farmer; Dr Basil Mustafa, bursar and Nelson Mandela fellow in educational studies in the Oxford Centre for Islamic Studies: (Jewish) Rabbi Norman Solomon; Rabbi Sybil Sheridan of the Wimbledon Reform Synagogue and lecturer at Leo Baeck College; Dr Alison Salveson, fellow of the Oxford Centre for Hebrew and Jewish Studies, and university research lecturer; Revd Jonathan Gorsky, education adviser to the Council of Christians and Jews; (Christian) Revd Professor Keith Ward; John Barton, Old Testament scholar and Oriel and Laing professor of the interpretation of Holy Scripture, University of Oxford; Rt Revd Kallistos Ware, an Assistant Bishop in the Orthodox Archdiocese of Thyateira and Great Britain and also a monk on the island of Patmos; Dr Paul Joyce, a fellow of St Peter's College, Oxford; Marcus Braybrooke and Harries.

Once again Harries was exemplary as a convenor, facilitator and contributor, this time in the relaxed atmosphere of his home. Again the key word is dialogue. As Harries tirelessly explains: 'Dialogue does not mean obliterating differences as a precondition. On the contrary it means bringing those differences into a relationship of mutual respect and trust.' Tim J. Winter, university lecturer in Islamic studies, University of Cambridge, an active member of the British Muslim community, who studied under traditional authorities in Egypt and Morocco and leads Friday prayers in the mosque, reflects the importance of the environment in which they met. 'The comparative informality of the encounters, and the genial hospitality of the host, also allowed the formation of friendships across denominational lines through the discovery of less intellectual but no less personal affinities and interests. To launch a passionate defence of the Cappadocian view of the Trinity, and then to find that one's interlocutor has children at the school where one's wife is a teacher, provides a calming reminder that one never disputes with doctrines; one disputes with those who hold them, and that no belief which is important to evidently good people can be undeserving of respect. It is to this that one should attribute the persistent courtesy of the encounters, helped by what one can only describe as a kind of English reserve.'

Jo Harries was superb at providing culinary hospitality with a variety of dietary requirements – everything needful to ensure that members were made welcome, as they knew they were!

All religions are almost irredeemably and irreconcilably deficient at stereotyping one another. The key to mutual comprehension in the Abrahamic Group was to let each religion speak of and for itself. Harries knows that in any relationship with Muslims it is vital to be scrupulously fair and let them define themselves and their beliefs in their terms, listening with a view to understanding rather than refuting. The inspiration for the success of this group was not at first in alighting on current controversies and being glued to them, but in focusing on what the three religions had in common, starting with Abraham. Muslims regard Abraham as the first Muslim, the one who submitted his life to God. Islam means submission to the will of the one God, Allah. Closely associated with this act of submission is acceptance of the seventh-century prophet Muhammed as the last and final Messenger of God, the 'seal of the prophets'. Those who submit – who 'fear God and obey, His messengers' – which scripture, the Qur'an, frequently admonishes humans to do, are known as Muslims.

An absorbing and detailed account of the Oxford discussions, *Abraham's Children: Jews, Christians and Muslims in Conversation*, edited by Norman Solomon, Richard Harries and Tim Winter, was published in 2006.

The following brief extracts are the personal views on 'life after death' from Jewish, Muslim and Christian perspectives from the hands of Rabbi Norman Solomon, Professor Yaha Michot and Harries, which illustrates the type of dialogue Harries has sought to initiate:

(Solomon) Religious language about life after death is metaphor. That is why there is so much confusion about what it 'refers' to, whether this-worldly resurrection or other-worldly immortality of the soul. It is why attempts to portray it, whether as 'the righteous sitting with crowns on their heads and absorbing the divine radiance' or in grosser terms of two regions, one inhabited by angel harpists and the other by pitch-forked devils, lapse into childishness and absurdity. To explain the 'meaning' of the metaphor results only in another metaphor. Yet to dismiss traditional ways of talking about the afterlife entirely, and to speak of death simply as the final end, fail to do justice to the sense that many people have of being part of what lies beyond each of us as individuals. The 'Yizkor' ceremony that takes place in many Jewish rites on certain festivals conveys this powerfully: as parents and others are remembered, one feels a bond that binds the 'community of saints' (to use a Christian term) and transcends the generations. But even a phrase like 'what lies beyond' is a spatial metaphor; it seems that any attempt to articulate 'life after death' in words comes up against a language boundary that cannot be crossed. Humility is necessary to see oneself not as an independent, disconnected individual, but as a focus of limited self-awareness within an inconceivably vast universe, every part of which interacts with every other. Death is a melting back, a re-absorption into this wholeness . . . Belief cannot be justified solely on the grounds that it generates a positive attitude to life; a belief not grounded in reality is worthless. The reality conveyed by afterlife talk is of the totality and interconnectedness of creation, and of the enduring significance of the life-work of the individual.

(Michot) Our trial in this life has an end at an appointed term. 'I do not hesitate about anything I do,' God says in a famous *hadith qudsi*, 'as I hesitate (to take) the soul of the believer. He hates death and I hate to harm him.' However, as confirmed in the Qur' an, 'every soul will taste death'. 'Lo! we are God's and lo! unto Him we are returning.' There is no transmigration.

Faith in the afterlife is one of the fundamental principles of the religion, like faith in the one God and the prophethood of the Prophet (peace be upon him). We do not survive death because of some everlasting essence of our soul but exclusively thanks to the will, the power, the providence, the justice, and the mercy of God. 'As He originated you, so you shall return.' 'Have they not seen that God, Who created the heavens and the earth and was not wearied by their creation, has the power to bring back life to the dead?'

Humans are servants accountable to their divine Lord . . . Their deeds are weighed on the day of judgement and 'whoso does good an atom's weight will see it then, and whoso does ill an atom's weight will see it then'. Ethics, which are at the core of revelation and prophethood, would have no meaning without the final reckoning leading to a reward or a punishment . . . We do not investigate this secret of God but have faith in God's justice, wisdom and mercy.

(Harries) The prospect and possibility of heaven still remains fundamental to Christian belief, however often it has been caricatured and disparaged. This is not to be seen in terms of a reward, like a medal stuck on the chest, but as the destination of the road of godliness. Of course, we cannot imagine now what heaven will be like; there can only be hints and guesses taken from the most fulfilling and worthwhile human experiences. But heaven remains, because, as Paul said, nothing, not even death itself, can separate us from the love of God in Jesus Christ. Heaven is inseparable from the glory of God in God's saints. For the great goal is not simply human fulfilment but a community of persons upheld and bonded together within the love of God. In the New Testament, the risen Christ is inseparable from his body, the Church, with every Christian being a limb or member of that body. So the abiding reality of heaven is the glory of God, which is that sublime conjunction of love, truth and goodness, glimpses of which we have in this life and which point to their source and standard in God's own self. Above all, this glory is revealed in the self-emptying of Jesus Christ, a theme which is profoundly explored in the Gospel of John. The glory irradiates and suffuses the whole communion of saints.

Karl Marx criticized religion in general and Christianity in particular for offering a misplaced hope. Instead of getting people to change this world for the better and hoping for a new future, religion directed their hope to another world. That is a salutary criticism, which many churches have taken on board. The Kingdom of God is not limited to this world but we have nevertheless to strive to make it reality within this world. Christians pray daily, 'Our Father in heaven, hallowed be your name, your Kingdom come, your will be done on earth as in heaven.' The Kingdom of God has to be built up in this world, even though it has its consummation beyond space and time . . .

Christians believe that God created the universe out of love and wisdom. So much that happens in the world seems directly to contradict this meaning and purpose. Christians, like Jews and Muslims, hold out the hope that, in the end, God's loving wisdom will prevail. For us, the humility of the self-empty-ing God revealed in Jesus Christ will be revealed in all its glory in those who share Christ's character and purpose whether they are aware of it or not. In the words of Julian of Norwich, quoted by T. S. Eliot,

> And all shall be well and
> All manner of things shall be well.

So much theory. Is that where it ended? An 82-page booklet was published in 2001 'Friends in Faith: Some Examples of Good Interfaith Practice in the Thames Valley Area'. It is a compendium covering activities and initiatives of the Christian Churches in dialogue and at work with Muslim, Sikh, Hindu and Jewish communi-ties, as well as a number of Buddhists, Baha'is and members of newer religious move-ments. And the key Christian player on the stage is the diocese of Oxford with its Committee for Interfaith Concerns. The pages of 'Friends in Faith' are full of stimu-lating information – mixed-faith marriages, education, health concerns, links with society, theological reflections, guidelines, interfaith prayer, all interwoven with per-sonal experiences.

On an intellectual level much has been done in the last decade to build bridges between religions. There is a view that the Muslim community in Britain has been accepted but not understood. The Muslim Council of Britain is well and creditably established, although it comprises about a third of the Muslim institutions. An increasingly educated Muslim community has developed a religious identity that has little time for zealotry. Another view is that Islamaphobia – the dread or hatred of Islam – is widespread. Scaremongering about Islamaphobia promotes a Muslim victim-culture and allows some community leaders to exhibit a sense of injury while suppressing internal debate. A third view, more a series of photographs, portrays something quite different. At a local level in parts of Lancashire and Yorkshire, British-born second generation Muslims feel alienated from mosque and community. Is it any wonder when many imams come from rural villages in Mirpur, Pakistan and speak little or no English? Is it possible that major barriers between religions have not been so much touched or removed but reinforced among 'ordinary' Muslims, Jews and Christians? The position has changed beyond all expectations and forecasts over the last 40 years.

In Oxford, the Abrahamic Group brought the three faiths together for intellectual dialogue. This was in part the result of being in a university setting where the 'meeting' though not the 'clinching' of minds was easier; more congenial. Harries' leadership was evident in practical results in the diocese, as mentioned above. What of the limits of interfaith action? What of the theological tensions? Muslims look to the Qur'an and Jews to the Old Testament for their Law, which is explicit and unchanged and rules the minutiae of the lives of those who practise the religion. Although an increasingly vocal, but not necessarily representative or numerically strong number of fundamentalist Christians look to the Bible for rules to undergird their convictions or prejudices, they still have to distinguish between Law and Gospel – the Gospel of Grace.

In this milieu Harries follows a middle way between the dogmatic, authoritarian, laying down of hard and fast rules likely to provoke to sin rather than to save, and the announcement of a 'free-for-all', in which everybody has to start building up a morality for themselves, as though they were newly created and placed in the Garden of Eden without even the one commandment given to Adam and Eve. Is this 'middle-way' or *via media* something which can be accommodated or at least comprehended in the practice of Islam today? Dr F. A. Nizami is the director of the Oxford Centre for Islamic Studies, the Prince of Wales fellow in the study of the Islamic world, and a member of the Abrahamic Group. He says his early education 'benefited from attendance at a Roman Catholic school and the Mother Superior became a lifelong friend from whom I have learned much. Subsequently my experiences at university, in India and at Oxford, brought many opportunities to learn about the faith of others and to explain my own.'

He thinks the major benefit of the Abrahamic Group was less when theological issues were discussed but more when, encouraged by Harries' leadership, 'an exploration of ethical values derived from the three faiths, and a realization of the manner in which these faiths underpin a large common ground of such values, took place. I view consideration of the practical implications of such shared values as being a more useful aim of interfaith dialogue than a concentration on the specific differences of the faith traditions themselves . . . It is for this reason that I have admired the active engagement of Bishop Richard in the task of achieving better understanding of ethical issues . . . In Britain today I believe that such discussion can be most helpful if it focused on the rights, responsibilities and obligations of citizenship.'

In the case of Richard Harries, the man subsumes the bishop, and not the bishop the man. Nowhere is this better illustrated than in his concentrated study and energetic action in Christian, Jewish and Muslim relations. He has a noble voice, one of faith and hope, in an age of fragmentation and hate.

Chapter Sixteen
Right Gladly

When Michael Ramsay was appointed Archbishop of Canterbury people asked him if he was 'in good heart about being Archbishop?' His response was 'Yes'.

> I'm going to do it right gladly, to carry out my duty. But the phrase 'in good heart' sometimes gives me pause, because after all, we are here as a Church to represent Christ crucified and the compassion of Christ crucified before the world. Because that is so, it may be the will of God that our Church should have its heart broken, and if that were to happen it wouldn't mean that we were heading for the world's misery but quite likely pointing to the deepest joy. (*The Christian Priest Today*, 1972)

Harries entered the bishopric of Oxford 'right gladly'.

A well-run diocese is like a well-made spider web, the result of meticulous weaving of tiny strands that criss-cross and intersect, so that if you happen to touch the web at any one time, it is instantly felt throughout. Harries did not spend his time in the diocesan office dreaming or wrestling with matters of discernment about the direction in which the diocese should move. There was work to be done. Part of this was an 'executive' function, managing the diocese. He was successful in inducing others, area bishops, senior staff, boards and committees, to undertake responsibility for the bulk of administration. A large diocese attracts willing, competent and responsible people. He was not the kind of democratic supervisor who manipulates and manoeuvres. Once a function was delegated, he left people to work things out for themselves, alone with their responsibility. This was not people-management. Harries was not always sensitive to people's feelings about being asked to do or stop doing a role. He seemed to expect people to take a pragmatic rather than emotional approach and some people, especially volunteers, did not react in that way. But he never bore grudges. When apologies were made by staff for errors the matter was forgotten, never mentioned again.

Decisions were usually reached by consensus, which was effective because it achieved goals and built mutual trust. A survey of American episcopalian bishops has revealed that those most respected for presiding over well-run dioceses were those bishops who seemed least likely to feel the need for the wisdom of other bishops, or for communicating with other bishops about specific aspects of 'bishoping'. In contemporary parlance Harries was 'his own man'. This is confirmed again and effectively by Canon Keith Lamdin, director of Stewardship, Training, Evangelism and Ministry (STEM). He had a very great respect and support for Harries' leadership, though was not blind to potential pitfalls.

As a diocesan bishop, Richard has always believed in the goodwill of people and in their natural desire to belong and help. He seems always surprised by bullies and has that upper-class English optimism that everybody will see sense and behave in the end. This has meant that people he has appointed have always had his support in public and have been trusted to bring their own leadership to the fore. It has also meant that he has not found it easy to challenge colleagues when he thinks they are out of line. This has happened with his senior staff and that has brought both innovation and some flair but has often meant that there has been little accountability between them.

There are occasions when Richard is the kind of leader who appoints somebody and gives them their head and maybe could give a little more supervision when the person causes a stir. I remember this happened to me after running a training workshop in which people were invited to talk or speak to the bread before it became the bread in the Communion service. Someone did not like this and reported it to the *Telegraph* and it had a little flurry of interest reaching even to the *News Quiz*! On another occasion I wrote a very brief opinion in *The Door* supporting the view that God created and affirms and blesses people of a homosexual orientation. I am sure that Richard came under pressure to either discipline or sack me. On both occasions he was understanding and completely supportive, not only of my right to have such views and to engage in such activities, but also I sensed some delight that he had staff who were full of energy and able to cause a stir.

Richard has a quick mind that works well and grasps issues quickly and thinks them through. Often he assumes that once thought through and agreed, everybody is on board and should get on with it. He would not be too interested in the emotional support aspect. He has probably only been upstairs to our department once or twice in the last five years. He is definitely not a 'leadership by wandering around' person. You make an appointment and do the business and all that works very well. There are one or two little things that Richard has a fine reputation for. One of them is tipping his chair back until he is in an almost horizontal position, closing his eyes and either going to sleep or appearing to be deeply concentrating on the topic in hand. I have never known him not to sit up and contribute vigorously to the debate. The second thing is the capacity to become quickly bored with a topic of conversation about which he has already reached a conclusion and it has not been unknown for him to open his briefcase and start looking at other papers while other people are still engaged in the discussion, although this has not happened as much, more recently.

Richard's natural inclination is Establishment, a benign light touch on the tiller and the all-sufficiency of the parochial system when there is a good incumbent in charge. Demands for him to lead the diocese into the new age of consumer spirituality and purpose-driven Church has been alien to him. However, although he will never do the 'I'm the leader – come and follow me into the new world', he has grasped the need for radical change and in his own way he has released and empowered people in the diocese to be entrepreneurial. In stable times that has been fine, but in the more urgent need for change he has been less easy with grasping the rudder, steering with vigour and demanding some common assent. Those bishops who have wanted to be in more of a common enterprise have often been frustrated and others have run their episcopal areas with a good deal of independence.

Within days of his enthronement Harries, after consulting his senior staff, appointed a working party to consider the range of training for ministry then being offered in the diocese. Under the able and reliable chairmanship of the Archdeacon of Oxford, Frank Weston, and five members, the group began its work in October 1987, had eight meetings, and its unanimous report was signed on 23 March 1988. The result was the gathering together of work into one single board, with four councils: ministry, parish development, training and the Board of Education. Education was difficult as it needed to have autonomy not least because of its statutory establishment. STEM, as it is known, is regarded by many other dioceses as a centre of excellence. None of this would have come to pass without Harries' huge breadth of vision, intellectual and physical energy, capacity for listening and noting and for not forgetting people and places.

In June, the bishops of the diocese set forth a vision – Harries' own vision! – in which the priorities were personal spirituality; Christian generosity; the integration of faith and work; clergy development; sharing the faith; solidarity between those in need; work with children and young people; and working together. If proposals failed they were withdrawn and another way forward was found. In 1994, the drastic fall in the Church Commissioners' grant to dioceses triggered the need to consider how the Church would be resourced in the future. With alacrity, Oxford produced 'Mission and Ministry in the Diocese of Oxford' which each deanery needed to study. A Parish Share scheme was prepared. In 1995 there was a 'Vision and Priorities Statement'. Harries prepared 'A Vision for the Diocese', which encapsulated his desires as leader and enabler. Two extracts are sufficient illumination of this vision:

The Church has been called into being by God. It exists to offer worship, to make known, by deed as well as word, the love of God in his Son Jesus Christ and, through the Holy Spirit, to draw people into a loving and ever deepening relationship with God and one another. The Church strengthens us to work for a world in which all human beings are able to flourish, physically, emotionally and spiritually, and in which the environment is cared for. It thereby acts as a sign of that divine Kingdom in which the whole created order will find its proper fulfilment. So our vision of ministry is of a Christian congregation in each centre of community. This congregation, whilst assuming responsibility for its own life, particularly financing its own life, will seek to serve the wider community. This congregation will have a number of people with gifts for ministry, trained for the purpose. In some of these congregations there will be an increasing number of non-stipendiary clergy, able to help each congregation realize its full potential. These people will be able to work collaboratively at parish and deanery level as well as ecumenically. In a number of areas the deanery will play an increasingly important role enabling the local congregations to do together what they are not able to do apart. We anticipate that 'major benefices', involving a team of clergy and lay people, will play an increasingly important role.

By 1997 the five strands of mission were:

1. Proclaim the Good News of the Kingdom.
2. Teach, baptize and nurture new believers.
3. Respond to human need by loving service.
4. Seek to transform unjust structures of society.
5. Strive to safeguard the integrity of creation and sustain and renew the face of the earth.

These were not the vapourings of working parties, but urgent impulses, impelling necessities for a diocese ever responding to the original vision and always on the move.

Oxford was the first diocese to appoint three parish development advisers, one for each episcopal area, and did so because it believed that any kind of training intervention in the life of the parish, whether it be children's or youth work, stewardship or parochial church council training, always affected the life of the whole parish.

When the mounds of paper subsided from Harries' desk, the motivating factor of it all was clear, calling the people of the diocese to a renewed awareness of the world. He endeavoured to stir the consciences of people on pressing claims of the moment. He was skilled in making public statements on how the faith relates to moral, social, community, national and international issues. Progress was made in all areas except one: the integration of faith and work. 'We never succeeded in achieving anything in that sphere,' said Harries.

One form of spiritual bounty was available to Harries and the diocese of Oxford. Nowhere else in the Church of England are there as many Religious communities. The mixed Benedictine Community of the Priory of Our Lady, Burford, was a special place for him. He gained strength from the spiritual energy found in the consecration of lives wholly dedicated to the glory of God and the benefit of the Church. His admiration for monks and nuns was immense. In a world which resents authority and discipline, they take the life-vow of obedience; in a world preoccupied with materialism and consumerism, they take a vow of poverty; in a world obsessed with human sexuality, they take a vow of chastity. When Harries first arrived in Oxford he was official visitor to five communities, but two closed down leaving him the Communities of the Sisters of the Love of God at Fairacres, St Mary the Virgin, Wantage, and St John the Baptist, Kidlington.

Harries recommended quiet days, retreats and spiritual direction in the knowledge that Religious communities are powerhouses, places of unexpected disturbance, not cosy cocoons or havens from the turbulence and crises of daily living. Many Sisters have a bracing, uncomfortable directness about them. Harries knew he was held in remembrance before God in these communities which leaven the Church with spirituality and action.

 Christian unity has been a fundamental feature of diocesan life since the time of Harry Carpenter. Several successful local initiatives serve as examples. The Church of the Holy Family at Blackbird Leys in the city of Oxford, built in 1965, became a shared church used by several congregations. The new city of Milton Keynes was planned ecumenically from the earliest days, with the development and building of shared churches and community centres, the most prominent of which is the Church of Christ the Cornerstone. In 1993, Harries led an ecumenical mission in Witney: all Christians in the town, from evangelical House Church members to Roman Catholics, participated. Christians in Abingdon have been united in outreach and service to the town over a long period. Trinity Church, Lower Earley, Reading, was opened in 1988 with the United Reformed and Methodist Churches: there is one congregation that receives the Sacraments together.

Harries had good relations with most other Christian leaders. For a few years he chaired the Church leaders' meeting for Oxfordshire and also the main ecumenical body for that county, now Churches Together in Oxfordshire. Relations with the Roman Catholic Church were the exception to the mutual understanding and cordiality developed with other denominations. The size of the Anglican diocese of Oxford meant that Harries had to relate to the Roman Catholic Archbishop of Birmingham and the bishops of Northampton and Portsmouth. Oxford city itself is mostly in the Birmingham archdiocese but part is in Portsmouth. From 1982 the archbishop was an urbane, courteous, erudite, traditionally minded archbishop whose Huguenot cousin was one of De Gaulle's Prime Ministers – Maurice Noël Léon Couve de Murville. He had been the Catholic chaplain at two universities, Sussex and Cambridge, for 21 years before being catapulted to Birmingham. If the appointment was unexpected and strange it was also misjudged. There is no evidence that the life and cultural surroundings of a university chaplaincy, Roman or Anglican, provides the best grounding for episcopal life. Moreover, Couve de Murville was unwise in the way he dealt with serious cases of clerical abuse in his archdiocese. The result, now revealed, was the protection of priests in their criminal misdeeds coming before care of the victims of abuse. Once the cloud descended upon him it never lifted. Vincent Gerard Nichols, one of Cardinal Hume's auxiliary bishops in Westminster, was appointed to succeed him as archbishop in 2000. Was it possible that relations between Oxford and Birmingham would improve? Nichols was relatively young at 55, had charm, ambition and proven abilities and, like

Harries, had the capacity to communicate with all ages. But Nichols was essentially illiberal. Although there was not much chance of Harries and Nichols reciting the rosary together, Harries feels that if it had not been for the disagreement over St Augustine's School they would have developed good relations. The decision about the school was made before Nichols had arrived.

As for ecumenicalism overall, Harries has a sceptical view:

> One of my reasons for disappointment with the whole ecumenical movement is the way that the then Cardinal Ratzinger pumped cold water out of the Vatican cellars onto the Anglican–Roman Catholic International Commission (ARCIC) reports. That reflects what I have discovered in other circumstances, namely, I don't think the Roman Catholic Church actually has any real will to unity, except very much on its own terms. This reminds me of a saying of Austin Farrer, that he was neither a Slav nor a Greek, and the papacy was a great fact-producing machine, so the Anglican Church was the only possible spiritual home. There is also a remark of Father Percy Coleman, a much revered Anglo-Catholic of a previous generation, who, shortly before he died, said to Mother Rosemary SLG, 'The Church of England is the only part of the Catholic Church which is open to the future'. I suppose these are the reasons why though I'm enormously attracted, spiritually and aesthetically to the Orthodox Church, and though I hugely admire the internationalism of the Roman Catholic Church and its ability to produce genuine saints (which may or may not overlap with those who are canonized) and though I have good friends amongst non-conformist Churches of various kinds, the Church of England for all its many faults, seems the only possible place to be.

Whilst at Fulham, Harries made good friends with the local Roman Catholic parish priest of St Thomas of Canterbury Church, Fr Adrian Hailer. 'He did a wonderful job renewing his parish round serious Bible reading and reflection. He eventually left and married a parishioner, indeed one who was divorced, and I had the interesting experience of marrying him, after a civil ceremony, in an Anglican church using, if I remember correctly, the Roman rite! We have remained friends.'

While Fr Hailer was still a priest, he and Harries met and agreed to their parishes developing an ecumenical relationship. But the kind of work Hailer believed in was sometimes regarded as an optional extra in Roman Catholic clerical circles. As Adrian Hailer reflects:

> You could get by without engaging in it. As one Irish bishop, frustrated in his attempts to put his priests to work and conscious of their far-flung interests, remarked, 'if it is not ecumenism they are interested in, it is beekeeping'. Richard's position was a world away from this because his starting point was so utterly different. Richard had grown up in an Anglican world where ecclesiastical dispute was deep-seated and endemic. I sometimes felt at a meeting of a clerical fraternal that the Anglicans were able to mark one

another's cards by word and attitude rather as Catholics and Protestants in Northern Ireland are able to suss one another out by address, schooling etc. I sensed, perhaps wrongly, that Richard felt that the Anglican Church, however mighty its endurance, was like a ship in a storm looking for a safe haven. Historically, theologically that haven was most likely to be the Roman Catholic Church. I always thought he saw Rome, for all its failings and clumsy dealings, as a strength and stay, upholding Church life in the West. The clerical fraternal in Fulham thrived during his time. At least we were all talking to one another and appreciating one another's works. One day there was a lively discussion about soteriology – what Christ did, above all on the Cross that was of saving effect. A Methodist present argued very forcefully that he did not accept a substitutionist theology – roughly that Christ died instead of us, in our place. Then he explained what he did think. After the meeting was over, as we were going, Richard observed in his usual kind and calm manner that the Methodist did indeed hold a substitutionist theology though he did not seem to be aware of it.

Richard and I became friends and we would sometimes go walking along the towpath that runs from Putney to Barnes. There you can pick up the muddy smell of the tidal Thames and glimpse what the river used to look like. We would pass St Paul's where his son was at school. It would be easy to overlook how much of a family man Richard is. When an evening meeting ended I noticed that he would soon be away and I felt that there was a sense of responsibility in his doing so. I imagine he wanted to get back to his wife and family. Richard had married a beautiful woman whose health was delicate. I was with them once when the discussion turned on how to manage family life in a vicarage where the parishioners came in as though it was their own home. I am not sure how easy they found family life in a busy vicarage. I missed Richard when he moved on, and the fraternal meetings and joint services gradually became harder to sustain.

One existing ecumenical opportunity was smashed. In 1996 a new schools' adviser was appointed for Buckinghamshire, Milton Keynes and Slough and, in 2000, was appointed the diocesan director of education. What was unusual was that Danny Sullivan was a Roman Catholic. He had been head teacher of a Roman Catholic primary school, worked as an adviser to the Roman Catholic Bishop of Portsmouth, Crispian Hollis, and had taught religious studies to student teachers at La Sainte Union College in Southampton. In addition he had been chairman of the Thomas Merton Society of Great Britain and Ireland and was actively engaged in Christian/Buddhist dialogue. A major controversy and difficult struggle surrounded the future of the joint Church of England and Roman Catholic St Augustine's Secondary School in Oxford city. This popular and successful school had been in existence since 1980. The archdiocese of Birmingham, which held the trust deeds, wished to withdraw from the school. Legally the Church of England was in a weak position. Harries gave an excellent defence of the school and worked long and hard to retain it. He won the support of Oxford City Council and the majority of people active in education in Oxford. Danny Sullivan was in the unique position of being able to argue for the joint school:

> ... as Anglican director of education, using as my references documents from Vatican II and consequent Catholic documents on education and ecumenism – no doubt ruling myself out of any chance of a Papal medal for services to Catholic education!!

The archdiocese's' campaign at times against the school was scurrilous and great use was made of parts of the Catholic media to rubbish the school and by implication its staff and students. Bishop Richard held to his integrity in this matter and never responded in kind. He once confided in me his hope that the school could remain a bridge between the two Churches. For my part as director, I received a flood of messages of support for the diocese's commit-ment to the school from fellow Catholics whom I had previously worked with. Each Sunday when I went to Mass in my local Catholic parish, the parish priest would encourage me (and the Oxford diocese) not to give up the fight for the school. Of course, we lost that fight but I believe we, with Bishop Richard's lead, modelled to the students and parents and staff of St Augus-tine's why the concept and reality of that joint school was worth fighting for as long as we did. Once the school was to close, Archbishop Nichols invited Bishop Richard to join him in a farewell to the school. Given some of the scurrilous behaviour of some in the archdiocese over the school, Bishop Richard declined to appear with Archbishop Nichols, as he thought it would simply be hypocritical. He was right, I believe.

While the Roman Catholic Church faced revelations of clergy sex abuse – acting only when forced to do so – the Anglican Church, in the 1990s, had its own scan-dals, mostly with adults, not children. A number of these were connected with and arose out of charismatic worship, speaking in tongues, healing and exorcism. Apart from the *News of the World* entrapment of Brian Brindley, Oxford was not involved in any which featured in the glare of publicity, such as the notorious 'Nine O'Clock Service' in Sheffield, which, with a number of other infamous cases, prompted the bishops to act!

In an *Ad Clerum* (June 1995) Harries suggested a safety code:

> From time to time the area bishops and myself have to deal with a sexual scandal involving a priest. This is painful and distressing for all concerned. Those who find themselves in this sad situation do not usually set out to do wrong. Rather, through a combination of circumstances, involving what the ASB Confession well describes as negligence and weakness, they find them-selves caught up in a relationship from which it is difficult to extract them-selves. I would like to suggest the following safety code. First, to be aware of our own emotional needs. We all have a desire for intimacy, whether

expressed in marriage or through close friendships. If we are isolated and lonely but not really aware of this, it is easy for our unconscious needs to trip us up. We find ourselves overstepping the bounds of professional conduct or developing an illicit relationship. Secondly, there are occasions when we all need counselling. We need a trained person to help us think through our disappointments and frustrations . . . Far better to take preventative action and seek help if you feel the tremors of a mid-life or other crisis coming upon you.

This developed into a detailed draft 'Code of Ministerial Practice' (September 1995), written by the Revd Simon Baker, principal of Berkshire Churches Training Scheme, as part of the process of review of ministerial training in that archdeaconry. At Pentecost 1996, it was adapted and adopted for the whole diocese and, not for the first time, Oxford led the way in the Church of England. 'The Greatness of the Trust' focused on the important and sensitive area of sexual abuse of adults by ministers, and was complemented by the national 'Guidelines for the Professional Conduct of the Clergy'; and later the 2004 edition of the House of Bishops' policy on child protection, 'Protecting All God's Children'.

There is a clear distinction between pastoral care and counselling. Counsellors, like financial consultants, have been a growth industry of very uneven practice and equally varied results. An advertisement in a local newspaper or a plaque on a door is not evidence of a qualification. Appending the adjective 'Christian' may be a way of duping an anxious client. Harries and his area bishops had names of good people that could be passed onto clergy, without any questions being asked at that stage, with, usually, half the cost being met from discretionary funds.

The Revd Michael Wright, chairman of the Association for Pastoral Care and Counselling, considered the Oxford guidelines, not without criticism (*Church Times* 4 October 1996):

Counselling training has a secular ethic with humanist values. These values are widely seen as being the unchallengeable orthodoxy of counselling, but they do challenge some of the values and practices of Christian faith ethics. The non-judgemental approach of the counsellor feels very safe for the client. In pastoral care it is also important, but not necessarily as an end in itself. It can be a stage towards growth in understanding, in acceptance of a difficult path to tread, and in finding the strength to tread it. Pastoral care aims to find a proper path between the values of hedonism and the values of Christ. It is not a matter of using biblical texts as a kind of Elastoplast on deep and painful wounds: it seeks rather to provide the troubled Christian with a safe place in which to explore dilemmas, and to look realistically at Christian values and principles, without being overwhelmed by feelings of judgement and condemnation.

It was increasingly common for individual dioceses in the Church of England to have links with dioceses in the worldwide Anglican Communion. Oxford's formal link with Kimberley and Kuruman in South Africa owes its formation to what may be called the personal chemistry between Harries and Njongonkulu Winston Hugh Ndungane, Bishop of Kimberley and Kuruman from 1991 to 1996. Although the son, grandson and great-grandson of Anglican priests, Winston's call to serve God came when he was for three years a prisoner in a cell on Robben Island. He was one of the first political prisoners and was set to work building the actual prison – 'hell on earth' he called it – which later housed Nelson Mandela.

> (Ndungane): I think African culture affirms life and we are people whose identity is founded on '*ubunto*' – which translates as the essence of community, the essence of affirming people, the essence of belonging, and so worship, which is the coming-together, is an enjoyment. In the African world-view there is no separation between the religious and the profane. All life is one – God the Creator is the source of all. The whole question of eternal life is rooted in the being of an African, in the sense of the presence and the awareness of the living dead.

Kimberley is one and half times the size of the United Kingdom, sparsely populated (500,000), arid with large areas of desert, economically poor despite important diamond and copper mines and vast deposits of manganese, asbestos, lime and gypsum. There are 40,000 Anglican Church members, hundreds of churches, 35 parishes, but only some 40 priests and no money to pay for more. The diocese's borders include Namibia and Botswana.

Harries' flame of affection for South Africa has never burned low. On a private visit to the country in 1993 he laid the foundations for the diocesan link with Kimberley which was formally inaugurated at the 1993 Ascension Day Eucharist at Christ Church Cathedral. It is a wonderfully creative and fruitful link. The original vision was not just about handing over money to 'our brothers and sisters'. Parishes in the diocese made their own links with particular parishes in Kimberley. African priests came to Oxford, computers were bought to help isolated and lonely clergy to have email and other facilities; there was support for work with women (58 per cent of women in South Africa are HIV positive). Richard and Jo Harries visited Africa and hosted the bishops in Oxford. In 1996 Winston Ndungane was elected Archbishop of Cape Town, succeeding Desmond Tutu. Itumeleng Moseki was elected Bishop of Kimberley and Kuruman. He had earlier been director for Justice and Reconciliation in the diocese of Johannesburg. He too formed a close relationship with Harries and reflects, 'I was at first intimidated by having to be in the presence of such a leader and servant of the Church but all my anxieties soon disappeared. He was a patient listener when our discussions tended to betray my woundedness and sometimes an awkwardness in trying to spell out the needs and challenges in my home diocese. Through him I got to know what empathy was all about; a capacity to draw nearer into the felt needs and pains of others and work alongside in search of relief and restoration.'

Another link is with the diocese of Växjö in the Church of Sweden. There are parallels with England. Traditional values of Church and society have yielded, through the odyssey of modernization, to postmodernism. The authority of the Churches has eroded, but so has that of the State. There are also contrasts. In Sweden 87 per cent of burials are according to Church rites; 71 per cent of parents have their children baptized, even if confirmation of 15-year-olds dropped to 50 per cent by 2000. Sweden is a classless society and social democracy is social democracy! Christian parties take part in political life. In 2000 after a long process there was the separation of Church and State. The ordination of women in the Nordic Churches pre-dates England, for example 1947 – Denmark; 1960 – Sweden; 1961 – Norway. By the millennium one third of the clergy in Sweden were female and there are women bishops at Lund and Stockholm.

The exchange between Oxford and Växjö is welcomed in each Church. The bishop, Anders Wejryd, who was also elected Archbishop in 2006, observes, 'many Swedes, lay and ordained, find Church-life in our Lutheran sister Churches in Germany and Denmark less familiar than Churches in England' and he provides a glimpse of Harries through their first meeting:

> Some of us were going to take part in a confirmation service at Greyfriars Church, Reading. The confirmands were adults and the Church was charismatic. We met the bishop (Harries) outside and his aristocratic posture (obviously accentuated by an aching back and hip) went well together with what we expected from a member of the House of Lords. The church was an experience to us, being so to say turned 90 degrees, with a podium at what used to be the side-wall. We realized that was practical for the band and also gave a good view for the congregation, not only through the monitors. This was perhaps not the most natural liturgical environment for the bishop, but he successfully built bridges between expressions and traditions. On his question, what this confirmation would mean to the newly confirmed, they all witnessed that they were going to let the Christian witness play a large part in their lives and they were all reflecting on going into mission on a more full-time basis. Reflecting on that, the bishop noted that some Swedes were in church.
>
> 'They are Lutherans. Does anyone know who Luther was?' – No one knew – or volunteered, so he went on:
>
> 'Well Luther had an idea that you could serve God by serving your fellow man. He even said that a hangman could serve God, if he did his job properly. Maybe I don't mean to go that far, but Luther has a point when saying you serve God where you are. Maybe you don't have to go somewhere else?'

In Oxford there were ordained women deacons awaiting the grace of priestly orders. On 16/17 April 1993, 66 were ordained priest at six separate services in different churches throughout the diocese. At last women were canonically and legally ordained as priests. It was more than a moment to savour for Harries. When he voted 'Yes' at the 1991 Diocesan Synod, he did so for a positive reason. It was not primarily for justice, nor even for theological rectitude, but because he knew the

Church would be enriched by gifts from the ministry of women, and so it has proved. A number of clergy and laity, some high-profile ones, left the Church of England for the Roman Catholic Church or other Churches. The extended alternative or parallel episcopal oversight for those priests who were opposed but remained was welcomed by Harries. 'I believe the position we are adopting does have a theological basis. Apart from that, a compassionate muddle is preferable to a tyrannical tidiness. Indeed, I think the Church of England at this point has much for which, under God, it can be thankful. For the first time in the long history of bitter religious division in the world, a real attempt is being made to include opponents of a majority decision rather than giving them the straight choice of "accept or leave".'

By 2006 there were more than 200 women priests in the diocese. When the House of Bishops met to consider the next logical step, women bishops, Harries wondered if positions had again polarized: 'But at the early morning meeting of the House of Bishops on 9 February 2006 the House was at its best, with much shared wisdom. Later that morning at the General Synod, the Transferred Episcopal Arrangement (TEA) was passed with only one vote against.' Once again with the Act of Synod, the Church of England took the historic step in seeking to be inclusive of those who disagreed though, as Harries recalled, 'we have to remember that it is women priests who then and now bear much of the pain of this inclusiveness. On the day that Synod took its historic vote on the ordination of women to the priesthood, I wrote a prayer, the sentiments of which will still be much needed in the years ahead:

> Most holy and gracious wisdom,
> Illuminate the deliberations and decisions of this day.
> Our view is narrow; you encompass the whole of humanity;
> Our horizon is bounded; you see far beyond all limits;
> Our sight is clouded by self-concern;
> You are wholly given over to the well-being of your creation.
> In the radiancy of this true and only light
> Guide our deliberations and decisions today.'

The consecration of women as bishops remains at this time of writing some way ahead. There were two debates at the General Synod meeting in York in July 2006. For the first time a motion was passed 'that admitting women to the episcopate in the Church of England is consonant with the faith of the Church as the Church of England has received it and would be proper development in proclaiming afresh in this generation the grace and truth of Christ'. Voting figures were Bishops 31–9; Clergy 134–42; Laity 123–68. Following a second debate General Synod agreed to set up a legislative group to explore the way forward, after the House of Bishops had reached an impasse on the subject. The vote was Bishops 27–11; Clergy 118–67; Laity 103–92. Only a simple majority was required. Legislation will require a two-thirds majority. On this basis mitres on women's heads is not assured as the House of Laity did not reach a two-thirds majority.

If a Swan Hellenic cruise is blissful paradise for Harries, what would be his nightmare? 1,300 people, 90 workshops, 30 seminars, fun and fellowship and six different forms of worship for four days at Butlins' South Coast World Holiday Camp at Bognor Regis? That is where he went for the Oxford Diocesan Conference 2001 'Setting Course for the Future'. Laity outnumbered clergy by more than three to one and there was an age-span of eight weeks to 90. It had been meticulously and imaginatively planned. All Harries had to do was to turn up! Taste and see was endemic among the delegates. Evangelicals dropped into the New Promise Sung Eucharist in the Manhattan nightclub and amongst clouds of incense found inspiration in Anglo-Catholic renewal. Some who had opposed women priests attended services where a woman presided and did not walk out. *Book of Common Prayer* devotees sat alongside children in an all-age service with drama and dance. There was a daily *Door* newspaper, rivalled by *Catflap*, a newspaper written and distributed by children. Speakers included Sara Maitland, feminist, novelist and author of *A Big Enough God* ; Michael Nazir-Ali, Bishop of Rochester, on contemporary communities under God; and Richard Holloway, a former Primus of Scotland, redirecting delegates to a missionary Church on the move, 'We are not here to preserve the old but to follow Christ who is always new and young'. For Harries 'the God in whom we believe took us by surprise and surpassed our expectations. The combination of serious Christian learning, the joy of the worship and the warmth of the fellowship left an indelible impression'. Christine Zwart, then editor of *The Door*, adds, 'Bognor proved to be the most amazing experience for us all – charismatic filled with all the excitement of the Holy Spirit and the closing worship (at which Harries preached) was a taste of heaven. The bishop was quietly delighted. This kind of thing happened a few times and so I began to wonder if God was not using him rather wonderfully despite himself and his claim to be a cynic about things charismatic.' When a large number of people went down with a bug immediately after the conference, people jokingly referred to this as the 'Bognor Blessing'.

In 1999 when visiting the diocese, the Archbishop of Canterbury, George Carey, was asked what Christians could do to celebrate the millennium. His reply was that it would be excellent if everyone in the diocese wore the Cross as a token of his or her Christian commitment. No sooner suggested than done! A special diocesan millennium Cross was designed and made available for £1 to every member of the electoral roll of every parish in the diocese. With the Cross was a prayer card. Harries was always encouraged when he saw people wearing it. With the millennium came fresh 'visions': in 2001 a 'Sharing Life' programme and in 2003 'Shaping the Future Together'. The consistent theme throughout Harries' episcopate was 'The Way Forward'. The mission of the Church was uppermost in his thinking. He worked hard with 'Sharing Life'. The principles of this vision were simply expressed: Centred on God, Father, Son and Holy Spirit; orientated towards the world and its needs; connecting to people, both their communities and their culture in new ways; serious about Christian discipleship. Harries' words of farewell at the Eucharist with the blessing of oils and renewal of ministerial commitment on 11 April 2006 at Christ Church Cathedral, echoed 'Sharing Life':

So, dear friend, like Jacob, there is no escape from wrestling with the issues of our time, especially what the preface to the declaration of assent refers to as the faith which 'The church is called upon to proclaim afresh in each generation'. Wrestling to do this will mark us – and makes us a bearer of blessing. For this great task we have been assured the gift of sacred love on the altar of our heart, one which the spirit yearns to fan into flame. This will enable us not to be too bothered about whether we are a somebody or a nobody, because we are focused on the other and their well-being, after the pattern and in the spirit of the one who came amongst us and is still amongst us as the one who serves.

From the beginning to the close of his episcopate Harries' purpose was to create a caring, sustainable and growing Christian presence in every part of the diocese of Oxford.

Chapter Seventeen
Waiting and Journeying

Richard Harries has a profound sense of Christian hope. The seasons of Advent and Epiphany unexpectedly and paradoxically reveal and explain much about his priesthood and episcopal ministry. Advent is about waiting but there is waiting and waiting. Human beings with and without hope. There is religious faith and there is stoic courage. A symbol of Advent is a pregnant woman about to give birth. Heavy with child, out of balance, cumbersome, she waits, confronted with certain truths about life and death, pain and joy. It is ironic that Advent is entered when the world around dives into a frenzy of shopping and consumer activity. Lasting things happen in God's good time.

Anglicans are inclined to shun away from talk of the 'the last day' when all the trophies of our competence and gall become debris and we are naked before God. How far is Harries a 'last day' person? When deacons, priests and bishops look at their diaries and calendars (maybe for several years ahead), they should be reminded that there is only one certain appointment. That is with God on the subject of life. At the heart of whatever in this world is on a downward spiral, slipping, eroding, suffering, dissipating, plans and initiatives coming to naught: there at the bottom is the life-giver declaring, 'And I will raise him up at the last day'. A hard word – and lesson – for any Christian leader is contained in a single word – restraint. Restraint is the secret of Jesus' power. Accordingly a leader, instead of having a heart fully occupied with agendas, manoeuvrings, self-aggrandizing imaginings and a will to power, finds a space for restraint, room to be expanded, a waiting area, a location from which to weigh ultimates, and a place to surrender one's will for the sake of God's.

One of Harries' early *Prayer for the Day* broadcasts opens with the words:

Advent is, I think, my favourite part of the Church's year: which is odd. For the traditional themes of Advent, death, judgement, heaven, hell hardly fill us with delight. Advent is a time of spare beauty. It perfectly matches nature at this season. The trees are stripped of their leaves and they stand alone, silhouetted against the winter sky, austere of line, mysterious and haunting. Advent reflects this . . . Advent is a time of expectation, of hope, which, like cheerfulness, keeps breaking in. This hope is no illusion. For there is something to look forward to; and for this future, God's future, we were made.

Harries cared deeply for his clergy, more than the majority would ever know as it was not overtly obvious. He also understood the grind and joy of parish life, the unreal expectations of clergy and the difficulties they have in ordering priorities. Several times he has quoted G. K. Chesterton's adage, 'If a job is worth doing it's worth doing badly', which he regards as 'a very salutary antidote to the perfectionist streak within us which wants to do a job perfectly or not at all. We cannot, and do not have to make ourselves perfectly acceptable to God. He takes us as we are, and because he takes us as we are, we can, while still doing our best, live with the fact that everything we do is less than the best'. One priest responded, 'If a man is any good at his job, for every one thing he does, he sees two he ought to do, and four he would like to do. Do what you can and leave the rest to God.'

Harries was scarcely known to be downcast, broody, moody or glum. St Teresa used often to exclaim, 'God deliver me from sour-faced saints'. Harries had to an unusual degree a serious countenance and a beaming wide smile, exuding a warm, not sunny, persona. Behind this is there an Advent element of holy fear? Fear is not meant to induce a sour-face, but it saves people from being shallow or slack and lazy, something Harries abhors in priests; not to make them weary, but to save them from being frivolous. Fear may, of course, drive people to God, not fearing his harshness but knowing their own need and dependence on his strength.

There is always fruitful friction relating to the so-called 'role' of the clergy in society. In his 1992 Maundy Thursday homily Harries is clear: 'We do not receive our vocation from society. Our role and ministry is inextricably bound up with that of the Church, with the generous outgoing of our Lord himself, which fitted no definable category in his own time. As he was obedient to the Father, struggling as we do for the way ahead, not always certain about the direction, the value or the purpose of what he was doing, he committed himself in trust to the Father. His identity, the very meaning of his mission, which was only given in hints and guesses, was retroactively validated in the Resurrection. So with us.' A priest in society has opportunities of noticing the unnoticed; celebrating the non-celebrities; empowering the powerless; putting in touch the out-of-touch. A bishop has other opportunities if he is prepared to recognize and act on them. Harries was there to encourage, cheer and sustain his clergy, in his own way.

The clergy are not united in their impressions of Harries, except in a near unanimity of acknowledging that he is demonstrably a kind and humane man, serious and supportive, and someone who seeks the will of God in prayer. Even at times of ferocious conflict when barbed arrows were aimed, they were directed at his views or actions and not at his person. That is reflected in words of the Revd Anthony Ellis, Area Dean of Oxford: 'The one thing which I have come to recognize in Richard Harries is his extraordinary kindness and his ability to see good things in people whom I would want to criticize. The generosity of spirit is what I value most in him. He takes the Gospel imperative to love his neighbour seriously and does so to the best of his ability.'

Harries was good at building up new clergy and then leaving them alone. As they were appointed to their new parish he enjoyed that part of being a bishop. He read their files before visiting each parish, trying to ensure he knew something of their lives and interests. And what he read he retained. To those who felt he was not approachable the evidence to the contrary is apparent. He was usually at his best when there were specific needs, when his patient listening and gentle direction was exemplary. A priest breaking down was helped to find a way forward. Another who became ill with depression gave Harries permission to speak to his psychiatrist so that the best could be done for him. Harries was so trusted that he alone knew where the priest was staying. His own pastoral sensitivity and action speeded recovery. The simple and friendly hospitality provided by Jo and Richard Harries helped many priests through rough and scarring times. They understood. Canon Beaumont Stevenson, adviser in pastoral care, thinks of Harries as 'probably one of the most unpompous people going. He had vision, but a down-to-earthness and practicality, which is a good combination'. He provides two examples:

> Meeting in the hallway when I had an office at Diocesan Church House, he said: 'How are you today?' 'I feel like hell,' I said, 'would you take me out to lunch?' 'Of course,' he replied. We went off to a local pub, and had a lunch and chat, and then he insisted I have a 'scrumptious chocolate dessert' to round things off. I felt beautifully supported – just what I needed. Similarly a monastic friend said that he was kneeling next to the bishop during the singing of some psalms. The monk was feeling under stress, and really belted out one of the lines. 'That felt good, didn't it?' Richard said with a smile. He said it was nice to have his anger affirmed.

Work appraisal and the importance of continuing ministerial education for clergy in the diocese was emphasized and strengthened. Harries wanted clergy to work through their difficulties, supporting and reassuring one another. 'It was a way of clergy not only being able to share on a peer level their concerns and stresses about the way they would like to exercise their ministry, but also to share what they do best and feel is going well.' In 1990 a Spirituality Network was started for people who acted as spiritual directors, counsellors and soul friends.

On several occasions Harries stressed that to be ordained was to run the risk of losing identity rather than gaining it: 'It means facing a world that tries, and fails, to press us to be socially acceptable categories.' How does this accord with his own admitted need to have a recognizable and public identity? He exudes a gratifying glow. In the words of the novelist Henry James, 'He reminds me . . . of one of those lucent match-boxes which you place, on going to bed, near the candle, to show you, in the darkness, where you can strike a light: he shines in the uneasy gloom – vaguely, and has a phosphorescence, not a flame.'

The 'phosphorescence' was evident in Harries' approach to renewal in the diocese and methods of bringing people into the life of the Church. There was a common policy with the area bishops by which Harries encouraged open, welcoming baptism and Communion before confirmation, subject to appropriate safeguards. 'This (latter) practice should certainly not be regarded as a panacea for all ills but I certainly want to encourage and support those parishes which, with a strong emphasis upon the nurture of children, wish to pursue this policy.'

'Charismatic' is another word purloined and subsumed for partisan use, draining much of its original meaning. It is not confined to evangelical Churches but is found within the whole spectrum of Anglicanism. It is not difficult to understand its rise and rise when lethargy befalls a Church. There is something impressive about a 'movement' which does plainly succeed in arresting people, and giving them a vivid and operative religion, one that is at once demanding and exciting. It is an antidote to institutionalism, to Christianity becoming so organized that it ceases to be personal. A number of Anglican bishops were swept along with the charismatic movement and saw its permanent place in the Church of England. Harries neither fulminated against it, nor greedily swallowed the bait offered by its enthusiastic adherents. He recognized its gifts and its deficiencies.

Harries responded to the growth of evangelical charismatic parishes where there was a need for a service in which people could make an adult act of commitment. 'Sometimes, people who are confirmed young, later undergo a powerful conversion experience. Sometimes people who have undergone a conversion experience are at another time conscious of a special baptism or blessing of the Holy Spirit. Occasionally, in response to the New Testament emphasis on baptism, people are tempted to seek re-baptism as an adult believer. Personally, I wish there were more opportunities to offer confirmation to adults who are seeking some public expression of their new-found or re-found Christian faith. It may be that those parishes that are particularly conscious of this situation might advise me how it might be appropriate for bishops to be involved in recognizing and affirming the experience and conviction of such people.'

An abiding characteristic should here be reckoned and stressed. There were clergy and laity who were strenuously critical of specific views and actions of their diocesan bishop. They consumed his time and caused grief and pain. These were troublesome times for the Church of England. In the 1970s and 1980s there was a resurgence of biblical fundamentalism and doctrinal fanaticism. Fanaticism is the disease of faith not its fullest expression. It hungers ever for certainty, tokens and signs, refusing to recognize God's presence in what is normal, unexciting and commonplace. Further, the effects following the emergence of the charismatic movement were frequently divisive, dangerous and delusory. However, more recently some of the ill-fated traits of the movement have been tamed as more rigorous theology, accountability and leadership are evident, though not always and everywhere. Throughout his episcopate Harries' support and personal warmth never wavered towards those with whom he had theological differences or who were harshly critical of his position on specific issues. When he retired they openly expressed their gratitude for his kindness and support. Only the frozen-hearted were incapable of acknowledging his 'generosity of spirit' which is both a remarkable gift and lasting legacy.

Whereas Harries enabled and supported experimentation and innovation and was known as an adaptor of the faith, was he less efficacious as a preserver and guardian of the faith? He had a natural affinity with the Catholic aspects of Anglicanism. But he neither stands with the Church's ultra-conservative section, which cannot believe that any new teaching is true, nor the ultra-modern section, which is ready to accept any new hypothesis as true because it is new. The general sense of the Church of England – 'the beauty and crown of the Reformation' – still lies at its best in a balance between those extremes. It is difficult to decide in particular cases what is central and what is circumferential in Christian belief. Harries was on guard whenever he heard the bleat 'What the Bible says is . . .' The biblical record is not the last word on any subject, it is the first word; the last word has yet to be uttered. The New Testament gives us the first word; the Holy Spirit gives us the last word of Jesus. On belief, Harries, along with most bishops, thought some latitude may be wisely allowed, so long as speculative discussion and authoritative teaching were kept strictly apart. But doubt, or even heresy, is better met by argument than by official reprobation. The problem arises when consideration is given to the claims of the Church of England as not only soundly Catholic, but also purely apostolic. It is a reformed branch of the Catholic Church, standing for the great positive principle of a non-papal Catholicism. It holds to the apostolic faith, it venerates the apostolic sacraments, it continues the threefold ministry of bishops, priests and deacons. It has neither mutilated them by subtraction nor adulterated them by addition.

Had Harries shifted his position from the times of his curacy at Hampstead and his incumbency at Fulham? He had always been careful not to become a 'paid up member' of any party. He sees positive developments in many movements and is probably nearer to 'Affirming Catholicism' than anything else. But had he departed in any way from the 'faith once delivered to the saints'? That is what many people think and there is little to counter it in his words and writings. Even so, dissatisfaction was not as deeply entrenched as that which came from biblical fundamentalists.

From Advent to Epiphany. The Church of England by law established is an inheritance and a challenge. There are assets and liabilities. As rich as is the heritage, there is the possibility it can veil the richest treasure of all, which is the life of our Lord himself. Harries was not drawn by the panoply or trappings of the Establishment. He was allured by the possibility of influence in and near the corridors of power and on the wider stage of the House of Lords. Of the Establishment of the Church of England the words of Isaiah could be echoed by Harries: 'Destroy it not; for a blessing is in it'. Nevertheless the Epiphany temptation for Anglicans is to shy away from the awful moment of religious confrontation and bask in the partial glories of accumulated riches. A concern for glorious inherited treasures may prevent the Christ story to unfold. The real wisdom is to carry the treasure just far enough and then leave it. Then let the Christ moment happen beyond our ability to guide or predict.

As a custodian of the Anglican treasure, Harries carried his words in writing and speech, and offered his life of service, left them and returned whence he came by another route for fresh endeavours. That was his Epiphany moment.

Chapter Eighteen
The Final Sanction

In 1957 the report on 'Homosexual Offences and Prostitution' was published by the Government. A major recommendation was that homosexual behaviour between consenting adults in private should no longer be a criminal offence. The committee, known as the 'Wolfenden Committee' (after its chairman John Wolfenden), was clear that the criminal law was quite separate from personal morality, a view with which the Church of England concurred. A report of the Church of England Moral Welfare Council, 'Sexual Offenders and Social Punishment', which comprised the Church's evidence to the Wolfenden Committee, concluded: 'We would submit however, that it is not the function of the State and Law to constitute themselves guardians of private morality, and that to deal with sin as such belongs to the province of the Church.' When the subject was debated in Church Assembly on 15 November 1957 the Wolfenden proposals were accepted by a small majority of 155 to 138 – an unexploded time-bomb. Fear ruled the minds of advocates and opponents alike. It was ten years before the Sexual Offences Act (1967) became law. It removed criminal sanctions from the conduct known as buggery and gross indecency when (with certain exceptions) this took place between consenting adults in private. Homosexual behaviour began to be discussed publicly. The Homosexual Law Reform Society and the Gay Christian Movement were active in pushing for greater reform. The word 'gay' was a strange and spurious description to use for a minority who still thought of themselves as persecuted and discriminated against. Thus hijacked, it entered common parlance, extinguishing its original meaning.

This was a time when the House of Bishops, not used to thinking or speaking corporately, should have acted. Instead, in 1974 the Conference of Principals of Theological Colleges approached the Board for Social Responsibility for a study to be made of the theological, social, pastoral and legal aspects of homosexuality. In a few theological colleges, homosexuality was rife with the same features to be regretted in heterosexually-orientated society – casual relationships, promiscuity, parties for 'pick-ups', excessive drinking (for persuasion or drowning of sorrows), 'missionary' endeavours on the part of strong-minded homosexuals determined to persuade the immature. A working party was formed under the chairmanship of the Bishop of Gloucester, John Yates. The report was unanimous. Among its findings was a declaration that there were circumstances in which some people may justifiably choose a homosexual relationship with the hope of enjoying companionship and sexual love similar to that in marriage. Thus physical or genital expression was recognized. Nonetheless, it rejected casual and promiscuous alliances and found that the concept of homosexual 'marriage' could not be validated. Being a homosexual should not hinder membership of the Church of England nor the receiving of Communion. Responsible homosexual unions, if not scandalous, should not be criticized. The working party also proposed that the age of homosexual consent should be lowered from 21 to 18, and that a priest who was a practising homosexual should offer his resignation to his bishop, who would then decide whether it should be accepted or not. As for ordinands:

> We do not think that a bishop is justified in refusing to ordain an otherwise acceptable ordinand merely on the ground that he is (or is believed to be) homosexually orientated. But an ordinand would be wrong to conceal deliberately from his ordaining bishop an intention existing in his own mind to live openly in a homosexual union after ordination or to campaign on behalf of a homophile organization.

Before the report was published it was placed before the members of the Board for Social Responsibility, chaired by the Bishop of Truro, Graham Leonard. When the working party met selected board members on 20 April 1978, a grenade was thrown in their direction. The board was not prepared to accept the report without amendments being made. This was not agreed. Accordingly, when it was published on 19 October 1979 it carried eight pages of critical observations (which had been formulated by Harries' old 'mentor' Professor Gordon Dunstan) and a foreword by Graham Leonard with these words: 'The question of homosexuality raises questions to do with authority of Scripture and the Church's tradition. Because of this, we do not think that the Church of England is yet ready to declare its mind on the subject of homosexuality.' But at least this report was published, unlike two earlier ones on 'The Problem of Homosexuality' (1954) and 'Homosexuality: A review of the situation after the passing of the Sexual Offences Act' (1970) which were 'confidential' and 'not for general release'.

Although the Gloucester report was direct in its findings it had theological and other weaknesses which could have been avoided with a stronger working party. There was only one diocesan bishop (Gloucester), no parish priest and no prominent theologian, whereas the board was strong, argumentative and thorough with four diocesan bishops, three parish priests and experts from the fields of medicine, biology, psychiatry and law. And, importantly, the conservative evangelical voice was represented. The report received a public buffeting with muted satisfaction from some and boiling indignation from others. It was 16 months before it was debated at Synod on 27 February 1981. Much of the discussion and debate at this time highlighted a trend in contemporary Church affairs. Does the Church change the standard in order to accommodate individual propensities? In order to love the sinner, is it necessary or desirable to deny that the sin is sinful? That was one argument. Another, and growing, view was that in the Church of England moral questions could be decided on the basis of the evidence of Scripture. Moral theology has never properly been conducted in this way.

A friend of Harries' from undergraduate days, John Halliburton, put his finger on another weakness, the almost total absence of reference to the question of conscience:

> I feel almost sure that in the case of the communicant member of the Church who is involved in a faithful homosexual relationship, his (or her) conscience is such as to have made a judgement that the state of life chosen is acceptable in the eyes of God. The Church may judge such a conscience erroneous, but if the individual cannot accept this, then he must continue to obey his conscience; provided that he does not cease to realize that his conscience does not square with the objective standard presented by his religion, though clearly he judges this to be in error.

There was a lapse of time before there was another development, although the opposing forces were gathering strength in numbers. On 11 November 1987, the General Synod debated a private motion tabled by the Revd Tony Higton, rector of Hawkwell in Essex and founder of Action for Biblical Witness to our Nation, which described the Lesbian and Gay Christian Movement as a 'pornography-peddling subversive organization which is undermining the Church'. It was a time when there was also an accelerating national fear and gathering panic about the emerging worldwide AIDS epidemic. Higton, supported by an organized stentorian clamour, asked the Synod to 'reaffirm' that sexual intercourse should be restricted to marriage, that in all circumstances fornication, adultery and homosexual acts were sinful, that as a condition of being appointed to or remaining in office 'Christian leaders' should be 'exemplary' in all spheres of morality, including sexual morality, and that the ministry of healing should be offered to all who suffered physically or emotionally as a 'result of such sin'. The march of biblical fundamentalism had begun. Pages of the book of Leviticus were like processional banners. The interventionary, and slightly softening, amendment proposed by the respected evangelical Bishop of Chester, Michael Baughen, allowed the following motion to be passed by 403 votes to 8:

> This Synod affirms that the biblical and traditional teaching on chastity and fidelity in personal relationships is a response to, and expression of, God's love for each one of us, and in particular affirms
> 1. that sexual intercourse is an act of total commitment which belongs properly within a permanent married relationship.
> 2. that fornication and adultery are sins against this ideal, and are likewise to be met with a call to repentance and the exercise of companionship.
> 3. that homosexual genital acts also fall short of this ideal, and are likewise to be met with a call to repentance and the exercise of compassion.
> 4. that all Christians are called to be exemplary in all spheres of morality, and that holiness of life is particularly required of Christian leaders.

This became the benchmark for members of the Church of England who wanted to maintain tradition. Resolution 64 of the 1988 Lambeth Conference moved little further than the statement of the 1978 conference, reaffirming and 'recognizing the continuing need in the next decade for deep and dispassionate study of the question of homosexuality, which would take seriously both the teaching of Scripture and the results of scientific and medical research'.

Meanwhile, another working party, chaired by the Revd June Osborne, was set up in the summer of 1986 to advise the House of Bishops. The Osborne Report was received in 1989 and was found unacceptable to the House of Bishops who, unwisely, refused to publish it although there were many leakages. The report carried insights and foresights which deserved to be aired and was frank in its portrayal of the existing situation of homosexuals in the Church. It had the advantage of drawing on direct testimony from homosexual Christians.

Harries' involvement with this issue really began in 1987: 'The House of Bishops realized that it had been caught off guard by the Higton motion, and we were likely to be in an increasing state of disarray, being picked off one by one by the press, unless we could come to some kind of a common mind. With that end in view a working party was set up. In addition to myself this consisted of John Lucas (fellow and tutor of Merton College, Oxford, one time member of the Archbishops' Commission on Christian Doctrine and of the Lichfield Commission on Divorce and Remarriage) – a very good philosopher indeed but a person of deeply conservative outlook; the Suffragan Bishop of Doncaster, William Persson, not I think technically a conservative evangelical, but a very conservative evangelical nevertheless.' The chairman was the Bishop of Salisbury, John Austin Baker. Not without significance for the future, there was another member, Rowan Williams, then Lady Margaret professor of divinity and canon of Christ Church, Oxford, who attended the first two meetings.

'Issues in Human Sexuality: A statement by the House of Bishops', was published in December 1991. The report had been in danger from within its membership. Its chairman, John Baker, gives a reason and asks a question:

> When Rowan Williams left the working party this changed the inner dynamics of the group very considerably, because it left us with two conservatives of different types – John Lucas and William Persson. In fact I was myself steadily moving towards a liberal position, but had not yet arrived, and I would guess that Richard was appointed to fight the liberal corner. He certainly had major personal bridges to gay clergy. In the end working on the report made me the spokesman for an inclusive stance on ordaining members of gay couples, but the group refused to wear this in any form. I had hoped Richard might support this line, but he did not. Had he done so, we would have had to split and fail to deliver a clear message, but with hindsight even that would have been better than the feeble and untenable compromise we in fact ended up presenting. For that I must take much responsibility, but many years of eirenic Church drafting meant that I was conditioned first and foremost to produce an agreed text. My question is simply: 'What did Richard really think?'

Harries' response to Baker:

> We had got nearly to the end of the drafting, just the last chapter, when John
> suddenly announced to members of the group that he had changed his mind
> and could no longer go along with the kind of consensus we had achieved. We
> were amazed. John asks 'What did Richard think?' That's always a very diffi-
> cult question to answer, looking back. However, first, I am both by tempera-
> ment and philosophy a 'don't tell, don't ask' kind of person. I have a deep
> respect for people's private lives and inner life, and I hate even to label people
> of being of a particular sexuality. This means that I have never been an active
> campaigner on the issue. I realize now of course that my previous position,
> that of the United States armed forces, is no longer tenable.
>
> Producing a text around which we might be able to unite was in the fore-
> front of my mind. John refers to the text as a 'feeble and untenable compro-
> mise'. I strongly disagree with that judgement. First of all, that text did in fact
> achieve its purpose. The House of Bishops united round it and it has stood the
> test of time for some 12 or 13 years. It is still the one around which the House
> of Bishops could actually unite. Secondly, not long after its publication I
> received a letter of warm congratulation from Jack Spong (the Bishop of
> Newark, USA), hardly a compromising moderate. He was enthusiastic in his
> praise of the document, clearly believing that it had moved the Church of
> England's position onwards in a very significant way. I think it did. First, in
> the priority we give to conscience, and in particular to lay people who wish to
> enter into same-sex relationships and all that we say about that. Secondly, in
> firmly eschewing any idea of a witch-hunt against clergy. In addition, the
> whole tone of the document is sane and pastoral. For this we thank John
> Austin Baker himself. He did a wonderful job drafting the document, every
> word of it himself. And amazingly, even though he disagreed with the con-
> clusions, he agreed to draft that final part in order to accord with the mind of
> the group as a whole.

The essential points of guidance given in the report included:

> The Church in its pastoral mission ought to help and encourage all its mem-
> bers, as they pursue their pilgrimage from the starting-points given in their
> own personalities and circumstances, and as they grow by grace within their
> own particular potential. It is, therefore, only right that there should be an
> open and welcoming place in the Christian community both for those
> homophiles who follow the way of abstinence, giving themselves to friend-
> ship for many rather than to intimacy with one, and also for those who are
> conscientiously convinced that a faithful, sexually active relationship with
> one other person, aimed at helping both partners to grow in discipleship, is
> the way of life God wills for them. But the Church exists also to live out in the
> world the truth it has been given about the nature of God's creation, the way

of redemption through the Cross, and the ultimate hope of newness and full-ness of life.

If 'Issues in Human Sexuality' had concluded at that point, its reception might have been 'inclusively' different. The statement makes it clear that homosexuals who are convinced that they 'have more hope of growing in love for God and neighbour with the help of a loving and faithful sexual partnership' are entitled to the respect due in Christian tradition to 'free conscientious judgement', and should find 'in every congregation' 'friendship and understanding'.

However, the statement also concluded:

> We have, therefore, to say that in our considered judgement the clergy cannot claim the liberty to enter into sexually active homophile relationships. Because of the distinctive nature of their calling, status and consecration, to allow such a claim on their part would be seen as placing that way of life in all respects on a par with heterosexual marriage as a reflection of God's purposes in creation. The Church cannot accept such a parity and remain faithful to the insights which God has given it through Scripture, tradition and reasoned reflection on experience.

This stuck in the gullets of many practising and non-practising homosexual clergy. For some it was as crude as saying you can have sex on the mind but nowhere else; to others it was double-edged, providing double-standards which would become untenable and unbearable. In C. of E. *The State It's In* (2000), Monica Furlong even went so far as to claim that the 'new diktat' placed homosexual clergy 'in an impos-sible position. Some resigned, others carried on feeling very vulnerable. Some com-mitted suicide. Bishops, who knew very well that they had ordained homosexuals in the past and that many had made a fine contribution to the Church including some at the highest levels, suddenly became cautious'.

'Issues in Human Sexuality' was the first document signed by the new Archbishop of Canterbury, George Carey, in April 1991. He admitted that it could not be the last word on the subject although it would be difficult to find a stronger document. His personal support was essential to contain the evangelical stance. He rather suggests that Harries was a wild card and more unreliable when the pack was shuffled:

> In the House of Bishops Richard took a leading and positive role where he argued his point with great energy and ability. I was concerned however that his independent streak often led him to maintaining his position outside the House of Bishops and not going along with agreed policy. For example in the area of sexuality Richard was not happy with 'Issues in Human Sexuality'. Although he was willing to keep to our agreed policy within the Church and within his own diocese, he did not and would not maintain this publicly. In the House of Lords I felt he was at fault in arguing strongly for his own view-point and thus giving the public the impression that the Church of England

had no agreed policy. Of course, Richard argued cogently that he was there in the House of Lords not as a representative but there in his own right as a bishop. That was not a view I shared because, clearly, he was not there as an independent but because he was a bishop in the Church of England. On social, sexual and political matters Richard reacted instinctively as a liberal. The Bible was important to him as a source book of the Church but not, as it is for the evangelical, as the primary authority in his own life or that of the Church.

'Issues in Human Sexuality' was not debated in General Synod until 14 July 1997 when only a minority of members wished the Church to change its stance on homosexuality. The remarkable gap between the publication of the report and the debate in Synod is explained by Harries: 'The House of Bishops was totally united in wanting it discussed as it was in the Church as a whole, with no amendments in either a conservative or more radical direction. The result was that at the General Synod, when any amendment came up, we simply stood up as a block to block it! As we all sat together in the front and took people by surprise by this tactic, it sent a tremor round the assembly and there was quite a lot of muttering about the deployment of this tactic!'

In 1997 Harries asked Jo Saunders, the Oxford Diocesan Social Responsibility officer, to head an educational process in the diocese on issues in human sexuality. There were study days in different parts of the diocese involving Bible study and a lecture from Harries on different aspects of the issue, either in person or on CD, and a study session where two openly gay people, one taking a traditional and one a more radical view, had a conversation in front of the audience. Educational work was the key for Harries, deliberately not declaring any position publicly on the grounds that this would frustrate what was important, namely getting people to listen to one another and look seriously at the arguments to which they were opposed. Raising awareness is always a risky course to take on this subject. Jo Saunders expanded the original group to include two theologians, an influential evangelical layman and a local member of the Lesbian and Gay Christian Movement. She remembers, 'Meetings were often long, tense and confrontational as we grappled with sociological, theological and emotional issues. At each stage as the process emerged I shared our conclusions with Bishop Richard, and twice we met as a whole group. We decided that we would hold three seminars in each of the three archdeaconries and that it was essential for a bishop to invite the clergy and to chair each session, in order for the clergy to respond. This involved over 400 clergy, finding nine venues (where the subject of the day was not considered so controversial that the PCC would refuse to have us).' A summary of the process appeared as an Appendix to 'Some Issues in Human Sexuality: A guide to the debate' (2003).

Were these study days useful and successful? The key facets were Harries' introduction, the presence of gay Christians having the courage to speak of their experiences in the Church, and the opportunity to study Scripture with this issue in mind, but not relying on the 'seven' texts always used when discussing the subject of homosexuality. Jo Saunders does not think that the minds of many people were changed; either way, 'what we had achieved was an understanding of how the other person feels and reacts and why, and a freeing up of the subject so that it can be discussed without embarrassment.'

By the mid–1990s Harries had become the 'authority' on human sexuality in the House of Bishops. His next major appointment was at the tenth meeting of the Anglican Consultative Council (ACC) in Panama in October 1996 and he wrote the Preface to the official report 'Being Anglican in the Third Millennium' (1997). He is something of a sun lizard, so being cooped up in a hotel conference room under chilly air conditioning was not his idea of fun. Islam, sex and the structures of the Anglican Communion were on the agenda. The pressures on Churches in different countries varied, but all accepted that the growth of Islam, with its substantial resources, was a worrying challenge, as was the growth of Pentecostal sects. Of the former, Bishop Mark Dyer of Bethlehem (USA), a former Roman Catholic Benedictine monk, referred to Islam as the fastest-growing religion in the deprived areas of American cities which had the power to wean young blacks away from drugs and crime. The global perspective of Islam was provided at one of the hearings by the Bishop of Lahore, Alexander Malik. There were new encounters – uncomfortable for some – such as the celebration of the Eucharist by a woman priest, the first time at an ACC meeting. Harries was responsible for the presentation on Human Sexuality on 17 October. Theoretically he was prepared for the divide between what became known as the Churches of the southern and the northern hemispheres. But, as never before, he appreciated that on the subject of homosexuality there was a clash of cultures rather than theologies. He recognized that in a number of Churches it was not an issue; even the word homosexuality was unknown. By contrast, for Churches in the United States and Canada, not yet in England, this was the most persistent and deeply divisive issue facing these provinces. He was able to weave into his presentation both conflicts and the need for the gay community to have role models of faithful, stable, same sex relationships. His paper was well received. He appeared at ease in such a gathering, but were there signs of isolation and insecurity? One observer noticed he always had to be the first person on the 'plane or 'bus and the first person off.

Between Panama and the Lambeth Conference of 1998, the cracks in the Anglican edifice were beginning to show in an ominous way. Hammers were widening the cracks. Some 80 delegates, bishops and lay leaders, representing the Anglican Church of the 'Two Thirds World', met in Kuala Lumpur in April 1997 and issued the 'Kuala Lumpur Statement on Human Sexuality'. Mission united them – as did the 'sinful' issue of homosexuality. A concerted, united and conservative, even fundamentalist, voice set forth traditional sexual norms in clear, unambiguous terms and expressed great concern about any contrary teaching or practice. The statement said that, 'The Holy Scriptures are clear in teaching that all sexual promiscuity is sin. We are convinced that this includes homosexual practices, between men or women, as well as heterosexual relationships outside marriage.' The delegates came from Africa, Asia, Latin America and Oceania. There could be no doubt of the influence of Africa, which claimed 40 million members against the Church of England's 2.6 million members and the United States' 2.4 million. But some over-vocal provinces hung on to the coat-tails of the larger provinces. The Anglican Church of the Southern Cone of America is a case in point. It covers Argentina, Bolivia, Chile, Paraguay, Peru and Uruguay. It was a big mouth with a puny body – total Anglican membership was 22,400, about the size of the electoral roll of Sheffield. Moreover, at this time, of the seven diocesan bishops covering these countries all but one were citizens of the United Kingdom.

The evangelical groups in Oxford, not yet at full flight, spread the Kuala Lumpur statement and Harries received many letters from parochial church councils urging him to accept and support the 'statement' at Lambeth.

As chairman of the English House of Bishops Working Party on Human Sexuality, Harries went to the 1998 Lambeth Conference with the prime intention of listening carefully to what was happening in other parts of the Anglican Communion. Unfortunately an overexcited and manipulated – and manipulative! – media alighted on the single issue of homosexual relations which dominated proceedings at the conference. This was alarming and predictably divisive.

The vociferous voices came from the side determined to get a ringing denunciation of homosexuality as a sin. The liberal American bishops were remarkably quiet. Harries was frankly and rightly appalled at the venom unleashed in a gathering of Christian leaders. Even from the start, any thought of reconciling opposing views was dead in the Nile and Niger waters.

The conference of some 750 bishops met at the University of Kent (Canterbury) between 18 July and 19 August. Harries was a member of Section I, Call to Full Humanity. Even the venue for the subsection dealing with homosexuality did not presage a good outcome in Harries' expectation:

Meeting in a lecture room with sharply banked benches, the chairman, the Bishop of Johannesburg, Duncan Buchanan, announced that he had invited members of a gay organization for Anglicans to make a presentation. There was immediate and fierce opposition. The meeting voted to postpone the presentation – but in the event it never took pace at all. Duncan Buchanan, fired in the struggle against apartheid, pronounced himself 'traumatized'. Another room was found and, sitting in a circle, the business of meeting one another as fellow human beings, let alone Christians and Anglicans, could begin. It was quite clear that there was a very strong tide in favour of a conservative report and resolution. A draft outline, drawn up by the theological adviser, Canon Robin Gill (Michael Ramsey professor of modern theology at Kent University), which made a distinction between those things we all agreed were good, those things we all agreed were sin and a third, problematical category containing practices such as homosexuality and polygamy was roughly pushed aside as not meeting the bill. The Bishop of Grahamstown, David Russell, in a very conciliatory way, and the Suffragan Bishop of New York, Catherine Roskam, with passionate concern, argued for the full inclusion of gay people in the life of the Church. But however deeply felt their position, this was a minority voice. Eventually, at an impasse, a small sub-group, of which I was a member, was formed in order to draft a very short report which would frankly acknowledge the diversity of opinion. After a good number of hours and a fair amount of further debate such a report was indeed produced. Everyone present could at least recognize their own position as being fairly stated. But then came the question of the resolution. All agreed on faithfulness in marriage and chastity outside it as being the Christian way. All could agree on pastoral sensitivity to homosexual people. Beyond that there was much disagreement.

If Harries, with many other like-thinking bishops, was to agree a resolution, how-ever imperfect, it would require his deft skill at drafting. He proposed a sub-clause, a paragraph saying that this Conference:

recognizes that there are among us persons who experience themselves as having a homosexual orientation. Many of these are members of the Church and are seeking the pastoral care and moral direction of the Church, and God's transforming power for the living of their lives and the ordering of relationships. We wish to assure them that they are loved by God and that all baptized, believing and faithful persons, regardless of sexual orientation, are full members of the Body of Christ.

Another sub-clause was accepted, reading that this Conference 'cannot advise the legitimizing or blessing of same-sex unions, nor the ordination of those involved in such unions'. Harries managed to persuade the sub-section to drop the call for a mora-torium on these practices and to use the word advise rather than anything stronger.

In the afternoon of Wednesday 5 August, potential chaos loomed when a series of fierce resolutions and endless amendments from other sections and regional groups was put forward. It was fortunate that the chairman of the session was the Archbishop of Armagh, Robin Eames, even more well known than Harries for his capacity to bring people together and present business and debate in an orderly fashion. On the chairs of the bishops as they went into a plenary session, was a new amendment inserting the words 'While rejecting homosexual practice as being incompatible with Scripture' before the condemnation of homophobia. That amendment was passed by 389 to 190. Harries understood that if this amendment had not been in and accepted, great numbers of bishops from the African Churches would have walked out. This amendment was brokered by the Archbishop of Canterbury, George Carey.

There were two other significant amendments. The word homophobia was rejected in favour of 'irrational fear of homosexuals' and the clause 'we commit our-selves to listen to the experiences of homosexual people' was voted in. Eventually the conference approved the following resolution by a vote of 526 in favour, 70 against and 45 abstaining:

This Conference:

(a) Commends to the Church the subsection report on human sexuality;

(b) In view of the teaching of Scripture, upholds faithfulness in marriage between a man and a woman in lifelong union, and believes that abstinence is right for those who are not called to marriage;

(c) Recognizes that there are many among us persons who experience themselves as having a homosexual orientation. Many of these are members of the Church and are seeking the pastoral care and moral direction of the Church, and God's transforming power for the living of their lives and the ordering of relationships, and we commit ourselves to listen to the experience of homosexual people. We wish to assure them that they are loved by God and that all baptized, believing and faithful persons, regardless of sexual orientation, are full members of the Body of Christ;

(d) While rejecting homosexual practice as incompatible with Scripture, calls on all our people to minister pastorally and sensitively to all irrespective of sexual orientation and to condemn irrational fear of homosexuals, violence within marriage and any trivialization and commercialization of sex;

(e) Cannot advise the legitimizing or blessing of same-sex unions nor the ordination of those involved in same-gender unions and same-sex unions;

(f) Requests the primates and the ACC to establish a means of monitoring the work done on the subject of human sexuality in the communion and to share statements and resources among us;

(g) Notes the significance of the Kuala Lumpur Statement and the concerns expressed in Resolutions IV.26, V.1, V.10, V.23, V.35 on the authority of Scripture on matters of marriage and sexuality and asks the primates and the ACC to include them in their monitoring process.

The resolution represented a conservative interpretation of 'Issues in Human Sexuality'. For Harries, 'One thing Lambeth has convinced me of, if I needed any convincing, is that this is a Gospel issue. Without the statement in the resolution that gay and lesbian people "are loved by God and that all baptized, believing and faithful persons, regardless of sexual orientation, are full members of the Body of Christ", there would for me have been no Gospel at all.'

It would have been understandable if Harries had had a surfeit of discussing homosexuality. But no! At the eleventh meeting of the Anglican Consultative Council in Scotland 1999, the subject came naturally and correctly under the aegis of the Anglican Peace and Justice Network. There was a presentation from both lesbian and gay organizations from Seoul, Korea. The emphasis was on the human rights aspect and the speakers noted that the Church is a major source of repression of homosexuals. A task force was created on 'Human Sexuality', with three members from the United States, South Africa and Aotearoa/New Zealand.

After the Lambeth Conference another group was set up by the House of Bishops which Harries chaired. 'The purpose of this was twofold. First, many people were wanting to see the Archbishop of Canterbury about this issue. Our group deflected them and we could give them time to discuss in a way that would have been difficult for the archbishop. So we met a range of people, of very different points of view. Secondly, we kept abreast of new writing and developments on the subject. We did not set out with the intention of writing a new report but eventually came to the conclusion that we might be of use if we did that, trying to set out the main arguments on either side, particularly in relation to the Bible, which had emerged as the key issue, not just for what it said but how the Bible should be interpreted today. Members of the working party in addition to myself were the Bishops of Chester, Peter Forster, a clever theologian but of conservative stance; Winchester, Michael Scott-Joynt, a very kind-hearted person, courageously committed to the welfare of Congolese people, but who has become increasingly conservative; and John Gladwin, first of Guildford and now of Chelmsford, who is associated with a more radical position. If we were to produce a truly open, balanced report, the difficulty was that the secretary was Dr Martin Davie, a very competent theologian, who was recently on the staff of Oak Hill and fundamentally conservative. The good side of this was that any report we produced would reflect something of the outlook and quotations of those writers to whom conservative evangelicals look. It would therefore have some credibility in their eyes. However, there is no doubt that the report had a somewhat heavy, conservative feel to it. The struggle all the way along was to keep the arguments open, not to close them on the conservative side. We were helped in this by our theological consultant, the Revd Dr Jane Shaw, fellow, chaplain and dean of divinity at New College Oxford, who is a historian of gender issues, though she got somewhat frustrated by the process at times.' After over 30 meetings 'Some issues in human sexuality: A guide to the debate' was published on 4 November 2003.

The strength of the report was its dense packing of helpful material to inform discussion and debate. Those who sought conclusions and recommendations were disappointed, regarding it as inconclusive and bland. They missed the point of this 358-page book of reference which included every conceivable biblical reference, and precisely traced the tortuous Anglican progression on the subject. It had the Harriesesque touch confirmed by Bishop John Gladwin:

'Although I am sure Richard, if he exercised his own personal view, would have taken a more relaxed and liberal view of the issues, I think the report is testimony to his style of working in its thorough attention to theological method and its willingness to go deeply into all the issues that confront us.' The interpersonal relationships on the working party may have hampered mutual understanding. Peter Forster is the most independently-minded bishop in the Province of York. He ploughs few partisan furrows. He sees through the passing breezes of intellectual fashion and is not flustered by the discordance on ethical issues. He uses a theological spanner to tighten – or loosen – nuts. It was unfortunate that he did not work in critical harmony with Harries as neither skates on the surface of issues which they confront. Michael Scott-Joynt's primary concern was with the way in which Government legislation was moving in a liberal direction and bemoaned the divided views of bishops in the House of Lords.

Harries attended the twelfth meeting of the Anglican Consultative Council in Hong Kong in 2003. Pushed to the forefront were grievous world problems – up to 50 million people suffering from HIV/AIDS in South Africa; atrocities in the Congo; children as labourers, soldiers, prostituted and abused; globalization and poverty. At the same time it was humbling for many countries to hear of the great and practical efforts made by Churches in living out the Gospel by helping those in poverty and dire need, challenging governments without fear of consequences and acting as effective reconcilers between warring people. Internally, the Archbishop of Canterbury (George Carey's final appearance) proposed a motion that dioceses should not undertake unilateral actions. The Bishop of New Westminster, Michael Ingham, had agreed to sanction same-sex blessings on the basis that 'a blessing is not a sacrament, and thus it falls within the jurisdiction of the diocesan bishop whether to authorize such blessings'.

Harries was not untypical of his generation and upbringing, shaped by a very conservative culture towards the issue of homosexuality, and it is still his instinct. Yet he has looked on this subject in as rational a way as possible. Cultural changes cannot be ignored and there was the possibility that the Church of England might take up a contra-cultural view. That would consign the Church to a sect. Harries has consciously related to the gay phenomenon in a positive way and has changed some of his views. These are less to be seen in the ecclesiastical setting than in the House of Lords. A few examples will suffice to underline the point.

Harries changed his mind over the age of consent for homosexuals. He had supported an age of 18 but in 1997 indicated he was in favour of reducing the age to 16. The House of Commons passed the Crime and Disorder Bill lowering the age of consent to 16 which was subsequently voted down by the House of Lords in July. The former Archbishop of York, John Habgood, had a different and interesting perception in opposing the change:

Should we never discriminate? Before the word was given a bad flavour, the ability to discriminate between things which are different was regarded as one of the marks of an educated mind. It is not hard to think of circumstances in which discrimination is essential.

He swatted the 'rights' argument:

The appeal to rights is always at its most powerful when people feel that they have been oppressed or marginalized. Rights act like trumps in a moral card game. They are used to override opposition by the assertion of absolutes amid all the ifs and buts of actual decision-making. Sometimes this may be necessary, especially in the absence of proper democratic means of redress. But if presumed rights are allowed to displace the careful weighing of pros and cons, and if they rely for their effectiveness on faulty logic, they can pave the way for even worse decisions in the future.

The Sexual Offences Amendment Bill came before the Lords in 1999 when the redoubtable, not to be trifled with, Baroness Young moved against the Government's wish to reduce the age of consent to 16. She was supported by the Archbishop of Canterbury, George Carey, and the Bishops of Manchester, Christopher Mayfield; Norwich, Peter Nott; Southwell, Patrick Harris; and Winchester, Michael Scott-Joynt. Voting for the Government were Harries and the Bishops of Birmingham, Mark Santer; and Bath and Wells, James Thompson.

In January 2000 there was considerable opposition to the repeal of Section 28 of the Local Government Act (forbidding local authorities to promote homosexuality). The most vociferous clerical voices came from the Roman Catholic Church, led by Cardinal Thomas Winning of Glasgow. Among Anglican opponents were the Archbishop of Canterbury and the Bishops of Blackburn, Alan Chesters; and Liverpool, James Jones. For its repeal Harries was clear. In an article in *The Independent* (25 January 2000) with the provocative title 'Heterosexuals are the cause of problems, not homosexuals' he referred to the failure of Section 28: 'Whatever ills it was designed to stop, it has certainly done nothing to prevent homophobic bullying of young people. On the contrary, it is likely to have reinforced negative attitudes and given them an illicit veneer of respectability . . . The real problem in our society is not the small percentage of gay and lesbian people who are trying, sometimes under very difficult circumstances, to make a decent life for themselves. It is the casual attitude to sexual expression generally but particularly by heterosexuals. Indeed I sometimes think that the hysteria generated in relation to gay issues is in fact a displacement by the heterosexual community of their own unease about such loose, promiscuous relationships . . . I believe that we need to take fully into account the feelings of vulnerable teenagers, of both sexes, conscious that their sexual longings are directed towards members of their own sex and who are in a school environment which is full of the usual cracks and innuendoes about gay people. Teachers need the authority and confidence to be able to address such situations.'

In April 2004 the controversial Civil Partnership Bill, which Harries welcomed, was debated in the Lords. Harries saw the bill as rectifying a range of unfair anomalies. He did not think the Bill denigrated or downgraded marriage. 'If the prime responsibility of the Church today is to communicate something of the sublime vision of faithful loving human relationships as reflecting the divine love . . . the possibility of fully committed, faithful same-sex relationships, or covenanted partnerships, will, I believe, strengthen rather than undermine what is at the heart of the Christian faith, as is reflected in the marriage covenant.' In the debate Harries expressed a particular concern that when the partnership was registered there was 'no indication of what it is that the couple are committing themselves to . . . I would like to see the registration of a civil partnership involving not only a written statement that such a partnership now exists, but some verbal understanding that this is a commitment of two human beings to one another through all the vicissitudes of human existence. I believe that that conforms to the deepest desires and longings of those people who do in fact commit themselves to one another in such a relationship, even though, until the bill becomes law, there is no way in which their commitment to one another can be legally recognized.'

However, for many Anglicans and other Christians, civil partnerships appear to be a step towards homosexual and lesbian 'marriage', which would be a final breaking point for them. Homosexuality has become a paralysing obsession for the Church. Standing away from the morass and taking a wider view, how does it look? Has religion become merely a synonym for morality, philanthropy and self-improvement; faith reduced to feelings; the Christian life regarded as an activity rather than an act, doing rather than being; the intellectual and moral side exalted to the exclusion of the spiritual and affective; nature opposed to grace; a riot of conflicting and ultimately anti-Christian tendencies, a spiritual malaria which it suffers?

Harries has been an articulate voice in difficult times, having the ability to focus on absolutes. Christian morals are beyond reason, so too they are beyond regulation. Christian conduct is the spontaneous self-expression of a personality really united with Christ. St Augustine's famous aphorism *Ama et fac quod vis* (Love – and do what you like) is the perfect summary statement of the idea. Christians may never reach to such a condition of spontaneous saintliness, because they never reach to such a level of holy love. But at least they know the line along which to aspire for moral growth. Religion – the love of God – is the only secure avenue to morals – the love of persons. Laws, codes and commandments and the use of discipline and obedience are undeniably stages of Christian living. However, in the end it is love, not rules and duty, which is the final sanction of Christian morality.

Throughout Harries' time as Bishop of Oxford he had comparatively few problems of a scandalous nature to confront and resolve – until 2003 – although there would be the conviction in 2006 of his former director of communications for downloading indecent images of children from the Internet.

Chapter Nineteen
2003

Following the retirement of one Archbishop of Canterbury and the arrival of another there is a restless pause. In 2002 the Church of England was in the doldrums, needing fresh impetus and new bearings. This is no sleight on the outgoing archbishop who served and led the Church of England and guided the Anglican Communion with all his abilities and strengths. George Carey was a brave man endeavouring to do his best to hold the Church he loved in bonded togetherness.

Whilst the rumour-mongers flourished, the Church prayed that God would break through the machinations of the elaborate and long-winded appointments' procedure and touch and call someone hesitant and worthy to sit in St Augustine's Chair. The announcement of the translation of Rowan Douglas Williams, Archbishop of Wales and Bishop of Monmouth, to Canterbury, was greeted with widespread disagreement. Acclaimed by many and condemned by many, he was enthroned in Canterbury Cathedral on 27 February 2003. How easy it is to alight on particular issues with which one disagrees, magnify them out of proportion and propagate and spread them with technological ease and speed to every corner of the globe. Little was mentioned of his spiritual qualities. He is only the second Archbishop of Canterbury in 100 years – Michael Ramsey was the first – who is indubitably a man of God, prayer and deep spirituality. Though personally modest, he does not hide his theological brilliance under his mitre. Any bishop worth his crosier uses it to prod and guide his flock into the way of truth. It may be a thankless task but that is what God has given him to do.

In 2003 two new area bishops for Oxford were required following the translation of Dominic Walker of Reading to succeed Rowan Williams at Monmouth, and Michael Hill of Buckingham to Bristol. In accordance with the 1995 House of Bishops' code of practice for senior Church appointments, Harries set up an advisory group. It was not a selection committee, but one formed to give Harries advice. It consisted of the chair of the House of Clergy, Simon Brown; chair of the House of Laity, Penny Keens; the Archdeacon of Buckingham, Sheila Watson; the Archdeacon of Berkshire, Norman Russell; and a person experienced in appointments, Philip Giddings. Giddings was particularly important for the group. He was senior lecturer in politics at Reading University and a member of the Bishop's Council. He was also an influential national lay figure in the Church of England – chairman of the Mission and Public Affairs Council (General Synod), a member of the Archbishops' Council, a member of the Crown Appointments' Commission

Review and a licensed reader at the evangelical stronghold of Greyfriars, Reading. Harries and Giddings had worked together for many years and, in most cases, knew each other's position very well. Harries' chaplain, Michael Brierley, acted as secretary to the group.

This consultation was primarily directed at defining the nature, duties and responsibilities of the area bishops, and the gifts, skills and personal characteristics to be looked for in the person appointed. A job description was drawn up and approved by the Bishop's Council.

Harries had been successful in providing a collegial team of bishops from different backgrounds and churchmanship with complementary gifts and skills. The continuing Bishop of Dorchester was Colin William Fletcher whom Harries had appointed in 2000. His face was well known throughout the Anglican Communion as the Archbishop of Canterbury (George Carey)'s chief 'prop', carrying the Primatial Cross before him, and acting as domestic chaplain since 1993. Like Margate rock – he was vicar of Holy Trinity there for nine years – he was a rock solid evangelical. St Paul's words, 'May I never boast of anything except the Cross of our Lord Jesus Christ by which the world has been crucified to me, and I to the world' were quoted by Harries in one of the readings at Fletcher's episcopal ordination in Westminster Abbey. From that moment Colin Fletcher moved throughout Oxfordshire, the area covered by Dorchester, as an outgoing, energetic, enthusiastic and effective evangelist and pastor, living the refrain of Daniel Schutte's contemporary hymn *Here I am, Lord* (1981).

Following best practice in accordance with the 1995 code, Harries encouraged people to send him names of anyone they would like considered for Reading and Buckingham. It was a typically open and generous gesture, though in retrospect perhaps unwise as over 90 names were received, each with 'backers' who hoped their candidate would be one of the two area bishops. Did it encourage an election atmosphere in a Church which does not elect its bishops? The names included those on the list received from Anthony Sadler, the Archbishops' Appointments secretary. Sadler had a background in personnel and employee relations and was author of *Human Resource Management: developing a strategic approach* (1995).

From the outset Harries was certain and made it crystal clear to others 'what I was looking for in Reading, where there are large numbers of rather run-down Anglo-Catholic churches, was a definite Anglo-Catholic with a heart for mission'. He would have short-listed two priests but did not initially do so. One was Stephen Cottrell, Canon Pastor and Vice-Dean of Peterborough, aged 45, married with three sons. Cottrell was previously diocesan missioner in Wakefield and bishop's chaplain for evangelism, before becoming a missioner with Springboard, the archbishops' evangelistic initiative. He had written books on prayer and helped to write and develop the *Emmaus* evangelistic programme. However, the Bishop of Peterborough understandably blocked further exploration as Cottrell had been in his new post less than two years. The other was 50-year-old Jeffrey John who was unmarried. John was canon chancellor and theologian at Southwark Cathedral, previously fellow and dean of divinity of Magdalen College, Oxford (1984–1991), then for six years parish priest at Holy Trinity, Eltham (Southwark). But Harries says, 'I originally ruled Jeffrey out because of his controversial views.' Jeffrey John's position on Christian same-sex partnerships was well known. His book *Permanent, Faithful, Stable* was first published by Darton, Longman and Todd in 1993 in association with Affirming Catholicism. Further editions were published in 2003 and 2004.

John opened his introduction, 'This booklet has a straightforward aim. It argues that homosexual relationships should be accepted and blessed by the Church, provided that the quality and commitment of the relationship are the same as those expected of a Christian marriage. It argues that the theological, ethical and sacramental status of such a partnership between two men or two women is comparable to that of marriage, whether or not the word marriage is used to describe it. It also argues that the self-discipline and self-sacrifice, which are required to make a Christian marriage a way of holiness, are equally required of a homosexual partnership which deserves the name Christian.'

Although Harries initially had ruled out John's name, as early as December 2002 he had received a persuasive letter from the Dean of Southwark, Colin Slee, pressing John's name for consideration as an area bishop and enclosing a lengthy reference he had prepared for the Diocese of Monmouth as John had been a strong candidate to succeed Rowan Williams there.

Slee said, 'There is no doubt whatsoever that one reason Jeffrey did not get the job is that he is single and has been brave and clear about the "gay issue". This made some people in Wales very nervous, particularly because of Rowan's known views and potential embarrassment to him whereby the press might have decided Rowan had "fixed" his own succession.' John had a South Wales background, was born in the Rhondda Valley and educated there before going to Hertford College, Oxford.

When Anthony Sadler produced his list of 12 names, two of them were starred: that is those who would be particularly suitable for a bishopric. At that stage Harries included John on the initial shortlist of eight which, with the advisory group, he then reduced to five including Alan Wilson, aged 48, rector of Sandhurst and Area Dean of Sonning in the Reading jurisdiction. The impetus for Jeffrey John came from outside, from Colin Slee, Tony Sadler, the Bishop of Thetford, David Atkinson, and the Archdeacon of Durham, Stephen Conway (appointed Bishop of Ramsbury in 2006). Wilson's name was put on the shortlist by Philip Giddings. Wilson received a personal approach by telephone: 'He (Harries) was just off to the House of Lords, but "there were couple of jobs going here in the diocese" and would I be offended if he sent me the job descriptions.'

In the case of John, Harries 'looked again at his references and being reassured about his lifestyle I decided it would be wrong to exclude him at this point'. And, significantly, he telephoned the archbishop, checking whether, if John eventually emerged as the best candidate for one or other of the jobs, he would agree to consecrate him. The archbishop said he would. That confirmed John as a potentially favoured candidate. Harries explains the procedure. 'The two archdeacons (Berkshire and Buckingham) and myself interviewed the shortlisted candidates but as it did not seem clear at that point who were the best two, I arranged for the final four to do a presentation to the advisory group. The candidates had to choose one of the job descriptions and describe how they understood the episcopal role in furthering the diocesan strategy in that area.' The presentations took place on 1 May. Harries considered that John made an excellent presentation. His perception was 'Simon Brown and Penny Keens were supportive, Sheila Watson rather non-committal (for reasons other than Jeffrey John's stance on homosexuality) and Philip Giddings warned that there would be opposition from evangelical parishes if John were appointed.' This was a moment when Harries should have sat down with Giddings to probe and ascertain the force of the opposition.

At Harries' request, Giddings then took some soundings amongst Southwark evangelicals. Whilst a number were affirming about the work John had done in that diocese, none was happy about the idea of him becoming a bishop. And opposition was not confined to conservative evangelicals but stretched right across traditions of churchmanship including strong criticisms of the nomination from traditional Catholics who were not members of Forward in Faith. After further reflection and discussion with others it seemed to Harries, 'that Jeffrey had just the gifts I was looking for, for the Reading area'.

Harries telephoned the archbishop for a second time, saying he would like to nominate John if the archbishop were still prepared to consecrate him. 'I fully expected that we would meet up and talk the matter through; indeed I said over the telephone that he would want time to think about Jeffrey's nomination. In fact by the end of the telephone conversation he had agreed to it.'

The public announcement of the appointments of Alan Wilson to Buckingham and Jeffrey John to Reading came on 20 May. When did the rumblings of unease begin and increase to such avalanche proportions that they engulfed the whole of the Church of England and the wider Anglican Communion? Before turning to consider this there were two further unforeseen events which would influence the outcome.

On 29 May the Bishop of New Westminster (Canada) authorized a rite for the celebration of gay and lesbian covenants for use by clergy in six parishes within the diocese, including Christ Church Cathedral, Vancouver. The central words in the rite are: 'I give myself to you. I love you, trust you and delight in you. I will share your burdens and your joys. I will go with you wherever God calls. This is my solemn promise.' Harries did not agree with this action.

Then on 7 June Canon Gene Robinson was elected bishop coadjutor of the diocese of New Hampshire (USA) on the second ballot and would succeed Douglas Theuner as diocesan bishop. He was the first openly gay man to be elected as a bishop in the Episcopal Church in the USA. Previously married with two adult daughters, he had been living with a gay partner for 13 years. It was his third 'run' for episcopal office in five years. It was a popular election as Robinson was well known and well liked in New Hampshire, already serving as assistant to the retiring bishop.

Returning to Oxford, Harries was deluged by unfolding events without letting the daily postbag, telephone calls and emails drown him. He carried on with his duties and commitments. In a single chapter it is impossible to give a daily sequence of events but only to provide a number of the crucial markers. The heather was already ablaze but the heat spread like wildfire following the discovery on a website of an address John had delivered in September 1998 to the Affirming Catholicism Conference and the Southwark Chapter of the Society of Catholic Priests which came into Giddings' possession. Its title 'The Church and Homosexuality: Post-Lambeth Reflections' included an account of his own gay experience in the Church and of the Church's stance on homosexuality. The address had been an angry and provocative response to the Lambeth Resolution and had been written in haste, pointing out the hypocrisy of the double standards for laity and clergy. It had been written five years previously and was not intended for publication. John had no idea how it had come to be on a website. Significantly, this piece also revealed that John himself was in a relationship.

On 22 May Giddings sent this to Harries, who had not previously seen it, hoping it would help him to understand why some people would be troubled by the appointment of John and find it difficult to accept the assurance Harries had been given about his conduct. The conservative evangelicals were torpedoed into action and organized their opposition to the appointment. The archbishop and Harries were equal targets. John's address came to the notice of *The Daily Telegraph*, and from there to other newspapers.

Within ten days of the appointment, 120 signatures were gathered expressing dismay and great concern at the appointment: 'From within the Oxford diocese we wish to put on record our astonishment that someone can be entrusted with the responsibility of a bishop in the Church of Christ when they have so strongly and consistently opposed the Church's moral teaching in relation to same-sex unions.' The major clerical figures involved in Oxford itself were, in descending order of stridency, the Revds Vaughan Roberts, rector of St Ebbe's, Charlie Cleverly, rector of St Aldate's and Andrew Wingfield Digby, vicar of St Andrew's. The Revd Andrew Goddard, tutor in Christian ethics at Wycliffe Hall, and Canons (not of Christ Church Cathedral) Christopher Sugden and Vinay Samuel, preachers in the diocese, were likewise in the forefront of confrontation. Among the prominent organizations fuelling opposition were the Oxford Diocesan Evangelical Fellowship and its secretary, the Revd Piers Bickersteth, rector of Aborfield and Barkham; the Oxford Centre for Mission Studies and Reform, an evangelical network of clergy and laity in churches throughout the country which came into being in 1993, campaigning for biblical integrity. Most evident of all was a newcomer, Anglican Mainstream, which was formed as a result of the opposition. Philip Giddings was its convenor and he provides a characterization: 'In a sentence we seek to bring together orthodox Anglicans who are united on the controlling authority of Holy Scripture for the life and work of the Church and carrying out of the Lord's mission. I confess to inventing the term when, in the middle of the Jeffrey John crisis, we were struggling to find a way of describing ourselves which wasn't as long as "a group of clergy and laity opposed to the nomination of Jeffrey John as Bishop of Reading".

As we included folk from both Catholic and evangelical traditions, and indeed some who characterized themselves as "liberal" but were deeply upset by the manner in which Richard Harries went about '"selling" the appointment, "mainstream" seemed apt. I have been disappointed that in some media circles it is assumed to be just conservative evangelicals (though I have no hesitation in describing myself as a conservative evangelical).'

Harries responded to the 120 signatories on 2 June, defending his choice of John as 'a mission-focused priest, with an excellent track record and a strong sense of vocation to help struggling congregations grow'. He indicated that John was 'more than willing to meet people on an individual basis' and Harries had set aside 20 June for anyone who wished to talk with him.

On 7 June Harries defended his decision to his Diocesan Synod meeting at High Wycombe, outlining the selection process and 'after further consultation, reflection, and prayer, it seemed to me that Jeffrey's gifts were the ones we needed in the episcopal area of Reading'. He explained that he had received many assurances that John, although in a long-term relationship with another man, had not been sexually active for a long time and that his lifestyle as a priest was in accordance with the teaching of the Church of England as set out in 'Issues in Human Sexuality'.

On 10 June, Harries met 12 evangelical clergy. There was little meeting of minds. Questions on the significant central issues of justice and the pastoral response to gay people were raised. By this time the wider Church of England was in uproar and the secular press was recording every move and inventing some of its own. Harries received several thousand letters and emails. Then, to his surprise, on 16 June a letter appeared in the press from nine diocesan bishops, representing a range of churchmanship – Bradford, Carlisle, Chester, Chichester, Exeter, Liverpool, Rochester, Southwell and Winchester. It reiterated the House of Bishops' position that any departure from fundamental teaching must be viewed with grave concern, especially in the case of those who are ordained and called to be examples to God's people.

'We are glad at the reassurances from the Bishop of Oxford that Jeffrey John's life is now celibate. But it is the history of the relationship, as well as Dr John's severe criticism of orthodox teaching, which gives concern.' A number of these bishops wrote to Harries personally in a more vituperative vein.

On 19 June a lengthy statement prepared by John was made public, largely to clear the air which was by now rife with rumour. He was candid in recognizing that his personal view on homosexuality was not that of the majority of Christians, nor the official view of the Church of England, but claimed he would 'not act as a maverick against the Church's teaching and discipline'. He had never hidden the facts of his relationship from his confessors and his canonical superiors 'and have obeyed their direction':

My partner and I have never lived together (apart from one brief period while he was moving house) because our separate ministries have never made it possible to do so. However, we rely on each other for support and spend as much free time together as possible. I am therefore making this statement (despite my distaste for having to make such a private matter public) for the avoidance of any doubt about what this closeness implies.

It may have been unwise of John to agree to a lengthy interview in *The Times* on 19 June. By this time it was known that his celibate partner was the Revd Grant Holmes, a senior hospital chaplain and an honorary curate at St Michael and All Angels, Barnes, in south west London.

On 20 June a letter from a further eight diocesan bishops to the archbishop, giving full support to the appointment, was released to the press. The signatories were the bishops of Worcester, Hereford, Leicester, Newcastle, Ripon and Leeds, St Edmundsbury and Ipswich, Salisbury and Truro. Suffragan bishops, both pro and con, were also on each list. Other bishops were in touch with Harries privately, assuring him of their prayers, confidence and support and a number publicly, such as the Bishop of Norwich, Graham James, who devoted part of his diocesan synod address specifically to the Jeffrey John affair. More than 100 clergy in the Oxford diocese signed a letter 'rejoicing' in the appointment. It was not made public to avoid triggering yet more correspondence. The Very Revd Robert Jeffrey, sub-dean of Christ Church, was a signatory and said that it was 'quite clear that the diocesan clergy are not all of one mind. The issue is reduced to two sentences. Anything that undermines the value of friendship cannot be part of the Gospel. And none of us is ruled by the Book of Leviticus, however we interpret it'.

On 20 June there was another meeting between Harries and conservative evangelicals, this time pleading with him to withdraw John's name. The opponents thought it was beyond the bounds of belief that John could be expected to remain silent once consecrated. An openly gay bishop is a Christian symbol. The question they wanted answering was that although he may have been against promiscuity, was he against homosexual sex? This touched on something which was not fully understood by John's supporters. There were many Church people who were revulsed by homosexual sexual actions. It may have been wrong or irrational thinking, but it was there. There was underlying hysteria too, that the Church of England would be unrecognizable in a short time and evangelicals would not want to join it. Harries thought it was healthier for the debate to take place in the open. He knew that some of those present were already distancing themselves from him as their diocesan bishop, but even if people chose to go out of communion with him, he would continue to support them. Equally he made clear that he would bring no pressure on John to withdraw. He still believed that when he had been a bishop for two years John would win the people's trust. It was an idle thought!

An impression was conveyed outside the diocese that Oxford was a seed-bed of conservative evangelicalism. It was not. Under Harries' leadership it was remarkably liberal, probably more so than any other diocese, which is confirmed by the provincial episcopal visitor in the province of Canterbury, the Bishop of Ebbsfleet, Andrew Burnham, who lives in Abingdon. 'My impression is that Oxford is a diocese which has thoroughly embraced liberalism. During Richard's time there has been a substantial decrease in traditional Anglo-Catholic belief and practice. To some extent this is a national phenomenon but Oxford has been at the forefront of the new mood, and to be fair, has shown a healthy vibrancy which is not always associated with liberal theology.' But the Catholic tradition remained strong, though more 'Affirming' than 'Forward in Faith'. The majority of Churches were of the *via media*, comprehensive and tolerant.

The archbishop was under pressure from every side, even from erstwhile friends who, whatever they may say in private, were keeping their mitred heads well below the parapet.

There was no question of containment of the controversy. On 23 June, Rowan Williams, in his capacity as Archbishop of Canterbury and chairman of the House of Bishops, sent a letter to all diocesan and suffragan bishops. Some extracts need quoting:

> The concerns of many in the diocese of Oxford are theologically serious, intelligible and by no means based on narrow party allegiance or on prejudice. They must be addressed and considered fully. Confidence in the ability of a new bishop to minister to those in his pastoral care is a centrally important matter, and it is clear that serious questions remain in the diocese. To consider these with prayerfulness and maturity needs time and a measure of calm. It is not for anyone outside the diocese to override or pre-empt what is obviously a painful and complex process, and I can only ask your prayers for the diocese as it struggles with this and tries to find a right discernment. Finally, it would be a tragedy if these issues, in the Church of England and in the communion, occupied so much energy that we lost our focus on the priorities of our mission, the priorities given to us by Our Lord. What we say about sexuality (and not just the same-sex question) is a necessary part of our faithfulness, but the concentration on this in recent weeks has had the effect of generating real incomprehension in much of our society, in a way that does nothing for our credibility. In the world where we are called to offer the Good News of Jesus, we need to reflect on this dimension of the situation – not to surrender to alien standards, but to keep our eyes on those central revealed truths without which other matters of behaviour and discipline will never make sense.

Few people were prepared to consider the issues at stake with a 'measure of calm'. Quite the opposite. On the date the letter was sent, the archbishop had a further meeting with Philip Giddings and Charlie Cleverly and realized that they and those they represented were not prepared to budge an inch. He gave a depressing report of the meeting to Harries on 24 June.

The question of 'alternative episcopal oversight' had been discussed for the Reading episcopal area for those unable and unwilling to accept John's ministrations should he become bishop. In sum, Harries remained the 'chief pastor' throughout the diocese at all times. He may delegate to the other two area bishops (Dorchester and Buckingham) specific authority in the Reading episcopal area.

He may invite other bishops from within or outside the diocese to assist in limited ways in relation to disaffected parishes. He may inhibit unauthorized episcopal intervention. Fortunately it became unnecessary to implement this divisive 'oversight'.

On 4 July, a letter with 254 signatures of both clergy and leading lay Anglicans from the diocese was sent to the archbishop. 'We believe this crisis threatens the unity and mission not simply of our diocese, but the Church of England and the worldwide Anglican Communion. For this reason we request an urgent meeting with you at which a representative group from the diocese might inform you further of the extent and nature of our concerns for unity and order in the diocese.'

No meeting was needed. By this time tumult surrounding the archbishop had reached intolerable proportions. And then Harries was summoned to Lambeth Palace for a meeting at 8 am on Saturday 5 July. He arrived to find a draft statement by the archbishop 'to be agreed by 09.00 hours'. Harries thought he 'was there to discuss how best we could handle the issue. In fact, it was to tell me that the archbishop was not going through with the nomination. Jeffrey then had a separate meeting with the archbishop and was told the unpalatable truth. We were both pretty shell-shocked. The morning was spent drafting a suitable statement for Jeffrey to make. Lambeth of course wanted him voluntarily to withdraw. Jeffrey was very reluctant indeed to do that. He had no intention of withdrawing. However, in the end he acted in a remarkably Christian spirit, recognizing that it would be easier for the archbishop if he issued a statement saying he was withdrawing because of the divisive nature of the appointment, rather than a statement from the archbishop saying that he was not prepared to consecrate Jeffrey. We both felt pretty hollowed out after all that, though of course it was much worse for Jeffrey, who went through a terrible time'.

John wrote to Harries expressing his profound gratitude 'to you for having placed such confidence in me, and to all those in the area and diocese who have so warmly welcomed and supported me in recent weeks'. Harries wrote to John respecting his decision, made in the interest of wider Church unity. 'However, I would like you to know that not only did you have my unswerving support, but also that of a great many others in the diocese. I have no doubt about your episcopal gifts, on the basis of which I nominated you; nor about your commitment both to the lifestyle and principles set out in "Issues in Human Sexuality". I am very sad that we are not going to be blessed by your ministry as I know the diocese of Southwark has been.'

The morning after John's withdrawal was announced Harries went into hospital for a long-arranged hip operation. From his hospital bed, after a successful operation, he wrote to all the clergy in the diocese enclosing a pastoral letter to be used in churches on Sunday 13 July. For one long moment Harries considered resigning. The archbishop wrote to Harries intimating that he had never in his life taken a decision he so much disliked and hope that he and Harries would salvage a working relationship which was of immense value and importance to Rowan Williams. Harries' stature was not one whit decreased – quite the opposite.

In April 2004 Jeffrey John was appointed Dean of St Albans succeeding

Christopher Lewis who was the new dean of Christ Church Cathedral, Oxford. Jeffrey John and Grant Holmes registered their civil partnership at St Albans Register Office in July 2006. The Archbishop of Canterbury continues to be mired in the morass of problems concerning human sexuality.

Afterthoughts

A. Harries: 'I'm not critical of the role of the archbishop, because I understand very well the pressures on him and his deep desire to hold the Anglican Communion together.'

Observations: The time for a face-to-face conversation and correspondence between Harries and the archbishop was at the first time of asking. Rowan Williams was a friend of John, knew him and his views. They were associated with the inauguration of Affirming Catholicism. They knew the Anglo-Catholic movement needed a radical overhaul, which was unlikely to be achieved within existing structures and organizations. The position was reached when Anglo-Catholics knew only how to apply the brake instead of pushing the accelerator, bringing to mind one of Cardinal Newman's sayings that 'every organization seemed to start with a prophet and end up with a policeman'. Affirming Catholicism injected life and vigour into an increasingly active and inclusive segment of the Church of England. John appears to feel intensely and passionately and may be easy prey to 'events'. He is a publicist with a tongue and pen which is occasionally used to caricature those he cannot convince or coerce. He also has fire – not that of a fire-raiser – which has the effect of stripping people of some of their accumulated mental and emotional possessions, exposing them to risk and uncertainty: in a word – a challenger. Would an area bishopric be able to harness, use and contain him? Would the wider Church be well served by consecrating him bishop? The Archbishop evidently thought so.

Were Anthony Sadler's papers on candidates deficient? It was not for Harries and members of his advisory group to quarry material and assemble facts. Did Sadler have all the facts? Should he have known about a five-year-old obscure address? Did he? If so, why was it not disclosed in his paper? There are sufficient examples, now on public record, to show how patronage secretaries, whether of the Prime Minister or archbishops, have sometimes exceeded their responsibilities. Owen Chadwick has observed: 'A man who consults a lot of people gets a lot of different opinions. Therefore it matters how he reports on those opinions, with what bias if any, conscious or unconscious.' John Hewitt, son of an evangelical clergyman and missionary, was patronage secretary to Prime Ministers from 1961 to 1973. In Chadwick's words, 'He cared about the welfare of the Church of England, especially as a force in preserving and promoting the moral strength of the English people' in the turbulent 1960s. Three people at least were effectively blocked by him for diocesan bishoprics – Ambrose Reeves, Eric Kemp and Hugh Montefiore. After Hewitt's retirement Kemp and Montefiore became Bishops of Chichester and Birmingham respectively.

The Reading debacle leaves disconcerting and unanswered questions. Who 'starred' Jeffrey John and made his name leap to the front of a queue, even when his personal history was largely or wholly known? Or was it fully verified?

Harries is 'not sure about the role of the apparatchiks at Lambeth Palace. There was one rather unhelpful press statement in the middle of the furore, dwelling on opposition within the diocese of Oxford, which exaggerated its extent, and which took no account of my conviction that that could be contained. Its style was such it clearly wasn't written by Rowan himself.'

B. Harries: 'There was a mistake that the archbishop made and clearly I shared in, in that we didn't anticipate the extent of opposition from the Anglican Communion. I did anticipate and take fully into account the opposition from the diocese of Oxford, though I didn't anticipate the degree of distress which people felt about the ensuing disunity. But I believed it could be contained. Particularly influential with me was a letter of support from a conservative evangelical vicar in the diocese of Southwark who strongly supported Jeffrey John. I took that as an indication that if Jeffrey had won round conservative evangelicals in Southwark he could do the same in Reading within a couple of years.'

Observations: Rowan Williams (then Bishop of Monmouth) and Harries attended Lambeth 1998. They witnessed the rising tide of antagonism on the issue of homosexuality. As Archbishop of Wales, Williams attended Primates' Meetings and would hear first hand of discontent and anger, not least from provinces in Africa, the West Indies, South East Asia and the Southern Cone of South America. Orchestrated opposition to his appointment as Archbishop of Canterbury, as a result of his known views on homosexuality, is well attested.

Harries over-used the single splendid letter from the conservative evangelical incumbent. This encouraged opponents of John's appointment to seek contrary and numerically greater testimonies. Nonetheless, there was also much evidence that John had won respect from evangelicals in Southwark, and the essence of such a process was clearly perceptible in his various meetings in Berkshire.

C. Harries: 'On one matter, I'm undecided. I decided not to keep members of the senior staff, except for the Archdeacons of Buckingham and Berkshire who were members of the advisory group, in the picture about Jeffrey or consult them. This was I think for a good reason, namely I felt I had to take responsibility for the nomination myself and it would be unfair to ask them to share in the responsibility in any way. One result of Jeffrey's nomination was that as the pressure mounted two senior members of staff privately (possibly semi-publicly) disassociated themselves from the nomination and were not prepared to support it. They too were under huge pressure from evangelicals in the diocese and elsewhere.'

Observations: Having established an open procedure it was a mistake not to share everything with the whole of his senior staff. He would, for example, have heard at an early stage the misgivings of the Bishop of Dorchester, Colin Fletcher, which ultimately led to him confirming to Harries that he could no longer offer his support in public or in private to the appointment of John. Within the advisory group the Archdeacon of Berkshire, Norman Russell, eventually wrote to the archbishop directly without speaking to Harries first, saying it would be in the best interests of the Church if John could be persuaded to withdraw. Penny Keens, chair of the House of Laity, at first supported the appointment but later became fearful of the consequences as fissures in diocesan unity began to show.

The general opinion of Harries' senior colleagues is that there should have been more discussion and agreement about the way forward. This would have broadened the views and perhaps affected the outcome. There was a view that Harries conceded too much to the conservative evangelicals. It is questionable whether Harries should have allowed, for reasons of harmony, evangelical curates of St Ebbe's who, post-Reading, refused to be ordained by him, to be ordained by a 'sound' evangelical, the Bishop of Dorchester. This was an example of Harries graciously keeping the peace. It did not do so.

D. Harries: 'If we had met, and fully taken into account the opposition from the Anglican Communion, then we would have made a decision either not to put Jeffrey's name forward in the first place or, if we did put it forward, to stick with it. It was clearly not at all good that his name was first put forward and then he was forced to withdraw.'

Observations: Harries is precisely correct. A lesson should have been heeded from the experience of the former Archbishop of York, John Habgood, who was besieged with criticisms over his decision to consecrate David Jenkins as Bishop of Durham in 1984.

(Habgood) Richard has made his mistakes (as we all know) and his inability to get Philip Giddings on his side in the John affair was a major tactical error. But it has also become obvious that he was to some extent misled by Lambeth, and found himself trapped. I compare this with my own baptism of fire with David Jenkins when it seemed to me that a proper decision, once made, should be carried through if the Church of England was to retain its integrity. Admittedly the lobbies have become better organized since my day, but I detect a certain unwillingness to lead at a moment when leadership was vital.

E. Harries: 'I should stress that I nominated Jeffrey because, by his own admission, he had been celibate "for a considerable period", and his lifestyle seemed to me to conform to that required by the Church of England. As we know, this was not enough for his opponents, who wanted a public act of repentance. They were also sceptical that someone who so strongly disagreed with "Issues in Human Sexuality", would have credibility in defending them publicly as a bishop. Jeffrey and his partner were put under huge pressure by the media, which were highly intrusive into their private life and the whole situation was inflamed by the appearance on a website of an address which Jeffrey John had once given which contained a number of sentences in it that incited further opposition. The address had in fact been on the website for some time. When the row broke out it was taken off but people had seen it and made a copy of it.'

Observations: If John's address had been placed before the advisory group is it possible, or more likely probable, that they would have been more cautious about his candidature or even rejected it? Philip Giddings would not have been the sole antagonist. The language and tone was not that of someone who had gained a reputation and accumulated widespread trust as a thoughtful pastor, matched by theological expertise, a gifted teacher and preacher. John encouraged clergy in Southwark and elsewhere to help their parishes grow spiritually as well as numerically. As an interpreter and expositor of the Christian faith he was skilled and effective. The 1998 address revealed more of a campaigner for a cause about which he felt deeply without any compensating discernment. Would this have re-emerged at Reading?

Whatever the position, it is certain that John was exposed to venom and hatred, a form of uncharitable wickedness in a Christian Church. The media were fed not with crumbs but red meat, devoured with disgusting glee as his privacy was appallingly invaded to the point that only a few entrails were left. Hard-faced henchmen in deep clerical collars were not good Protestants but Puritans, smacking their lips with each new revelation followed by denunciation. The words they used, 'submission' and 'struggle', were reminiscent of crowds around a scaffold. 'Repentance' they shouted. The quiet voice of a sinner repenting and being forgiven was absent . . . It was shameful episode.

It may have been necessary for John to issue his 'statement' on 19 June, but it was a distasteful step to take and a highly dangerous one as a precedent for the Church of England. How replete would be the bench of bishops if each and every one of them had to hang their dirty washing out on a line for the public to see.

F. Harries: 'There was great distress in the diocese, not just because of the issue itself but by the fierce division it was causing in particular deaneries. The divisive nature of the nomination really upset a lot of people, particularly those charged with the responsibility of holding clergy chapters together, area deans and lay chairs and the area bishops.'

Observations: Canon David Winter, Harries' officer for evangelism 1989–1995, speaks for many correspondents:

I have sometimes winced when I have heard Richard being interviewed on a controversial topic, fearing that he was swimming out of his depth, but by and large he has the *nous* to avoid disaster, usually by his ability to see a verbal landmine lying in his path. All of this makes his handling of the depressing Jeffrey John affair inexplicable. It is hard to believe that he was unaware of the strength of feeling in the diocese; and although personally I could see why he wished to appoint such a gifted man to be Bishop of Reading (and cannot see any rational objection to the appointment of a celibate gay man) I was also aware that this, more than any other, was a subject likely to divide rather than unite the diocese, and so it proved. It was almost as though Richard felt that this was an issue that had to be faced, at whatever cost.

This brings us to another issue, articulated by Alan Wilson who was successfully nominated as Bishop of Buckingham:

Richard was deeply committed to what he was doing as a justice issue. This was wide flaring nostrils stuff. I was reminded of fellow students 20 years before who sold their houses for God, or the torpedo run in *Das Boot!* I had been an equal opportunities employer in my last job, and was fully supportive of Richard's intentions. Having taken careful soundings, it seemed to me that, within the Berkshire archdeaconry, some 5 per cent were passionately, intellectually against. This included a very small element whose style reminded me of animal rights activists! One or two had big global agendas riding on it. The theory was rather like Charlie Manson's *Helter Skelter* – their victory in excluding Jeffrey from being Bishop of Reading would initiate a cascading process of realignment for world Christianity around the gay issue. Some 20 per cent were viscerally unhappy, and another 30 per cent unsure. Some 50 per cent were broadly supportive, including a large number who could not see why it was an issue, and a small (5 per cent?) group who were passionately supportive. The vast majority of people in parish and deanery were, frankly, rather embarrassed that the question had been raised, and just wanted it to go away. At the end there was some degree of guilt and shame among many mid-range clergy in Berkshire that they had not stood up more boldly for Jeffrey early on. I am sure that the notion he had been turned down for another see on the grounds of his orientation would have been a powerful incentive to Richard's instinct for justice and the underdog.

Meanwhile I had to spend some time after 20 May *not* being Jeffrey! I found Richard extremely helpful and personally supportive, as Rowan Williams also was. On a visit to New York, New Jersey and North Carolina that summer I experienced a high degree of interest in what was going on in the Oxford diocese. It may be that we all underestimated the extent to which the Oxford name carried its own cachet abroad, as well as the disproportionate power modern communications technology can give essentially small and marginal groups. I sometimes wonder, had we not been living in the age of the internet and emails, the appointment would have rolled through, and we would now, à la St Albans Abbey, be wondering what all the fuss was about. This has become such a key issue for those who involve themselves with it as single-issue fanatics that this may be not the case.

It struck me increasingly, during the Nineties, how Richard's leadership was about enabling seemingly incompatible people to work together as colleagues. As Bishop of Buckingham, I have really enjoyed working with a wise, engaging, humorous and loyal chief. In his own essentially hands-off way, he has done all I would have expected to facilitate my new role in the diocese – were I new to the diocese, it could have seemed extremely laid-back. In disciplinary dealings he can seem slightly soggy (where the modern fashion is often to act more defensively and formally) but his approach is founded clearly on a strong view of grace and habits of personal kindness. As someone new to the job, it has been immensely helpful to feel I was trusted and supported to a high degree that may not be characteristic of all English

bishops and their suffragans. At a time when the Church has become introspective, he has an eye to the big picture. Surrounded as we all are sometimes
by Adullamite whining, he always works hard to be kind and to think the best
of people. His approach reminds me of the Quaker discipline of 'speaking to
that which is of God in the other'. If the role of bishops is becoming more
focused on organizational hygiene factors, Richard has bucked the trend.

Most, rather than few, clergy and laity in the diocese were shocked and dismayed by
the suffering inflicted on Harries and his wife Jo over the Jeffrey John drama. At
diocesan meetings in the summer and autumn there was a palpable feeling of
warmth and love for Harries. Earlier, on the day of the announcement of John's
withdrawal, Sunday 6 July, the annual ecumenical St Birinus pilgrimage (12 miles
from Churn Knob, Blewbury to Dorchester Abbey) was taking place. News of
Jeffrey John's announcement reached the pilgrims by mobile phone. Canon John
Crowe was participating in the 6 pm service at which the preacher was the Bishop
of Winchester, Michael Scott-Joynt. Canon Crowe:

> I found myself alone walking across a field with Michael Scott-Joynt who
> started saying how the whole situation was the fault of +Richard who should
> have had 'more street cred' than to rouse up a hornets' nest by making such an
> appointment. I told him I thought his remarks were unfair and that +R had
> found the right man for this appointment and had acted according to the rule
> book. I felt an announcement would have to be made before the service so
> that everyone should know what JJ had said and that at that time, before the
> service, we should have brief prayers for JJ and all hurt by the situation.
>
> +MS-J said if I was to ask him as my bishop what to do he would advise me
> to say nothing. We walked on in silence and I followed my own conscience
> and gave out the notice and led brief prayers including +R and the diocese
> before the service started. I am glad that +R, not +M, was my diocesan
> bishop!'

Harries concludes with a reflection, 'I found myself amazingly serene and tranquil
through all this turmoil. I mentioned this fact to one of the archdeacons, who was
rather suspicious and harped back to claims of charismatics he'd known who stress
the validity of their religious experience. I'm the last person in the world to look to
religious experience as evidence of anything. It's just that I was very surprised
myself how totally calm I felt.'

Forward

There would be no extensive and convoluted procedures for Harries' final episcopal
appointment, which was to Reading. Harries returned to his best method and was
again 'himself'! Let Stephen Cottrell, then canon pastor of Peterborough Cathedral, tell his story.

Towards the end of November 2003 – Friday afternoon – I came home and my secretary had left a message saying that the Bishop of Oxford had 'phoned and could I ring back. I kind of knew straight away what it would be about. The previous week I had been talking with a friend about what the Church would do now that Jeffrey John had been pressurized into standing down as the next Bishop of Reading. We talked about the sort of person the Church would look for next and reckoned it would need to be someone who was an Anglo-Catholic and with some background in mission. We also reckoned that it would need to be someone who held similar views to Jeffrey. The Affirming Catholic wing in the Oxford diocese would be feeling quite defeated and so it would need someone whom that wing of the Church could identify with as 'one of theirs'. But it also needed to be someone who understood evangelicals and was respected by them. They, after all, had revealed their strength of feeling of this issue. We agreed that it was a job that no one would want and one hardly anyone could be expected to do. But as I walked away from this conversation I couldn't help but conclude that while I didn't presume to have the personal qualities that would be needed to do such a job, I did tick most of the other boxes. Somehow this planted something within me, so that when I phoned the Bishop of Oxford back and quickly discovered that he did, indeed, want to talk with me about becoming Bishop of Reading I knew in my gut (rather than my heart) that this was meant to be. To close friends I have described it as one of the easiest decisions I have ever made – though the hardest to live out. I can only describe this as a call. It seemed of God that I would say yes. At this point I should say that I had never met Richard Harries. Never heard him speak (except of course on the radio). In a strange way this increased my sense of call.

After they met, in the House of Lords, Cottrell was asked to meet the Archdeacon of Berkshire to see if they could work together and then the senior staff of the diocese. 'Richard assured me this was not an interview, but of course this is exactly what it was. I gave a short presentation about developing mission in the Reading episcopal area. I was quizzed a bit, and later on that day was 'phoned by Richard and offered the post. I said yes.'

The diocese of Oxford was breathing again. Were lessons learned? One bishop expressed the view that Harries was the only bishop who could have attempted the appointment of Jeffrey John at the time. Another supporting bishop did not doubt the integrity of those on all sides in the dispute, but believed that wisdom and discernment of the mind of Christ comes from stillness, and much waiting upon God and upon each other, which was not allowed to happen. Another bishop was clear that once the Crown has nominated, the appointment is *de facto* made. Is not that how it should have concluded?

In writing this chapter, words of Dorothy L. Sayers on Ira or Wrath hovered in the atmosphere:

The average English mind is a fertile field in which to sow the dragon's teeth of moral indignation; and the fight that follows will be blind, brutal, and merciless. That is not to say that scandals should not be exposed, or that no anger is justified. But you may know the mischief-maker by the warped malignancy of his language as by the warped malignancy of his face and voice. His fury is without restraint and without magnanimity – and is aimed, not at checking the offence, but at starting a pogrom against the offender. He would rather the evil were not cured at all than that it were cured quietly and without violence. His evil lust of wrath cannot be sated unless somebody is hounded down, beaten, and trampled on, and a savage war-dance executed upon the body. (*The Other Six Deadly Sins*, 1943)

Chapter Twenty
Leader of the Pack

Fortuitous and coincidental with Harries' entrance into the Lords was his appointment from 1996 to 2001 to the chairmanship of the General Synod's Board for Social Responsibility. On questions of morality this is the most public arena in the Church of England for debate and controversy. Unlike the Roman Catholics, Anglicans do not have authoritative papal encyclicals, many of them impressive, on social and ethical teaching. Anglican moral statements, usually *ad hoc*, are essentially intended as contributions to a continuing debate in Church or society towards the reform of statute law. It is characteristic of statements produced within the Church of England, that the appeal to reason and experience is as strong as the appeal to the tradition of the Church and to Scripture. There is a history of authoritative reports which have made major contributions to changes in the law of the land, for example, 'Ought Suicide to be a Crime' 1959; 'Decisions about Life and Death' 1965; 'Putting Asunder (A Divorce Law for Contemporary Society)' 1966; 'Abortion' 1966; 'On Dying Well, an Anglican contribution to the debate on euthanasia' 1975 (2nd edition 2000); 'Personal Origins: Report on Human Fertilisation and Embryology' 1985 (revised 1996).

Harries followed a line of very capable people chairing and guiding the board, formed in 1958. Recent chairs, sat upon by bishops, have been Graham Leonard of Truro and London (1976) serious, deficient in humour and rather self-indulgent. He always had to give his opinion first. The Revd Professor Oliver O'Donovan remembers it as a 'rather tense body in those days. Graham Leonard chaired with an extremely strong hand. He was determined that the board should not get itself into a position which he could not possibly defend, and would himself speak for considerable periods at each plenary meeting, laying down a line which he thought the board could successfully hold. It was difficult to find oneself in disagreement and the chair's line was usually sound sense, either practically or theologically or both'. Hugh Montefiore of Birmingham (1982) was loveable, fluent, speaking as incessant thought and proposals flowed from his pen and mouth, occasionally bulldozing them onto others. Yet with a more relaxed style and humour from the chair, it was easier for members to say what they thought. But as a result the board seemed to fall apart with centrifugal pressures. David Sheppard of Liverpool (1991) had considerable stature with deeply embedded social concerns: outwardly charming, he was given to sudden flashes of temper. And then came Richard Harries (1996). It is recognized that he stands apart from the rest. On every topic which came or erupted for consideration he had something sensible to contribute with genuine depth. His characteristics of loftiness, realism and humour were held together in commendable equipoise.

In Harries' period the board functioned in a vastly changed context compared to what some regarded as the 'Golden Age'. It was not a product of the Archbishops' Council, as such. But, like that development, it is probably reflective of a significant ecclesiological shift within a much more secular public policy environment. Harries puts it this way: 'Major reports may have had their day. One of the main aspects of the board's work is responding to a whole series of government consultation papers. This is done to a very high standard, for example, briefing papers on abortion, hunting, drugs, alcoholism, animal welfare. Their purpose is to ensure that bishops and other church spokespeople have the facts readily available and also any relevant Synod decisions.' This does not mean that Harries, as chair, necessarily had any direct input to every topic, but there were exceptions, of which abortion is a prime example.

Now to Harries as a member of the House of Lords. There are 26 Lords Spiritual, including the Archbishops of Canterbury and York. One of the bishops reads prayers whenever the House of Lords is sitting. This bishop is, therefore, theoretically available to speak on any matter which arises during his week of duty.

One of the main characteristics of the Lords' debates is their informed nature. It is worth noting some observations by Robert Cecil Mortimer, Bishop of Exeter 1949 to 1973, the last of the 'Lord Bishops', never a proud prelate, though not without a dash of patriarch and potentate. He was impressive for his humanity, which is why he was an outstanding moral theologian – 20 years at Christ Church, Oxford. There was not a trace of populism in his being. The impression was of intellectual power and aloofness, a person whose bite could be worse than his bark. His style was clear, strong, fearless, never sentimental, verbose or ostentatious, yet with a retiring, almost embarrassingly shy persona. His scorn for whatsoever was unreal added an edge to many of his phrases. In the House of Lords he was one of the very few bishops of his time who was listened to with attentiveness and respect. That was because he carried both knowledge and authority on the most pressing moral and ethical subjects of the time. He expressed himself in a way that is a warning any contemporary bishop should heed, including Harries. Mortimer reflected on his report 'Putting Asunder' (1968):

> Christians living in a secular and plural society increasingly find themselves called on to encounter and cooperate with their fellow men, not on any specifically Christian basis of faith and morals, but on some other basis that enjoys wide recognition in society as a whole. In order to do what is required of them, they have to learn and practise the art of putting themselves in the place of secular man and seeing the demands of the right and the good through his eyes. This can be an absorbing and even exciting undertaking, as we have found in our study of divorce, but one of which the effect on the Christian concerned may be curious. He may grow so engrossed in, so

habituated to, the formerly strange mental world which he has entered, that in the end he comes to be dominated by its concepts and cabined by its logic. In short, while he is in that world he stops thinking as a Christian and forgets all about the possibility of a Christian contribution that might extend its horizons. It is therefore salutary for us, at the end of our immersion in the secular law of divorce, to call to mind some words of T.A. Lacey, speaking of a Christian's duty to work for the reformation of state laws, he said:

> In doing this he has no right to put aside, what he has learnt as a Christian, and in the quality of citizenship to act as a mere natural man. Such a division of personality is intolerable . . . He is bound . . . to use his Christian illumination for ascertaining what is naturally just.

No bishop of his time has been so regular in attendance and contributed to as many debates on a vast range of legislation and subjects as Richard Harries. He was introduced into the House in 1993 and made his maiden speech on 23 February 1994. The subject was 'The Family'. Harries urged the Government to look at all areas of policy with the likely impact on the family in mind. It was a period when the Conservative Government under John Major was rocked with scandals. A maiden speech is a moment when a new member has the opportunity of being noticed as a promising and effective Lord, a hesitant or loquacious flop or someone neutered by political partisanship. And if knowledge of the subject is seasoned with humour, the maiden will not remain one for long. Harries may have been the first person in the Lords to show an amusing side to Lenin, in his illustration that human nature does not change very much:

> After the 1917 Revolution in Russia, people used to consult Lenin about life in a socialist society. One peasant tramped hundreds of miles to ask:
> 'Comrade Lenin, is it permissible in the new society for a man to keep a mistress?' 'Comrade,' replied Lenin, 'it is not only permissible, it is obligatory, for then a man can tell his mistress that he has to be with his wife and can say to his wife that he is with his mistress. Meanwhile he can be getting down to some solid work in the library.'

From November 1995 to March 1996 Harries was active in the ensuing Family Law Bill. Indeed, for a period he was in the House day after day because he had time blocked out to be away from his diocese. The Bill was proposed by the Lord Chancellor, Lord Mackay of Clashfern, an honest and decent man from a devout Free Presbyterian background. The Bill contained the most radical package of changes for a quarter of a century. The 'quickie' divorce for unreasonable behaviour and adultery would be swept away – in 1993 there were 178,000 divorces in Britain, one for every two marriages that year, and 70 per cent of the petitions were filed by women. In its place was proposed a 'no fault' divorce after a minimum 12-month period of reflection, and a new emphasis on mediation rather than court battles.

For Harries, marriage is a vocation. It is also a human institution. He was dismayed by the level of divorce. He offered Christian insights in a pastoral letter to his diocese – 'Marriage – A Christian Understanding'.

Romantic love is wonderful but it can set up some dangerous illusions. Sometimes people feel if only they can meet the right person and there is a mutual falling in love, all their previous frustrations and discontents will fall away. Everything is staked on this one relationship. But it is God alone who is meant to be the most important factor in our life, as the ground of our being and the goal of all our longing. Unless we have this as our first priority then everything else becomes out of balance. If we invest everything in one human relationship as the most important thing in our life, then we are asking of it more than it can bear. Then we have to face the fact that none of us is perfect. As the poet W. H. Auden put it: 'We have to love our crooked neighbour with our crooked heart.' This means we have to love our less than perfect husband/wife with our own less than perfect heart. Christians believe that God is love and that, in Christ, this love is available to help us grow in love. Most marriages have minor difficulties: some go through periods of crisis which have to be worked through by the couple themselves. But the grace of God is present and available to help us grow in love towards God, our spouse and other people.

On faithfulness, Harries reaches for an apposite quotation to express his feelings. In the highly popular novel *Captain Corelli's Mandolin* by Louis de Bernières, Dr Iannis gives his daughter Pelagia this advice:

And another thing. Love is a temporary madness. It erupts like volcanoes and then subsides. And when it subsides you have to make a decision. You have to work out whether your roots are so entwined together that it is inconceivable that you should ever part. Because this is what love is. Love is not breathlessness, it is not excitement, it is not the promulgation of promises of eternal passion, it is not the desire to mate every second minute of the day, it is not lying awake at night imagining that he is kissing every cranny of your body. No don't blush, I am telling you some truths. That is just being 'in love', which any fool can do. Love itself is what is left over when being in love has burned away, and this is both an art and a fortunate accident. Your mother and I had it, and grew towards each other underground, and when all the pretty blossom had fallen from our branches we found that we were one tree and not two.

Harries proposed various amendments to ensure not only that information about marriage counselling was available to the couple but that this was offered free and that the agencies received the necessary financial support for their work. Another amendment was for the strengthening of high-class mediation as a key feature of the Bill. Everything should be done to prevent an angry dispute burning into an entrenched bitterness, thus hardening the couple against any possibility of reconciliation. The effect on children was likewise a paramount consideration. When he proposed that grants to cover the cost of marriage counselling should be mandatory rather than discretionary, he was strongly supported in the Lords by two former archbishops, Lords Runcie and Habgood, and the Bishops of Lichfield (Keith Sutton) and Worcester (Philip Goodrich). But when Baroness Young tabled an amendment calling for 'fault' to be reintroduced she had the support of the Bishop of London (Richard Chartres), Lord Jakobovits and 34 Tory Lords.

The opposition came from those who argued that taking fault out of the divorce process would lead to a no pain, no blame, no shame attitude to divorce. They wanted a Bill that buttressed marriage rather than civilized divorce. A small number of right-wing MPs was vociferous, including some Roman Catholics who, unlike the Catholic bishops who were sympathetic to the Bill, acted as a Tory rump, wagging the dog. In March 1996 the Bill had its third reading and the Lord Chancellor bowed to demands from Harries to introduce regulation to control marriage counselling.

In the space of four months Harries had established himself as an important House of Lords figure. It is no exaggeration to say he had taken to the Lords like a duck to water. This, rather than the General Synod and all its tributaries, is where he felt at ease. And this is the environment in which Harries would be noticed, make his presence felt and voice heard. He does not have inflated views on the presence of bishops in the Lords. 'I try to pop into the Lords for a short period whenever I am in London. The reasons I do this are because I feel some bishops need to take an active interest and I am very handy living in Oxford. Also I have to be in London quite a lot anyway. I think bishops are listened to with respect and I would judge that the level of their contribution is well above average. Nevertheless, I certainly would not exaggerate their influence. We are very rarely able to speak on the detailed committee stages of Bills, because of the sheer time and technicality involved.' Harries became what the Archbishops of Canterbury call 'The Leader of the Pack' in the Lords. This means convening such meetings as are necessary for spiritual peers and acting as a link person with 'the usual channels'.

In 1997 there was another fortuitous event, a General Election and political change. On 1 January *The Guardian* led with the views of five bishops (Durham, Birmingham, Coventry, Liverpool and Oxford) on the subject of public policy and personal responsibility. Harries was in primary place and prominence:

John Major's big idea of 'Back to Basics' poked its head out of its hole and then scampered down a burrow, never to be seen again. This was partly because Mr Major was badly let down by the scandals, sexual and financial, of some of his colleagues. It was also because of the suspicion that Tory class interest emphasizes personal morality because it wishes to resist the fundamental economic and political changes that threaten the privileged position of its supporters. Yet there are now clear signs that people right across the country want a renewal of personal responsibility.

If Labour takes office, the time for this will be more propitious than any other since the postwar Attlee Government. Public policy and personal morality will no longer be seen as antithetical. Both could receive equal emphasis. This is partly because Labour is not open to the kind of class criticism levelled at the Tories. More important is the fact that Labour has rediscovered its moral, as opposed to Marxist, roots. If Mr Blair is elected, I suspect there will be an equal emphasis upon changing the conditions which depress and degrade the lives of so many of our fellow citizens, and on our personal duty to live decently. Both the Pope and the Archbishop of Canterbury have tried to get people to see that fundamental moral values are there to be recognized, not made up as we go along. We need to get away from a pick and mix attitude to morality, to acknowledge that certain fundamental moral insights are inherent in the nature of things, and are essential for the well-being of both individuals and society. The voice of the Church has not yet prevailed. We too can look hypocritical or ridiculous. But individuals with integrity, both in business and in politics, are increasingly recognizing the link between an objective morality and its expression in the community of faith. The Church of England, which now seems to have picked itself up off the floor, will have an important role in the years ahead in supporting people in all walks of life as they grapple with these issues for the Churches have never ceased proclaiming that public policy and personal morality go together.

Economics and politics shape the conditions in which we live and these in turn shape (but do not condition) our whole outlook. But politics is not everything. The personal struggle to live with integrity, honestly and faithfully, especially in sexual and financial matters, is equally crucial. The Church is a rich resource for individuals and organizations determined to bring a more coherent ethical structure to their lives. For all its failings, it will still be trying to give people a vision to underpin and strengthen this morality, helping them to live with decency and hope. And when they fail, as the Gospel recognizes they will, it will provide a framework within which they can be forgiven and restored, rather than thrown out in favour of the next 'big idea'.

A national debate was fuelled by the press moving into their predictable positions of party entrenchment from which leader writers launched their missiles of severe criticism or praise!

Harries had long been an advocate of 'The Third Way' approach to politics. Promoting and reconciling the four values of equal worth, opportunity for all, responsibility and community were as embedded in him as they were defined and defended by the director of the London School of Economics, Anthony Giddens in *The Third Way and Its Critics*.

Harries' sure touch was recognized in the Lords, so the chamber did not empty when his name was called. A few of his contributions are mentioned here as further fragments towards the mosaic.

The debate on 'The Mentally Ill: Care in the Community' (15 May 1996) followed a number of highly publicized cases of murder by severely mentally ill people. Harries came with statistics from Oxfordshire which he used sparingly. He knew how to insert and establish a few facts without drowning his 'audience' with an endless monotony of figures. How best could care in the community be made to work? What were the ideals behind such a concept? 'There must be, first, a systematic assessment of health and social care needs; secondly, nomination of a key worker to coordinate the package of care offered to the client; thirdly, a written care plan; fourthly, regular reviews of need; fifthly, inter-agency and inter-professional collaboration and care planning; sixthly, consultation with users and carers; and, seventhly, effective coordination of packages of care to support individuals in the county. Care management is to be fully integrated into the care programme so that people will have only one key worker, and full joint paperwork is planned.'

The Government was planning small homes for between eight and 20 people, ideally for 12. The need was for approximately 5,000 places, meaning more than 400 homes. Harries questioned the Government's political will in this matter, not least because of the huge financial implications. During a debate on the Housing Bill (16 May 1996) Harries spoke as president of the National Federation of Housing Associations. The Government's policy of encouraging more housing to be met by the private rented sector was a sound aspiration, 'But can it really meet the need for good quality, permanent, low-cost rented accommodation for all our citizens?' Harries was sceptical of the results when the Bill proposed the abolition of the duty by local authorities to provide permanent accommodation and limited their obligation to ensuring that accommodation of some kind was found for a two-year-period – double the period originally specified in the Bill. 'But two years at a time is not the kind of security that anyone, especially a family with young children, can be easy about.'

From his detailed knowledge, Harries was also unhappy about the availability of land to build low-cost housing. Previously generous landowners, the Church or some other trust, had given land or sold it at below market value. They did so because they wished to help those who could not afford to purchase houses and also wished to ensure the mixed social character of their community. 'I understand that the diocese of Hereford and the diocese of Salisbury, as well as my own diocese, are having reservations about making any more land available for such schemes. Reassurance is needed that land made available for low-cost rented accommodation, in order to ensure the continuation of a mixed community, will continue to serve that purpose.'

Penal policy was always important to Harries and there were regular opportunities for expressing himself. In 1997 the Oxford Diocesan Board for Social Responsibility published a report from its Criminal Justice Group – 'Beyond Redemption'. Restorative justice was its theme and it asked, 'Upon whom does the burden of crime fall?' giving a short answer, 'It falls upon the entire community. The task of the Church in this diocese, at all levels and in all areas, is to help others bear that burden, by a willingness to bear part of that burden too.' Penal Policy was debated in the Lords on 27 October 1997. Harries had visited a number of prisons and met

governors and prison staff. A too-large prison population in overcrowded conditions concerned him as did the number of untried prisoners remanded in custody,
over 4,000 on any one day. He proposed a three-month time limit on custodial
remands. He described the criminal justice system as neither fully humane nor
Christian. 'If we look carefully at why we need containment, what constitutes
punishment, how we can best deter and what we need in order to change people's
behaviour, we see that there is a massive imperative to find an alternative to prison;
to make prison itself a context to which people can be enabled to face up to the
harm that they have done to others and where they can be helped to change their
behaviour. From a Christian point of view we must never lose hope of that possibility.'

In an earlier debate on the Crime (Sentences) Bill (27 January 1997) Harries
agreed, momentarily, with Lord Tebbit about the importance of deterrence. 'There
is no doubting that this is crucial in the kind of fallen society in which we all live.
But it is well known that the length of a sentence is not in itself a deterrent. The
only real deterrent for a criminal is the high probability that he will be caught. As
Lord Tebbit put it, it is the prospect of being nicked.' Harries quickly collected himself and prevented Lord Tebbit from a heart flutter at the thought of a spiritual
peer's agreement on 'lock 'em up', as Harries continued, 'In the long term, and one
of the advantages of being a bishop is that we can and should think in the long
term, there are still more fundamental and more effective ways of tackling crime.
The additional annual expenditure eventually needed to finance the proposals in
the Bill would be equivalent on a conservative estimate to the annual cost of
200,000 nursery school places . . . Money spent at an early age helping parents and
nursery schools provide an ordered, caring environment is the only way in the long
run in which a government can tackle the roots of crime, for people's patterns of
behaviour go awry at a very early age and it is both difficult and costly to change
those patterns later in life. The Bill is disappointing because in the judgement of
many in the Church it takes penal policy in totally the wrong direction: one that is
costly, unlikely to work and potentially unfair.'

Detention centres were a running sore for Harries. Before the debate on the
Asylum and Immigration Bill 1996 he was one of a small group who visited asylum
seekers who received no benefits and were sleeping on the floor of Rectory Road
United Reformed Church, Stoke Newington. When the Labour Government came
to power in 1997 he was encouraged by the Government's attitude towards the
issue of asylum seekers after leading a delegation of the Churches' Commission for
Social Justice to meet the Home Secretary, Jack Straw, and the Immigration Minister, Mike O'Brien. His pleasure was short-lived when he realized that although
temporary detention was probably a regrettable necessity there could be no justification for detaining or imprisoning people who had committed no crime, let alone
keeping them locked up for six months, 12 months or even longer. During a debate
on Campsfield House Detention Centre (20 April 1998) following an extended
visit, he referred to the importance of the chaplaincy service in what had been
described as 'the most religious place in Oxfordshire. This is first, because many of

the detainees come from countries where religion is a crucial aspect of life. Secondly, because the whole experience of coming to this country and detention throws people back upon their inner resources, and this has the effect of highlighting any religious dimension. At Campsfield there is a special room for Muslim prayers, another for Sikh prayers and regular, vibrant worship by Christians from Africa'.

Harries was more likely to reveal his convictions in the Lords than anywhere else. He was against the National Lottery in principle. He thought its existence and huge popularity was a 'sign of a fundamental malaise in our society' one in which the culture of getting replaces the culture of giving. He accepted it is here to stay but when the National Lottery Bill was debated on 22 January 1998 he endeavoured to insert an amendment that the minimum age for play should be raised to 18. The Churches had a common view on this.

Harries intervened in most of the Lords debates on Iraq. He did not speak off-the-cuff. Before talking part he telephoned some of the wisest strategists and military experts concerned with the possibility of military action. In the end his position arose out of the accumulated wisdom of Christian civilization, reflecting on the morality of law which began with Augustine and was refined by Aquinas and others well into the twentieth century. His criteria for military action were those shared by those who would ultimately support the Government in an act of war, as set forth in a debate on Iraq (17 February 1998):

> First, there must be legitimate authority. In any action against Iraq, that means the authority of the UN. Secondly, every attempt to resolve the dispute by peaceful means must have been tried and exhausted. Thirdly, a calculation must be made so that military action would not cause more harm than would be the case if such action did not take place. But that calculation depends very much on what is trying to be achieved, the goal of any action.

In February 1999 a Royal Commission was appointed on the Reform of the House of Lords. Its report 'A House for the Future' was published in January 2000. Lord Butler of Brockwell, former Cabinet Secretary and then master of University College, Oxford, was invited to chair the commission but declined because of a heavy commitment at the college. The Prime Minister, Tony Blair, then asked Lord Wakeham, chairman of the Press Complaints Commission, to chair. Members were: The Rt Hon Gerald Kaufman MP; Lord Butler of Brockwell; Baroness Dean of Thornton-le-Fylde, former trade union leader; Lord Hurd of Westwell, former Conservative Northern Ireland, Home and Foreign Secretary; Sir Michael Wheeler-Booth, former clerk of the Parliaments who was involved with the Richard Crossman plan 30 years previously; Anthony King, professor of government at the University of Essex, and former member of the public standards watchdog; Bill Morris, general secretary of the Transport and General Workers' Union; Dawn Oliver, constitutional lawyer at University College, London (said to be the second choice for the Liberal Democrats after Julia Neuberger turned it down);

Ann Benyon, national manager of BT Wales; Kenneth Munro, chair of the Centre for Scottish Public Policy and former European Commission representative in Scotland; and Richard Harries. This was the kind of work which Harries relished.

Of the 128 recommendations in the report the most far-reaching were: cutting the number of peers from 1,213 to about 550; a 'significant' minority directly elected from the regions, with three options – 65 seats, 87 seats or 195 seats; the majority to be appointed by a new independent appointments committee; at least 30 per cent of all appointments should be women – 5–6 per cent would go to ethnic minorities, 20 per cent for non-party cross-benchers; the Prime Minister would lose control over the appointments; no decision was made on what the new House or its members should be called; they would be paid according to attendances; seats would be kept for Law Lords; there would be a 'spiritual' bench with 26 seats for Christian Churches in the United Kingdom – 21 for England, five for Scotland, Wales and Northern Ireland. Of the 21 places in England, 16 should be assigned to the Church of England and five to members of other Christian denominations in England. In addition, at any one time, there should be at least five members specifically selected to represent different non-Christian faith communities.

Harries had the unique, responsible and onerous task of providing foundation material to support a specifically religious presence in the new House. His independent trait was essential for there were pressures from all sides, from the view that the two archbishops and 24 bishops of the Church of England should be untouched, to those who would like to oust the bishops altogether from the chamber. In a self-assured submission – 'The Role of Bishops in the Second Chamber' – prepared by the Archbishops' Council, the point was made that 'the Church has become, and remains, a unique institution located still at the centre of our national life and thinking nationally as a result'. Without specifying the number of bishops for a new Lords it was plain where the Church stood: 'Reducing the number of bishops available to the chamber risks compromising the service of the Church of England by impoverishing the range of contributions – regional and otherwise – that it can offer.'

There was never any question that the status quo would or should be continued. If the Church of England was to maintain an influence, it could only do so by opening the door to other Churches and different faiths. A prominent national Christian leader was Cardinal Basil Hume who had repeatedly declined a seat in the Lords, partly because his Canon Law ruled it out and partly because it would have overturned the proper distinction between what was appropriate for a Catholic bishop and for a Catholic lay person. It was with great surprise that the submission to the Royal Commission took the opposite view. The Roman Catholic hierarchy said that if they were offered seats in the reformed second chamber and provided certain criteria could be met (above all by a legal dispensation from Rome), they would accept.

Harries was anxious to have the religious element widened out beyond the Church of England to include leaders of other Christian denominations and members of other faiths. How to do this in a way that still left the Church of England a significant presence required agreement by persuading the chair and members of the commission that it was just! Sixteen bishops in the new chamber was realistic, not mere compromise.

The Royal Commission report had what may be termed a bad press. That was less important than the Government's reaction to it. When the White Paper was published in November 2001 the main points were: the remaining 92 hereditary peers to be abolished; only 120 members to be elected by the public; 120 non-party political peers to be nominated by a Commission; 320 political peers to be nominated by party leaders; the lion's share of nominations to the Prime Minister; a golden handshake for older peers – possible age limit of 75; more women, and ethnic minorities guaranteed by quotas; Church of England bishops reduced from 26 to 16; a cross-party Appointments Commission to oversee the political balance. It was clear that there would be no requisite and comprehensive reform. It was as if the Prime Minister and his Cabinet gave the impression that, having set out with grandiloquent plans to modernize Britain, they grew bored by the intricacies of the Constitution. What the Prime Minister wanted from a reformed House was a combination of echo chamber and chamber of 'cronies'. The existing situation would continue. The Prime Minister had already succeeded in creating the largest number of peers since the Life Peerages Act, 1958. Comparisons are Tony Blair, 248 in four years; John Major, 171 in seven years; Margaret Thatcher 216 in 11 years, Harold Wilson, 326 in eight years; Harold Macmillan, 90 in five years.

Harries questioned the seriousness of the Government in putting forward these reform proposals. 'The last thing Tony Blair wants is a dust-off with the Establishment. He would prefer to let sleeping dogs lie.' The work of the Royal Commission was effectively dead. The Government acted discreditably. How soon the dogs will awaken and bark is not known. Harries and Lord Wakeham always believed that people would come back to their proposals. In 2006 reform is again on the agenda with at least some momentum. Perhaps the Royal Commission's proposals will not be wholly ignored!

On 9 April 2003 Harries proposed the debate on 'Religion and Global Terrorism'. As usual he studied the background of Al'Qaeda. He acknowledged that it was essential to understand what is fundamental to the religion the terrorists purport to practise: that there should be an *Umma*, a united worldwide community of Muslims united by Sharîa law. Western states are based on a particular territory, the rule of law and democratic processes. What and who could bridge the chasm, search for a common language, a particular landscape and a shared way of life in a multi-ethnic, multifaith society? What could interfaith groups do to strengthen moderate, mainstream, majority Muslim opinion? What might it mean for a Muslim to be a faithful Muslim in our society? On the successful answers to these questions 'depends the extent to which Al'Qaeda is ideologically isolated and dies out, or has an increasing resonance within the wider Muslim world, so much of which at the moment is alienated.'

After a vigorous and wide-ranging debate, Harries returned to the understandable attitude of Muslim societies and communities feeling alienated in our world today, hostile to US power, disgusted by Western lewdness, sometimes oppressed, the young resentful and marginalized, excluded from the hope of a better future. 'That, as we are all aware, is the breeding ground of terrorism. When these communities take religion seriously, as they do, when terrorists speak to that sense of alienation by offering an alternative better world that can come about only by destructive acts of violence, and when they can gain the allegiance of those alienated young people by a religious call to commitment to kill and be killed, we have a very serious situation indeed. Religion is being misused. However, we must face the sad brutal fact that misused religion is a powerful destructive force. It is a rage against the established order and against corrupted states. It is a creed for the discontented.'

Harries chaired a working group of the House of Bishops on 'Countering Terrorism: Power, Violence and Democracy Post 9/11' whose report was published in September 2005. Other members were the Bishops of Coventry, Colin Bennetts; Worcester, Peter Selby; and Bath and Wells, Peter Price. Harries wrote in the preface to this good and sadly under-reported 100-page document, 'All governments have a proper responsibility to take the necessary steps to safeguard their citizens. People in Britain are acutely aware of this following the London bomb attacks of July 2005. But citizens need to be vigilant that these steps do not infringe hard-won civil liberties, particularly the right to due process of law. The Churches have a particular message here based on biblical insights about fear and how playing on the fears of enemies makes for unwise policies. The report also examines the United States' sense of moral righteousness and questions the way some American Christians have used biblical texts to support a political agenda in the Middle East. We argue, "There is no uniquely righteous nation. No country should see itself as the redeemer nation, singled out by God as part of his providential plan." The report calls for a strengthening of the United Nations as "the legitimate authority for military intervention" and opposes democracy being "imposed on any other country by force", saying it must be adopted by a nation "in culturally appropriate ways".'

The bishops examined the controversy surrounding Iran's nuclear ambitions and thought the arguments against nuclear proliferation needed to be made more compelling. They concluded: 'The non-nuclear weapon states need to be presented with rather more convincing arguments and incentives than they have been up to now, as to why it might be in their best interests not to go nuclear.' There were those who thought Harries and his co-authors were committing the House of Bishops to a *de facto* pacifism – a rather absurd accusation to level at Harries who supported the Falklands War and the first Gulf War, who long championed military intervention in Bosnia and Kosovo, and who for 40 years tried to expose the crypto-pacifism in Church documents!

There were lighter moments in the Lords. On 14 January 1999 Harries asked the Government what action they were taking to encourage the contribution of poetry to national culture!

Chapter Twenty-One
Life and Death

The question of when the soul enters the body is hotly disputed by philosophers and theologians. When the soul leaves the body is not so doubted.

Harries' published contributions to composite works include: *Attitudes to Death in the Twentieth Century* (1991); *The Beginning of Life* and *The End of Life*, two lectures for the Liddon Trust (1999); *Staying Human* (2001); *The Moral Status of the Early Embryo* (2003); *Delivering Public Policy: The Status of the Embryo and Tissue Typing* (2004). There are many unpublished lectures, newspaper articles, sermons, reviews: for example, *Is the Human Embryo a Person?*; *The Human Genome Project – Being Human or Playing God*; *The Moral Status of the Pre-Implantation Embryo: Reading the Christian Tradition*; *Physician Assisted Suicide*.

The Abortion Act 1967 effectively, not intentionally, allowed abortion for personal and social reasons where two physicians agreed that it was indicated. By 1997 more than 170,000 (rising to 181,600) legal abortions were carried out and the Act in some places was interpreted so literally that in practice there was abortion on demand. Christian opposition to abortion is associated in the public mind with the Roman Catholic Church, which has directness and clarity as its rule. Abortion is wrong at all times and under all circumstances, even when the life of the mother is at risk. By contrast the Church of England's position is thought to be weak, woolly or inconsistent. That is not the case. The theological basis is that the foetus is God-given life, with the potential to develop relationships, think, pray, choose and love.

There is continuing debate, disagreement and anxiety amongst Anglicans about the circumstances in which it is right to perform an abortion. Harries indicates: 'Most would agree that in a direct choice between the life of the mother and the life of the unborn child, the mother should be chosen.' The Church of England combines strong opposition to abortion with a recognition that there can be strictly limited conditions under which it may be morally preferable to any available alternative. However, the position is not static. In 1991 a clause in the Human Fertilisation and Embryology Act lowered the time for abortion from 28 weeks to 24, except for severely abnormal foetuses or when the life of the mother is threatened. There are many advocating a limit of 20 weeks or less. One thing is certain, namely, abortion will not be banned. Harries regrets the placarding of the debate into 'pro-choice' and 'pro-life'.

In 1997 the General Synod acknowledged the moral legitimacy of abortion if the abnormal foetus was not likely to live long if the pregnancy were brought to full-term. But some Anglicans would go beyond this and argue for the legitimacy of terminating a pregnancy in the case of any severe foetal abnormality. Here questions of the quality of life for the potential child should be considered. Harries' position is, 'I myself believe it would be wrong to force a teenager who has been raped to bear a child conceived in that way. It would be sheer cruelty to impose what could only be seen as a distasteful burden upon the suffering already endured as a result of the rape. So there are exceptions to the general opposition to abortion, but the point is that they are few, and truly exceptions.'

On March 2001 a Select Committee of the House of Lords was appointed to review issues arising out of the Human Fertilisation (Research Purposes) Regulations 2001. The Regulations extended the purposes for which research – not treatment – on human embryos could be undertaken under licence from the Human Fertilization and Embryology Authority (HFEA): (a) increasing knowledge about the development of embryos, (b) increasing knowledge about serious disease, or (c) enabling such knowledge to be applied in developing treatments for serious disease.

Harries had the exceptional privilege for a bishop in being invited to chair the Select Committee, whose members were Baronesses Cumberlege, McIntosh of Hudnall, Northover, O'Neill of Bengarve, Perry of Southwark, Platt of Writtle, Warwick of Undercliffe and Lords Dahrendorf and Donoughue. (Baroness Cumberlege and Lord Donoughue are Roman Catholics.)

In his contribution to *Public Life and the Place of the Church*, Lord (Douglas) Hurd writes:

Richard Harries himself provides a striking example of how a bishop can use his experience and authority to influence through the House of Lords the policy of our Government. The question of stem cell research involves issues that are scientific, legal, ethical, philosophical and theological. Those who are knowledgeable on the subject, and many who are not, approach it with strong moral feelings one way or the other. A select committee of the House of Lords is exactly the sort of place where these issues can be thrashed out in a calm and reasonable manner with proper recognition both of the moral anxieties and of scientific enthusiasm. The chair of that select committee has the duty of presenting its report to the House of Lords and thus a unique opportunity to influence the debate on which decisions will be based. Richard Harries has earned wise admiration for the way in which he carried out that duty and used that opportunity.

Baroness Perry had a ringside seat on the Select Committee:

Bishop Richard showed a grasp of the complexities of the subject which was admirable. He was able to understand the issues clearly, and guide the committee's work well. He used the 'expert' advisers intelligently, enabling their advice to the committee to enhance our conclusions without determining them.

The fact that the chair was a bishop was of course helpful to the credibility of our report. It was, I think, the first time that a bishop had chaired a select committee inquiry, and all the more important that it should be done well and impartially. He and we were all aware of that, and I think Bishop Richard was brave to ignore the lobbying of some members of the Church of England who had strong views against such research. I don't know at what personal cost he was able to move ahead with our recommendations, but I think he was helped by the fact that our two Roman Catholic members of the group (who were 'leant on' somewhat by their Church) both supported the conclusions on intellectual grounds. The overwhelming weight of the evidence was to accept that the research should be permitted, within the safeguards of legislation. All members of the group reached that conclusion independently, and were prepared to sign up to the conclusions.

The report from the Select Committee 'Stem Cell Research' was printed on 13 February 2002. Its conclusions and recommendations included:

Stem cells appear to have great therapeutic potential for treatment of many disorders that are both common and serious and for the repair of damaged tissue. Recent research on adult stem cells, including stem cells from the placenta and umbilical cord, also holds promise of therapies; and research on them should be strongly encouraged by funding bodies and the Government.

(Status of the Early Embryo) Whilst respecting the deeply held views of those who regard any research involving the destruction of a human embryo as wrong and having weighed the ethical arguments carefully, the committee is not persuaded, especially in the context of the current law and social attitudes, that all research on early embryos should be prohibited. Fourteen days should remain the limit for research purposes.

(Cell Nuclear Replacement – CNR – and Cloning) Even if CNR is not itself used directly for many stem cell-based therapies, there is still a powerful case for its use, subject to strict regulation by HFEA, as a research tool to enable other cell-based therapies to be developed.

Given the high risk of abnormalities the scientific objections to human reproductive cloning are currently overwhelming. The committee unreservedly endorses the legislative prohibition on reproductive cloning. The Government should take an active part in any move to negotiate an international ban on human reproductive cloning.

It is interesting that an Appendix was included on 'The moral status of the early embryo: reading the Christian tradition', clearly from Harries' hand. The report was introduced in the Lords on 5 December 2002. A major issue was the approval of cloning for medical research. Harries, supported by some of the committee members, argued that it was legitimate to do so and did not believe that the ethical objections, which were not few, stood up to scrutiny.

Harries was and still is a member of the Nuffield Council of Bioethics which examines ethical issues raised by new developments in biology and medicine. It has achieved an international reputation for providing independent advice to assist policymakers and to stimulate debate in bioethics. Under the chairmanship of

Professor Ian Kennedy and subsequently Professor Sir Bob Hepple, QC, its council members comprise some of the best brains and practitioners available on bioethics. Once again Harries loves working in these mind-stretching surroundings.

Following interviews according to 'process' Harries was appointed by the Department of Health as a member of HFEA from 24 November 2003. It absorbs a great deal of his mental and diary time. HFEA was established in 1991 following the coming into law of the Human Fertilisation and Embryology Act. It is both adjudicator and policeman. Why is the authority necessary and what does it do? It came in the wake of the 1970s and 1980s IVF revolution and the Warnock Committee set up in 1982 to investigate social, ethical and legal implications of developments in 'Assisted Reproduction Technologies', i.e. all 'artificial' techniques used to assist women to conceive. In 1984 the 'Warnock' Report of the Committee on Inquiry into Human Fertilization and Embryology recommended establishing a statutory licensing authority.

In 2005 one in seven couples in the UK had a problem conceiving a baby – approximately 1,750,000 couples. About 30,000 will have had IVF and more than 8,500 babies will be born as a result. HFEA exists to ensure that the treatment patients receive is safe and conducted to a high standard. It also regulates research on embryos, making sure it is safe, necessary and ethical. Accordingly, HFEA licenses and monitors clinics carrying out IVF and donor insemination; regulates the storage of eggs, sperm and embryos; provides information and data about the services, treatments and techniques that clinics provide; keeps a register of treatments to enable people born as a result of IVF or donor insemination to obtain information about their origins; and, controversially, licenses embryo research to ensure science can progress in a responsible way. It advises the Government on all aspects of assisted reproductive technology and produces a Code of Practice. Dame Suzi Leather succeeded Ruth Deech as chair of HFEA in March 2002. Suzi Leather is an attractive person, highly intelligent and knowledgeable, forthright, imaginative, a Christian Socialist, well trained in working on public bodies. She is unfearful of controversy as when at the HFEA annual meeting on 21 January 2004 she said the law should be changed to remove a clause requiring doctors who assess infertile women to take account of the 'need of a child for a father' before offering treatment. One in four families is now headed by a single parent. The reaction of some of an excitable media was predictable – giving the green light to single women including lesbians to seek treatment on equal terms with heterosexual couples!

In 2006 Dame Suzi Leather left to be chair of the Charity Commission and Harries was appointed interim chair.

What does Harries bring to HFEA, in particular to the Ethics and Law Committee which he now chairs, and as a member of one of a team of Licence Committee members? Clear-sighted analysis of issues and understanding of the human predicament; determination; sharp observation of human nature; non-judgemental of moral positions linked with compassion in not driving through a moral line, making him acceptable and attractive to non-Christians – there are some vociferous atheists on HFEA: a person of integrity, liberal and weighty, a problem-analyst not a problem-solver.

Harries is not confined to 'round the table' discussion. He speaks on his work with HFEA at the drop of an invitation and will go, as he says, like 'a lion in a den of Daniels' where he knows the opposition will be fierce but fair, as for example, when he debated embryo research at St Mary's College, Strawberry Hill (University of Surrey) in 2005 with Dr David Albert Jones whose book *The Soul of the Embryo* (2004) is a learned, authoritative and accessible work on the topic. Professor John Wyatt of the Royal Free marshalled the exchanges before an audience of clergy, laity, medical practitioners, lecturers, students and sixth-formers. Whether lecturing, debating or writing, Harries is consistent. He argues that the concept of respect for the early embryo does have substance because of the strict regulatory regime of the HFEA. He considers the arguments that the early embryo 'enjoys the full rights of the human being and should be accorded the respect owed to a human being'. He concludes that these arguments are not finally convincing. He also looks at the moral status of the early embryo in Christian tradition and argues that perhaps from the fourth and certainly from the seventh century in the West until 1869, offences against the early embryo were regarded as less serious than offences against the embryo when developed further. It was in 1869 when Pope Pius IX declared that all mothers who had survived an abortion were to be excommunicated. Harries concludes that there should be no absolute prohibition against research on an early embryo up to 14 days. He also looked at cases involving pre-implantation genetic diagnosis (PGD) and tissue-typing with a view to obtaining matching tissue from an early embryo for a sibling suffering from a life-threatening disease. Although a distinction has been made between what might be licit in the case of a genetic disorder in the sibling, but illicit if the disorder is not genetic, he argues that it could be in the best interests of the early embryo, the child that is to be, if in either case it were selected with a view to matching the tissue of a sibling.

As new developments and regulations follow each other with rampant momentum, it is imperative that he continues to recognize the red as well as amber and green in the bioethical traffic lights.

At the other end of life, death is certain. The 1965 Board for Social Responsibility report 'Decisions about Life and Death', concluded with some salutary remarks which are even more pertinent 40 years on:

> The central affirmation of the Christian faith is that Jesus died and is alive for evermore. The Christian places an absolute value on life, though not on life in this world. He values death, therefore, as a necessary gateway through which men must 'pass into life', must move on towards the fulfilment of God's purpose for them in the vision and fruition of himself. They must, therefore, be prepared for death. *Disce mori* [learn to die]. Perhaps the Church, in its self-conscious attempt in recent decades to preach a gospel 'for this world' – in its desire to be and appear to be 'relevant' – has neglected this 'other-worldly' element in its gospel, and in its pastoral care of people. But death also is relevant to all men; and as relevant to life as life is to death. A recovery of balance between these two points of reference may make more distinctive the Christian contribution to the discussion of the matters of life and death.

By the 1990s there were many opportunities for facing proposals, voluntary or otherwise, for euthanasia. 'Dying with dignity' has become something of a euphemism. 'Dying well' is not much discussed. In 1994 the House of Lords created a Select Committee to investigate the issue of euthanasia in the light of the Bland case. Tony Bland was a patient in a persistent vegetative state, whose artificial feeding and hydration were withdrawn after a ruling from the House of Lords. The Select Committee report of 17 February 1994 decisively rejected changing the law to permit euthanasia. In a Lords' debate on euthanasia (6 May 1998) the peers were divided, following developments in Holland. Harries continued to make his clear conviction heard against any form of euthanasia. His plea was how to improve palliative care and how to bring it to everybody in society.

On 6 June 2003 the Lords debated the Patient (Assistant Dying) Bill. Harries was clear that 'assisted death is wrong in itself however compassionate the motive behind it might be.' In 2004 Lord Joffe introduced a private member's bill – Assisted Dying for the Terminally Ill Bill followed by a Select Committee established to scrutinize the Bill. The Church of England House of Bishops and the Roman Catholic Bishops' Conference of England and Wales made a joint submission (2 September 2004). Their conclusions were clear and simple:

> It is deeply misguided to propose a law by which it would be legal for terminally ill people to be killed or assisted in suicide by those caring for them, even if there are safeguards to ensure it is only the terminally ill who would qualify . . . It would risk a gradual erosion of values in which over time the cold calculation of costs and caring properly for the ill and the old would loom large. As a result many who are ill or dying would feel a burden to others. The right to die would become the duty to die.

Church leaders were very active in print, in conversations and behind the scenes, notably the Roman Catholic Archbishop of Cardiff, Peter Smith; the Archbishop of Canterbury, Rowan Williams; the Anglican Bishops of London, Richard Chartres; St Albans, Christopher Herbert (who was a member of the Select Committee) and Harries. When the committee report was published on 4 April 2005 it did not conclude for or against changing the law on euthanasia.

When The Mental Capacity Bill was published in 2004 its aim was to set out a legal framework for living wills: instructions to doctors to withdraw treatment should patients become incapable of communicating their wishes. It would also enable third-party advocates to tell doctors when to stop treatment of incapacitated relatives. Again Harries and other Church leaders recognized the unfortunate consequences of this Bill. In the House of Commons on 14 December 2004 the Labour Government unwisely applied a three-line whip. Roman Catholic MPs had deep-seated, irreversible convictions which no whip could touch. Iain Duncan Smith MP attempted to defeat the Bill but failed by 297 to 203 votes. However, he managed to draw from the Lord Chancellor, Lord Falconer, a commitment to make explicit in the Bill that it would not authorize any decision where the motive was to kill. However, the Bill passed its third reading in the Commons by 354 to 188 votes. Doctors have an influence, for even after a new Act they would always prefer ILR – indefinite leave to remain, than DNR – do not resuscitate. Harries wrote to a number of medical organizations to see whether they had any evidence and material which would sharpen his position and presentation. When the Bill came to the Lords, Harries spoke on various amendments (25 January and 1 February 2005).

The Lords debated the Select Committee Report 'Assisted Dying for the Terminally Ill Bill' on 10 October 2005. The debate reflected the diverse views of members. Harries opposed the Bill, 'Not just because of its social effects and impact on doctor/patient relationships, but because, at its heart, is a flawed understanding of what it is to be a human being, an excessive emphasis on personal autonomy to the neglect of our mutual interdependence'. The Bill was defeated but Lord Joffe has every intention of rising again or being resuscitated! Indeed, the Joffe Bill in its new form came back to the Lords on 12 May 2006 and was again defeated.

Harries has a postscript: 'I did not share the great worry of the Roman Catholics over this Bill. I felt that there was some scaremongering, which is why I tried to get some hard evidence from medical bodies. There is much confusion around because of the unwillingness of some to grasp the moral distinction between refusing burdensome treatment that is useless and direct killing, and also the distinction between pain-reducing drugs that also shorten life and direct killing. There is also disagreement with the judgement that feeding tubes in the stomach is a form of treatment, not basic medical care.'

Very few people hear Harries in the Lords and fewer still read accounts of the proceedings. His widest and most personal appeal is in *Thought for the Day*. He cannot know how many people are helped in their anxieties and influenced by his words. There is no better example than his words broadcast on 17 February 1994.

When my time comes to go I don't want endless treatment; just to be kept free of pain and comfortable; and supported by family and friends. So I'm glad that there will be support for research into pain, and the development of palliative care in hospices, hospitals and the community, as well as special regard to the maintenance of individual dignity for those in long-term care.

I also want to be spiritually sustained by the prayers of good people. A couplet in one of Charles Wesley's great hymns always gets me pondering. It prays that our lives might show faith and love:

Till death thy endless mercies seal

And make my sacrifice complete.

It implies that death, as part of nature, at the proper time, is within the providence of God; and that a life offered to God and others in love can find its proper culmination at the end – and I think especially of the last prayer of Jesus, 'Father, into thy hands I commit my spirit.' Not a usual way of looking at death these days, or an easy one. But I find it a hopeful ideal for which to aim.

Chapter Twenty-Two
Via Negativa *and Beyond Compare*

Harries' friends and acquaintances include some of the brightest and most interesting people of our time, some who make guest appearances in this work. They are not necessarily those who have had the greatest influence on him. One does not have to dig to locate them. No sermon, address or lecture is complete without several quotations from their works. The procession includes, notably, Julian of Norwich, George Herbert, Samuel Johnson, Gerard Manley Hopkins, Dostoevsky, T .S. Eliot, Samuel Beckett and R. S. Thomas.

Harries cannot be accused of using any of the chosen few in order to massage his ego or to seek solace in their words. What draws him towards lives so different from his own? Or are they so different? Here there is room to mention only a handful and to alight on a few characteristics which may help in probing Harries.

T. S. Eliot (1888–1965) is pre-eminent. Harries is selective in his choice of Eliot's poetry and plays. He would not subscribe to Eliot's social criticism. Portions of *The Idea of a Christian Society* (1939) and *Notes Towards the Definition of Culture* (1948) are alien to his own thought. Eliot's polemical Anglican tracts, for example, *Reunion by Destruction* and *Thoughts After Lambeth*, reflect a 'high and dry' Anglo-Catholicism, antipathetic to the liberalism for which Harries is known. *After Strange Gods* (1934) was 'a primer of modern heresy', assuming a paradigm of sound doctrine, which Eliot believed he possessed. Even Gerard Manley Hopkins, whom one might expect to find praised, fails to win much approval: 'Hopkins has the dignity of the Church behind him, and is consequently in closer contact with reality. But from the struggle of our time to concentrate, not to dissipate, to renew our association with traditional wisdom; to re-establish a vital connection between the individual and the race; the struggle, in a word, against liberalism: from all this Hopkins is a little apart.' Harries would have been uncomfortable amongst some of Eliot's close associates. They included Philip Mairet, Maurice Reckitt, V. A. Demant and William Travers Symon, whose thinking was enfolded in the pages of *The New Age* and *The New English Weekly*, where some of Eliot's poetry first appeared. Harries would have been disconcerted by the bluntness of their exchanges. Eliot's views on leadership are contrary to those expressed by Harries.

Poetry and Truth, on George Herbert and T. S. Eliot, is John Drury's magnificent contribution to *Public Life and the Place of the Church: Reflections to Honour the Bishop of Oxford*. He observes: 'The person and the poet go along together in both instances. In offering it to Richard Harries, I mean to honour a steadfast friend and

241

a person who believes in poetry as a primary vehicle (perhaps sacrament) of that most valuable and hardly-won thing, religious truth.' Can Harries associate or empathize with Eliot the person? There is little help from Eliot himself who once said, 'The critics say I am learned and cold. The truth is that I am neither.' He furnishes no further explanation, deliberately hiding his own life, even from most of his friends. He could have been referring to his afterlife when he contributed to *Reminiscences of Virginia Woolf* (Horizon, May 1941), but even here he is exclusively elusive:

> It seems to me that when a great writer dies – unless he has already outlived his life – something is in danger of vanishing which is not to reappear in the critical study, the full-length biography, or the anecdotal reminiscences. Perhaps it is something that cannot be preserved or conveyed: but at least we can try to set down some symbols which will serve to remind us in future that there is something lost, if we cannot remember what; and to remind a later generation that there is something they do not know, in spite of all their documents, even if we cannot tell them what . . . While the feeling cannot be communicated, the external situation can to some extent be outlined. Any dead author of long ago, an author on whom we feel some peculiarly personal dependence, we know primarily through his work – as he would wish to be known by posterity, for that is what he cared about. But we may also search and snatch eagerly at any anecdote of private life which may give us the feeling for a moment of seeing him as his contemporaries saw him. We may try to put the two together, peering through the obscurity of time for the unity which was both – and coherently – the mind in the masterpiece and the man of daily business, pleasure and anxiety as ourselves: but failing this, we often relapse into stressing the differences between the two pictures. No one can be understood: but between a great artist of the past, and a contemporary whom one has known as a friend, there is the difference between a mystery which baffles and a mystery which is accepted. We cannot explain, but we accept and in a way understand. It is this, I think, that disappears completely.

The religious thinker, who was also a mathematician, physicist and man-of-letters, whom Eliot found congenial above all others was Blaise Pascal (1623–1662) – 'as the type of one kind of religious believer, which is highly passionate and ardent, but passionate only through a powerful and regulated intellect, is in the first sections of his unfinished *Apology for Christianity* facing unflinchingly the demon of doubt which is inseparable from the spirit of belief'. These are intertwined in Eliot. His belief according to Anglican precepts and practice came in 1927 when he was baptized in Finstock Church, Oxford, with the doors locked, then whisked to Cuddesdon to be confirmed in the bishop's chapel. Finstock, the village where Barbara Pym lived, is on the route of one of Jo and Richard Harries' favourite walks, and they never passed through without reflecting on both Eliot and Pym. On 13 June 2004 Harries preached during choral evensong at Finstock in celebration of the life and work of Barbara Pym. The outward sign of the sacraments bestowed was evident in Eliot's dramatic monologues reflecting spiritual struggle – *Journey of the Magi* (1927) and *A Song of Simeon* (1928). In both poems the advent of Christ is seen as involving a painful rather than a joyful transformation.

In an unpublished lecture on the *Four Quartets* Harries makes an accentuated point that 'a fundamental assumption and major theme of the four poems is that human life is a life in time with a history. Right at the beginning of *Burnt Norton* Eliot states:

> If all time is eternally present
> All time is unredeemable.

'This suggests that it is the movement in history, the movement from a past to a present, which allows for the possibility of our experience being changed.'

It is also evident that Eliot was the least time-bound of his contemporaries. He regarded tradition as the coexistence of the past with the present, like places geographically separated from one another coexisting in time. To him the traditionalist was not the remote heir of a disintegrated inheritance, but a missionary travelling from a civilized area – the past – into a fragmentary and incoherent one – the present.

Harries conviction is:

In the Christian life there are two possible ways in which human experience can be transfigured. The first is by appreciating the good things in life and blessing God for them. This is the way of the Hebrew Scriptures and, within the Christian tradition, particularly of Thomas Traherne, the seventeenth-century Anglican writer. For Traherne, the whole world and everything in it shimmers with divine glory and our problem is not so much that we love the wrong things but that we don't love the good things intensely and whole-heartedly enough. The other route is the *via negativa*. Eliot prefaced the *Four Quartets* with a quotation from Heraclitus to the effect that the way up and the way down are one and the same. They may be, but for Eliot there was only one way, namely the way down. No doubt this had something to do with his own temperament, his fear of certain aspects of life. It certainly had to do with what he saw as the futility of modern urban existence, which he explored to such powerful effect in his pre-Christian poetry, especially *The Waste Land*.

Eliot's religious preoccupation long predates his formal acceptance of Anglican faith. Even in *Prufrock and Other Observations* (1917) and *Gerontion* (1919) he revealed his understanding of that forlorn riverside region of the spirit, peopled by souls who have refused to make any decisive choice between good and evil, where earthy lives have incurred neither praise nor blame.

Picasso could paint ruptured images of mankind, painful because true. In *The Waste Land* (1923) Eliot wrote of disorientated and disintegrating humanity. It was like the shrill note of a seagull, a voice crying in the wilderness of our civilization. The facsimile and transcript of the original drafts, published in 1971, reveal the poem coming to birth painfully, a self-emptying but not a discarding. The mind is awesome as a receptacle. The inexpressibly wonderful moments of life are inclined to slip through the mind's mesh leaving the body without the background, like fish struggling in a net after the water has disappeared, whilst the shadowy aspects of living remain in the mind forgiven by others but not by ourselves and rarely forgotten.

Harries accepts 'the way of renunciation, the journey into the dark, is indeed tough for us today' although he thinks 'Eliot would certainly want to argue that his valuation of ordinary human experience, including ordinary human love, is a true valuation and a higher valuation than pertains in the modern world'. But Eliot contends that 'the judgement of God, though not his mercy, is a possibility in the mind of this "dull head among windy places"'.

Eliot's first marriage to Vivien Haigh-Wood in 1915 cannot be separated from any commentary on Eliot the person. She was a mixture of melancholy, disillusionment, fragility, sensitivity, giddy liveliness and startling intelligence. Eliot was attracted by her sparkle, frivolity and gaiety which seemed to complement his rather puritan upbringing, classical education and inherent austerity. He failed to see the delicate hold Vivien had on reality. She was a person of great mental instability. It was a marriage of tense torment. He appeared helpless, unwilling or impotent to assist his wife in her periods of insanity. Eliot himself suffered a severe breakdown and went to Switzerland for treatment. In 1933, whilst giving the Charles Eliot Norton lectures in America, Eliot instructed his solicitor to draw up a Deed of Separation and take it to his wife. That was indeed that! They never met again. When Vivien died in 1947 Patrick Heron painted a double-faced powerful portrait of Eliot – *Jekyll and Hyde*.

Eliot's second marriage to his secretary, Valerie Fletcher, brought him great happiness. But in the seven years of this marriage he wrote neither poetry nor plays of distinction, in contrast to the outpouring from the 'sacred wood' which had marked his 17 years with Vivien. Her biographer, Carole Seymour-Jones, closes *Painted Shadow*: 'He died at the age of 76 on 4 January 1965, comforted by the impregnability of his reputation; Vivien, meanwhile, lay forgotten in the Pinner Cemetery.'

Harries would like to see Samuel Johnson (1709–1784) commemorated in the Anglican calendar. Why? Are we helped by a few extracts from his Presidential Address to the Johnson Society in 1988?

> For most of his life Johnson inhabited a mental hell . . . He suffered from that most modern of diseases, severe depression. It never left him and twice it resulted in virtually incapacitating breakdown lasting several years . . . At the centre of the depression there was Johnson's fear of losing his reason . . . Yet out of this mental hell came humour, wisdom, laughter, great generosity and a profound faith. While Johnson was inwardly wrestling with the beasts of

dread, outwardly he was throwing himself into life. It will do a man no good to whine, he said: earning a living for much of his life by a pound here and a pound there, writing his poems and above all the dictionary . . . For Johnson it was only grace, the help of God, that enabled him to survive. What held his life together, and which was even more fundamental than the dread, was his faith. Yet even this was not an unmixed blessing.

Does Harries share Johnson's belief in universal optimism but not in divine governance? He advances Johnson's earning his living in the rough, tough world of journalism. 'He had to scramble to survive and make his way in the world and at the same time maintain his integrity as a Christian believer. If ever there was a religion of the workplace his is it.' Harries finds Johnson curiously modern 'in his capacity to face life as it is, without illusion, romanticism or cant'. He 'represents a form of Christian life that does not fit into stereotyped notions of sanctity'.

But faith, the Christian religion, was central to his life and what kept it, just, together. Johnson has suffered from the general low estimate of eighteenth-century religion and the caricature of him as a Church of England man, meaning someone concerned to defend the outer status and forms of the Church but with little true religion. Nothing could be further from the truth. His outward religion was reasonably tolerant and his churchgoing unenthusiastic. But his inward religion was intense. And his Christian discipleship firmly aligned with the generosity from poverty of Jesus.

There are many 'howevers . . .'! In a lecture on 'Johnson and Unbelief' Harries brought David Hume (1711–1776) the Scottish philosopher into the picture. Hume, who got under Johnson's skin, attempted to introduce the experimental method of reasoning into moral subjects. Johnson's infrequent bouts of happiness were undermined. As Harries says, 'Disappointment lurked around every corner.' A depressive nature was a cloud which rarely lifted. 'He knew that life was hard and though he himself had achieved worldly success, misery stalked most human beings. The only way such a life could be seen as a blessing was by viewing it as a testing ground for eternal happiness.' This was the only way for Johnson 'to view this life in a positive and courageous way'. It saved him from perpetual torment and a terrifying aversion to dying.

Harries makes a strange claim for Gerard Manley Hopkins (1844–1898), recognizing him as the 'best ostensibly Christian poet since George Herbert' (1593–1633). Hopkins was born into a devout Anglican family and converted to Roman Catholicism in his final year at Oxford. He became a member of the Society of Jesus and was ordained in 1877. The problem for the Jesuits was in knowing what to do with this academically brilliant member who painted, played an instrument, composed music and wrote poetry! His poetic creativity was difficult to reconcile with religious devotion. But through the teaching of Duns Scotus (c. 1265–1308), the Scottish Franciscan philosopher and theologian, he came to recognize the importance of allowing individual talent, and hence his poetic gifts, to be exercised in the service of the Church. Sadly, his poetry was rejected for publication in his lifetime. It was his university friend Robert Bridges who arranged for their posthumous publication in 1918.

Once again Harries is drawn to someone who thinks, 'God's providence is dark and we cannot hope to know the why and wherefore of all that is allowed to befall us . . . but though he knows and remembers all the harm we have done he will not be our accuser; where he cannot help us he will be silent; he will speak but of our right deeds and plead in our defence all the good he has observed in us. His whole duty is to help us to be saved, to help us both in body and soul.' (Sermon preached in Liverpool on the Feast of St Raphael, 25 October 1880.)

For Hopkins himself there were terrible periods of darkness, expressed in some sonnets. Yet Harries records the note of hope in Hopkins' anguish. Delivering the 1992 brilliant annual lecture of the Gerard Manley Hopkins Society 'Away grief's gasping' Harries claimed, 'some of his phrases, wrought out of his darkness, are the most eloquent prayers of our time. "Mine, O thou Lord of life, send my roots rain." . . . We may wish that Hopkins had experienced more human happiness: but that he knew Christian joy I have no doubt; a foretaste of that revealing of the immortal diamond, which was his own unique suffering, struggling, amazingly creative self.' And the essence of his mystical vision!

Samuel Beckett (1906–1989) provides the title for this book: 'A heart in my head' (*Endgame*). Beckett called it 'the play I dislike the least'. It is a typical Beckettian phrase. There is a mixture of mind and feeling in there. He is not just the factual rationalist on a high intellectual plane. He once said, 'All I am is feeling.' This Irish writer, playwright and Nobel Prize winner has very great appeal for Harries and is of particular importance for Christians. Again, why? For a time Beckett was secretary to James Joyce, with whom he shared the same tantalizing preoccupation with language, and the failing of human beings to communicate successfully, mirroring the pointlessness of life yet striving to make it purposeful. For Beckett friendships were always possible, sustained relationships less so. 'Lives are never interesting in themselves: . . . the work is all that matters.'

When Harries gave the 1982 Drawbridge Memorial Lecture in London his subject was 'Astride of a grave' – Samuel Beckett and Christian hope. He quoted Malcolm Muggeridge – it could have been himself – 'I believe that at all times and in all circumstances life is a blessed gift'. Beckett has written: 'Life is a punishment for having been born.' A favourite line of Beckett states that 'the sun, having no alternative, shone.' Reflecting on three of Beckett's books – *Molloy*, *Malone Dies* and *The Unnameable* – Salmon Rushdie is convinced that: 'These books, whose ostensible subject is death, are in fact about life, the lifelong battle of life against its shadow' (*The Independent*, 24 February 2006). Harries would concur, and says, 'There is a strange paradox that, despite everything, Beckett's characters, though tempted, do not commit suicide.' In challenging Christian hope Harries concludes, 'The beauty of Beckett's works is, for those who are predisposed to see it, a sign of the capacity of creatures to share in their creator's power and skill. It would be absurd of course to try and make Beckett a crypto-Christian, an anonymous believer. But the mystery in his plays is akin to the mystery of life itself, with their door not finally closed; the way the characters struggle on without killing themselves; the compassion and the art itself, with its unique blend of truthful insight and poetry, are for the believer signs which are underpinned and have their proper place in a view of the world that includes more than Beckett brings into his plays. Augustine once wrote: "Do not despair; one of the thieves was saved. Do not presume one of the thieves was damned".'

Beckett's art will endure. For Harries it is a sign of hope itself, 'the fact that out of all that he has experienced himself and been sensitive to in others, he has produced works of art'. Of course, it is language – and in Beckett's case its minimal use – that compels. Despair is never vanquished. Neither is it ultimately enthroned.

In the 1662 *Book of Common Prayer* when mourners come to the grave, while the corpse is made ready to be laid into the earth, the priest says, 'Man that is born of a woman hath but a short time to live, and is full of misery. He cometh up, and is cut down, like a flower; he fleeth as it were a shadow, and never continueth in one stay.' These words united most of the lives of poets and writers who have such an abiding influence on Harries. They knew the *via negativa* of St John of the Cross. Perhaps there are traces in Richard Harries?

From *via negativa* to beyond compare is to contemplate Harries from the outside in and outside again, receiving and giving. There is not only a heart in his head but eyes that unite the two. Nowhere is this more evident and profound than his life-long interest in and knowledge of the pictorial art. He is a finely organized observer; not in the sense of brooding and burrowing, but in that of seeing, storing up and elaborating what he has seen. He is the ideal companion, seeking works of art in cathedrals, churches and art galleries. He never says, 'This must mean to you what it means to me'. He helps unfold one's imagination by suggesting and nudging rather than directing and judging. Although he is a regular commentator and reviewer of works of art and books on art, he made his debut as art book author with *Art and the Beauty of God: A Christian Understanding* (1993), which was chosen as Book of the Year by Anthony Burgess in *The Observer*. Burgess is another of those brilliant, versatile people – novelist, critic and composer – whom Harries would have found both uplifting and abrasive, friendly and difficult with his dark and violent vision of the future. Burgess believed 'you can't have both stability and freedom' and 'It won't work – this pretence of us understanding one another.'

Beauty, goodness and truth form a triad of transcendentals in the Christian Church, though beauty has been neglected and underexposed in a Church often predominated with and by the Word. Harries' book is a *tour de force* in arguing for a distinctively Christian approach to art which tingles with the spiritual dimension. The Church needs art to lead believers – and could-be and would-be believers – into the beauty and mystery of God by using its unique power to translate the Gospel message into colours, shapes – and sounds. Harries salutes the power of music.

Three further publications contribute to the gathering momentum of Harries' deposit, *A Gallery of Reflections: Devotional reflections on the Christmas story in art* (1995); *The Passion in Art* (2004) and 'Art' – his 40-page contribution to *Jesus in History, Thought and Culture*, edited by Leslie Houlden (2006). Art history is a burgeoning business. At the same time there is a dearth of spiritual reflection on particular pictures. Harries brings the two together with pertinacity and success. His approach is clear, 'To do this is, I believe, neither illegitimate nor forced, because for the vast majority of artists, painting a religious scene was itself a religious act. They did not think of religious pictures simply as cultural adornments or status symbols. These were expressions of faith and devotion. The art expressed the faith, and the faith flowed into shapes, colours and arrangements.'

His travels have familiarized him with Christian art in icons, mosaics, frescos, paintings, sculpture and glass from the second century to the present day. He knows that most truth is communicated through symbol and image. The good symbol is a servant, behaving as a good symbol should, in self-effacement that it may face two ways, both towards the greater reality it exists to symbolize, and also towards the person for whose enlightenment it exists. Self-consciousness may obscure the thing symbolized.

The rare phenomenon called genius consists of the outer faculty of observation, highly developed, and the inner core, sensitive, restless and anguished, disappointed with its work. Anything else is complacency. Accompanying Harries through his books is to be guided in understanding the essential character of a work of art, of how to look for it and at it: to look for its essential character. Is it to be found in its reverence for truth? Does its secret abide in its understatement of latent power? Is it to be recognized by concise expression and reticence in form and colour? Is it attractive because it recalls memories of themes far grander and more profound than the commonplaces of everyday living? Are we stunned into silence by the expressive beauty of a work of sculpture, picture or fresco; does it purr like a cat making us feel contented and comfortable or does it roar like a lion moving us away from our complacency to fear? Or are our eyes prised open and our senses startled and disturbed so that our vision is extended, deepened and widened? Harries is capable of tapping into all these characteristics.

Harries' books unite his reader-pilgrims in seeing and accepting that the Christian faith does not simply express the beauty of God and Christ Incarnate, but is itself an uncomfortable, even shocking faith. It requires to be accepted and lived with in complete surrender and we should not be surprised if its most vital servants, the prophets and the artists, ask to be accepted on their own terms, or rather on the terms of uncompromising faith, and not on our own more placid terms. Many artists have lived in familiarity with the truth, and the truth is rarely an easy companion, even when it makes us free!

In *The Passion of Art* Harries asks: 'how else can we dare approach the agony depicted in Grunwald's Isenheim altarpiece? We can only stare and stoop in front of our Lord's Passion and the cruel vitality of thorn branches. It is majestic in suffering, even though the figure is crushed, drawn and mutilated by the agonies of the Passion. It is an artist's vision of the utmost the Incarnate can embody of human pain, transfiguring it in divine submission.'

Imagine going into an art gallery and discovering a bold notice, 'It is prohibited to pray in this gallery'. A similar command may as well be in churches as visiting voyeurs rush past fresco and painting. *The Adoration of the Kings* by Giotto (1313) in the Scrovegni Chapel, Padua, draws us to our knees and Harries is the prompter. 'There is in this scene a sense of genuine devotion, reverence, piety and gentleness. One of the standing kings seems almost to be shying away with a sense of the unutterable humility of God becoming man. It is this atmosphere of tender reverence, which is at the very heart of the religious spirit, which makes this so special. Because our capacity for awe, reverence, even respect is so diminished in the modern world we need Giotto to remind us what genuine devotion before the Holy One is like. Yet, in all of us, something of that capacity for tender reverence is still alive.'

Harries avoids fairy-tale wonder. Andrew Mantegna's *Adoration of the Magi* (c.1497–1500) brings us right into the picture alongside the Magi. Again Harries pokes us into reality, more effectively than a hundred sermons. 'They are people who know the world, people who have had positions of responsibility in it, people who have had to struggle and make hard decisions, people who have developed a range of sophisticated skills. Yet together with this, they have retained a certain directness which they bring to bear from their hearts through their eyes to the Christ Child. Our closeness to Christ reveals us as we are. But Christ wants the real person, not a pretence or fraud. We are to come as we are, with all our experience of the world, lessons hard-won, skills acquired: with, Jesus said, the wisdom of serpents and the gentleness of doves.'

Turning to a modern painting, Harries admits Roger Wagner's *Menorah* is 'vitally fresh and morally challenging'. It is used on the cover of *Public Life and the Place of the Church* in which Wagner has an essay on 'Art and Faith'. Harries describes its magnetic pull:

The cooling towers of Didcot Power Station dominate the landscape for 20 or more miles round Oxfordshire and the former West Berkshire. Though obtrusive they are not beautiful. In an association that is at once striking and dangerous, Wagner sees them as both the gas ovens of the Nazi extermination programme and the Jewish Menorah, the seven-branched candlestick which gives its name to the picture. In the foreground are figures that are recognizably Jewish without being stereotypical. They convey an impression of utter, abject grief. To the left, a man, staring in horror, comforts his wife. One man hides his head and bends low, unable to look anywhere; two others cover their faces with their hands. A woman looks away while she and the man next to her hold out their arms in anger and dismay. The sense of impotence and despair make them speechless . . . Across the painting (1.5 metres by 2 metres), in the middle ground, are three crucified figures; the central figure is clearly the Jesus of Christian iconography. What is Wagner saying? These are victims, Jewish victims, of State power: victims belong together whether killed by the Romans or the Nazis. Four figures gather round the Cross in the centre, three of them lifting their arms and pointing. The pointing could be accusatory, for the Cross has too often been used as an instrument of anti-Judaism, to bludgeon psychologically (and sometimes physically) the Jewish people. But Wagner is a devout Christian, so there will be more in this gesture than an accusation. For Christian believers, the Crucifixion is a sign that God suffers in all human suffering and especially this must be true of the suffering of the chosen people . . . The light on the flooded loam, shining on the clay, gives the landscape a bleak, unearthly feel. The reflection of the giant cooling towers in the water almost overwhelm. Light, because it is God's light, uncreated and created, can never be without hope, so the light on the towers, even the light on the clouds of steam/smoke presages something better . . . But this hope, if it is received as such, cannot be seen apart from the light that lays everything bare, the terrible cruelty, the unspeakable grief.

In his own artistic 'Pilgrim's Progress' Harries recognizes and rejects 'The name of the Slough was Despond' and is confronted by the Passion of the Crucified One. 'Yet the Christian conviction is that, through his life, death and Resurrection, Jesus has won a decisive victory over evil and death, that he has made our redemption possible, and that we have a vocation and destination whose consummation is beyond space and time. Is it possible still to convey that joyous faith in visual form?' The victory of the Cross was the theme of the early Church. Harries has a challenge, 'as to how the victory of the Cross and in particular the Resurrection, can be conveyed in artistic terms in a way that does not take away from the reality of human agony. Even more testing from a visual point of view, is how to depict Jesus as a human being in a human culture, while at the same time indicating that, from the standpoint of Christian faith, he is more than a human being.'

The former John Bunyan Baptist Church in Cowley, Oxford, is a venue for transforming lives. In 1997 Jo and Richard Harries were strongly supportive patrons of the Ark-T Centre which takes its motif from the biblical story of Noah. Every kind of living creature found refuge in the Ark when the world was at its most chaotic. The message of hope – a word at the apex of Harries' vocabulary – speaks to all and underpins the work of the centre. Each week around 900 people come into the centre, which is equipped with a recording studio for young musicians, rehearsal space for theatre and dance, a performance and concert area and studios for eight resident artists, musicians, painters and textile artists. A garden provides a working space for a sculptor and is home to three studios for a film-maker, musicians and visual artists. Fair-trade coffee, drinks and home-cooked food are available in the Broom Tree Café. Much of the creativity happens with those who are or feel excluded, sometimes by physical or mental circumstances or simply by lack of opportunity. The Oxfordshire Youth Offending Team works in partnership with the centre, offering creative alternatives for young people caught up in crime.

Harries reaches a different audience on his annual Swan Hellenic cruises. It is another example of his continual stretching of his own knowledge and inner resources. David Wright, an Oxford solicitor and member of General Synod, refers to Harries' deeply impressive ability to master subjects. 'Soon after he arrived in Oxford, we invited Jo and Richard to dinner along with another clergy couple. My wife, Anita, is an actress, and was at the time heavily involved in a one-woman play, *The Belle of Amherst*, about the American poet Emily Dickinson. To pursue this, Anita had acquired and read much of the published work about Emily Dickinson, and Richard was fascinated and asked to borrow a book about her, and I remember him specifying that he wanted not a slim volume but a major work. This we duly lent him, and a few weeks later there was a knock on the door, and there was Richard returning book, dressed in running kit, as he was jogging (we live about a couple of miles from his house) . . . I remember one friend telling us that he once visited Richard at home, and found him in his study surrounded by large books on some obscure subject, Turkish art or something of that nature, and Richard told him that he was reading it up from scratch for his next Swan Hellenic cruise. He told me once, with a twinkle in his eye, that his practice was, on these cruises, to talk right to the end of the lecture period, so that there was no opportunity for hard questions from the kind of culture buffs who go on those cruises.' Harries' style and language is accessible in the arena of art where art historians and theologians tend to dispense jargon and talk to themselves.

Somewhere, Kenneth Clark refers to the danger of training one's eyes on the great works of the past and becoming blind to the work of the present. Not Harries! He loses few opportunities to visit exhibitions of works by contemporary artists and his appraisals should appear in future books.

Harries' approach to the subject may find expression in an unexpected place – *Sonnet 15* by Michelangelo, the poet:

> Not even the best of artists has any conception
> what a single marble block does not contain
> within its excess and that is only attained
> by the hand that obeys the intellect.

Chapter Twenty-Three
A Cross-Bench Mind

The mosaic of Richard Harries cannot be completed until several decades after his death. At this juncture no more can be achieved than to gather a few further scattered fragments where there are gaps capable of being filled.

Harries has a rational explanation of his faith. He lives at a time when people ask of every opinion and idea presented to their judgement, 'Is it true?' and reason is on their side in being sceptical concerning the records of the past. They ask, is age to be a test of truth? Is devotion to a formula to count as an argument? Harries is not afraid to examine his faith, bringing his mind as well as his heart and his soul to the place of judgement.

Theologically he remains within the broad parameters of orthodox belief. He should not be thought of as one who wishes to adapt religion to the needs of the day, but as one who believes that, thoroughly understood, religion is adequate to the needs, not only of our day but to the needs of all time. This is not to suggest that he is unaware of the struggles people have in believing today. He also knows that for the majority, Christianity has not been tried, tested and rejected, but is outside their interest, of no importance. The language of Christianity is simply unintelligible outside the circles of its adherents. The enthusiasm and certitude of Christians are incomprehensible.

Harries' faith is not based on vision which can be a very narrow kind of faith depending upon personal experiences. Faith must be attainable along the lines of commonplace living or not at all. And that faith is so attainable is the promise implied in Christ's last and greatest Beatitude, 'Blessed are they who have not seen, and yet have believed'. Such faith stands firm when theologies grow obsolete and churches totter to their ruin, for it draws its life from no earthly fountains but from the everlasting hills.

Harries' book *God Outside the Box* (2002) is a response directed at those who reject Christianity as anti-life and guilt-ridden, but who at the same time have strong values and beliefs and follow different spiritual pathways. The book was a surprising and satisfying success, in effect an apologia for the Christian faith, relating to God rather than the Church. In his inimitable way, Harries faces objections to the traditional Christian view of God and delves deeply to reveal that 'Christianity has within its treasure store enormous spiritual riches'. He inclines quietly towards optimism, believing in the providence of God, thinking that there are an increasing number of seekers, and to seek is eventually to find. Much contemporary theology is positive. To keep abreast of truth Harries neither goes back nor stands still. He rarely lets an opportunity pass on radio discussion or in reviews to puncture the hocus-pocus views of 'professional' atheists such as Richard Dawkins and Daniel C. Dennett. He is also very good with individuals. Professor John Barron recalls an occasion when 'Richard and Jo came to dinner at home in Oxford, and our firmly agnostic daughter Helen, then an undergraduate, was present also. Sitting next to Richard, Helen somewhat belligerently (I felt – and I caricature only slightly) asked, "So why do you believe all that stuff, then?" Pin-dropping silence all round. Unabashed, Richard proceeded to tell her, quietly, calmly and straightforwardly. She was hugely impressed (and had not meant to be) both by what he said and by the mere fact of being taken seriously.'

There are few subjects on which Harries does not have an opinion to express. Remarkably, he is not accused of having the 'gift of the gab' or of speaking 'off the cuff'. Each subject is thoroughly researched from a deep motive. One subject prompted his book *Is There a Gospel for the Rich? The Christian in a Capitalist World* (1992), the Hughes-Cheong (St Peter's) Lectures in Melbourne, Australia in 1991 and his Pall Mall Lecture of the same title, delivered to the Institute of Directors in 1993. In giving the Sir Robert Birley Lecture in 2000, Harries asked 'Can a Market Economy Serve the Poor?' Earlier he wrote, with Lord Laing of Dunphail, life president of United Biscuits, a booklet 'The Value of Business and its Values' which was the outcome of a working party where they were joined by Geoffrey Brand, former under-secretary, Department of Employment; Charles Green, former deputy chief executive of National Westminster Bank and the Revd Norman Russell, rector of Gerrards Cross and Fulmer, now Archdeacon of Berkshire. Their case was that 'there is no point in having moral guidelines for an enterprise unless the enterprise itself has moral legitimacy. Again, if the enterprise – in this case the world of business – does have a moral justification, then consistency demands that the values which underlie it in the first place should be expressed in all its activities.' Their concern was the necessity of increasing the resources of society (wealth creation) in order that the quality of life for all might be improved and 'the necessity of underpinning and suffusing the whole of our commercial life with clear moral principles'.

Money is power. No one can ever altogether prevent wealth, which is frozen opportunity, from exercising an influence on the course of the events of a globalized world. Yet there are limits to the kind of influence that it should exert, and to the sphere in which it ought to be permitted. These limits are perfectly well capable of being enforced by a rational and enlightened society. If only that were the universal case!

Harries commends and preaches the Gospel to the rich, telling them not only to be good, serviceable as real people can be, but also to be uncomfortable in the enjoyment of their wealth, which under the system of capitalism and the market economy, they enjoy at the cost of unfairness to the poor. If they are Christians they will want not only to mitigate the system but also to change it. They will not be content with ambulance work at the foot of the cliff, if they can effect a change which will stop people from falling over it. In *Is There a Gospel for the Rich?* Harries is deliberately adept at disturbing the consciences of the rich. But as he does not use the shibboleths of socialism he does not alienate his audience. And he was speaking within his territory, for the three counties of Berkshire, Buckinghamshire and Oxfordshire were crammed with those who have leading positions in the world of commerce, finance or industry.

Harries was initially one of the great welcomers of New Labour which was endeavouring to work with a market economy as no other Labour government had done before. But could such an economy, in conjunction with liberal democracy, alleviate the suffering of millions and truly serve the whole of humanity? Elitists everywhere always hope to concede as little power as possible whilst retaining maximum economic power.

In *Is There a Gospel for the Rich?* Harries is motivated by the Beatitudes:

> We truly help the poor, and become the poor who are blessed, not so much by action, in their situations (though that be part of it) as by standing with them *in our own situation* and confronting the institutions and organizations and attitudes which maintain a system of impoverishment. The Church will be a centre of resistance, or a multi-cellular structure made up of a number of centres of resistance.

The thrust of Harries' thinking is that pietism does not do justice against the political and economic policies that crush the poor and powerless. If a market economy fails 'some other spectre will arise to tantalize and beguile the starving and oppressed masses with the hope of some solution to their misery.'

Harries' favourite mission statement is that from the constitution of Dayton Hudson, an American retailing group. 'The business of business is serving society, not just making money. Profit is our reward for serving society well. Indeed, profit is the means and measure of our service – not an end in itself.'

The creation of wealth properly motivated can be a good in itself and is a social good because it benefits society. Harries encourages charitable giving when the accumulation of wealth in private hands is vast beyond the precedents of history. Here Church members of all denominations are in the forefront. The unadvertised self-sacrifice of many wealthy people, sincere, unaffected, unambitious, unshakeably loyal to their principles, is on the increase. State action must in the nature of the case be impersonal. This is its justice, and this is its weakness. No personal sacrifice enables it; no personal sympathy sweetens it. Therefore, being impersonal, State action can rarely or never be morally regenerating. The benefits provided by the rates and taxes carry to their beneficiaries no influence which can quicken self-respect or stir affection.

It is difficult to think of Harries being bishop of any other diocese than Oxford. We have already observed how it allowed him, not simply to be the person he is, but to be the bishop he was determined to be. Bishops should be men or women who are thinkers rather than administrators, pastors rather than organizers – and leaders! Present conditions find them so immersed in the business of the institution – purple-bibbed executives – that their intellectual and spiritual lives become things of accident, luxuries to be squeezed into the odd moments, if there are any, of an almost breathless day. This is not good for the Church. The world is not asking for mechanism. It is asking for light. An over-organized, manipulated and directed world walks in the dark.

Harries is one of the episcopal exceptions with a full stack of candles on the votive stand! The Archbishop of Canterbury, Rowan Williams, paid him extravagant tribute at the General Synod in November 2005: 'I think it is fair to say that, in Richard, the twentieth-century Church of England – and the twenty-first-century Church of England for that matter – has had one of its truly great and memorable figures.' 'Truly great' is premature for, 'truth is the daughter of time'. Whereas Harries is unlikely to rank alongside the established 'greats' of William Temple, George Bell, Herbert Hensley Henson and Michael Ramsey, he will be in the forefront of those near or actual contemporaries who will be shuffled by history into their abiding places, amongst them, Ian Ramsey, John Habgood, David Jenkins, Hugh Montefiore and David Sheppard. For the moment it is sufficient to describe him as one of the most distinguished diocesan bishops of the past 20 years and distinctive for his recognizable range of gifts and stature.

Rowan Williams suggests Harries deserves to be remembered in at least seven areas:

He'll be remembered as a broadcaster; 11 years on *Prayer for the Day* on Radio 4 and of course one of the most familiar and indeed you could say definitive voices on *Thought for the Day* and insiders tell me, authoritatively, that he was regarded (and still is regarded) as one of the great stars of *Thought for the Day*. More than any other individual I suspect, he has shaped what that means for the nation.

He might be remembered for his writing: as the author of – I think – 37 books; he makes even those others of us who try and write occasionally look rather Trappist. His books on Christian doctrine and social order, on the frontier between Christianity and the arts and on prayer, remain as a formidable deposit of wisdom.

Or then we might think of his pioneering work in interfaith relations . . . there's also his work in the House of Lords; his work and focus there – 'gaffer' you might say – of the Lords Spiritual; he's the first person who's organized the work of the bishops in the Lords on a portfolio basis. Within the House of Bishops he has been a hard worker, a wise counsellor and somebody to whom difficult tasks are relegated with great relief and delight by the rest of us . . . and his work on the Board of Social Responsibility. Not many bishops have a legal judgment named after them but the Oxford judgment, arising from his case against the Church Commissioners in respect of investment in South Africa, will go down in the history books and the law books as well.

But I hope that we will most of us remember him most warmly as a guide, a friend, a pastor. When I was first elected Bishop of Monmouth, Richard gave me memorable and sound advice on how to exercise my ministry which has stayed with me.

Rowan Williams refers to the House of Lords – a place and function that Harries has never neglected, indeed he has grown into a prominent figure in that place. A former Archbishop of Canterbury, E. W. Benson, confided to his diary (22 June 1889): 'The bishops of England will soon be a name without a meaning. They are bishops of dioceses, and make an immense fuss about their business and their letters, so that people groan over their lamentations about their work – they are good diocesan bishops, but bishops of England, no!' It was Archbishop Randall David-son's position that archbishops should have a 'natural and friendly access to the men to whom is given the responsibility for the nation's affairs'.

Harries would have seized every possibility of accessing the accessible, and not so accessible, if he had become archbishop, although it is not an office he would have found satisfying. The daily, heavy and intolerable burden of institutional work and personal exposure would have cramped his style, mutilated his talents and circumscribed his activities. Moreover, he would have been caught between his liberal conscience and the conservative obligations that come with the Primacy and the worldwide communion being far from at ease with itself.

The bishopric of London would have been enticing had it not had such a large constituency of those opposed to the ordination of women.

The archbishop he knew well and liked was Robert Runcie who still awaits a just verdict, despite too many biographies and numerous books of tributes. Harries defended him in the press when he was being maligned and contributed 'The Beauty of God in Tradition and Unity', to sermons published in the archbishop's honour in 1991: *A Developing Style* in *Robert Runcie – a Portrait by His Friends*, 1991; and 'The Pastoral Pragmatist: Runcie as Communicator' in *Runcie: An Archbishop Remembered*, 2002. Principally Harries most admired in Runcie what he lacked to the same degree in himself, 'a great human being, very simpatico, with an extraordinary ability to relate to a wide range of people and make them feel better for being alive'. As Primate, Runcie endeavoured to make the Church of England and the Anglican communion a community of faith. His hope and vision were nowhere better expressed than in a sermon preached on Commemoration Day at the Community of the Resurrection, Mirfield, in 1982. It contains everything that Harries will applaud, as the following extract shows:

There are four ingredients which are needed to achieve true community. First, it needs to cultivate the family virtues of acceptance, tolerance, forgiveness, welcome, companionship.

Second it needs standards and discipline, a readiness to undertake tiresome duties and stick at them, as well as the proper development of talents and gifts.

The third ingredient for true community is loyalty. Communities, like individuals, only thrive if they are loved. But loyalty on its own can be narrow, exclusive, complacent. If so, it should be mocked. And this community (Mirfield) has never lacked a sense of humour. People who lack humour have no judgement, and therefore should not be trusted with anything. So be prepared to laugh at your loyalties.

Fourth – Vision. Christians can never be obedient to their Lord if they rest content with things as they are. Without vision a people perishes, and Our Lord was always leading people to look beyond Himself into looking for and working for the Kingdom of God. It is so characteristic of so many institutions today, whether secular or religious, that they are defensive, anxious to protect their rights or obsessed with the necessary management of limited resources. It can mean that narrow planning blocks generous vision.

As Bishop of Oxford, Harries took opportunities for the Church to bridge chasms, keeping open lines of communication across all the frontiers that divide the human family. For him the Church's responsibility is to show the way, through fears, conflicts and perplexities to the Kingdom of God by first walking in that way himself. He may find it tough in his discernment to pronounce that the Word of God is not the word of the world, but he never fails in his duty to face the ultimate paradox, 'My ways are not your ways: neither are my words your words'.

Harries' liberalism has never been in doubt though, unprotected and unharnessed in retirement, there may be literary fireworks. Yet inherent reasonableness will not desert him. He resembles the French writer and moralist Joseph Joubert who wanted 'to infuse exquisite sense into common sense, or to render exquisite sense common'. Harries' mind has always been hospitable to growth, tentatively searching for new ideas and expressing them with hesitant passion. Emotional Christianity is not safe without an intellectual background. Supreme in his character is that virtue Dr Johnson observed and praised in a Duke of Devonshire – 'a dogged veracity'. Harries' reforming liberal friends are the salt of the earth, but he is salted by Christ, and thus he is a witness of God to other people. His lecture to the Trollopian Society was entitled 'The Modesty of the Church of England'. There is something of Harries in that, for his heart is full of modesty as his mind is of unclouded clarity. That does not exclude thinking well of himself – but without arrogance, for he has a gracious nature.

There have been many references to Harries' semi-detachment from people. With some people he has a reputation of being 'cold'. A priest recalls the time when the bishopric of London was vacant and Harries was rumoured as a possible candidate. An Oxford priest went to a 'do' at Southwark Cathedral and one of the canons came up to ask if Harries was likely to move to London. He told him that he seriously doubted it, because he loved Oxford. 'Thank God for that,' said the canon, 'You could catch pneumonia from that man.' It is an undeserved remark. We have observed that reticence and a degree of shyness prevent Harries from opening up to those he works with, let alone those who work for him. That is how he is!

Harries left the diocese of Oxford in a much healthier state than he found it. Despite minority and jaundiced views to the contrary, it is far more unified and spiritually alive than it was in the 1980s, and the ministry of women has transformed its 'feel'. The old saying that behind every great man there is a great woman, is emphatically true of Jo Harries. It is wrong to think that her periodic terrible suffering with bipolar disorder is wholly burdensome, restricting, negative. She is an example of strength in adversity. She enables Richard to 'be' and his loving care, known best only to her, has been transforming to both of them. Jo is a kind of spiritual 'earth mother', a real force in Richard's life and ministry.

The gift of a wooden statue of a saint from a South American bishop stood on Harries' desk at Diocesan Church House. Christine Lodge, his indefatigable personal assistant, christened the statue 'Dolores'. It would be found lying on a towel in his office wearing sunglasses when he went on holiday. 'Dolores' would pack her mini-suitcase when he went travelling, and was even found with a pirate's hat on during the Jeffrey John debacle. One April Fool's day some wag decided to run a skull and crossbones flag up the diocesan flagpole. It was visible from the busy A34, and amidst the resulting furore (which included a cross telephone call from a governor at the neighbouring Church of England primary school), few people in the office saw the funny side. One of his chaplains had three in-trays labelled 'mad', 'completely mad', and 'barking'. A former vicar of Littlemore's parrot was called Archdeacon Paley, who somehow had found his way into the diocesan directory as an extra archdeacon. The bishop's chaplain wrote a letter of complaint to the vicar, whereupon the parrot promptly fell off its perch and died.

There was what became known as 'the conspiracy of humour' around the Bishop's office. On one occasion there was a serious conversation about whether BBC Radio Oxford should be allowed to run an April Fool joke announcing that the Bishop of Oxford had decided to buy the ailing Oxford United Football Club. They decided against it, only to find a few years later that Harries was on the front page on *The Sun*, having apparently 'exorcised' the same football ground. 'It's a normal part of a bishop's ministry,' he retorted. Harries has wit and humour, but is not frivolous.

It is time to take leave of Harries who retired on 2 June 2006 aged three score years and ten. Simultaneously, one of the best and most deserving appointments of the Prime Minister, Tony Blair, was made – Lord Harries of Pentregarth of Ceinewydd in the County of Dyfed who was reintroduced into the House of Lords on 25 July 2006. Lord Harries sits on the cross-benches where he belongs and has really always belonged, his true place! He will be confronted by the different and conflicting claims of Caesar and God. It is unlikely that he will fail to distinguish between the two as he continues to serve both Church and nation.

Bibliography

Books – sole author
Prayers of Hope, BBC 1975
Turning to Prayer, Mowbray 1978
Prayers of Grief and Glory, Lutterworth 1979
Being a Christian, Mowbray 1981
Should a Christian Support Guerrillas? Lutterworth Press 1982
Praying Round the Clock, Mowbray 1983
The Authority of Divine Love, Blackwell 1983
Prayer and the Pursuit of Happiness, Fount 1985
Morning Has Broken, Marshall Pickering 1985
Christianity and War in a Nuclear Age, Mowbray 1986
C.S. Lewis: The Man and His God, Fount 1987
Christ is Risen, Mowbray 1987
Evidence for the Love of God, Mowbray 1987
Shalom and Pax: Christian Concepts of Peace, Oxford Project for Peace Studies 1990
Is There a Gospel for the Rich? The Christian in a Capitalist World, Mowbray 1992
Art and the Beauty of God: A Christian Understanding, Mowbray 1993
Is There a Role for Charity in a Modern State?, Association of Charitable Foundations 1993
The Real God: A Response to Anthony Freeman's 'God in Us', Mowbray 1994
Questioning Belief, SPCK 1995
A Gallery of Reflections: The Nativity of Christ, Lion / BRF 1995
In the Gladness of Today, Fount 1999
God Outside the Box: Why Spiritual People Object to Christianity, SPCK 2002
After the Evil: Christianity and Judaism in the Shadow of the Holocaust, OUP 2003
The Passion in Art, Ashgate 2004
Praying the Eucharist: Prayers for Personal Use, SPCK 2004
Abraham's Children: Jews, Christians and Muslims in Conversation jointly with Norman Solomon and Tim Winter, T & T Clark 2006

Booklets/pamphlets
Religious Education and English Literature
Hockerill Lecture, King's College, London, 26 November 1982. Hockerill Education Foundation 1982
'Astride of a grave' – Samuel Beckett and Christian Hope
The Drawbridge Memorial Lecture, City of London 1982 (in *Questioning Belief* 1995)
Bias, Commitment and Value in Education
The Mary Roberts Memorial Lecture, Rougemont School, Newport, 15 May 1986
Has religion a future?
W. H. Smith Contemporary Paper No. 13 1993

A sermon preached in the Chapel of All Souls College, Oxford 11 June 1995

Issues in human sexuality

Severn Forum Lecture, University of Gloucestershire, Cheltenham 27 May 2004

Books edited/jointly edited

What Hope in an Armed World? Harries contribution 'The Morality of Nuclear Deterrence', Pickering & Inglis 1982

Seasons of the Spirit: Readings through the Christian Year with co-authors George Every and Kallistos Ware, SPCK 1984

Reinhold Niebuhr and the Issues of our Time Harries contributed 'Introduction' and 'Reinhold Niebuhr's Critique of Pacifism and his Pacifist Critics', Mowbray 1986

The One Genius: Readings through the Year with Austin Farrer, SPCK, 1987

Two Cheers for Secularism with Sidney Brichto. Harries contributed 'Introduction' and 'The Moral Case Against God', Pilkington Press 1998

Christianity: Two Thousand Years with Henry Mayr-Harting. Harries contributed 'Prospect', OUP 2001

Contributions to composite works

'True Unbelief', in Eric A. James (ed.) *Stewards of the Mystery of God*, Darton, Longman and Todd 1979

'Conventional Killing or Nuclear Stalemate?' in David A. Martin and Peter J. Mullen (eds), *Unholy Warfare: The Church and the Bomb*, Blackwell 1983

'Power, Coercion and Morality' in Francis W. Bridger (ed.) *The Cross and the Bomb: Christian Ethics and the Nuclear Debate*, Mowbray 1983

'Penitence' in Gordon S. Wakefield (ed.), *A Dictionary of Christian Spirituality*, SCM 1983

'Contemplation' in Alan Richardson and John S. Bowden (eds) *A New Dictionary of Christian Theology*, SCM Press 1983

'The Strange Mercy of Deterrence' in John W. Gladwin (ed.), *Dropping the Bomb*, Hodder and Stoughton 1985

'On the Brink of Universalism' in Robert C. Llewelyn (ed.) *Julian: Woman of Our Day*, Darton, Longman and Todd 1985

'The Resurrection in Some Modern Novels' in Elizabeth Russell and John Greenhalgh (eds) *If Christ be not risen: Essays in Resurrection and Survival*, St Mary's, Bourne Street 1986

'Praying with the Church' in James F. Butterworth (ed.), *The Reality of God: Essays in Honour of Tom Baker, Dean of Worcester 1975–1986*, Severn House 1986

'Tuesday / Lent 1' and 'Wednesday / Lent 1' in Shelagh Brown (ed.) *Lent for Busy People*, Bible Reading Fellowship 1987

'"We Know on Our Knees . . ." Intellectual, Imaginative and Spiritual Unity in the Theology of Austin Farrer' in Brian L. Hebblethwaite and Edward Henderson (eds) *Divine Action: Studies Inspired by the Philosophical Theology of Austin Farrer*, T & T Clark 1990

'AIDS and Tolerance' in Peter Byrne (ed.) *Medicine, Medical Ethics and the Value of Life*, John Wiley 1990

'Introduction' in Malcolm McCall and Oliver Ramsbotham (eds), *Just Deterrence: Morality and Deterrence into the Twenty-First Century*, Brassey's 1990

'A Developing Style' in David L. Edwards (ed.), *Robert Runcie: A Portrait by His Friends*, Fount 1990

'Attitudes To Death in the Twentieth Century' in Julia Neuberger and John A. White (eds), *A Necessary End: Attitudes to Death*, Papermac 1991

'Human Rights in Theological Perspective' in Robert Blackburn and John Taylor (eds), *Human Rights for the 1990s: Legal, Political and Ethical Issues*, Continuum 1990

'Foreword' and 'Evidence for the Love of God' in Gillian Ryeland (ed.), *Beyond Reasonable Doubt*, Canterbury Press 1991

'Introduction' in Duane W. H. Arnold (ed.), *Praying with John Donne and George Herbert*, Triangle 1992

'Jewish–Christian Dialogue' in (various eds) *Dictionary of the Ecumenical Movement*, WCC & Council of Churches for Britain and Ireland 1991

'The Beauty of God' in Dan Cohn-Sherbok (ed.) *Tradition and Unity: Sermons Published in Honour of Robert Runcie*, Bellow 1991

'Theodicy Will Not Go Away', in Tony Bayfield and Marcus C. R. Braybooke (eds) *Dialogue with a Difference: Manor House Group Experience*, SCM Press 1992

'A Sermon Given in Commemoration of the Founders and Benefactors of Keble College' in D. Geoffrey Rowell (ed.), *The English Tradition and the Genius of Anglicanism*, IKON 1992

'The Beauty of the Cosmos and the Beauty of God' in *In Being Human in a Cosmic Context*, Westminster College 1993

'The Arts' in David Gillett and Michael Scott-Joynt (eds) *Treasure in the Field: The Archbishops' Companion for the Decade of Evangelism*, Fount 1993

'Judaism and Christianity' in Alister E. McGrath (ed.) *The Blackwell Encylopedia of Modern Christian Thought*, Blackwell 1993

'World Population and Birth Control: An Anglican Perspective' in Bryan Cartledge (ed.), *Population and Environment: The Linacre Lectures 1993–4*, OUP 1995

'Preface' and 'On Human Sexuality' in James M. Rosenthal and Nicola Currie (eds), *Being Anglican in the Third Millennium: Panama 1996 – The Official Report of the 10th Meeting of the Anglican Consultative Council*, Morehouse 1997

'The De-Romanticisation of War and the Struggle for Faith' in Martin Gilbert (ed.) *The Straits of War: Gallipoli Remembered*, Sutton 2000

'Rochester's "Death Bed Repentance"' in Nicholas Fisher (ed.), *The Second Bottle: Essays on John Wilmot, Earl of Rochester*, Manchester University Press 2000

'Lancelot Andrewes' Good Friday 1604 Sermon' in Michael Hattaway (ed.), *A Companion to English Renaissance Literature and Culture*, Blackwell 2000

'Staying Human' in Marshall Marinker (ed.), *Medicine and Humanity*, King's Fund 2001

'The Presence of Justice' in Anna Kiernan (ed.), *Voices for Peace: An Anthology*, Scribner 2001

'The Pastoral Pragmatist: Runcie as Communicator' in Stephen Platten (ed.), *Runcie: On Reflection*, Canterbury Press 2002

'The Moral Status of the Early Embryo' in Timothy Bartel (ed.), *Comparative Theology: Essays for Keith Ward*, SPCK 2003

'Ringlets' in Anna Jeffery (ed.), *Five Gold Rings: Powerful Influences in Prominent People*, Darton, Longman & Todd 2003

'The Last Word' in *For the Life of the World: The Official Report of the 12th Meeting of the Anglican Consultative Council, Hong Kong, 2002*, Morehouse 2003

'Art' in J. L. Houlden (ed.) *Jesus: The Complete Guide*, Continuum 2006

'Application of Just War Criteria in the Period 1959–1989' in Richard Sorabji and David Rodin *The Ethics of War: Shared Problems in Different Traditions*, Ashgate 2006

Contributions to journals and periodicals

'The Tygers of Wrath Are Wiser than the Horses of Instruction: The Alternative to Christian Pacifism' *Theology* 75, 1972

'Are Non-Revolutionaries Living in Mortal Sin?' *New Fire* 2, 1972

'The Religious Dimension of Humour' *New Fire* 2, 1973

'The Criterion of Success for a Just Revolution' *Theology* 78, 1975

'Alternative Services: The Test of Practice' *Theology* 79, 1976

'Ivan Karamazov's Argument' *Theology* 81, 1978

'Re-review of Reinhold Niebuhr, Moral Man and Immoral Society' *Modern Churchman* 25/1, 1982

'Nuclear Weapons: The General Synod Decision in the Light of Day' *Crucible* April–June 1983

'"The Church and the Bomb": A Reaction' *Christian* 7, 1983

'Reflections on Religious Broadcasting' *Kairos* 9, 1984

'The Christian Churches and the Pacifist Temptation' *World Today* 40, 1984

'Death and After Death' *New Fire* 8, 1984

'Chanter le Chant de la Mort' *Parole et Pain* 65, 1984

'Human Rights in Theological Perspective' *King's Counsel* 37, 1988

'Power and Powerlessness in Judaism and Christianity' *Christian/Jewish Relations* 21, 1988

'Stewart Sutherland on Suffering' *Theology* 91, 1988

'Friendship: A Thought for the Day' *Chrism* 26, 1988

'Johnson: A Church of England Saint?' *Johnson Society*, 1988

'Sermon Preached in Lichfield Cathedral, Sunday 24 September 1989' *Johnson Society* 1989

'The Response of the Churches to Israel' *European Judaism* 25, 1992

'The Morality of Warfare' *General Studies Review* 1, 1992

'The Morality of Good Business' *The Stockton Lecture Business Strategy Review* 4/1, 1993

'Commemoration Sermon' *Tyndale Society Journal* 1, 1995

'No Other Alternative' (Complex problems of Israel) *Common Ground* 1995

'The Anglican Acceptance of Contraception' *Transformation* 13/3, 1996

'When the Gods Ceased to Be' *Theology* 100, 1997

(and Peter H. Sedgwick), 'Anglican Moral Teaching Today' *Crucible* October–December 1997

'Public Health – Everybody's Business: Inequalities in Health' *Journal of Public Health Medicine* 19, 1997

'The Rt Revd Lord Runcie (1921–2000)' *Oxford* 52, 2000

'The Beginning of Life' Liddon Trust Lecture 1999 *Ecclesiastical Law Journal* 2000

'The Third Way' *Crucible* January–March 2001

'Tuning into the World before Turning it Upside Down: A Response to Michael Banner' *Crucible* April–June 2001

On Jonathan Sacks' 'The Dignity of Difference: How to Avoid the Clash of Civilisations' *Scottish Journal of Theology* 2004

'Delivering Public Policy: The Status of the Embryo and Tissue Typing' *Studies in Christian Ethics*, Spring 2005

'Religion and Science – Old Enemies or New Friends? *Modern Believing* 47:1, 2006

Articles in national newspapers and magazines

'Towards a Life in Grace' Evelyn Waugh's Brideshead Revisited. *Church Times* 27 November 1981

'Face of apartheid as ugly as ever' *Church Times* 10 September 1982

'The Christian and Apartheid' *The Times* 25 September 1982

'4 Major Questions on Nuclear Report (The Church and the Bomb) *Church Times* 22 October 1982

'Peace on earth and peace within' *The Observer* 18 December 1983

On Women Priests: An Open Letter to the Bishop of London *The Tablet* 8 February 1986

'A protective cloak for Brother Durham (David Jenkins) *The Observer* 8 June 1986

'Anglicanism's New Image (Justice and Peace) *Church Times* 5 September 1986

'A dagger in the back' (Universities) *The Observer* 4 October 1987

'Dr Runcie's bravery is greater than Crockford's' *The Independent* 5 December 1987

'What the resolution on violence should have said' (Lambeth Conference) *The Times* 6 August 1988

'More talk than listening' (Homosexuality – Lambeth Conference) *The Tablet* 15 August 1988

'Does the State of Israel need a Jewish liberation theology' *The Independent* 10 September 1988

'Historically unlikely and morally unattractive' (on Martin Scorsese's film *The Last Temptation of Christ*, *The Independent* 27 August 1988

'A myth that will not die' (Evolution and Religious Belief) *The Observer* 4 September 1988

'A Truly Christian Poet. Salute to T.S. Eliot on Centenary of his Birth. *Church Times* 23 September 1988

'An event unique and of cosmic significance not a mere detail' *The Independent* 29 March 1989

'The Our Father for Jews and Christians' *The Independent* 22 July 1989

'Finding the Soul in Hare's New Drama' (*Racing Demon*) *Church Times* 19 February 1990

'Obituary – The Revd Joseph McCulloch' *The Independent* 10 March 1990

'Why I am resolved to take the Church Commissioners to the High Court' *Church Times* 30 March 1990

'Prophet not honoured in his own land' (Robert Runcie) *The Observer* 1 April 1990

'A just war, not a crusade' *The Observer* 20 January 1991

'Danger's Edge' (An assessment of the work of Graham Greene) *Church Times* 12 April 1991

'Our God-given self interest' *Church Times* 5 May 1992

'A painful search for greater good' (The case of Tony Bland) *The Times* 21 November 1992

'The royal split: does it matter?' *The Independent* 10 December 1992

'In the same boat" (Ordination of Women in the Church of England and the Roman Catholic Church) *The Tablet* 27 January 1994

'Time to balance up the good books' *The Times* 16 February 1994

'Reliability, Sympathy, Purposefulness' *Church Times* 25 November 1994

'Plunged back into the Passion' (Norman Adam's Stations of the Cross) *Church Times* 21 July 1995

'Humanising the divorce law' *The Tablet* 27 January 1996

'How to find fault in the wreckage' (Divorce Law) *Church Times* 15 March 1996

'Goodness is not a lot of good without enchantment' *The Times* 13 July 1996

'Why it is time to return to morality' *The Guardian* 1 January 1997

'Pointing children towards the path of God' *The Times* 3 February 1997

'New Labour, new decency' *Church Times* 9 May 1997

'Termination and determination' (The Church of England on Abortion) *Church Times* 31 October 1997

'The year of Diana' *The Tablet* 20/27 December 1997

'Churches have rights too' (Human Rights Bill) *Church Times* 13 February 1998

'Why freedom needs cages' *The Tablet* 28 November 1998

'Christianity and politics do mix' *The Independent* 1 February 1999

'For a Christian this is a just war' *The Independent* 2 April 1999

'Why Hume is our favourite churchman' *The Independent* 9 April 1999

'Answers to soul-searching questions' *The Independent* 26 April 1999

'Nato's deadly mind-game' *The Tablet* 17 July 1999

'Opinion Research Statistics' *The Observer* 23 December 1999

'Does it really matter if our miraculous story of Jesus is not the Gospel truth?' *The Independent* 24 December 1999

'Heterosexuals are the cause of problems, not homosexuals' *The Independent* 25 January 2000

'A new chamber, and our place in it' (House of Lords) *Church Times* 28 January 2000

'Lord Runcie' *The Observer* 30 July 2000

'Child-abuse: be aware, stay charitable' (Anti-paedophile violence in Portsmouth) *Church Times* 18 August 2000

'The Lottery is a symptom of a malaise that impoverishes us all' *The Independent* 24 August 2000

'The new government we deserve' *Church Times* 15 June 2001

'Why we need faith in the Lords' *Church Times* 24 May 2002

'Iraq war would fail just-war test' *The Observer* August 2002
'How to decide what is doctrine' *Church Times* 27 September 2002
'It's too soon for war' *The Tablet* 18 January 2003
On the 'Jeffrey John' controversy *Sunday Times* 29 June 2003
'In blood stepp'd in so far' (Damien Hirst exhibition) *Church Times* 19 September 2003
'Why limited cloning is right and necessary' *Church Times* 20 August 2004
'With arms outstretched '((Art – Christ and Mary Magdalene) *The Tablet* 26 March 2005
'Talking ethics' *The Tablet* 4 June 2005
Assisted Dying (opposing Joffe) *The Observer* 7 October 2005
'We need more rational argument and less polemic on euthanasia' *The Guardian* 25 October 2005
'The female mitre' (women bishops) *The Tablet* 15 July 2006

Reports of commissions and working parties of which Harries was chairman or member
Member – 'Teaching Christian Ethics: An Approach' The Advisory Council for the Church's
    Ministry, SCM 1974
Chairman – 'Peacekeeping in a Nuclear Age' Board for Social Responsibility of the General
    Synod, Church House Publishing 1978
Member – 'Human Rights and Responsibilities in Britain and Ireland: A Christian Perspective'
    Macmillan 1988
Member – 'Issues in Human Sexuality: A Statement by the House of Bishops' Church House
    Publishing 1991
Chairman – 'A very light sleeper: The persistence and dangers of anti-Semitism'
 Runnymede Trust 1994
Chairman – 'Christian and Jews: A New Way of Thinking' The Churches' Commission for Inter-
    Faith Relations Council of Churches for Britain & Ireland 1994
Chairman – 'Jews, Christians and Muslims: The Way of Dialogue' Group for Lambeth Conference
    1988. Published as Appendix to *The Truth Shall Make You Free*, *The Lambeth Conference 1988*,
    Church House Publishing 1988
Member – 'A House for the Future' Royal Commission on the Reform of the House of Lords,
    Stationery Office 2000
Chairman – 'Stem Cell Research' Report from the Select Committee (House of Lords),
 Stationery Office 2002
Chairman – 'Some issues in human sexuality. A guide to the debate'. A discussion document from
    the House of Bishops' Group on Issues on Human Sexuality, Church House Publishing 2003
Chairman – 'Countering Terrorism: Power, Violence and Democracy Post 9/11. A report of a
    working group of the House of Bishops, Church House Publishing 2005

House of Lords
(This is restricted to Harries' speeches, interventions and questions. It does not include the great
number of occasions when he voted without speaking)

1994
23 February The Family (Maiden)

1995
1 March Income and Wealth: Rowntree Report
1 May Human Rights Bill
31 May Bosnia
30 November Family Law Bill

1996
22 January Family Law Bill
23 January Family Law Bill
4 March Family Law Bill
15 May The Mentally Ill: Care in the Community
16 May Housing Bill
5 December Human Fertilization and Embryology

1997
27 January Crime (Sentences) Bill
30 January Geneva Conventions (Amendment) Bill
9 July Jubilee 2000 Scheme
27 October Penal Policy
17 December Nuclear Weapons: Papal Policy

1998
22 January Bosnia: Mine Clearance
22 January National Lottery Bill
17 February Iraq
29 April Campsfield House Detention Centre
6 May Euthanasia
11 December Debate on the Address (Modernization)

1999
14 January Poetry
18 January Citizenship and Democracy
8 March World Poverty Elimination: Role of Women
28 April Human Embryos and Cloning
6 December Local Government Bill
14 December Race Relations (Amendment) Bill

2000
7 June Tobin Tax
11 December Debate on the Address (Climate change)

2001
4 April Foot and Mouth Disease
25 April Iran
27 June Debate on the Address (World trade and arms exports)

2002
20 March Corporate Regulation
10 June Adoption and Children Bill
24 June Immigration Policy
5 December Stem Cell Research: Select Committee Report

2003
15 January Sentencing Policy
26 February Iraq
12 March Patients Protection Bill

18 March Iraq
9 April Religion and Global Terrorism
6 June Patient (Assisted Dying) Bill

2004
22 April Civil Partnership Bill
7 September Iraq
? October Pornography on the Internet
24 November Debate on the Address (Presidency of G8 – debt – trade)

2005
25 January Mental Incapacity Bill
1 February Mental Incapacity Bill
9 March European Union: UK Presidency
16 March Iraq
10 October Assisted Dying for the Terminally Ill Bill: Select Committee Report
11 October Racial and Religious Hatred Bill
12 October United Nations Convention Against Torture
19 October Indonesia: Human Rights
31 October Identity Cards
8 November Racial and Religious Hatred Bill
16 November Iranian asylum seekers
30 November Pension Commissioning Report
5 December Terrorism Bill

2006
17 January Immigration, Asylum and Nationality Bill
19 January Education
19 January Kalahari Bushmen

Forewords
'Foreword' in James W. Woodward (ed.), *Embracing the Chaos: Theological Responses to AIDS*, SPCK 1990
'Foreword', in Christopher J.E. Moody, *Eccentric Ministry: Pastoral Care and Leadership in the Parish*, Darton, Longman and Todd 1992
'Foreword' in Alexander Men, *Awake to Life!: The Easter Cycle*, Bowerdean 1992
'Foreword' in Richard P. Thomas, *An Introduction to Church Communication*, Lynx Communications 1994
'Foreword' in Elizabeth Roberts and Ann Shukman (eds), *Christianity for the Twenty-First Century: The Life and Work of Alexander Men*, SCM 1996
'Foreword' in Christopher Irvine (ed.) *Celebrating the Easter Mystery: Worship Resources from Easter to Pentecost*, Cassell 1996
'Foreword' in John Drane, *Revelation: The Apocalypse of St John*, Lion Hudson 1997
'Foreword' in *Prisons: A Study in Vulnerability: A Collection of Essays from the Board for Social Responsibility*, Church House Publishing 1999
'Preface', in *Cybernauts Awake! Ethical and Spiritual Implications of Computers, Information Technology and the Internet*, Church House Publishing 1999
'Introduction' in Edmund J. Newell (ed.), *Seven Words for the 21st Century*, Darton, Longman and Todd 2002
'Foreword' in Bernard H. M. Palmer *Serving Two Masters: Parish Patronage in the Church of England since 1714*, Book Guild 2003

Index